THE LIBERTY SHIPS

The *Patrick Henry,* the first Liberty ship, on trials
December 26, 1941. (Bethlehem-Fairfield, Yard
no 2001)

L.A. SAWYER and W.H. MITCHELL

THE LIBERTY SHIPS

THE HISTORY OF THE 'EMERGENCY' TYPE
CARGO SHIPS CONSTRUCTED IN THE
UNITED STATES DURING WORLD WAR II

Drawings by John S. Lindsay

CORNELL MARITIME PRESS, INC.
Cambridge   **Maryland**

First published in the United States of America
in 1970 by Cornell Maritime Press, Inc.
Cambridge, Maryland
© 1970, in England, L.A. Sawyer and W.H. Mitchell
Library of Congress Catalog Card Number 70-124469
International Standard Book Number 0-87033-152-3

Printed in Great Britain

CONTENTS

ILLUSTRATIONS

Cover illustration: A Liberty Ship at dusk (North Carolina Ports Authority)

INTRODUCTION

Liberty ships were the product of certain shipyards in the United States during the eventful years between 1941 and 1945 and formed the 'emergency' part of a shipbuilding programme which had been started by the United States government some five years previously, in 1936, with the advent of the United States Maritime Commission.

The initial government orders for tonnage were quite considerable, but with war becoming almost inevitable, the need for America to safeguard her own interests became a priority.

The original programme was, therefore, greatly expanded, even before the devastation at Pearl Harbour in December of 1941.

Then, with war declared, it quickly became evident that vast numbers of cargo ships would be needed for the transport of food and war materials the world over, and an emergency type of ship which, of necessity, could be speedily constructed in vast numbers and by unskilled labour was urgently required.

Thus, the 'Liberty' ship was born.

The following pages give details of these ships and also brief details of the history of each vessel up to, generally, April 1970.

The sequence of details for each ship are:

Yard number, original name of ship, completion date, engine maker and history.

Within the text the names of the engine makers have been abbreviated in accordance with the key shown elsewhere. Some entries in the history details indicate that certain ships were/are attached to the United States Navy (USN) and the group letter/number designation following the Navy name indicates the USN classification and type. Again, the key to these abbreviations will be found separately. Also under history a reference to 'reserve' status indicates the present situation of a given vessel, and an explanation of the different 'site numbers' shown will be found under the heading of Part Seven of this book. An entry shown without change of name or change in status generally indicates that such vessel had remained under Maritime Administration jurisdiction. It will be noted that some vessels, subsequent to a casualty, have been declared as constructive total losses; this fact is indicated by the abbreviation CTL.

Generally the scrapping dates shown indicate the commencement of scrapping. But for some ships these dates were not available and, therefore, the dates given indicate the completion of scrappings.

The index not only lists the original and/or completion names of the ships but, for special interest, includes the complete list of Liberty ships transferred to Britain on lease lend terms and which were known as 'Sam' ships.

The authors wish to acknowledge with thanks the assistance given them, particularly by Lloyds Register of Shipping; the Corporation of Lloyds (Lloyds of London); the United States Maritime Administration; the United States National Archives and Record Service; the United States Naval Institute; Messrs Bill Hultgren of Erie, Pennsylvania, and Captain Bob Childs of Rochester, Kent, and also all other persons who have contributed facts towards the compilation of this record.

London and Southampton
April 1970

L.A. Sawyer
W.H. Mitchell

THE LIBERTY SHIPS

In the United States of America up to the years 1919-20 some 2,500 merchant ships, built both of wood and of steel, and totalling nearly 6½ million deadweight tons, were constructed under the impetus of First World War conditions, but thereafter the American shipbuilding industry declined rapidly.

In the fifteen years from 1922 until 1937, only two dry cargo ships were constructed in American shipyards, although a few tankers were also built and twenty-nine passenger-cargo liners were constructed under the subsidy provisions of the 1928 Merchant Marine Act.

However, the lost art of shipbuilding was somewhat revived by the Merchant Marine Act of 1936, for this provided for the formation of a maritime commission and a policy of which three salient features were:

a) ......that it is necessary for national defence and for the development of both domestic and overseas commerce to have a new, modern and efficient merchant marine......

b) ......that such fleet should be capable of serving as naval or military auxiliary in time of war or national emergency......

c) ......that the ships should be constructed in America and owned and operated under the US flag......

Therefore, disregarding any previous methods of aiding the failing shipping industry, the Act frankly authorised construction differential and operating differential subsidies, so that American builders and operators found themselves on a competitive parity with foreign-flag ships. The maintenance of a building nucleus and of operating capacity for emergency use could not be met in any other way, for it was generally agreed that the (then) cost of constructing a cargo vessel in an American shipyard was, on the average, twice as much as paid by foreign competitors and that American operating costs were fifty per cent more.

When the United States Maritime Commission was established in 1936, there were only ten shipyards and forty-six slipways in the United States capable of building ocean-going ships more than 400 ft long, and half of these yards were then engaged on naval construction. In 1937 a ten-year peace-time programme was begun by the commission, this calling for the construction of fifty ships a year to rehabilitate an ageing merchant fleet whose average remaining economic life was less than five years. It proposed to replace these over-age ships with high-speed tankers and with three standard types of freighter, the latter being fast units powered by geared turbines and designed for economical operation.

The original maritime commission programme was indeed an ambitious one. Contracts were 'let' for the first hundred ships and the five hundred ships planned were expected to place a total of just under four million gross tons of new shipping on the high seas.

At that time the commission itself determined which services should be maintained between American and foreign ports, and its survey of trade routes indicated the types of vessel best suited to each. All the varied requirements were taken into account by the commission's design teams and the result was the early C1, C2 and C3 standard type ships. It was perhaps fortunate that large scale planning and its execution had always been a dominant feature of the American way of life, for this far-sightedness in instituting quantity production in shipbuilding was of immense importance to the speed with which the nation was able to turn to mass prefabrication during the following critical years.

In its original concept the shipbuilding programme made history with its attempt at 'standardisation for individualists', for although it produced three standard types of ship, there still remained the necessity of adapting them to the needs of various owners and operators. These individual needs showed, not only in trade requirements but also in the fact that, for example, some owners still demanded a tall circular funnel whilst others insisted upon a squat pear-shaped structure.

By the year 1939, even before the European declaration of war, and whilst the old-established American shipbuilding yards could muster only the bare nucleus of a skilled labour force totalling no more than 20,000, the original building schedule was doubled. In August of 1940 it doubled yet again, to two hundred ships a year, by which time the commission's building programme was distributed between nineteen different yards.

These standard ships proved to be excellent turbine vessels with no equal. In 1940 one averaged nearly 17 knots on a transatlantic voyage. Another completed in November of the same year was the commission's first all-welded vessel. It showed that this technique and modern building ideas could save some 600 tons weight in any one ship.

However, American shipyards were still not geared to a war programme, and even during the following year, when the commission was five years old, some 92 per cent of the 1,422 US-flag ocean-going ships of over 2,000 tons were more than twenty years old. Of a similar vintage, too, were 225 American government-owned ships, the majority of which had been laid up 'in reserve' since the First World War.

In 1940 Britain alone was fighting the enemy. In the Atlantic the menace of the submarine was increasing and in the tally of destruction one hundred and fifty ships, totalling one million tons, had already been sent to the bottom in the first nine months of conflict. The U-boats were sinking ships at a faster rate than British yards could build them.

Clearly the menace had to be overcome and the balance restored.

So it came about that in September of 1940 a British Merchant Shipbuilding Mission headed by a representative from the Sunderland shipbuilding yard of J.L. Thompson & Sons left for the USA with the sole motive of ordering ships to be built there. Ships were needed urgently if the Battle of the Atlantic was to be won, and America with her safety and neutrality was the obvious supplier.

Already Britain had been too slow, for during the early days of the war hundreds of the laid-up American ships could have been acquired. Yet only 178,000 deadweight tons had been purchased from these First World War-built stocks — and only then after urging by Winston Churchill 'to delay no longer but to make the best possible bargain'.

The plans which the mission took to America were based on the Thompson-designed and Thompson-built *Dorington Court* of 1939. But these plans were less complicated and the ship not so beamy as the prototype, but nevertheless had the same classical hull lines as the ship which had previously impressed the British Admiralty by its ability to drive some 10,000 tons at 11 knots on a modest 2,500 ihp. These same plans were, in fact, used in the United Kingdom as the basis of the first British 'emergency' war-built ship, the *Empire Liberty* of 7,157 grt.

In New York waited Admiral Emory Scott Land, Chairman of the United States Maritime Commission. He was well aware of the fate facing Britain and considered it pointless that American energy should be diverted to build 'slow' ships for a country facing disaster. His view was that the commission should disassociate itself from these 'simple, slow' ships by permitting Britain to purchase their planned sixty ships outright.

This they did, but the mission found no working berths were available and quickly concluded that the ships would either have to be welded, and in new shipyards, or not built at all.

And so, for the two thirty-ship 'Ocean' contracts, new yards had to be specially laid out by a syndicate formed by Todd Shipyards Inc and Henry J. Kaiser's group of West coast construction and engineering firms known as Six Services Incorporated.

Other spheres of ship construction in America were not keeping pace with the upsurge of hull construction at that time and it soon became obvious that the propelling machinery needed for all their C (cargo) type ships was just not available on a large scale. At the same time the rapidity with which the war was spreading pointed to a need for even greater tonnage.

In January 1941 a change of policy came with the announcement that a new shipbuilding programme would be started. It was realised that slick, sophisticated vessels must await better times and that British thoughts of quantity rather than quality — 'ships built by the mile and chopped off by the yard' — was the only possible answer in the circumstances.

But traditional diehards still favoured commission designs and argued against the British drawings. They declared that the new 'Ocean' type hull was not suited to mass production and would not compete in speed or equipment, and in an attempt to justify their point they even cited a World War I design as a promising plan, and suggested its use instead. This was the 'Los Angeles' class of vessel, of which some 238 had been built at the end of the war. It was of the same deadweight as the planned British ships but on slightly smaller dimensions, with triple expansion engines, water tube boilers and a speed of 10½ knots. At first glance it was, perhaps, just what was needed, but the plans would have needed very much revision for the application of welding. Also, this type of ship had suffered from known defects, the main ones being a weak skeg and an unrigid engine foundation. They also had heavy and expensive boilers, the engine builder no longer existed and no plans of the machinery had survived.

Time was of vital importance. Therefore the choice had to be made from existing designs, with slight modifications to meet special needs, for it was obvious that to adapt any design other than the known British ones would bring further long delays in re-designing and testing. Some shipyards graciously conceded that with the backing of long experience, British ideas were basically sound. Also, it was estimated that the fabrication required for these ships in mass production would result in only a slight increase in man-hours over a USMC design.

With a change of heart Admiral Land then made the final decision — to copy the 'slow' British ships.

Later he was to boast of the rapid deliveries of the sixty 'Oceans' and on 15 October 1941 Mrs Emory Land named the very first of them as *Ocean Vanguard*.

In a February broadcast President Roosevelt announced this emergency 200 ship programme without disguising his contempt for their appearance in describing them as 'dreadful-looking objects'.

Immediately they were dubbed 'ugly ducklings', whilst one newspaper's headlines declared that 'Sea Scows with Blunt Bows will carry the tools to Britain' — this being a variation on the theme of a famous British wartime slogan.

Thus an emergency type of cargo steamer, based on British designs and which could be produced on a mass production basis by assembly line methods was adopted. But the use of derisive names was not the way in which to proclaim a new ship type, and Admiral Land, in an attempt to refute the bad image, gave the first reference to these ships as a 'Liberty Fleet' and nominated September 27, 1941, to be 'Liberty Fleet Day'.

After this there was great public acclamation of the ships and they were publicised by the press throughout the country. But by this time they had become 'Liberty Ships' and their new class name was adopted throughout America.

The Liberty ship is the type of vessel which, in its hundreds, is accredited with saving not only Britain, not only the Allied cause, but the whole world from disaster — for there was a grave fear that the war might be lost simply because Allied lifelines were stretched almost beyond limit owing to an insufficient number of ships.

The advent of America's Liberty ships was an undoubted relief at a time of dire distress. But this was perhaps no more than an unintentional and yet welcome reciprocal act which offset the years of 1940-41 when in Europe Britain remained undaunted against the might of the powerful and almost all-conquering German war machine, and stood virtually alone until late in 1941 when further acts of Axis aggression, culminating in the Japanese attack on Pearl Harbour, brought the United States of America into the conflict.

THE LIBERTY SHIP PROGRAMME

'The Liberty ship was an emergency product primarily for war use. It was classed with other materials of war; it was produced to be expendable if necessary — and if expended then it had served its purpose'.

But as subsequent events were to prove, it was neither a mistake nor a poor ship as its early critics averred, and it was in fact good enough to be regarded as something more than an expendable instrument of war.

In its early days the Liberty was still regarded as a doomed type and its emergency character was impressed upon Congress in a Committee Report of January 1941 which supported the special appropriation for construction, but described the Liberty as 'a five-year vessel' and added:

'It is slow and seaworthy and has the longevity of a modern steel ship, but for the demands of normal commerce in foreign trade it could not compete in speed, equipment and general serviceability with up-to-date cargo vessels. The design is the best that can be devised for an emergency product to be quickly, cheaply and simply built. They will be constructed for the emergency and whether they have any utility afterward will have to be determined then. The coastal trade may offer some possibilities in that direction.'

Built in the USA, Liberty ships were the same type as the 'Oceans' ordered by Britain from American yards and the ship 'which began it all' – the *Empire Liberty* completed in the United Kingdom in October 1941.

The Liberty ships, then, stemmed from a British design, and the basis on which the United States commenced their mammoth programme was greatly assisted by the 1940 visit of the British mission to that country, for the early mass production of 'Oceans' set the pattern for the whole of the subsequent American shipbuilding effort.

This effort consisted of a series of defined programmes or definite 'waves of expansion'. The first was that provided by the 1941 approval of nine new emergency yards – two of which were building the sixty 'Ocean' ships and the others the two hundred US-owned ships ordered on 3 January 1941.

The second followed in April of the same year, when Congress authorised the transfer of merchant ships and other forms of aid to Britain under a lease lend formula.

The remainder of 1941 saw the third expansion wave embrace not only major and minor types of ships, but also, accelerate the earlier programmes. The end of the year and Japanese attack in the Pacific opened the 'flood' of two even greater waves. The first of these two was, of course, the stupendous changes made as America entered the war, and the second one was the raising of the 1942-43 objective to a total of 24 million tons of shipping.

Many changes distinguished the Liberties from the British prototype, and in fact no British ships had been built exactly to the plans used as the basis of the new vessels. The plans brought from England had been quickly modified in the interest of fast construction, to facilitate welding and to avoid, as far as possible, the need for furnaced plates by giving a slight curvature to the whole ship. This eliminated many of the turns and twists and double curves at bow and stern and left only two plates, on each side of the forefoot, which still required furnacing and power-pressing.

Some of the larger changes, previously agreed by the commission, were embodied in the specifications, but others originated in the drawing of the working plans. Some, seemingly insignificant, turned out to be quite important – as for instance, the unstrengthened square hatch corners and the sheerstrake cut in the way of the accommodation ladder. Such features as these were the starting point of many subsequent hull fractures, but at the time of their approval there had been no experience of welded ships in wartime conditions of heavy deck loads, unusual stresses and poor ballasting.

One major hull alteration was to re-arrange the superstructure so as to accommodate the whole of the crew in a single midship house. This was not only the customary maritime commission choice but was considered safer for Atlantic voyages. It also economised on piping, heating and outfitting. The only other major modification was to eliminate deck-camber between the hatches and to have a straight camber from the sides of the hatches to the sides of the ship.

Minor alterations included steel decks instead of wooden ones, although wood was retained for furniture and fittings, some bulkheads, ceilings, linings and hatch covers, the latter so that they might, if necessary, act as life rafts. In addition the ships were given bulwarks instead of chain rails, bridge plating instead of canvas wind dodgers, access ladders to holds without the need to remove the hatches, an after steering position, searchlights, domestic refrigerators and running water in the cabins.

A major improvement was the new style contra rudder which increased speed and assisted manoeuvrability, but nevertheless the high standards previously set by the USMC were cut some three dozen times, so reducing the ships to severely austere ones. They were planned to have bar davits instead of mechanical ones, although before the first completion mechanical ones were again specified. The ships were not given radio direction finders, fire detection equipment, emergency diesel generators or lifeboat radios, and although it was known that degaussing equipment affected standard magnetic compasses, they were not fitted with gyro compasses — although each vessel had a wired gyro room as an integral part of the design.

A shortage of steel necessitated the reduction of the anchor chains from the original 300 fathoms to 240. Later this was again reduced to 210 fathoms, being divided so that one anchor had 135 fathoms and the other 75. Even so, many vessels still went to sea with only one anchor.

At times of such steel shortages wood was regarded as a good substitute for some items formerly made of steel, but by 1943, when lumber became scarce and the shortage of steel had eased, the substitution was reversed. This regular conserving and changing of materials is well shown in the problem of supplying cargo booms to the Liberty ships. The original plans specified 5-ton booms only, but increasing sizes of heavy cargoes made it necessary to put in some fifteen — then thirty and finally fifty-ton booms at Nos 2 and 4 hatches. The demand for steel booms was further increased by the failure of the wooden ones which were fitted to the first 122 Liberties built on the West coast. And so the introduction of a new cold-rolling process for tapered tubes produced a new-style, lightweight boom and nearly 17,000 of these, giving a total saving of over 2,300 tons of steel, were ordered subsequent to July 1942.

A paradoxical aspect of the shipbuilding situation was that whilst British-built vessels of the time were customarily being fitted with steam reciprocating engines and Scotch boilers, engineers in the USA had to learn the technique over again when similar machinery, designed in Britain by the North Eastern Marine Engineering Co Ltd. was installed in the 'Ocean' vessels.

Nevertheless, this same engine design was chosen for the Liberty ship programme, the only alteration being to turn the ships into oil burners and to install water-tube boilers instead of the Scotch ones. These engine units were of 2,500 ihp and standardisation was also applied here, so allowing not only the main engines but also the boilers, pumps and deck equipment to be fabricated by many different yards and factories with facilities readily available. Later new plants were constructed and existing ones expanded, so enabling, for instance, the Joshua Hendy Iron Works at Sunnyvale, California, to raise its output from ten to thirty engine sets per month, thus becoming the largest producer.

All engine parts were so completely interchangeable that during the following war years a few American-made machinery sets, temporarily surplus to immediate requirement, were fitted into some wartime Canadian-built ships (also using similar machinery), whilst in return certain Canadian-built machinery powered some of the Liberties.

The change to oil fuel also brought about other modifications. Fuel tanks replaced fixed ballast in the double bottoms and two deep tanks were added to No 1 hold for water ballast forward. The single midship house and the elimination of coal bunkers permitted the use of masts instead of king posts, and allowed the lengthening of No 3 hold.

The resultant ships from all the plans and modifications were 11-knot vessels with a standard tonnage of 7,176 gross tons (further technical details will be found under the respective sections) and these basic vessels were finally classified by the commission as the EC2-S-C1 type, this being a variation of the originally intended EC2-S-D1 design, such unused design being a simplified hull form of the type finally adopted.

This system of ship classification was based on three groups of letters and numbers. The first group — prefixed by E for emergency — indicated a type of vessel (ie cargo, tanker, passenger, etc) and its approximate waterline length (based on a scale wherein 1 represented less than 400 feet; 2 represented from 400 to 450 feet, etc). The second group indicated the type of machinery and number of propellers (ie S equalled steam; ST equalled steam, twin screw; M equalled motor, etc), and the third group indicated the particular design of the ship-type and its modifications.

There was later variation to the classification as differing Liberty types evolved. It may be noted here that the three-group system was adopted by the USA for certain of its wartime tonnage; prior to this a two-group classification applied.

Therefore, with Liberty ships, the first group of letters, EC2, indicated that the vessels would be about the same size as the normal C2 vessels but different from them in being of the emergency type.

The original style of nomenclature adopted for the emergency vessels was the bestowing upon them the names of persons notable in the history and culture of America. Later names included those of merchant seamen, military and naval nurses and other eminent Americans from all walks of life – although there were some notable exceptions to this.

Organised under the jurisdiction of the USMC, two new shipyards were created early in 1941. These were the Oregon Shipbuilding Corporation and the Bethlehem-Fairfield Shipyard Inc, and in January 1941 both were awarded contracts for the construction of shipyard facilities. As a result eight slipways (later increased to eleven) were built at Portland, Oregon, and thirteen (later sixteen) at Baltimore. On March 14 of the same year both yards contracted to produce Liberty cargo ships, and these and all subsequent Liberty ships from all yards were given a 'Maritime Commission, Emergency' hull number as well as the builder's yard number.

In the event, a total of 3,148 Liberty MCE numbers were allocated between different shipyards, but a total of only 2,710 ships were constructed, the balance of the numbers being either not used or the contracts cancelled.

The story here of one batch of cancelled contracts serves as the forerunner to the brief yard histories shown under their respective headings.

To meet the February 1942 directive from the President of the USA, the new Higgins shipyard at New Orleans was authorised. Of revolutionary design, it planned to have four assembly lines each a mile long and was to contain a total of 44 ships in various pre-launch constructional stages at any one time. Along with this grandiose scheme was the vision of New Orleans becoming the future shipbuilding centre of the world, and to set the pace the first five vessels of the 200-ship order were to be delivered in 1942 and the remainder during 1943.

But mounting costs gave rise to scepticism, for the original estimate of 25 million dollars had, within five months, risen to 59 million. Soon it was obvious there would be no 1942 output and that the yard would be the last to come into production. At the same time a shortage of steel was a limiting factor in shipbuilding, but whereas in a normal yard any delay would affect only 'a few' ships, shortages in this huge yard would have stopped work on all the many ships on the lines.

And so the yard was not completed and the 200-ship contract was cancelled. At the time of the cancellation no MCE hull numbers had been allocated to the vessels of this contract.

Elsewhere, rapid shipyard construction enabled Bethlehem-Fairfield to lay the first keel (of the *Patrick Henry*) on April 30th, whilst the Oregon Shipbuilding Corporation laid two, the *Star of Oregon* and the *Meriwether Lewis* on May 19th. Only eight months after the agreement to create these yards, each had launched its first ship and three months later, on December 30th and 31st respectively, each had delivered its first complete product.

Thus both the Pacific coast and the Atlantic coast participated in contributing to the war effort the first of the emergency cargo ships.

In all, during 1941, a total of nine new emergency shipyards were approved. From their original total of 65 ways it was expected to produce 260 ships (the first 200 Liberties and the British 'Oceans') within two years. Of these nine yards, two, at Baltimore and Wilmington, were in the hands of old established shipbuilders; one at New Orleans was in the hands of a Great Lakes builder and another, at Mobile, was managed by a large ship repair company. The remaining five yards, at Houston, Los Angeles and Portland, plus the two for British 'Oceans', were under the control of a Todd Shipyards/Bath IronWorks/Henry J. Kaiser group.

In the year 1775 Patrick Henry, the person, had cried 'Give me liberty or give me death'. The ship *Patrick Henry*, the first of the many Liberties, was launched on 27 September 1941, and on that day, called 'Liberty Fleet Day', and still some ten weeks before Pearl Harbour, there was presented a dazzling array of outstanding shipbuilding achievements.

Throughout the nation fourteen ships were launched with many notable persons speaking at the various ceremonies, and capped by a message from the President, directed especially to shipyard workers.

His speech was more than just praise of the occasion and an appeal for 'more ships and still more ships', for it contained the first reference to his determination to set aside the laws which prevented American merchant ships being armed and prevented their entering the combat zones. 'Each new ship', he said, 'strikes a blow at the menace to the nation and for the liberty of the free peoples of the world .... we propose that these ships shall sail the seas as intended, and to the best of our ability shall protect them from torpedoes, bombs or shells'.

Up to the time when the Neutrality Law was finally amended on 13 November 1941, none of America's merchant ships were armed. Under the amendment arming began, but at first progress was very slow. Not long after, the declaration of war temporarily brought about a critical situation, for enemy submarines roamed the Atlantic, the East coast and the Gulf of Mexico almost at will and ships were soon to be sunk in alarming numbers before the matter was resolved.

After the delivery of the *Patrick Henry* the shipbuilding programme swung into full scale production. Eighteen shipyards were ultimately involved and almost unbelievable records were made and broken again and again. A study of the production times at the two previously-named yards produce some interesting figures for their first year of operation.

At Fairfield the first vessel (yard No 2001) was on the slip for 150 days and spent ninety-five days fitting-out, a total building time of 245 days.

Yard No 2002 took five days longer to complete; twenty ships later the total was down to 120 days and at the fifty-ship mark was down to fifty-eight days, this being fifty-one days on slip and seven fitting out. This new yard maintained an average of 'more than' five launchings per month during their first year, and in August 1942 created a world record when twelve vessels (yard Nos 2044-2050 and 2056-2060) went down the ways. In the previous month another record was established at the yard, with twelve completions.

In the case of the Portland yard the average first-year monthly launchings was 'nearly' six ships, reaching ten vessels during August 1942 and attaining a peak for completions in May of the same year when thirteen vessels were handed to the maritime commission. Here, the first vessel (yard No 171) was completed in 227 days but the next vessel (yard No 170) took twenty-seven more days to finish. Up to August 1942 the fastest time for a completion was forty-seven days (yard No 236), this being a radical change from the 257 days spent over one of the first ships (yard No 173).

However, late in September 1942 a special assembly effort resulted in a ship (yard No 581) being launched after only ten days and delivered some five days later.

Also during this same month the American shipyards reached the promised goal of three ships a day, by delivering ninety-three new ships into service. These vessels totalled more than one million deadweight tons, and for the record it may be noted that sixty-seven were Liberties, seven were 'Oceans' for British account, seven were large tankers, ten were of the C1, C2 and C3 types and the remaining two were a passenger-cargo vessel and an ore carrier.

By October 1942 the American shipbuilding capacity had expanded more than 600 per cent over the 1937 figure, and there were more than sixty shipyards producing various types of ships for the maritime commission. Since February of the previous year, when President Roosevelt ordered the emergency programme, the commission had authorised and financed the construction of twenty new shipyards and also laid claim to some closed-down yards. A capacity of ninety-seven ways was authorised before 'Liberty Fleet Day' and a subsequent sixty-eight ways made a total of 165 ways in these twenty yards.

A further forty-five ways were added to existing yards, and this total of 210 slips, plus later expansion, permitted a schedule of more than 2,300 merchant vessels for production in 1942 and 1943 (of which more than 1,500 were Liberty ships) totalling in all some 27 million deadweight tons. From this total the 1942 figure is quite significant, for although some 11 million tons (including 8 million from America) of new merchantmen was constructed by the Allies, the Axis destruction of shipping was so widespread that there was a nett loss for the year of about one million tons.

Another event during 1942 – on February 7th – was the formation of the War Shipping Administration, set up by the President as a war emergency measure to control all American shipping and to take over, for the duration of the war, the vessels of the maritime commission. After the war, in September 1946, this administration was liquidated and all vessels reverted to the jurisdiction of the commission.

Initially the 1944 target of some 2,000 merchantmen included only about 800 Liberties, for by this time the trend of military requirement was for a greater proportion of faster ships – those which could run free of convoy and move quickly to fighting fronts and also those which would be more effective in post-war times. By August of this year the commission had 251 slipways at its disposal, of which 103 were being used by the USN.

In fact, by August of the previous year one yard, North Carolina, had already completed its last Liberty; had launched its first C type ship less than three weeks afterward and had laid its first 'Victory' ship keel two months later.

Also, for future invasion plans the Bethlehem and the new Kaiser yards built tank landing ships and escort aircraft carriers (respectively) on slipways designed for Liberties. All these and other similar factors account for subsequent breaks in some sequences of Liberty yard numbers, both in these and in other shipyards.

Nevertheless, as Liberty shipbuilding progressed still more records were made and broken with great rapidity. A special effort had launched one in only ten days and the response to this produced the world record of the assembly and launch of the *Robert E. Peary* in only four days, fifteen and a half hours after keel laying.

Henry J. Kaiser was undoubted 'king' of mass production shipbuilding in America. Previously his group had linked with Todd Shipyards and the combine controlled five of the nine new yards from 1941. In the early part of this year the importance of forthcoming Kaiser management was not foreseen, for in shipbuilding the Todd name still overshadowed that of its partner. Subsequently Kaiser formed new yards of his own, acquired full ownership of the west coast yards he managed and sold to Todd his interest in the Todd-managed yards elsewhere.

But in 1940 this one-time owner of a New York photographic shop was still unknown in Britain, was unknown in shipbuilding, but was well known in America as the head of a construction group. His business interests had changed, firstly to the sand and gravel one, and thence had progressed into giant construction work. Notable feats to his credit included a series of dams — Hoover, Grand Coulee and Bonneville, and also the famous San Francisco Bridge which crosses the bay to the city of Oakland.

Kaiser was a man with immense drive, ability and initiative and was always willing to tackle 'impossible' tasks — indeed he could readily have coined the boast 'that the impossible is performed at once, miracles take a little longer'. Fortunately he had been willing 'to have a go' at the impossible task of constructing for Britain not only the sixty 'Ocean' ships on the solid rock of Portland, Maine, and the mudflats of Richmond, California, but had even brought in his own experts from the dam projects to help construct the new yards as well. Henry Kaiser was in the forefront of knowledge when the calculated risk of welding the emergency ships was taken.

At the peak of his 'reign' he controlled many of the major prefabricating yards, and it was said that he did not build ships but simply produced them. Probably only one in every 200 of his workers had ever seen a shipyard before, and 25 per cent had not even seen the sea! Many of his executives had not previously faced ship construction problems, and so they approached their new tasks — as indeed the whole organisation did — with open minds and no preconceived theories about conventional shipbuilding, but with the determination to get things done quickly, efficiently and with the minimum wastage of time, materials and labour.

These men were hustlers within a group which considered no task to be too difficult.

The Kaiser theories on mass production — and the fact that he spoke of 'front' and 'back' ends of a product which just happened to be the shape of a ship — caused America's traditional shipbuilders much amusement, but nevertheless he fulfilled all his 'promises' on shipbuilding. One promise was the determination that California, a land of movies, fruit and sunshine, should have its own steel plant and so avoid the frequent frustrations of awaiting steel supplies from the eastern part of the States.

An enquiry regarding the source of a potential iron ore supply brought the retort 'we'll prospect for it out here' — and it was found, too, in Utah......

Praise for his methods; acclaim for his achievements; amazement at ever-reducing delivery times, stirring accounts of success constantly made big news:

......'Henry Kaiser, who knew nothing of shipbuilding only two years ago, has just completed a ship in 47 days......'

......'a Liberty ship launched on the West coast was not only the 75th from this Kaiser yard in a year, but was launched only ten days after keel-laying......'

......'Kaiser advertises for a 'mere' 20,000 additional shipyard workers......'

Speed of construction is typified by the amusing 'Kaiser' story of the lady asked to launch a ship, and who arrived at the launching platform to be confronted by the usual bottle of champagne but no ship. Asking if a mistake had been made, she was advised to start swinging the bottle immediately, for not only the stem but indeed the whole ship would arrive at any moment!

These, and many other similar facts, stories and anecdotes inspired both sides of the Atlantic to even greater efforts over the fateful years.

Many wartime Kaiser shipyards were laid out on quite revolutionary principles, as was one of the two which built the 'Ocean' ships, and whether in the sun of the State of California or the rain of the State of Washington, the efficiency was the same, for the yards were merely assembly plants for the 30,000-plus components produced en-masse in thousands of factories in more than thirty-two States which went into the making of a Liberty ship.

Some yards, for instance, had no slipways, the substitute being docks or basins. Ships were not launched; the docks were just flooded and the ships floated out. Every basin was spanned by giant cranes and the whole group was inter-connected by platforms at various levels.

Notable items missing from these revolutionary yards were ordinary shipyard tools and equipment.

Component parts were consumed virtually non-stop and it was quite commonplace to see, say, complete deck-houses erected upside-down on a wheeled trolley and then inverted and placed in position. Also it became quite customary to see stock-piles of double-bottom sections with all piping already installed, waiting to be dropped complete on to the keels. Other stock would include complete stern-frame assemblies and even complete bow units. For yet other yards fabrication was carried out in plant which, pre-war, produced bridges, structural steel-work and the like.

It has been suggested that the influence of welding made all such fabrication possible, but really this statement is no more than partial truth. It was really the speed of required deliveries which made welding necessary, and special portable welding plants which welded continuously whilst moving at walking pace were evolved for this purpose.

In general the Liberty hull was all-welded, although builders were given considerable latitude and between them produced several combinations such as rivetted frames, rivetted seams and in some cases rivetted deckhouses. Some yards, as for example the Delta Shipbuilding Co, elected to weld 100 per cent, for, being a new yard with mostly inexperienced personnel, they were able to establish the principle before their production commenced. With such welding they were able to eliminate both rivetting facilities and the necessary personnel. Later on, when rivetted gunwale bars and deck straps were fitted to the ships a rivetting section was established for this purpose.

As the shipbuilding programme continued, numbers of improvements were made to the Liberty design, most of which were for the purpose of giving the vessels greater protection against enemy action, but which included the addition of quick-release lifeboat gear, so giving a better chance to any crew forced to abandon ship. Ship-yards took alterations in their stride, but, as was only to be expected with such a vast mass-production programme, there were also some problems to be overcome. Undoubtedly the major one was some disquieting structural failures which occurred in these welded ships, whilst propeller-dropping also occurred quite frequently. The latter problem arose simply because of the mass building of the ships. Previously a ship's propeller was fitted tightly to the shaft without the use of a gland sealing ring; but such a tight fit was not readily achieved during mass produc-tion, and when not achieved corrosion often resulted as steel and bronze came together.

In the meantime the critics of welding had continued in their determination to discredit and undermine the nation's shipbuilding achievements. The climax to their campaign came early in 1944, when their growing fears for safety were publicly directed at the Portland, Oregon yard, builders of the *John Straub* — which had broken in two and sunk in Arctic waters. Previously, there had been a number of similar Liberty casualties (see the first vessel listed in this book), including two in quick succession in the December of the previous year — the *John P. Gaines* (qv) and the *Valery Chkalov*, (ex *Alexander Baranof*, qv). This latter vessel was, at the time, flying the Russian flag under lease lend terms, and the Soviet authorities were fortunate in that their demands brought them an immediate replacement vessel from the Oregon shipyard.

However, loss statistics showed that during the previous two years of 1942 and 1943 a heavy loss of life had in fact occurred due to the breaking in two of welded ships in Arctic waters. It was said that 12½ per cent of all Liberties had weld defects, nearly 10 per cent had already developed cracks and that one ship in every thirty had suffered major fractures.

Doubtless the statements that 'when they crack it sounds like an explosion'; 'the cracks run like ladders in a stocking' and 'the ships stand on a wave and the ends shake like jelly' were all founded on some fact, and perhaps even accounted for the early reports that the *John Straub* was 'sunk by explosion'.

Some alarm spread through the nation when, in Alaska, yet another Liberty (loaded with troops) split open whilst still moored alongside. Immediately the use of ten more Liberties, already converted into troopships, was vetoed until further investigations had been made.

It was found that plating fractures occurred from notches in the steel, defective welds or square hatch corners and were being accentuated by severe Arctic cold which turned ordinary mild steel brittle, like glass, and ships did in fact 'go bang and fall apart'.

During the winter of 1943-44 Kaiser-built vessels were the most affected by this cracking, but then many of his yards were near to the North Pacific and a large proportion of their output was, naturally, assigned to these cold waters.

As a preventive measure the 'crack-arresting' practice was introduced. This was in the form of special reinforcement to the hatches, strengthening with rivetted gunwale bars and deck straps, and the use of a tougher steel where stresses were concentrated. In addition the troopship conversions had additional girders fitted to their inner bottoms.

As designed, Liberties were 'stiff' ships; ie, stable but liable to roll violently in a seaway, especially when empty – which could lead to damage. (The alternative 'tender' ship would roll less but be less stable). Therefore, to take the stiffness out of Liberties in ballast, the practice grew during wartime (and subsequently) of putting a solid ballast in the 'tween decks to counteract the great weight down below.

This ballasting ensured a better performance, but under certain circumstances and conditions it was at the expense of stability and this, in fact, did lead to actual loss and to several near-losses. Further reference to this and referring particularly to ballasting in the United Kingdom, will be found under the heading of 'The Sam Ships'.

Many of the basic type of Liberty cargo ship were transferred to, or completed for America's allies; some 200 came to Britain under the terms of lease lend and these were all given the British style of nomenclature, having the prefix 'Sam' to their names.

Some fifty ships, mostly Oregon and Permanente built, were turned over to the Soviet Union on similar terms. But whereas the British lease lenders were all 'technically' returned to United States ownership, most of the Soviet ones subsequently suffered from a form of permanent detention, for that nation politely ignored the American request for the return of their ships, and most of those loaned some 25 years ago still trade under the Russian flag.

They are, of course, still technically on loan and yet have long-since been written off by the USA as a bad debt. At the current age and condition of the average Liberty, their return is perhaps not now so very desirable, for trading vessels of this vintage are no longer in demand and reserve fleet status would only briefly postpone a final trip to a shipbreakers yard.

Two major re-designs of the standard Liberty ship produced the Liberty tanker and the Liberty collier, whilst extensive conversion produced a further two (similar) types – these being transports for aircraft and for army tanks.

Further details of all these will be found under their respective sections.

In addition, other modifications fitted many vessels for use as troopships, hospital and training ships and a considerable number of others were taken by the Navy and Army and were extensively altered into other special naval and military auxiliaries. An example of a Navy conversion is the batch converted into floating repair shops (ARG), for these were given facilities for both major and minor repair and each had accommodation for a crew of 600 plus further accommodation for the crews of the ships being repaired.

Often the upperworks and superstructures of the converted and modified ships bore little likeness to the original vessel, although the standard Liberty hull always remained an easy point of recognition.

The letter Z used as a prefix to a design type was intended to indicate that the vessel was a modification of a standard type ship to make it a special purpose ship. The Z designation was not consistently used for this purpose, however.

The Z3-EC2-S-C1 designation refers to Liberty ships converted to training ships for use at marine schools.

WAR LOSSES

Despite early structural problems there was an overall soundness in the welded hulls and the Liberty ships as a whole gave tremendous and gallant war service, and they often sustained – and survived – terrific punishment under the most extreme conditions. A single example is the loss of the *Cornelia P. Spencer* (qv) which stayed afloat until a third torpedo sank her.

Doubtless many deeds of heroism remain untold, but rated very highly from those known must be the valiant action of the *Stephen Hopkins (I)* which, with her single 4-inch gun, engaged and sank the powerfully-armed German commerce raider *Steir*.

Nevertheless, all gallant services deserved recognition and this point was taken by the USA with her awards of 'Gallant Ship' plaques; the first vessel so awarded for its heroics was the *Samuel Parker* — under which name will be found a summary of her qualifying deeds.

The first vessel in the long procession of Liberty war losses was the *John Adams* which, as early as May 1942 when only a couple of months old, was caught in the Pacific by a Japanese submarine and torpedoed in No 4 hold. The ship was carrying cased petrol and 24 lucky survivors reached the safety of Noumea.

Luck also played its part when some vessels were under attack. In June 1943 when 50 miles south of Rio the *Charles Willson Peale* fought off an attack by the U-199. On another occasion the *Albert Gallatin* was struck by a salvo of three torpedoes — all of which failed to explode! But her luck ran out in the following year when she succumbed to another submarine attack.

Some Liberties were converted into differing types of trooper, and this in some cases led to heavy loss of life. During the war a grand total of 4½ million US troops embarked for Europe and Africa, of which 3,594 were lost at sea. A great loss of 504 men occurred when the *Paul Hamilton* (qv) exploded, whilst a further large loss of 76 troops occurred with the sinking of the *H.G. Blasdal*.

Similarly, the USN also suffered its share of losses; 196 persons were killed with the disintegration of its Liberty ship USS *Serpens* in January 1945.

An interesting group of losses were the seven Liberties, all previously war-damaged, which were used as 'Gooseberry' breakwater blockships at the 'Mulberry A' (American) harbour of the Normandy landings in June 1944. 'Gooseberry' was the code name for a shelter provided by sinking a line of blockships in 2½ fathoms or less, whilst a 'Mulberry' was an artificial harbour erected for the landing of stores off enemy beaches.

It may be noted that this 'Mulberry' harbour was formed under extremely adverse conditions. Nevertheless, it was constructed in only ten days instead of the estimated thirty days. But the very speed of its construction and the incorrect positioning of the ships told against the operation at the time when its strength was most needed. For in the most violent north-easterly summer storms for forty years which raged later the same month, breaches were torn in the breakwaters, Liberty and other blockships broke their backs and a great mass of wreckage was strewn ashore. Destruction was complete and the harbour, including the blockships, was officially abandoned.

The Liberty breakwaters have their own story. Invasion plans had deemed 'Utah' and 'Omaha' beach-heads as the sites for Gooseberries 1 and 2 — vulnerable positions both to the enemy and to the weather. Ferocious battles raged ashore as the first three ships were scuttled at 'Utah', including the Liberty *James Iredell*.

In the meantime five more vessels had formed the 'Omaha' spearhead. The *George S. Wasson* was hit by shell fire and an enemy bomber disintegrated above her decks whilst she was positioning. Her submerging hull was caught by the tide, tugs failed to hold her and she sank after drifting out of position. The following ship, the *Matt W. Ransom* took up her position whilst under dive-bomber attack. Her stern wire parted at the crucial moment, she drifted more than a thousand feet and sank in shallow water.

A third Liberty from the force, the *Benjamin Contee,* abandoned by her tugs when under heavy shell fire was fortunate to settle in her correct position.

Ultimately two smaller harbours were formed around these misplaced ships; the remaining Liberties were successfully scuttled and the lines of breakwater ships daily grew longer. Later, within these breakwaters, moorings for Liberty supply ships were laid.

Whilst serving in this capacity the *Charles Morgan* met her end. She received a direct bomb hit aft; this detonated her 5in ammunition lockers and the after end of the ship blew up with a shattering roar.

In all, a total of more than two hundred Liberty ships were lost during the war, of which some fifty vessels were lost whilst on their maiden voyage. An example of this, from the early days of Liberty shipbuilding, are the seven Liberties (Bethlehem-Fairfield yard Nos 2008, 2010, 2012, 2015 and 2018, and North Carolina yard Nos 4 and 5) which participated in the 35-ship PQ.17 convoy from Iceland to North Russia in June 1942. Twenty-three (including four Liberties) were sunk — taking to the bottom some 3,500 vehicles, 430 tanks, over 200 bombers and 100,000 tons of other war cargo. Only eleven vessels (including two Liberties) finally reached the 'haven' of Soviet shores. The remaining Liberty (the *Richard Bland*) had grounded off Iceland when the convoy sailed, and had returned to port.

Of course, during all the war years the hazard of normal marine risk was ever-present, and added its quota to the long list of wartime casualties. Nevertheless, many vessels were salved and repaired for further service — as for instance the *William B. Ogden* which was stranded for more than a year before being refloated by the United States Coastguard Service.

POST-WAR DISPOSAL

When the war ended the USA owned more than forty million tons of new ships and the disposal of this vast fleet posed two major questions. How many could be used commercially and what was to be done with the remainder?

America had again become a maritime nation and had every intention of remaining one! This, combined with the world need for moving enormous tonnages, suggested 'sale' or 'reserve' as the obvious disposal of their surplus ships.

The qualities of the ships made them a problem. Either they were a national asset or were to become a menace to post-war commercial shipping, depending on the point of view. For their economical fuel consumption, excellent equipment of cargo gear and deck machinery and a 27½ ft draft were sufficient qualities to make them highly desirable to operators both in the USA and abroad.

Also the ships required only very minor structural alteration, generally only the removal of armament, surplus liferaft equipment and gun tubs, to transform them into excellent tramp ships for service all the world over.

And so, in the immediate post-war years, America allocated numbers of the vessels for possible purchase by some of her Allies and also by her former foe, Italy.

At the same time she indicated her desire for the return of the lease lend vessels under the British flag.

And whilst Italy and Greece's allocation of 100 vessels each, France's seventy-five, Norway's quota of twenty-four and China's share of eighteen were all under prompt negotiation, Britain's long-delayed request to purchase tonnage was casually added to the very foot of the allocation list.

Later the American mood of nationalism eased under the pressure of a reminder of the wartime agreement whereby America had concentrated on the building of merchant ships whilst Britain directed her major efforts to warship construction, and she finally authorised the sale of 106 vessels to the United Kingdom.

Therefore, in the following years and before the authority for their 'trading' sale expired in 1951, many Liberties passed into world-wide commercial ownership.

Others were operated for a while for the United States Government by private American companies, but the balance of the surplus ships formed the basis of the National Defense Reserve Fleet, created by an Act of Congress in 1946.

Over the years many vessels from this fleet have been sold for scrap (see Part Seven), whilst those in private ownership produced many variations to owners account, including conversions to heavy-lift, self-unloaders, bulk carriers and even to container ships.

A few of the Italian-flag vessels were converted during 1949-50 into motorships by the use of Fiat direct-drive engines, and this raised their power output to 3,600 bhp.

It may be noted here that one or two vessels, sold to private buyers soon after the war, did in fact retain their original names throughout their careers. One, the *Richard D. Lyons*, passed to commercial ownership in 1946 and, still under this name, finally succumbed at the age of 23 years to the shipbreakers during 1968.

When the price at which America sold ships after the war was determined, the cost figures were broken down into direct and indirect charges and different items were included or excluded — the latter exemplified by the 'recovery' of the costs of the two yards (Wilmington and Vancouver) which were retained as standby yards for use in future emergency. And so, although Liberty costs were not accurately segregated for this purpose from the other ships built, the estimates of the 5,601 ships delivered between 1939 and 1945 (including Liberties) gave the total cost as 14.2 billion dollars.

The original price put on Liberties during their sale to Allied nations received severe criticism in some quarters.

Britain acquired her allocation of ships at nearly £140,000 each — but they were destined to establish historic fame during the following years as their price range and values fluctuated in alternate peaks and depressions at the dictates of shipping needs and world crises.

By early 1949 the ships were changing hands for sums approaching the £200,000 mark. Three years later the figure was treble this sum for a top-class vessel built by an experienced shipbuilder.

At the time of the Suez crisis in 1956 values again increased and reached an all-time high when one British-owned vessel was sold for nearly £700,000. But then they as quickly slumped again. By 1960 values were down to less than £60,000 or its equivalent. By late in 1961 they had risen to above the £130,000 mark and by 1963 were down yet again to the 1960 level.

All this time the vessels were ageing and ships in generally poor condition or those from the reserve fleets were levelling down to rock-bottom values. A then 'low' was reached in 1962 with the disposal of an active ship for only just over £30,000.

Of the many Liberties retained by the USN many of those of the Z-EC2-S-C5 (transports for boxed aircraft) type have in more recent times taken on such roles as radar picket ships, technical research ships and the like. Other interesting navy conversions occurred in the 1950s when a group became classified as Miscellaneous Auxiliary Service Craft (YAG). From these a group of five vessels, YAG 36–40, classified as the YAG 36 class, were used to evaluate differing radical minesweeping concepts at minimum cost. Some of them were also used during atomic tests in the Pacific.

Without doubt the greatest post-war group variation concerned Liberty tankers — for most of these were converted into dry cargo freighters. Many of them were also lengthened to a standard 511½ feet and to some 8,500 gross tons by the insertion of a new 70 ft midbody. In some cases, too, a third mast was added forward (*Sealady,* ex *Alan Seeger,* qv) whilst with others a mast-house and vents sufficed.

Both with these vessels before their conversion and the remaining few which retained tanker status for a longer period, their need for disguise had long-since passed and a customary change became the removal of the derricks and often of the fore or main-mast too, so leaving a single stump forward in a variety of positions. In at least one case all three orthodox masts were removed completely from the vessel and replaced merely by two slender pole masts.

It may be noted here that on 25 May 1950, the United States Department of Commerce (Federal Maritime Board) assumed the functions of the United States Maritime Commission. The controlling body then became known as the Maritime Administration. This body is often referred to in America as MARAD.

THE LIBERTY SHIP CONVERSION PROGRAMME

In the early 1950s the American Department of Defense became increasingly concerned over the reducing ability of the National Defense Reserve Fleet to fulfill its role as a potential and readily-available emergency fleet.

Rapid post-war improvements in warfare techniques and in commercial shipping indicated that vessels not capable of a sustained sea speed of 15 knots were inadequate for logistic support and were a negligible asset to national defence.

This point had been proven by the Korean emergency, for military requirements during 1950 brought about the re-activation of all suitable fast ships from the reserve, but only a limited number of Liberties. Additional requirements necessitated the chartering of nearly all the other fast ships then flying the US flag and this left world-wide shipping and trade to be implemented by the remaining, unsuitable, 11-knot Liberty ships.

In 1953 it was decided to commence a 'Liberty Ship Conversion and Engine Improvement Programme' with the objectives of upgrading to modern requirements and defence needs the speed of the Liberty ship portion (over 80 per cent) of the reserve fleet; to assist the American Merchant Marine with the development of new types of propulsion machinery; to improve the standard of cargo handling techniques; and to investigate the sea-keeping qualities of high-speed Liberties with and without a lengthened hull form.

Tank-testing had previously shown it possible to increase the speed of the ships to a sustained 15 knots by the use of an engine of 6,000 shp, and this fortunately permitted potential use of 'Victory' ship turbines, large numbers of which were readily available from stock.

In August 1954 funds for the programme were allocated under Public Law 663, and four trial conversions (Bethlehem-Fairfield yard Nos 2017, 2035, 2045 and 2050) of the basic EC2-S-C1 type were decided upon.

Upon the experience gained with these four vessels depended future conversions and re-activations from the reserve fleet, so each ship underwent a differing type of conversion.

The common factor was the replacement of their main propulsion machinery. One vessel was fitted with steam turbines, another with geared diesels, the third with gas turbines and the last with gas generators.

In general, the development of gas turbine types of main engines was based on the conviction that technological advances made possible the use of this type of machinery, which was expected to give greater efficiency and lower operating and maintenance costs than conventional steam turbine power plants.

Also, in the gas turbine field, there was in existence a considerable industrial capacity for such production, for similar machinery rated at 5,000 hp or more had already been produced in large quantities and used in commercial service throughout the world. Therefore, such designs needed only slight modification to make them more suitable for marine use.

One of the four conversions retained its normal hull whilst the other three vessels were lengthened by some 25 feet and given finer lines at the bow.

Interesting results were shown by all the ships in their new guise, but a final cost in excess of 12 million dollars spent on four ships with only a doubtful future was deemed sufficient reason not to proceed with general re-activation, and no further conversions were undertaken.

In fact the ships soon joined their comrades in the reserve fleet, and an interesting point to note is that at the peak of the Vietnam war in late 1967/early 1968 — when fast ships were again in great demand — only one of the four was actually returned to service.

Further conversion details will be found under the names of the individual vessels. Lengthened hulls really put these ships into the C3 scale, but in practice they retained the EC2 designation. No contracts were awarded for a conversion design EC2-GE-8f, nor were any for three other designs (all prefixed EC2-ME, but suffixed 8c, 8d and 8e) which were for diesel-electric conversions, or for the diesel conversion type EC2-M-8a.

THE BREAK-UP OF THE FLEET

Of more than forty million deadweight tons of wartime American construction, nearly three-quarters of the total was accounted for by the Liberty ships. Many of the latter went into 'reserve' lay-up, and over the years their numbers gradually declined until by mid-1967 only some 650 remained in this status. By the same date an overall total of nearly a thousand Liberties (including reserve and commercially-owned trading vessels) had been scrapped, whilst more than 600 still operated under the flags of many nations.

Two years later the total number of scrapped Liberties had risen considerably, for during this period the number in reserve had dropped to 428 and the number still in private ownership had reduced by some 50 per cent. In addition eighty-three other Liberties remained laid up in military reserve.

Post-war casualty losses whilst the ships were still only a few years of age were quite minimal, with the exception of a number of belated 'war damage' losses — usually caused by stray drifting mines. Commercial tonnage at this time, with the exception of the large stock held by the government in its reserve fleet, was still at a premium and, naturally, all but the most serious damage caused by marine hazard was worthy of repair. Losses remained low until 1961 — also the peak year for scrappings — but from this year, when the early-built vessels were approaching an age of twenty years, a disquieting frequency of major casualties increased to a rate which, by 1965, was double that of the previous year. Over this same period Liberty losses rose from 4 per cent to more than 9 per cent of the world's total losses.

By the mid-1960s then, all Liberties had reached a 20 year old retirement age, had already undergone or were due to undergo the stringent 'Special 20 year Survey' and were therefore on the brink of outliving their usefulness.

Thus a sudden demise commenced, due to a number of factors, of which the major ones were accelerated corrosion and severe structural deterioration. This is cited by a single case, included herein for interest, of the *Agios Giorgis* (ex *Frank H. Dodd,* qv) and the reports of her final casualty before she proceeded to the shipbreakers.

Profile of a Liberty cargo ship. The *St Olaf* later
became a hospital ship. (Bethlehem, Yard no 2020)

The launching of the *Patrick Henry*. The ship was under construction for a total of 245 days, this being 150 days on the slipway and a further 95 days outfitting. Her maiden voyage took her round the Cape of Good Hope with stores for the British Army in Egypt and she thus became the first American ship to pass through the Suez Canal after America entered the war. (Bethlehem, Yard no 2001)

Tritonia, ex *Samluzon,* a Bethlehem-built Liberty ship. Delivered to Hong Kong shipbreakers in July 1969. (Yard no 2371)

Thomas Nelson, as rebuilt under the conversion programme. (Bethlehem, Yard no 2017)

John Sergeant, as rebuilt under the conversion programme. (Bethlehem, Yard no 2050)

The launch of the *John Gallup* on March 3, 1943. (Bethlehem, Yard no 2101)

For, as ships aged and values dropped, it became no longer economically possible to meet the rising costs of maintenance or renewal, classification, or even the insurance surcharge for 'over age' vessels: in fact Liberties generally became not worthy of the expense of repair.

By 1967-68, when all prices were being based on mere scrap value, Liberties were still fetching around the equivalent of £50,000 when delivered to Far Eastern shipbreakers, but the useless vessels sold 'locally' from the US reserve fleets for scrapping in the USA were only raising sums below the equivalent of £20,000.

Towards the end of 1968 shipbreakers in the Taiwan port of Kaohsiung had, for some time, been figuring prominently in scrapping reports from the Far East. The deals were always the subject of negotiation between the vendor and the shipbreaker, the latter's price offers being based on the lightweight tonnage of the vessels involved.

But about this same time these shipbreakers began to give a very thorough check to some of the ships arriving for demolition before acceptance by them was confirmed. In some cases the letters of credit were withheld pending even further negotiation. This development probably resulted from the shipbreakers previous experience, for their sudden checking concerned such items as machinery and fittings, bronze propellers and other valuable metals, and occasionally the light displacement was disputed. Generally these last-minute disputes led to price reductions, for sometimes the ships were short of their allotted outfit and on other occasions advantages might have been gained from the knowledge that a prudent owner, with his ship newly arrived in the breaking port, did not wish to suffer monetary loss from delayed delivery of the ship or undue retention of the crew.

An example of the value of such outfit is shown by the sale, at the end of 1968, of the *Amalia* (ex *J. Frank Cooper,* qv) — albeit to Japanese shipbreakers — for the above-average price of 138,000 dollars. The sale included a spare bronze propeller, and this item alone was valued at about 5,000 dollars.

However, all the very many factors involved and concerning these now slow, obsolete and worn-out vessels with a comparatively high fuel consumption still steadily compels private owners and governments to scrap their surviving Liberty ships in favour of modern, fast, more economic tonnage.

During the years of 1966 and 1967 the world's shipbuilders suddenly produced more than twenty differing designs of vessels styled as 'Liberty replacement' ships. Only a few of these designs, and particularly the British and the Japanese ones, gained immediate popularity among shipowners, and it is of interest to note that whilst the first Japanese-built vessel of the type took over nine months from keel-laying to delivery in 1967, the first British-built one (of the SD 14 type) was completed in only fourteen weeks.

SHIPBUILDERS

Alabama Dry Dock Company, Mobile, Alabama.
Bethlehem-Fairfield Shipyards Inc, Baltimore, Maryland.
California Shipbuilding Corporation, Los Angeles, California.
Delta Shipbuilding Company, New Orleans, Louisiana.
J.A. Jones Construction Company, Brunswick, Georgia.
J.A. Jones Construction Company, Panama City, Florida.
Kaiser Company, Vancouver, Washington.
Marinship Corporation, Sausalito, California.
New England Shipbuilding Corporation, East Yard, South Portland, Maine.
New England Shipbuilding Corporation, West Yard, South Portland, Maine.
North Carolina Shipbuilding Company, Wilmington, North Carolina.
Oregon Ship Building Corporation, Portland, Oregon.
Permanente Metals Corporation (Shipbuilding Division), No 1 Yard, Richmond, California.
Permanente Metals Corporation (Shipbuilding Division), No 2 Yard, Richmond, California.
St Johns River Shipbuilding Company, Jacksonville, Florida.
Southeastern Shipbuilding Corporation, Savannah, Georgia.
Todd Houston Shipbuilding Corporation, Houston, Texas.
Walsh-Kaiser Company, Providence, Rhode Island.

ENGINE MAKERS

AME	=	Alabama Marine Engine Company, Birmingham, Alabama.
ASB	=	American Shipbuilding Company, Cleveland, Ohio.
CAC	=	Canadian Allis-Chalmers Ltd, Montreal, Canada.
CB	=	Clark Bros Company, Cleveland, Ohio.
DEW	=	Dominion Engineering Works Ltd, Montreal, Canada.
EMC	=	Ellicott Machine Corporation, Baltimore, Maryland.
F & S	=	Filer & Stowell Company, Milwaukee, Wisconsin.
GMC	=	General Machinery Corporation, Hamilton, Ohio.
HEW	=	Hamilton Engineering Works, Brunswick, Georgia.
HMC	=	Harrisburg Machinery Corporation, Harrisburg, Pennsylvania.

IFM	=	Iron Fireman Manufacturing Company, Portland, Oregon.
JHIW	=	Joshua Henry Ironworks, Sunnyvale, California.
JIC	=	John Inglis Company Ltd, Toronto, Ontario, Canada.
NT	=	National Transit Company, Oil City, Pennsylvania.
OWI	=	Oregon War Industries Inc, Portland, Oregon.
SMF	=	Springfield Machine & Foundry Company, Springfield, Massachusetts.
TS	=	Toledo Shipbuilding Company Inc, Toledo, Ohio.
VIW	=	Vulcan Iron Works, Wilkes-Barre, Pennsylvania.
WISC	=	Willamette Iron & Steel Corporation, Portland, Oregon.
WPM	=	Worthington Pump & Machinery Corporation, Harrison, NJ.

USN CLASSIFICATION AND TYPES

AG	=	Repair/Supply Ship, Electronics Research Ship.
AGR	=	Radar Picket Ship.
AGTR	=	Technical and Scientific Research Ship.
AH	=	Hospital Ship.
AK	=	Cargo Ship.
AKN	=	Net Cargo Ship.
AKS	=	General Stores Issue Ship.
AP	=	Transport.
APB	=	Self-Propelled Barracks Ship.
ARG	=	Repair Ship for Internal Combustion Engines.
ARV	=	Aircraft Repair Ship.
AVS	=	Aviation Supply Ship.
AW	=	Distilling Ship.
IX	=	Navy Station Tankers and Unclassified Vessels, the latter including damaged vessels used as Barrack Ships, Store Ships, Depot Ships, Hulks, etc.
T-AKV	=	Cargo Ship and Aircraft Ferry.
YAG	=	Miscellaneous Auxiliary Ship, including Experimental Minesweepers.
YAGR	=	Ocean Radar Station Ship.

PART ONE

Liberty Ships, Basic Design, Dry Cargo, EC2–S–C1 Type

The majority of the Liberty ships built were of the standard, or basic, design. The remaining vessels each conformed to one of the few types of complete re-designs, and these were given a different designation and type number; details of these are shown under the respective sections.

General details relating to design and construction are given in the foregoing text, but further pertinent details relating to the basic design of the dry cargo type are of importance.

The basic design was of a vessel of the full scantling type, with a raked stem, cruiser stern, a single screw and a balanced rudder. The second deck was continuous throughout and seven watertight bulkheads, all extending to the upper deck, divided the vessel into five cargo holds, fore and aft peak tanks and three deep tanks. The propelling machinery and boilers were located in a single midships compartment. The inner bottom tanks, six on either side, were fitted as fuel oil tanks but were also able to carry water ballast. Two forward deep tanks were situated under No 1 hold and the third was situated aft of the machinery space. The fuel oil settling tanks were located at the sides of the ship in the way of the boilers.

An illustration of the importance of the hull sub-division and the ability of Liberty ships to stand up to wartime conditions is the case of the *William Williams,* torpedoed in the Pacific and so severely damaged that it was estimated that no pre-war merchant ship could have taken similar punishment and survived the ordeal.

The torpedo struck the port side near No 5 bulkhead, shattered the plates and frames and blasted a hole on the starboard side of the ship. Bulkheads were destroyed, escape shafts blown away from holds and 'tween decks, the shaft tunnel smashed and the shaft pedestals blown away or damaged. In all, the damage aft was tremendous. The ship settled deeply by the stern, water lapped the deck forward of the after mast and the poop deck was completely submerged to the top of the gun deck atop the after house. Later, some 55 ft of after shell plating was found to be missing.

Steering was impossible and the vessel drifted for some days. Then, with tug assistance she was later able to proceed under her own steam of 42 'revs' to refuge at Fiji.

One of the most important attributes of this 'emergency' type of ship was its ability to carry a good deadweight of cargo. The deck space was as important as the under-deck areas and except for the midships house and the gun platforms there were no important obstructions for the whole of the Liberty's length. The unit deck load for the whole of the upper deck was 336 lbs per sq ft. For the second deck the loads ranged from 400 lbs per sq ft to nearly 700 lbs, and these applied from side to side of the vessel, including the hatches. Therefore it was to the latter positions that the smaller permitted loads applied. For the deep tank tops the load was 1,400 lbs per sq ft and for both the tank tops and the tunnel top recess it was 1,650 lbs per sq ft.

No 1 hold, with a length of 60¾ ft, had the least capacity due to the underlying deep tanks. These deep tanks

Key to Elevation

1 Stores
2 Fore peak
3 Deep tank No 1 (P & S)
4 Deep tank No 2 (P & S)
5 Fuel oil settling tank (P & S)
6 Machinery space
7 Refrigerated rooms & storerooms (P & S)
8 Fresh water tanks (P & S)
9 Deep tank No 3 (P & S)
10 Thrust recess
11 Shaft tunnel
12 Tunnel recess
13 Shaft tunnel escape trunk
14 After peak
15 Steering gear compartment
16 Void space

17 5-ton boom (P & S)
18 50 or 30-ton boom (CL)
19 30 or 15-ton boom (CL)

Double-bottom tanks:

20 Fuel oil or ballast tank No 1
21 Fuel oil or ballast tank No 2 (P & S)
22 Fuel oil or ballast tank No 3 (P & S)
23 Void space (P & S)
24 Reserve feed water tank No 4
25 Fuel oil or ballast tank No 5 (P & S)
26 Fuel oil or ballast tank No 6 (P & S)

P & S = Port & Starboard
CL   = Centre line

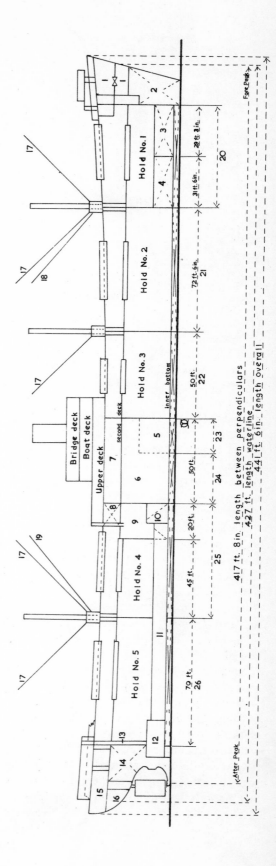

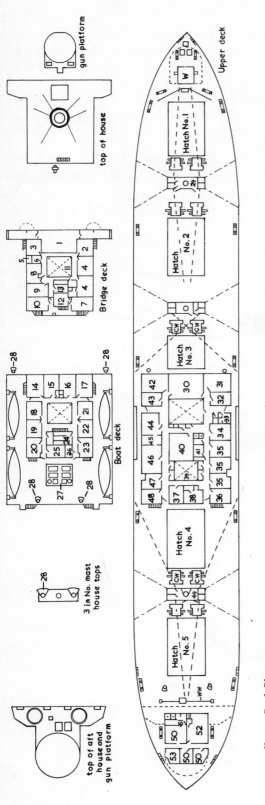

gun platform

top of house

Bridge deck

Boat deck

3 in No. mast house tops

top of aft house and gun platform

Upper deck

W

Hatch No. 1

Hatch No. 2

Hatch No. 3

Hatch No. 4

Hatch No. 5

CW   CW

CW   CW

WW

Key to Deck Plans

Bridge deck:
1 Wheelhouse
2 Chartroom
3 Radio room
4 Captain
5 Battery room
6 Toilet
7 Captain's office
8 Cadets – deck dept
9 Radio operators
10 Spare
11 Boiler casing
12 Generator room
13 Stores

Boat deck:
14 Chief engineer's office
15 Chief engineer
16 1st assistant engineer
17 Chief mate
18 2nd assistant engineer
19 3rd assistant engineer
20 2nd mate
21 3rd mate
22 Chief steward
23 Cadets – engineering dept
24 Showers & toilets
25 Gunnery officer
26 Locker
27 Engine room skylight
28 Ventilators

Upper deck:
29 Lamp room & deck lockers
30 Officers mess
31 6 gunners
32 Cooks & messman
33 Showers & toilets
34 Oilers
35 Seamen
36 Bos'n & clerk/typist
37 Messmen
38 Ships office
39 Engine casing
40 Galley
41 PO's showers & toilets
42 6 gunners
43 Steward
44 PO's mess
45 Scullery
46 Crews mess
47 Deck engineer & oilers
48 Firemen
49 Paint room & deck lockers
50 2 gunners
51 Showers & toilets
52 Hospital
53 Medical stores

W = Windlass
CW = Cargo winch
WW = Warping winch

LIBERTY DRY CARGO SHIP, EC2 – S – C1 TYPE

were used either for dry cargo or for salt-water ballast, whilst the third one (20 ft in length) could be used for dry cargo, cargo oil, or fuel oil. No 2 hold – the largest of all – had a length of 72½ ft, and No 3 hold measured 50 ft. Nos 4 and 5 holds – both with the shaft tunnel running through – were of smaller capacity and were 45 ft and 70 ft in length, respectively.

All the cargo hatches had a clear width of 19 ft 10 in. In length Nos 2, 4 and 5 were 34 ft 10 in, No 1 was 33 ft 7 in, and No 3 was 19 ft 10 in. Hatchways were fitted with portable hatch beams and the covers were of wood. This type of material was used as a ceiling on inner bottoms in the way of the hatches, for the joiner bulkheads and for the ships' furniture.

Accommodation was provided in a three-deck-high midship superstructure and in a single deck-house aft. Beneath the superstructure at second (or 'tween) deck level and to port and starboard of the engine and boiler casing were situated the refrigerated vegetable, dairy, meat and fish rooms, clean and soiled linen rooms, dry storerooms and the engineers stores. The after deck-house accommodated some of the gunners, but also included the ships hospital, medical store-rooms, toilets and showers and the watertight-trunk ammunition hoist. All these crew spaces were steam heated, this contrasting with the later Liberty colliers, where, from necessity, a different method was adopted.

The basic Liberty ship was originally intended to have a crew of forty-five, but this figure was later increased to include gun crews to a maximum of thirty-six men, so making a total of eighty-one persons. Subsequently the division of this figure was amended; ships crew was increased to fifty-two persons and the gun crews reduced to twenty-nine.

The cargo gear was subject to some variation, but as designed each hold was served by 5-ton booms. Later additions were a 50 ton boom at No 2 hold and a 15 or 30 ton boom at No 4. There were three steel masts each with a mast-house to which the booms were stepped. The outfit of steam-driven cargo winches consisted of nine 7 in x 12 in double-geared winches for the 5, 15 and 30 ton booms, and one 10½ in x 12 in double-geared winch for the 50 ton boom.

Amidships, on the boat deck, were located four steel lifeboats each 24 ft long. One (later, two) were powered and each had a capacity of twenty-five persons; the remaining pair each had capacity for thirty-one persons.

When the designs of the type were being studied by the American Bureau of Shipping for classification purposes it was found that their own requirements for a basic vessel with a maximum draft of 26 ft 10 in were exceeded, and consequently they were able to certify the Liberty with a greater draft – this permitting an additional dead-weight of some 430 tons.

Details

Measurements:	Length overall	441 ft 6 in
	" between perpendiculars	417 ft 8¾ in
	" registered	422 ft 8 in
	" waterline	427 ft
	Breadth moulded	56 ft 10¾ in
	" extreme	57 ft
	Depth, moulded, to upper deck	37 ft 4 in
	" " " second "	28 ft 7 in
	Draft, original	26 ft 10 in
	" as classed	27 ft 8⅞ in
	Freeboard	9 ft 8¾ in

Thomas F. Bayard as the liquified gas carrier
Ultragaz Sao Paulo, arriving at Rio de Janeiro
in August l952. (Bethlehem, Yard no 2139)

J. Fred Essary as the *USS Sagittarius* at Okinawa
in l945. (Bethlehem, Yard no 2283)

The Federal S.N.Co's *Leicester* (ex *Samesk*) arriving
in tow at Bermuda in October 1948. She encountered
a hurricane on the night of September 14-15 while
on a voyage in ballast from Tilbury to New York.
(Bethlehem, Yard no 2314)

The *A.J. Cassatt* in wartime guise, August 1944,
following her completion. (Bethlehem, Yard no 2394)

Tonnages:			
	Registered	7,176 gross,	4,380 nett
	US measurement	7,191 ”	4,309 ”
	Panama ”	7,223 ”	5,093 ”
	Suez ”	7,230 ”	5,399 ”
	Deadweight, as planned	10,414	
	” as classed	10,865	
	Displacement	14,245	
	” light ship	3,380 (at 7 ft 9 in draft)	
	Lightweight	3,401	
	Defence equipment	130	

Capacities:			
	Cargo, cu ft:		
	No 1 hold & tween decks	84,181 (grain)	75,405 (bale)
	” 2 ” ” ”	145,604 ”	134,638 ”
	” 3 ” ” ”	96,429 ”	83,697 ”
	” 4 ” ” ”	94,118 ”	82,263 ”
	” 5 ” ” ”	93,190 ”	82,435 ”
	Deep tanks (combined)	49,086 ”	41,135 ”
	Totals	562,608	499,573

	General stores, cu ft	11,626
	Refrigerated stores, cu ft	1,918
	Water ballast, tons	2,811
	Fixed ” ”	281
	Fuel oil, ”	1,819
	Freshwater, ”	188

Main engine:

Direct acting, condensing, three cylinder, triple expansion,
indicated horsepower (at 76 rpm)   2,500
Cylinders and stroke   24½, 37, 70 – 48 in

Daily fuel consumption, tons   30

Speed, knots   11

Boilers:

Two, of cross drum sectional sinuous header straight tube type,
fitted with superheaters burning bunker 'C' oil,
   pressure   220 psi
   temperature   450°F
   heating surface (two boilers)   10,234 sq ft

Auxiliaries:

Generators, three, type DC, 400 rpm, 167 amps, 120 volts, 25 Kw each.
Evaporator, one, vertical submerged type, capacity 25 tons per day.
Distiller, one, capacity 6,000 gallons per day.
Refrigeration system, one compressor,
   temperatures, meat and fish rooms   15°F
                vegetable room   40°F
                dairy room   30°F

| Masts: | Height above bottom of keel plate | 82 ft $0\frac{1}{4}$ in |
| Telescopic masts: | " " " " " " | 102 ft $0\frac{1}{4}$ in (not on foremast) |

Booms:	5 ton (at fore and after masts), length,	55 ft
	5 ton (at No 3 hatch) "	47 ft
	15, 30 and 50 ton (on centreline) "	51 ft

| Anchors: | Weight lbs, each | 8,400, with $2\frac{1}{16}$th in chain diam |

Propeller:	4 blade, diameter	18 ft 6 in
	mean pitch	16 ft
	surface	117 sq ft

BUILT BY ALABAMA DRYDOCK COMPANY

At times throughout the whole of the maritime commission's emergency shipbuilding programme certain 'waves of expansion' were put into effect, as dictated by military and shipping needs.

For some time the port of Mobile was not shown on the expansion lists, as it was considered that formation of new yards in the area would draw labour from nearby yards at Chickasaw and Pascagoula, which were already building C type ships. Nevertheless, in time it became necessary to develop more yards in the south and the management of a new emergency yard at Mobile was supplied by the Alabama Drydock & Shipbuilding Company. This company, already established, was then engaged on tanker newbuildings and also had much repair work in hand.

The new yard was located on Pinto Island, this allowing easy layout and giving ample water frontage. The four slipways were well spaced and the assembly platforms, instead of being in the customary position at the head of each slip, were placed between the ways. This shortened the distance over which the pre-assembled units were transported by crane. Owing to the heavy losses of tankers by enemy action eight more ways, for tanker construction, were later added to the layout. So this yard, originally planned for Liberty ship production, was developed for the multiple production of tankers.

By March 1943 the total labour force of 18,500 persons included some 6,000 negroes. The up-grading of some of the latter started a race riot, so causing temporary closure of part of the yard. But the problems were resolved and the negro craftsmen were confined to the production on only four of the ways.

However, in August 1943 the company acknowledged that the magnitude of shipbuilding operations was 'beyond the capacity of their management' and they offered its facilities solely for repair work. The maritime commission gave the task of new management to two engineering firms and the company formed a separate shipbuilding division. Thus there was no change in ownership but a complete change in management, and repair work was entirely separated from shipbuilding.

Liberty ship output: 20 vessels.

USMC hull numbers: MCE   1–13   (Yard Nos 231–243)
   740–746 ("   281–287)
   747–767   cancelled to permit tanker construction.

231 J.L.M. CURRY 5.42 GMC 8.3.43: Welded seam split during gale off Iceland. Broke in two, abandoned. Sank 66.53N 14.17W.

232 JOHN MARSHALL 5.42 GMC 12.55: Converted to YAG, same name, USN (conversion type EC2-S-22a). USN Reserve Fleet, site 1.

233 HENRY CLAY 6.42 GMC 8.67: Scrapped Kearny, NJ.

234 ARTHUR MIDDLETON 42 GMC 1.1.43: Sunk by submarine (U.73) torpedo off Cape Falcon near Oran, N.Africa, 35.45N 00.45W.

235 ALEXANDER H. STEPHENS 7.42 GMC Reserve Fleet, site 5.

236 THOMAS HEYWARD 7.42 GMC Reserve Fleet, site 4.

237 JUDAH P. BENJAMIN 8.42 GMC 1961: Scrapped Tacoma, Wash.

238 JEFFERSON DAVIS 8.42 GMC 2.61: Scrapped Bellingham, Wash.

239 THOMAS LYNCH 8.42 GMC 10.65: Scrapped Portland, Ore.

240 JOEL CHANDLER HARRIS 9.42 GMC 49: (sold commercial). 56: GRAIN SHIPPER. 58: PACIFIC EXPLORER. 60: MONTEGO SEA. 61: TOXON. 62: FANMAR. 65: FANLIL. 7.68: Scrapped Hirao.

241 NATHANIEL BACON 10.42 AME 24.11.42: Beached and submerged after collision with ESSO BELGIUM (37/10,529 grt) at New York. Refloated, repaired. 19.12.45: Struck mines, caught fire off Civitavecchia. 22.12.45: Beached 42.23N 26.30E. CTL. 1946: Stern part sold Italy for scrap. 1950: Resold and 31.3.50: Towed Genoa. 1951: Stern joined at Genoa to forepart of BERT WILLIAMS (II) (qv) and renamed BOCCADASSE (length 471½ ft, 7,740 grt). 1.63: Scrapped Spezia.

242 ISRAEL PUTNAM 10.42 F & S circa 65: Reported scrapped USA.

243 JOSEPH WHEELER 11.42 AME 2.12.43: Sunk during German air raid on Bari harbour, Italy. 48: Wreck sold to Genoa shipbreakers.

281 JAMES HOBAN 11.42 GMC 61: Scrapped Philadelphia.

282 CLARK MILLS 12.42 GMC 9.3.44: Damaged by aircraft torpedo off Bizerta, 37.20N 10.20E. Beached. CTL. Later salved and 24.9.49: Towed to Barcelona and scrapped.

283 BENJAMIN H. LATROBE 12.42 AME 47: VERCORS. 64: MANOLIS. 68: Scrapped Kaohsiung.

284 SIMON WILLARD 12.42 AME 7.69: Sold for scrapping at San Francisco.

285 COLIN P. KELLY JR. 1.43 GMC 4.6.45: Damaged by mine; towed to Tilbury thence to Sunderland. CTL, later sold. 4.48: Towed to Holland and scrapped Rotterdam.

286 WILLIAM C. GORGAS 1.43 F & S 11.3.43: Sunk by submarine (U.444) torpedo in N.W. Atlantic, 51.05N 27.35W.

287 LAWTON B. EVANS 1.43 AME 1.60: Scrapped Baltimore.

BUILT BY BETHLEHEM-FAIRFIELD SHIPYARD

When it was decided to establish an emergency shipyard in Baltimore the famous Bethlehem Steel Company was the obvious choice of leadership, for this company was already operating a large yard next to its Sparrows Point steelworks to the south-east of the city, and it also had important repair facilities within the harbour.

As with other builders, most of Bethlehem's berths were committed to naval work and in January 1941 it was arranged that a Bethlehem subsidiary should operate the new yard — Bethlehem-Fairfield — so named after the suburb in which it was situated.

The largest of the emergency yards, it originated with thirteen spacious ways, of which two were existing ways only in need of restoration. By using equipment in an idle Pullman rail-car plant 2½ miles from the slips the yard gained a start on other yards and was the first to launch a Liberty ship. At the Pullman plant steel was not only cut, rolled and even furnaced — in general, fabricated — but was also welded into sections, limited only in size by the capacity of the rail-cars which carried these units to the slipways. In the yard itself even larger sections were put together, some units from these early days of pre-fabrication weighing more than 22 tons. Later, the largest sub-assemblies at the yard were forepeak sections of nearly 50 tons.

In May 1942 the yard was ordered to give priority construction to the building of LSTs on the Liberty slipways, and were given contracts for 45 — later reduced to 30. These LSTs occupied twelve of the sixteen ways from August to December of 1942, for by the end of 1942 the original yard layout had been modified and an additional three slips added.

Some two years later, by January 1945, the total of employees at the yard had risen to a figure in excess of 27,000.

Generally, here, as in all yards, high productivity depended upon continuous production of a single type of ship without interruption. But despite the priority breaks and type-changes throughout the years the yard acquired one of the best speed records on the East Coast, and it maintained a consistently low production cost figure, the average per ship being in the region of 1¾ million dollars.

As with all shipbuilding, bonus wages were paid for fast work, and it was from this yard that some workers were put on trial in a civil court for deliberate bad welding, being convicted of *'making war material in a defective manner'*. Trials such as this were the deterrent to similar malpractices and also ensured that ships were constructed to the best possible standards.

After the war Bethlehem-Fairfield was given title to facilities which had cost in the region of 35 million dollars, although in June 1941 the anticipated cost had been less than 10 million. Before thus disposing of the yard the Maritime Commission had estimated that the cost of restoration of properties here (and at the California Shipbuilding yard) in accordance with the terms of the leases, would jointly total more than 44 million dollars.

Liberty ship output: 385 vessels

USMC hull numbers: MCE 14– 63   (Yard Nos 2001–2050)
    301– 312   (”   2051–2062)
    913–1022   (”   2063–2172)
    1755–1853 (”   2203–2301)
    2405–2419 (”   2302–2316)
    2585–2683 (”   2317–2415)

2001 PATRICK HENRY 12.41 GMC *The first Liberty ship built.* 7.46: Struck reef off coast of Florida, 25.08N 80.16W (voyage Sete/New Orleans). Refloated, proceeded New Orleans; later towed Mobile and laid up, damaged. 10.58: Sold to her builders and scrapped Baltimore. (See frontispiece and page 26).

2002 CHARLES CARROLL 1.42 GMC Reserve Fleet, site 1.

2003 FRANCIS SCOTT KEY 1.42 GMC 9.67: Scrapped Portland,Ore.

2004 ROGER B. TANEY 2.42 GMC 9.2.43: Sunk by submarine torpedo in S.Atlantic 23.00S 15.00W.

2005 RICHARD HENRY LEE 2.42 GMC 1965: Scrapped New Orleans.

2006 JOHN RANDOLPH 2.42 WPM 5.7.42: One of five ships mined and sunk in Allied minefield at eastern entrance to Denmark Strait (voyage N.Russia/ Reykjavik). Forepart later salved and towed Reykjavik. 1.9.52: Forepart broke adrift in position 59.20N 07.33W whilst being towed to Firth of Forth for scrapping. 5.9.52: Ashore and wrecked Torrisdale Bay, Sutherland.

2007 GEORGE CALVERT (I) 2.42 GMC Hull taken whilst incomplete and converted at Baltimore for USCG maritime training service; completed as **AMERICAN MARINER** (conversion type Z3-EC2-S-C1). Later transferred to US Army and still later to USAAF. 1961: Converted at Brooklyn to AGM 12 (Missile Range ship; same name). Used to observe by means of radar, infra-red tracker and optical instruments the missiles fired from Cape Kennedy and to follow their characteristics in the upper atmosphere and upon their re-entry. 1.7.64: Transferred to USN. 1.7.66: Stricken from USN. 10.66: Scuttled as a target ship in Chesapeake Bay.

2008 CHRISTOPHER NEWPORT 3.42 CB 4.7.42: Disabled by aircraft torpedo in Barents Sea. Torpedoed by HM submarine P.614 (part of convoy escort) but remained afloat. Later sunk by submarine (U.457) torpedo 75.49N 25.15E (voyage Reykjavik/N.Russia — war supplies).

2009 CARTER BRAXTON 3.42 CB 47: HERMAN FRASCH. 55: CILCO RANGER. 56: MURRAY HILL. 57: SEA SPRAY. 60: MELTEMI. 6.68: Scrapped Kaohsiung.

2010 SAMUEL CHASE 4.42 GMC 1.67: Sold for scrap. 27.1.67: Abandoned by tug TERN disabled with engine trouble 35.22N 75.19W whilst in tow for Philadelphia. Tug taken in tow; repaired. Tug later recovered tow and proceeded. 2.67: Scrapped Philadelphia.

2011 GEORGE WYTHE 5.42 WPM Reserve Fleet, site 2.

2012 BENJAMIN HARRISON 3.42 GMC 16.3.43: Sunk by submarine (U.172) torpedo in N.Atlantic 39.02N 24.15W (voyage USA/Gibraltar).

2013 FRANCIS L. LEE 4.42 WPM 2.65: Scrapped Savannah.

2014 THOMAS STONE 5.42 GMC Reserve Fleet, site 2.

2015 RICHARD BLAND 4.42 WPM 5.3.43: Damaged by submarine (U.255) torpedo in Arctic Ocean; proceeded toward Iceland, but 10.3.43: Sunk by (same) submarine torpedo off Iceland, 65.53N 14.10W.

2016 GEORGE CALVERT (II) 4.42 WPM 20.5.42: Sunk by submarine (U.753) torpedo near Cuba, approx 22.50N 84.30W.

2017 THOMAS NELSON 5.42 GMC 1956: Converted at Baltimore as trial-conversion type EC2-M-8b (7,259 grt) at a cost of 3,070,000 dollars. Reserve Fleet, site 2.

This was the second ship to be converted under the Liberty Ship Conversion Programme. She was lengthened, given finer bow lines and re-powered with two geared diesel engines manufactured by the Baldwin-Lima-Hamilton Corp, and these changes assured the minimum 15 knot sea speed – but this was only attained on a draft reduced to 26 ft.

Changes in the hull form involved the removal of 82½ ft of the existing bow and the addition of a new 107½ ft bow section of some 500 tons. Hull plating, especially at the stern, was reinforced and the vessel fitted with a new rudder.

Other alterations included the replacing of the standard cargo gear by five deck cranes and the use of two different types of sliding hatch cover. At each hatch was installed one crane and these are fully revolving, level-luffing, with a capacity of 5 tons and an outreach of 20 ft beyond the maximum beam of the ship. In other respects the three forward cranes differ from the after pair. The former are electro-hydraulic and are intended to operate as fixed cranes at a position 10 ft off the centreline, but are positionable by being mounted on sets of short athwartship rails.

The after cranes are electric, are of the gantry type and operate on fore-and-aft tracks. Mounted on the centreline,

their working radius is 10 ft more and so their boom length is greater. To take advantage of this mobility feature the No 4 hatch was lengthened to the greatest extent possible without major structural hull alteration – its new length being 47½ ft.

In the early stages of conversion design the designations EC2-S-8b and EC2-M-1b were allocated to the ship. No contracts for these types were awarded however, and the vessel was finally converted under the type number shown above.

2018 JOHN WITHERSPOON 4.42 GMC 6.7.42: Sunk by submarine (U.255) torpedo in Kara Sea, 70.30N 52.00E (voyage Reykjavik/N.Russia – tanks and ammunition).

2019 ROBERT TREAT PAINE 5.42 GMC 47: DIEPPE. 54: BROTHER GEORGE. 6.1.64: Aground Dry Tortugas 24.43N 83.00W (voyage Boca Grande/ UK – phosphates). 10.1.64: Refloated but later grounded off Key West. 12.1.64: Refloated, taken Port Everglades thence proceeded UK. 23.2.64: Aground in fog off Brook, Isle of Wight (voyage Ellesmere Port/Rotterdam – ballast). (Note: Smit tug WITTE ZEE struck rock and sank whilst assisting). 24.2.64: Refloated, severely damaged; towed to Rotterdam. Sold. 7.64: Scrapped Hendrik-Ido-Ambacht.

2020 ST. OLAF 5.42 WPM 1943: JASMINE (Assigned name of USN hospital ship – not used). 11.43: Converted at Boston to US Army hospital ship (7,940 grt). 11.45: Converted at San Pedro to transport for troops and military dependents (capacity 1,067 troops and 147 others). Later laid up. 4.63: Scrapped Portland, Ore.

2021 ESEK HOPKINS 5.42 CB 11.67: Scrapped Kearny, NJ.

2022 PETER MINUIT 5.42 TS 12.63: Scrapped New Orleans.

2023 ALEXANDER MACOMB 6.42 WPM 3.7.42: Sunk by submarine (U.215) torpedo in N.W.Atlantic, 41.40N 66.52W.

2024 HENRY ST. G. TUCKER 6.42 WPM 8.66: Scrapped New Orleans.

2025 ELEAZAR WHEELOCK 6.42 WPM 1964: Scrapped Philadelphia.

2026 THOMAS RUFFIN 6.42 CB 9.3.43: Damaged by submarine (U.510) torpedo in Gulf of Mexico.

Towed to Trinidad, thence to Mobile. CTL. Laid up. 1946: Scrapped Mobile.

2027 WILLIAM JOHNSON 6.42 GMC 1962: Scrapped Panama City.

2028 RICHARD BASSETT 6.42 WPM 47: CAROLYN. 61: Returned to US Govt; laid up. 10.62: Scrapped Panama City.

2029 OLIVER ELLSWORTH 6.42 CB 13.9.42: Sunk by submarine (U.408?) torpedo in Greenland Sea, 76.10N 10.05E (voyage Loch Ewe/N.Russia — war supplies).

2030 THEODORE FOSTER 6.42 WPM 3.70: Sold to Bilbao shipbreakers.

2031 JAMES GUNN 6.42 GMC Reserve Fleet, site 5.

2032 JOHN HENRY 7.42 WPM Reserve Fleet, site 2.

2033 SAMUEL JOHNSTON 6.42 WPM 2.68: Scrapped Green Cove Springs, Fla.

2034 WILLIAM MACLAY 7.42 VIW 10.67: Scrapped Kearny, NJ.

2035 WILLIAM PATTERSON 7.42 WPM 1957: Converted at Baltimore as trial-conversion type EC2-G-8g (7,275 grt). Reserve Fleet, site 1.

This was the fourth and last vessel to be dealt with under the Liberty Ship Conversion & Engine Improvement Programme.

Converted by Bethlehem Steel Corporation, she likewise incorporates the increased bow-length of her consorts (Bethlehem Yard Nos 2017 and 2050, qv), but unlike the JOHN SERGEANT — which was re-engined with open-cycle gas turbines, this vessel was refitted with six General Motors Soc Alsthom free-piston gas generators and two gas turbines geared to the single shaft as her main propulsion unit. This machinery was of 6,000 shp and increased her speed to more than 17 knots.

As with the third conversion under this programme the hull plating was strengthened and her existing cargo-handling gear retained, although the winches were renewed and she was given an additional pair at No 2 hatch.

In the early stages of conversion design the designations EC2-G-8h, C3-M8e and C3-S-8g were intended for this vessel. No contracts for these specific designs were awarded however, and the vessel was converted under the type number shown above.

As with the other hulls lengthened under the conversion programme, the ship should have been re-classed under the C3 scale, but in practice the EC2 prefix was retained to denote them as emergency type vessels.

2036 LUTHER MARTIN 7.42 WPM Reserve Fleet, site 4.

2037 WILLIAM WIRT 7.42 WPM 1966: Scrapped Kearny, NJ.

2038 REVERDY JOHNSON 7.42 WPM 10.67: Scrapped Kearny, NJ.

2039 JOHN H.B. LATROBE 7.42 WPM Reserve Fleet, site 6.

2040 RICHARD H. ALVEY 7.42 WPM 1961: Scrapped Beaumont, Texas.

2041 JOHN P. POE 7.42 EMC Reserve Fleet, site 4.

2042 BERNARD CARTER 8.42 WPM 1960: Scrapped Baltimore.

2043 JOHN CARTER ROSE 8.42 F & S 8.10.42: Sunk by submarine (U.201 and U.202) torpedoes and gunfire in Caribbean, 10.27N 45.37W.

2044 ANDREW HAMILTON 8.42 VIW 5.62: Scrapped Wilmington, Del.

2045 BENJAMIN CHEW 8.42 GMC 1956: Converted at Brooklyn as trial-conversion type EC2-S-8a (7,246 grt) at a cost of 1,079,000 dollars.

This ship was the first one to feature in the conversion programme. She underwent minimum conversion without lengthening or bow change, and this type evaluated the problems of driving the full lines and blunt bows of this type of ship at 15 knots. Seakeeping qualities proved to be rather poor and a maximum operating draft of only 24 ft forced the acceptance of a considerable loss of cargo deadweight.

Her propelling machinery was replaced by two AP2 Victory ship type steam turbines manufactured in 1945 by Allis Chalmers of Milwaukee, and here one of the problems was to determine how much of the original machinery and auxiliary systems could be used without change — for the increase from 2,500 ihp to 6,000 bhp was well beyond the normal overload margin.

The final design utilized the existing boilers and pumps, modified the condensers and gave new superheaters and reduction gear. This compromise arrangement, however, gave a fuel consumption rate very much higher than that acceptable in commercial practice.

The cargo-handling gear was modified to include additional derricks at No 2 hatch, replacement of all normal 5 ton booms with 10 ton ones and the 50 and 15 ton booms with 60 ton ones. Also installed was a removable 'tween deck in No 2 hold.

2046 WILLIAM TILGHMAN 8.42 GMC Reserve Fleet, site 8.

2047 JARED INGERSOLL 8.42 WPM 8.64: Scrapped Wilmington, Del.

2048 HORACE BINNEY 8.42 WPM 8.5.45: Damaged by mine 36 miles from Flushing, (voyage Flushing/Thames). Beached off Deal; broke in two. Subsequently salved and towed Thames, thence river Blackwater. 5.48: Scrapped Antwerp.

2049 WILLIAM RAWLE 8.42 WPM 47: ARLYN. 6.6.58: Aground on Silver Bank, north of Dominican Republic, (voyage San Juan/Philadelphia — sugar). 9.6.58: Refloated, severely damaged, returned to San Juan. CTL. 12.58: Scrapped San Juan, PR.

2050 JOHN SERGEANT 9.42 WPM 1956: Converted at Newport News as trial-conversion type EC2-G-8f (7,280 grt) at a cost of 2,450,000 dollars. Reserve Fleet, site 2.

When this converted Liberty ship commenced her crossing of the Atlantic on 3 October 1956, bound for Southampton and Bremerhaven, another milestone in the progress of marine propulsion was reached, for she was the first vessel propelled solely by gas turbine machinery to make this crossing. But it was not the first time that a gas turbine ship had made a transatlantic voyage, for in March 1952 the Shell tanker AURIS crossed from Plymouth to Curacao using her gas turbine only. But at that time she was also fitted with three diesel motors, which were normally used in conjunction with her gas turbine.

When the JOHN SERGEANT was converted to a gas turbine ship a new bow section was also added, this giving finer lines for increased speed and increasing her length by some 20 ft. The existing cargo-handling gear was retained, but added were new winches at No 2 hatch.

The vessel was also given one of the world's largest controllable-pitch propellers, this being 17½ ft in diameter, and this feature eliminated the necessity of reversing the ship's engines for astern movement. This propeller, as well as the turbine, is controllable from the bridge as well as from the engine room.

Her gas turbine was supplied by the General Electric Company of Schenectady, New York, and is a regenerative open-cycle gas turbine incorporating a combustion system, a high pressure turbine to drive the compressor and a low pressure one to drive the propeller through reduction gear.

The nominal rating of the unit is 6,000 shp, but on her speed trials off the Virginia Capes it developed some 7,575 hp and the vessel attained a speed well in excess of 18 knots.

2051 THOMAS McKEAN 5.42 WPM 29.6.42: Sunk by submarine (U.505) torpedo in Caribbean, 22.00N 60.00W.

2052 WILLIAM PACA 6.42 WPM 30.11.44: In collision with ss EMPIRE NESS, (41/2,922 grt), which sank, off Terneuzen. 12.69: Scrapped Mobile.

2053 BENJAMIN RUSH 7.42 GMC 1954: Scrapped Baltimore.

2054 JOSEPH STANTON 7.42 WPM 1964: Scrapped Philadelphia.

2055 JOHN WALKER 7.42 GMC 1961: Scrapped Jersey City.

2056 PIERCE BUTLER 8.42 GMC 20.11.42: Sunk by submarine (U.177) torpedo in Indian Ocean, 29.53S 36.28E (voyage Baltimore/Mombasa — general).

2057 TRISTRAM DALTON 9.42 WPM 47: ROSARIO. 54: ACHILEUS. 57: ANDROS LAUREL. 63: GRAND FAITH. 12.68: Scrapped Kaohsiung.

2058 JONATHAN ELMER 9.42 GMC 1960: Scrapped Baltimore.

2059 WILLIAM FEW 9.42 EMC 47: NORLANDIA. 2.69: Scrapped Osaka.

2060 WILLIAM GRAYSON 9.42 GMC 45: KERKYRA. 47: ANNA L. CONDYLIS. 57: ALEXANDROS. 62: THEONYMPHOS TINOU. 6.68: Scrapped Kaohsiung.

2061 JOHN MITCHELL 9.42 GMC 5.67: Scrapped New Orleans.

2062 JOHN W. BROWN 9.42 WPM 1946: Assigned to Board of Education, City of New York, as a training ship and moored at 23rd Street, East River. 1966: Towed to a new berth at Pier 42, North River, river Hudson. As the nation's only maritime high school, this vessel has, in more than two decades, trained very many seamen, engineers and catering staff.

2063 BENJAMIN HAWKINS 9.42 GMC Reserve Fleet, site 2.

2064 RALPH IZARD 9.42 GMC 4.65: Scrapped Panama City.

2065 JAMES CALDWELL 9.42 WPM Reserve Fleet, site 4.

2066 CAESAR RODNEY 9.42 EMC 11.59: Scrapped Portland, Maine.

2067 NICHOLAS BIDDLE 9.42 WPM 1963: Scrapped Beaumont, Texas.

2068 GEORGE WEEMS 10.42 GMC 10.1.48:
Ashore East Finngrund Bank, near Gefle. (voyage
Hudiksvall/Baltimore – pulp). 12.1.48: Refloated,
towed Stockholm. CTL. Sold. 48: MYKEN. 51:
CAVOLIDI. 53: COCLE. 59: WHITE EAGLE.
10.11.66: Aground on rocks South Point, San
Clemente Island, Calif., 32.55N 118.33W. (Voyage
Japan/San Diego – ballast). CTL. Abandoned.

2069 GRACE ABBOTT 10.42 GMC 9.67: Scrapped
Portland, Ore.

2070 CARDINAL GIBBONS 10.42 EMC Reserve
Fleet, site 4.

2071 THOMAS SIM LEE 10.42 WPM Reserve
Fleet, site 5.

2072 COTTON MATHER 11.42 VIW 1960: Scrapped
Boston, Mass.

2073 WILL ROGERS 11.42 EMC 7.4.45: Damaged
by submarine (U.1024) torpedo in Irish Sea (voyage
New York/Solent). Towed into Holyhead and
beached alongside ss JAMES W. NESMITH (qv). Later
refloated, towed Liverpool. Repaired and returned to
service. Reserve Fleet, site 4.
Note: These two vessels were the last to be torpedoed
by enemy submarines in this area.

2074 DANIEL CHESTER FRENCH 11.42 EMC
6.3.44: Sunk by mine off Bizerta 37.17N 10.22W
(voyage Philadelphia/Bandar Shapur).

2075 DANIEL WILLARD 12.42 EMC Reserve
Fleet, site 1.

2076 THADDEUS KOSCIUSZKO 12.42 EMC
47: MARINA. 54: ACRITAS. 10.5.56: Aground
south of Ilha Do Maio, Cape Verde Isles, (voyage
Kassa Isle/Port Alfred – ore). 26.6.56: Refloated.
CTL, sold, repaired. 56: ELIAS. 61: GEORGES.
20.9.62: Aground and wrecked in Kara Sea, N.Russia,
69.52N 61.10E (voyage Igarka/London – timber).
Vessel later broke up.

2077 PEARL HARBOR 12.42 WPM 62: Scrapped
New Orleans.

2078 LORD DELAWARE 12.42 GMC Reserve
Fleet, site 1.

2079 JAMES WOODROW 1.43 GMC 1.46:
Reported struck coral reef (no further details). Later

towed in and laid up at Suisun Bay, Cal. CTL. 6.54:
Scrapped Terminal Island, Cal.

2080 WILLARD HALL 1.43 WPM 66: Scrapped
Kearny, NJ.

2081 WOODBRIDGE N. FERRIS 1.43 GMC 3.65:
Scrapped Portland, Ore.

2082 WILLIAM McKINLEY 2.43 GMC Reserve
Fleet, site 2.

2083 THOMAS R. MARSHALL 2.43 VIW Reserve
Fleet, site 4.

2084 ANDREW G. CURTIN 2.43 EMC 25.1.44:
Sunk by submarine (U.716) torpedo in Barents Sea,
73.20N 23.30W.

2085 MOLLY PITCHER 2.43 GMC 17.3.43: Sunk
by submarine (U.521) torpedo in N.Atlantic, 38.21N
19.54W.

2086 HORACE GRAY 2.43 EMC 14.2.45: Sunk by
submarine (U.711) torpedo in Kola Inlet, N.Russia.

2087 SAMUEL BLATCHFORD 2.43 GMC
10.69: At Panama City for scrapping.

2088 HENRY B. BROWN 2.43 WPM 3.65:
Scrapped Philadelphia.

2089 GEORGE SHIRAS 2.43 GMC 46: ATLANTIC
BREEZE. 62: CETINJE. 3.68: Scrapped Split.

2090 RUFUS W. PECKHAM 2.43 GMC 51: SEA
GALE. 53: NICHOLAS C.H. 54: PITSA H. 58:
VALIANT EFFORT. 18.1.59: Struck reef, abandoned
during gale, drifted aground off Ras el Djebel,
Tunisia. 17.3.59: Broke in two; total loss. (Voyage
Galveston/Calcutta – wheat).

2091 WILLIAM R. DAY 3.43 VIW 12.59:
Scrapped Portland, Me.

2092 MAHLON PITNEY 2.43 WPM 64: Sold for
scrap, but 68: Converted at Portland, Ore., into a
crane barge, renamed TWIN HARBORS No. 2.

2093 LOUIS D. BRANDEIS 3.43 HMC 64:
Scrapped Kearny, NJ.

2094 NATHAN CLIFFORD 3.43 EMC 47:
AMERICAN ORIOLE. 57: ATLANTIC ORIOLE.
61: KYMA. 65: TASSIA. 9.5.65: Sprung leak, sank,
680 miles S.E. of Cape Race 36.36N 51.24W
(Voyage Antwerp/Houston).

2095 GEORGE SHARSWOOD 3.43 WPM 47: NEW ROCHELLE TRAILS. 50: NORTH LIGHT. 55: WILLAMETTE TRADER. 61: Returned to US Govt. 62: Scrapped Tacoma, Wash.

2096 HENRY L. BENNING 3.43 GMC 51: DOROTHY. 61: EMMA. 63: NANAK JAYANTI. 12.67: Scrapped Bombay.

2097 JOHNS HOPKINS 3.43 VIW 2.10.44: Damaged by aircraft torpedo in Mediterranean, towed to Marseilles (voyage Oran/Marseilles). Repaired. 46: THETIS. 52: SANTA ELENA. 60: ELINI K. 29.9.66: Broke in two in heavy weather, foundered in shallow water 8 miles from Thevenard, South Australia. (Voyage Port Lincoln/UK – wheat). 17.11.66: Refloated, beached Goat Island 32.18S 133.32E where vessel grounded and left tidal to deck level.

2098 THOMAS CRESAP 3.43 GMC 51: SUNION. 59: Lengthened at Tokio to 511½ ft (8,578 grt). 60: ZERMATT. 62: EPIROS. 66: TASSIA J. 67: PACTRADER. 12.68: Scrapped Sakaide.

2099 JAMES W. DENVER 3.43 WPM 11.4.43: Sunk by submarine (U.195) torpedo west of Canary Islands, 28.46N 25.40W.

2100 HENRY GILBERT COSTIN 3.43 WPM 51: JOSEPH FEUER. 55: EVY. 58: VALIANT FAITH. 61: HERMIONI. 63: ARYA JAYANTI. 12.66: Scrapped Bombay.

2101 JOHN GALLUP 3.43 GMC 63: Scrapped Kearny, NJ.

2102 CLIFFORD D. MALLORY 3.43 GMC 1.56: Converted to YAG, (USN, same name). (Conversion type EC2-S-22a). USN Reserve Fleet, site 4.

2103 WILLIAM H. WELCH 3.43 HMC 26.2.44: Ashore in storm at Black Bay, Loch Ewe. Broke in two, afterpart sank. Forepart beached and submerged. Total loss. (voyage London & Tyne/New York).

2104 WILLIAM OSLER 3.43 EMC 11.43: Converted at New York and renamed WISTERIA (US Army Hospital Ship, 7,940 grt). 1947: Returned US Govt; placed in reserve. 3.69: Scrapped Portland, Ore.

2105 HOWARD A. KELLY 3.43 GMC 49: TAINARON. 54: AKTION. 60: OLYMPOS. 62: lengthened at Maizuru to 511½ ft (8,593 grt). 66: OLYMPIAN. 68: BINKY. 11.69: Scrapped Kaohsiung.

2106 WILLIAM S. HALSTED 3.43 HMC 51: OCEAN C. 52: OCEAN LOTTE. 55: OCEAN NORA. 57: ANDROS LEGEND. 63: SAN REMO. 5.68: Scrapped Hirao.

2107 FRANKLIN P. MALL 4.43 GMC 3.65: Scrapped Philadelphia.

2108 JOHN HOWLAND 4.43 WPM 54: GALLOWAY. 61: KIN YUNG. 7.68: Scrapped Kaohsiung.

2109 WILLIAM H. WILMER 4.43 GMC 55: LOMALAND. 58: THEOPAN. 15.4.62: Afire in holds in Beirut harbour. Extinguished. 16.4.62: Aground in harbour. 19.4.62: Refloated. CTL. (Voyage Philippines/Beirut – copra). Sold 62: Scrapped Ambelaki, Greece.

2110 JOHN J. ABEL 4.43 EMC 3.61: Scrapped Hamburg.

2111 SANTIAGO IGLESIAS 4.43 HMC Transferred from reserve fleet to USN, and 14.7.65: loaded at Naval Ammunition Pier, Earle, NJ with 8,715 tons of obsolete ammunition and rigged for underwater demolition for measuring seismic travel-time. 16.9.65: Towed to deep water dump and scuttled. Thirty-one seconds after sinking, the cargo detonated at the 1,000 ft level as planned, and the scientific experiment was declared a success.

2112 JOHN BANVARD 4.43 WPM 31.10.44: Ashore in Praia Bay, Terceira, Azores. (Voyage Hampton Roads/Terceira). Refloated. CTL. 27.12.44: Towed to USA by US warship. 7.45: Towed to New York, thence Jacksonville. 8.45: Bids for scrapping rejected; vessel 'dismantled'.

2113 EDWARD N. HURLEY 4.43 GMC 57: Scrapped Mobile.

2114 CHARLES M. SCHWAB 4.43 GMC Reserve Fleet, site 1.

2115 CHARLES PIEZ 4.43 WPM 7.61: Scrapped Hamburg.

2116 BERNARD N. BAKER 4.43: WPM 8.64: Scrapped Wilmington, Del.

2117 WINFRED L. SMITH 4.43 GMC 11.59: Scrapped Portland, Me.

2118 BUSHROD WASHINGTON 4.43 GMC 15.9.43: Bombed and sunk at Salerno. Total loss, (no further trace).

2119 LEVI WOODBURY 4.43 WPM 8.64: Scrapped Philadelphia.

2120 WILLIAM STRONG 4.43 EMC 43: ROALD AMUNDSEN. 20.11.47: Ashore near Tretteskjaer, Skudesnaes. Broke in two. Total loss. (voyage Antwerp/Narvik — ballast).

2121 JOSEPH P. BRADLEY 4.43 EMC 49: JULES FRIBOURG. 50: LUMBER CARRIER. 59: MOUNT WHITNEY. 64: Scrapped Karachi.

2122 WARD HUNT 4.43 GMC 48: CAROLINAN. 50: HARPOON. 54: CENTAUR. 57: ANDROS FIGHTER. 63: Scrapped Dalmuir.

2123 JOHN WOOLMAN 4.43 GMC 10.60: Scrapped Baltimore.

2124 WILLIAM PEPPER 5.43 GMC 2.62: Scrapped Panama City.

2125 SILAS WEIR MITCHELL 5.43 GMC 8.66: Scrapped Panama City.

2126 JOSEPH LEIDY 5.43 WPM 46: ARISTO-MENIS. 48: MARIO C. 51: OCEAN RANGER. 10.66: Scrapped Hirao.

2127 WILLIAM W. GERHARD 5.43 WPM 21.9.43: Sunk by submarine (U.593) torpedo off Salerno, Italy.

2128 JOHN MORGAN 5.43 GMC 1.6.43: Exploded and sank after collision with USN tanker MONTANA (9,310 grt) off Cape Henry, Va., 36.53N 76.00W, (voyage Baltimore/Persian Gulf — ammunition).

2129 JAMES R. RANDALL 5.43 HMC 9.65: Scrapped Mobile.

2130 WILLIAM H. WEBB 5.43 EMC 2.1.46: Ashore on reef near Kildin Island. 15.1.46: Broke in two. Total loss. (Voyage Philadelphia/Murmansk — general).

2131 SAMUEL BOWLES 5.43 GMC Completed as LUZON ARG 2 (USN). USN Reserve Fleet, site 6.

2132 STEVENSON TAYLOR 5.43 GMC 1.70: Scrapped Panama City.

2133 ELBERT HUBBARD 5.43 GMC Completed as MINDANAO ARG 3 (USN). USN Reserve Fleet, site 5.

2134 JOHN E. SCHMELTZER 5.43 GMC 25.11.47: Ashore and wrecked 5 miles East of Pesqueiro Fundo, Santa Antao Island. (Voyage Rosario/Gothenburg — grain and cottonseed cake).

2135 CHARLES A. McALLISTER 5.43 GMC 60: Scrapped Baltimore.

2136 JOHN L. MOTLEY 5.43 GMC 2.12.43: Exploded and sank when hit by bombs in German air raid on Bari harbour, Italy. (Cargo: ammunition).

2137 HAYM SALOMON 5.43 GMC 47ᶜ ARISTO-PAIS. 51: CAPITAINE BROGNION. 63: KARPATY.

2138 FREDERICK DOUGLASS 5.43 WPM 20.9.43: Damaged by submarine (U.238) torpedo in Atlantic. Later sunk by submarine (U.645) torpedo, 57.03N 28.08W (voyage Avonmouth/New York — ballast).

2139 THOMAS F. BAYARD 5.43 EMC Completed as EDVARD GRIEG. 52: Converted at Kiel into liquefied gas carrier and renamed ULTRAGAZ SAO PAULO. 61: MUNDOGAS SAO PAULO. 2.69: In use as floating store at Santos.

2140 CONRAD WEISER 5.43 GMC Reserve Fleet, site 5.

2141 JOHN M.T. FINNEY 6.43 GMC Completed as CHRISTIAN MICHELSEN. 26.9.43: Sunk by submarine (U.410) torpedo 80 miles west of Bizerta. (Voyage New York/Bizerta — war materials).

2142 LOUISA M. ALCOTT 6.43 GMC Reserve Fleet, site 2.

2143 WILLIAM TYLER PAGE 6.43 HMC 3.64: Scrapped Mobile.

2144 JOSEPH H. NICHOLSON 6.43 GMC 47: JULES M. FRIBOURG. 48: PACIFIC WAVE. 57: MARIANTHE. 58: FREE MERCHANT. 59: FOTINI TSAVLIRIS. 60: EURO. 7.68: At Trieste for scrapping.

2145 THOMAS NELSON PAGE 6.43 GMC 47: ARISTOGITON. 51: CAPITAINE POTIE. 63: SIKHOTE ALIN.

2146 JAMES McCOSH 6.43 GMC Reserve Fleet, site 2.

2147 ALBERT C. RITCHIE 6.43 WPM 47: GLOBAL MILLER. 48: LESJE. 49: SOKNA. 59: Converted at New York to liquefied gas carrier. 64: ANGELA II. 66: Reconverted to dry cargo at New Orleans.

2148 GEORGE W. WOODWARD 6.43 EMC 60:
Scrapped Faslane.

2149 CHARLES BULFINCH 6.43 GMC
3.70: Sold for scrap.

2150 SAMUEL McINTYRE 6.43 GMC 66:
Scrapped Kearny, NJ.

2151 PIERRE L'ENFANT 6.43 GMC 46:
ATLANTIC WAVE. 61: MLJET. 65: KOLASIN.

2152 EDWARD L. GRANT 6.43 GMC 51:
LUCILE BLOOMFIELD. 54: SANTA ROSA.
1.65: Scrapped Hirao.

2153 ROBERT J. COLLIER 6.43 EMC 22.3.46:
Aground off Bieselingscheham, river Schelde. Broke
in two. 8.4.46: Refloated, towed Antwerp. CTL.
(Voyage Baltimore/Antwerp – coal). Sold. 1.47:
Scrapped Antwerp.

2154 JOSHUA W. ALEXANDER 6.43 GMC 17.10.45:
Ashore at Graves, Boston, Mass., (voyage Searsport/
Boston). Refloated, damaged. Later reported scrapped
USA.

2155 JOHN A.DONALD 6.43 GMC 64: Scrapped
Philadelphia.

2156 WILLIAM H. JACKSON 7.43 GMC 47:
ARISTOCRATIS. 51: SAN ROQUE. 60: AGHIOS
SPYRIDON. 60: SAN SPYRIDON. 12.68: Scrapped
Shanghai.

2157 JANET LORD ROPER 7.43 WPM 48: P.W.
SPRAGUE. 5.48: Shortened (forward) at Boston to
411 ft (loa) and converted to self-unloading coal
carrier (6,028 grt). 56: Converted to self-unloading
bulk cement carrier (6,278 grt), renamed FLORIDA
STATE. 68: Converted at Tampa to bulk carrier.

The conversion of this ship into a bulk cement carrier during
1956 was due to the need of her owners, the leading producers
of cement in Puerto Rico, to increase their fleet for the
transport of this product to Port Everglades in Florida.

The initial task of the conversion was the removal of
existing internal structures – such as transverse bulkheads
and decks – to provide two large unobstructed holds, the
forward one being 119½ ft in length and the after one 135 ft.
A third hold for general cargo was the ship's original No 1
hold. Web-frame sections were inserted to maintain the
transverse strength of the hull.

Each bulk cargo hold was divided by a centreline bulkhead,
and these bulkheads separated hoppered troughs containing
banks of airslide units. An individual airslide unit consisted of
a longitudinal steel channel enclosed throughout its length by

a taut canvas cover. Air pressure under the canvas aerated
and thus activated the bulk cement supported directly above
its surface.

These units were positioned on an incline within the
hoppered holds and further hoppering effect was gained by
the use of fore-and-aft deflector plates sloping transversely
both from the centreline and from the ship's sides. In the
space below these hoppers the cargo discharge machinery was
situated. Thus, the use of multiple units allied to the troughs,
also on an incline, created a flowing of the cement and
provided the means of conveying cargo directly through
hopper-bin gates into discharge pumps without the use of
other mechanical equipment. Compressed air forced the
cement through discharge lines rising vertically from pump
rooms situated at mid-length in each hold. On deck these
lines terminated at flange points which provided connections
for portable shore lines leading to the silos. The discharge
operation was such that all holds were stripped automatically
and no trimming or scavenging of residue bulk was necessary.

On the main deck the eight steel watertight hatches over
the cargo spaces remained sealed during all operations, but
two sets of dust collector units, located over the holds,
provided air release. Fitted with filter bags they not only
reclaimed cement which would otherwise have been lost into
the atmosphere, but automatically returned the trapped
cement dust into the holds. After this conversion the vessel
was able to transport some 9,000 tons of cement on each
trip.

2158 NATHAN TOWSON 7.43 GMC Reserve Fleet,
site 2.

2159 ROBERT ERSKINE 7.43 GMC 6.1.44: Ashore
and wrecked off Bizerta, Tunisia, during gale. Total
loss.

2160 JOHN WANAMAKER 7.43 GMC 1.69: At
Mobile for scrapping.

2161 JOHN STEVENSON 7.43 GMC 9.55:
Converted to YAG (USN, same name). (Conversion
type EC2-S-22a). USN Reserve Fleet, site 1.

2162 GEORGE M. COHAN 7.43 GMC 49: HARRY
T. 52: GENERAL PATTON. 54: NATIONAL
FIGHTER. 55: Lengthened at Kobe to 511½ ft
(8,537 grt). 61: MESOLOGI. 68: BLUE SAND.

2163 GEORGE H. PENDLETON 7.43 EMC
Reserve Fleet, site 4.

2164 GEORGE W. CHILDS 7.43 GMC War
damaged (no further details). 8.6.44: Sunk as
'GOOSEBERRY 2' breakwater blockship at
Mulberry Harbour A beach-head, St. Laurent,
Normandy. 16.7.44: Officially abandoned after
harbour was destroyed by the storms of 19-22.6.44.

2165 ROBERT EDEN 7.43 GMC 9.64: Scrapped Tacoma.

2166 JAMES A. FARRELL 7.43 GMC 29.6.44: One of four Liberty ships torpedoed by U.984 whilst in convoy in English Channel, 50.07N 00.47W, (voyage UK/Normandy). (Also H.G. BLASDEL, EDWARD M. HOUSE and JOHN A. TREUTLEN, qv). Towed in and beached Spithead. CTL. 10.44: Scrapped 'in situ'.

2167 JOSE MARTI 7.43 GMC 51: Sold commercial (same name). 57: MINOTAUR. 60: NATA. 10.66: Scrapped Hirao.

2168 CROSBY S. NOYES 7.43 GMC 4.65: Scrapped Wilmington, Del.

2169 LOUIS MARSHALL 7.43 GMC 51: MOUNT OF OLIVES. 52: SEAWIZARD. 53: GEORGE M. CULUCUNDIS. 56: PACIFIC OCEAN. 60: MARIA G.L. 15.3.64: Aground in fog 30 miles south of Yokohama, 34.53N 139.49E. 17.3.64: Broke in two, sank. Total loss. (Voyage Los Angeles/Chiba — phosphates).

2170 TOWNSEND HARRIS 7.43 GMC 9.67: Scrapped Philadelphia.

2171 GEORGE VICKERS 7.43 WPM 60: Scrapped Baltimore.

2172 JOHN W. POWELL 8.43 EMC 51: Sold commercial (same name). 54: JAMES MONROE. 63: EVAGELISTRIA. 10.67: Scrapped Hirao.

2203 EDWIN L. DRAKE 8.43 GMC 48: Sold commercial (same name). 54: PHOENIX. 57: ANASSA. 60: PRAXITELES. 62: DORI. 16.1.64: Sprung leak, beached, sank near Ponta Delgada, Azores, 37.44N 25.37W (voyage Emden/New Orleans — steel sheets).

2204 THOMAS U. WALTER 7.43 GMC 8.66: Scrapped Philadelphia.

2205 THORSTEIN VEBLEN 8.43 GMC 3.65: Scrapped Philadelphia.

2206 JOHN T. HOLT 8.43 GMC 62: Scrapped Philadelphia.

2207 ARUNAH S. ABELL 8.43 GMC 61: Scrapped Baltimore.

2208 JOSHUA THOMAS 8.43 GMC Reserve Fleet, site 5.

2209 WILLIAM S. THAYER 8.43 EMC 30.4.44: Sunk by submarine (U.711) torpedo off Bear Island, Arctic Ocean.

2210 DAVID DE VRIES 8.43 GMC Completed as SAMWATER. 29.1.47: On fire and abandoned 35 miles West of Finisterre, 42.41N 10.13W. Sank. (Voyage Sydney/Liverpool — general).

2211 HENRY VAN DYKE 8.43 GMC Completed as SAMHAIN. 47: CITY OF PORTSMOUTH. 59: EFCHARIS.

2212 JAMES M. GILLIS 8.43 GMC 11.62: Scrapped Panama City.

2213 LIONEL COPLEY 8.43 GMC Completed as SAMBRAKE. 47: CITY OF CHELMSFORD. 60: Converted at Newport, Mon. with two oil engines by Mirrlees, Bickerton and renamed SAN GEORGE. 68: SUERTE.

2214 MATTHEW BRUSH 8.43 WPM Completed as SAMOA. 47: EURYMEDON. 52: GLENLOGAN. 57: EURYMEDON. 58: ANGELOS. 64: MIMOSA. 66: ALPLATA. 67: ANKA.

2215 HOLLAND THOMPSON 8.43 GMC Completed as SAMITE. 47: Returned USA. 3.63: Scrapped Panama City.

2216 JOHN W. GARRETT 8.43 GMC 51: FRIBOURG TRADER. 56: FELIX R.P. 57: JANE B.L. 61: MARITIHI. 6.67: Scrapped Hirao.

2217 PETER COOPER 9.43 EMC Completed as SAMARKAND. 47: TALTHYBIUS. 54: GLENIFFER. 58: DOVE. 65: PATRAIC SKY.

2218 TENCH TILGHMAN 9.43 GMC Completed as SAMOS. 47: ZINI. 59: SAN SALVADOR. 12.68: Scrapped Spezia.

2219 JAMES BLAIR 9.43 GMC Completed as SAMARINA. 47: CITY OF ELY. 61: PAGET TRADER. 2.11.65: Fire in cargo in position 05.45N 94.00E. 6.11.65: Arrived Singapore, and later at Hong Kong (laid up). 8.66: Scrapped Kaohsiung.

2220 EMMA LAZARUS 9.43 GMC Completed as SAMARA. 43: SAMSHIRE. 47: CITY OF DONCASTER. 61: PEMBROKE TRADER. 66: GALLETTA.

2221 CHARLES C. LONG 9.43 GMC Completed as

SAMUR. 48: Returned USA. 3.66: Scrapped New Orleans.

2222 WILLIAM SMALLWOOD 9.43 GMC Completed as SAMPA. 27.2.45: Mined and sunk 9 miles North of Ostend.

2223 JAMES T. EARLE 9.43 WPM Completed as SAMAYE. 47: QUEEN VICTORIA. 48: HISTORIAN. 62: PARVATI JAYANTI. 6.9.67: Damaged by Israeli shellfire in Suez Harbour during Arab/Israel dispute. Repaired. 22.2.68: Grounded Azemmour, 50m from Casablanca. 23.2.68: Refloated, seriously damaged; proceeded Casablanca, (Voyage Alexandria/Bombay – cotton). Sold. 4.68: Towed Aviles and scrapped.

2224 JOHN H. HATTON 9.43 GMC Completed as SAMORA. 43: SAMPENN. 48: Returned to USA. 9.66: Scrapped New Orleans.

2225 ORVILLE P. TAYLOR 9.43 GMC Completed as SAMOTHRACE. 47: TALCA. 53: POPI. 61: LYDIA. 7.67: Scrapped Whampoa.

2226 MARIE M. MELONEY 9.43 GMC 65: Sold for scrapping at Philadelphia but, later, scrapping deferred due to Vietnam situation. 4.69: scrapped Philadelphia.

2227 ARTHUR P. GORMAN 9.43 GMC Completed as TUTUILA ARG 4 (USN).

2228 HEYWOOD BROUN 9.43 GMC 47: Sold commercial (same name). 61: CAVALIER. 8.69: Scrapped Hong Kong.

2229 PHILIP F. THOMAS 9.43 GMC 51: MOUNT VERNON. 52: SEAWORLD. 53: PELAGIA. 15.9.56: Swamped by heavy seas, broke in two and sank off Lofoten Islands, 67.15N 11.35E (Voyage Narvik/Baltimore – iron ore).

2230 CALEB C. WHEELER 9.43 GMC Completed as OAHU ARG 5 (USN). USN Reserve Fleet, site 6.

2231 HAWKINS FUDSKE 9.43 GMC 11.69: Scrapped Mobile.

2232 HENRY LOMB 9.43 WPM 51: WESTERN FARMER. 20.8.52: In collision with tanker BJORGHOLM (51/11,752 grt) 18 miles from Ramsgate. Severely damaged, broke in two. Bow sank, stern towed to Calais and beached. (Voyage Hampton Roads/Bremen – coal). 9.6.52: Stern refloated, towed to Dunkirk and discharged. 8.55: Stern part towed Burcht, Belgium, and scrapped.

2233 GEORGE UHLER 9.43 GMC 53: SOUTHERN TRADER. 54: NATIONAL TRADER. 55: Lengthened at Maizuru to 511½ ft (8,490 grt). 16.12.60: On fire and abandoned in Yucatan Channel off Cape San Antonio, Cuba 22.20N 85.22W (Voyage Vitoria/Mobile – iron ore). 23.12.60: Salved and towed Mobile. CTL. Sold 61: Scrapped, Japan.

2234 PATRICK C. BOYLE 9.43 GMC 2.60: Scrapped Baltimore.

2235 MARGARET BRENT 9.43 GMC 47: ELENA MARE. 49: ELENA PARODI. 61: KOPALNIA KAZIMIERZ. 67: Converted for use as floating warehouse in Poland.

2236 BEN F. DIXON 9.43 EMC 47: ANGELINA. 61: Returned US Dept of Commerce. 63: Scrapped Bordentown, Jersey City.

2237 FRANCIS VIGO 9.43 GMC 62: Scrapped Baltimore.

2238 JOHN J. McGRAW 9.43 WPM Completed as SAMARIZ. 44: JOHN J. McGRAW. 47: LASSELL. 62: AIOLOS II. 12.68: Scrapped Shanghai.

2239 ADOLPH S. OCHS 10.43 GMC Completed as SAMWYO. 43: ADOLPH S. OCHS. 48: Returned USA. 12.68: Scrapped Kearny, NJ.

2240 NIKOLA TESLA 10.43 HMC Completed as SAMKANSA. 47: CERINTHUS. 52: PHASSA. 53: URANIA. 64: CONCORD VENTURE.

2241 FRANZ BOAS 10.43 WPM Completed as SAMMEX. 47: SHEAF MEAD. 52: GERONTAS. 24.8.59: Aground off Gdynia. 27.8.59: Refloated, severely damaged. CTL. (Voyage Vitoria/Gdynia – ore). 59: Scrapped Hendrik Ido Ambacht.

2242 JOHN RUSSELL POPE 10.43 GMC Completed as SAMDAK. 47: ALPHA VAAL. 48: LEDBURY. 61: KOPALNIA CZELADZ.

2243 HORACE BUSHNELL 10.43 GMC 20.3.45: Damaged by submarine (U.995) torpedo; abandoned, later grounded off North Russia. Refloated and towed Murmansk; taken over by Soviet authorities.

The Liberty Ships

56: Rebuilt and converted to fish carrier, renamed PAMYATI KIROVA (8,491 grt), length 440 ft oa. Re-engined with C4 cyl. & LP turbine machinery built in Sweden. Converted at Murmansk 1948-1955.

2244 JOYCE KILMER 10.43 EMC 1.68: Scrapped Terminal Island.

2245 W.R. GRACE 10.43 GMC 1.66: Scrapped Philadelphia.

2246 JESSE DE FOREST 10.43 VIW Completed as SAMUTA. 47: KELVINBANK. 6.1.53: Ashore on reef at Sydney Point, Ocean Island. Refloated but held by tailshaft and propeller of wreck OOMA which penetrated bottom. Grounded again; became tidal. Total loss. (Voyage Ocean Island/Australasia — phosphate).

2247 LYON G. TYLER 10.43 GMC Completed as SAMNEBRA. 47: PENTIRE. 55: CUACO. 6.63: Scrapped Hirao.

2248 ADOLPH LEWISOHN 10.43 GMC Completed as SAMOTA. 47: ZUNGERU. 58: POROS. 66: MERY.

2249 EDWARD COOK 10.43 GMC Completed as SAMWIS. 47: SPECIALIST. 64: MITERA. 11.68: Scrapped Hong Kong.

2250 SIMON B. ELLIOTT 10.43 GMC Completed as SAMNESSE. 47: EUMAEUS. 52: GLENSHIEL. 57: EURYRADES. 61: MARINE BOUNTY. 25.2.66: Aground, refloated but grounded again at Hasieshan, China 25.20N 119.45E. Abandoned, broke in two. Total loss. (Voyage Chingwangtao/Singapore — coal).

2251 GEORGE M. SHRIVER 10.43 WPM Completed as VIGGO HANSTEEN. 53: ALKIMOS. 20.3.63: Aground 170 miles North of Fremantle. 25.3.63: Refloated, severely damaged: proceeded Fremantle. 30.5.63: Left in tow, bound for Hong Kong, but 31.5.63: Towrope parted in storm, vessel aground 31 miles north of Fremantle, 31.38S 115.41E. 11.2.64: Refloated and moored. 2.5.64: Broke moorings, again aground. Refloated. 1.7.65: Yet again aground. CTL. Wreck sold to Fremantle buyers for scrapping.

2252 STAGE DOOR CANTEEN 10.43 GMC 47: NORCUBA. 49: TRAMAR I. 55: SEANAN. 56: ALBATROSS. 61: Returned to US Dept of Commerce

— the first Liberty ship to be exchanged under the US Ship Exchange Act — in exchange for MORMACMOON (40/7,939 grt). 61: Scrapped Everett, Wash.

2253 FRANCIS P. DUFFEY 10.43 GMC Completed as CEBU ARG 6 (USN). USN Reserve Fleet, site 6.

2254 LEWIS EMERY, Jnr. 11.43 GMC 51: Sold commercial (same name). 61: CATCHER. 8.68: Scrapped Bilbao.

2255 HAROLD L. WINSLOW 10.43 GMC 64: Converted to depot ship and used as pier and floating warehouse at Nikishka, Alaska.

2256 J. WHITRIDGE WILLIAMS 11.43 WPM Completed as SAMSYLVAN. 47: TROPIC. 52: SAN FRANCESCO. 30.1.60: Grounded near Hainan Island. Refloated, damaged. Sold for scrap, (Voyage Whampoa/Yulin). 9.6.60: Foundered in typhoon at Hong Kong whilst awaiting demolition. Raised and scrapped locally.

2257 EDITH WHARTON 11.43 GMC Completed as SAMVERN. 18.1.45: Mined and sunk in Scheldt Estuary, 51.22N 03.02E (Voyage Antwerp/London).

2258 W. WALTER HUSBAND 10.43 EMC Completed as SAMYORK. 47: IVYBANK. 59: WINONA. 61: KONDOR. 63: GRAND. 13.1.65: Sprung leak in storm 320 miles east of Tokio 34.15N 145.10E. Broke in two, bow sank, stern presumed sank. (Voyage San Francisco/Kaohsiung — scrap iron).

2259 U.S.O. 10.43 GMC 54: COLUMBELLA. 61: EKALI. 65: LOYAL FORTUNES. 6.11.67: Aground in typhoon on Pratas Reef, 165 miles south east of Hong Kong 20.43N 116.43E. Abandoned, flooded buckled and fractured. Compromised total loss. Wreck sold for scrapping 'in situ'.

2260 JOSE ARTIGAS 11.43 GMC Completed as SAMOKLA. 48: Returned to USA. 62: Scrapped Newport News, Va.

2261 PRISCILLA ALDEN 11.43 GMC Completed as SAMLOUIS. 47: CORALSTONE. 59: ESMERA-LDA. 11.68: Scrapped Kaohsiung.

2262 THEODORE ROOSEVELT 11.43 GMC 43: INDUS AKN 1 (USN). 1946: THEODORE ROOSEVELT. 5.67: Scrapped Wilmington, Del.

2263 SAMUEL H. RALSTON 11.43 WPM Completed as SAMOIS. 47: CITY OF LICHFIELD. 59: CAMERONA. 61: CHEE LEE. 67: Scrapped Kaohsiung.

2264 EDWIN A. ROBINSON 11.43 GMC Completed as SAMSIP. 7.12.44: Damaged by mine 1 mile from NF 11 buoy, Schelde Estuary. Wreck sunk by gunfire of Allied warships.

2265 AUGUSTINE HERMAN 11.43 GMC Completed as SAMSETTE. 47: EURYPYLUS. 51: PEMBROKE-SHIRE. 57: EURYPYLUS. 60: KOTA BAHRU. 66: CRESTA. 2.68: Scrapped Kaohsiung.

2266 CHARLES SCRIBNER 11.43 GMC 47: SEA PRINCE. 48: JALAMAYUR. 68: SAMUDRA DAYA.

2267 EDWARD BRUCE 11.43 GMC Completed as SAMOINE. 43: EDWARD BRUCE. 47: Returned USA. Reserve Fleet, site 2.

2268 ISRAEL J. MERRITT 11.43 GMC Completed as SAMFLORA. 47: PRIMROSE HILL. 50: LONDON VENDOR. 52: CABANOS. 64: THEBEAN. 3.68: Scrapped Onomichi.

2269 FRANK A. VANDERLIP 11.43 GMC Completed as SAMBUFF. 44: FRANK A. VANDERLIP. 5.67: Scrapped Kearny, NJ.

2270 JOHN LA FARGE 11.43 EMC 49: OCEAN MARINER. 51: SEALIFE. 57: ANDROS LION. 63: SAN LORENZO. 4.68: Scrapped Tokuyama.

2271 JACOB H. SCHIFF 11.43 GMC Completed as SAMBURGH. 47: TIELBANK. 60: GIACOMO. 62: SORRELHORSE. 4.69: Scrapped Split.

2272 JOHN T. CLARK 11.43 GMC Completed as SAMCLEVE. 47: TANTALUS. 58: URBANIA. 65: COCLER.

2273 FRANCIS C. HARRINGTON 11.43 GMC 62: Scrapped Kearny, NJ.

2274 JAMES CARROLL 11.43 GMC Completed as SAMGARA. 47: TITAN. 50: FLINTSHIRE. 58: TITAN. 62: TITANUS.

2275 BARBARA FRIETCHIE 11.43 GMC 51: Sold commercial (same name). 63: Returned to USA. 64: Scrapped Hong Kong.

2276 DANIEL APPLETON 11.43 WPM Completed as SAMFIELD. 47: SOUTHMOOR. 50: MARINE PRIDE. 51: ST. SPERO. 53: ENDEAVOUR. 59: VALIANT LIBERTY. 60: SKYLLAS. 60: HWEI SUNG. 30.10.61: Aground at Naoyetsu, Honshu, whilst discharging. 7.11.61: Refloated, but CTL. Sold. 2.62: Scrapped Osaka.

2277 LEO J. DUSTER 12.43 GMC 47: F.S. BELL. 63: BAT. 66: DELURO. 4.69: Scrapped Kaohsiung.

2278 JOHN F. GOUCHER 12.43 GMC Completed as CULEBRA ISLAND ARG 7 (USN). USN Reserve Fleet, site 6.

2279 JAMES C. CAMERON 12.43 GMC 61: Scrapped Panama City.

2280 WILLIS J. ABBOT 12.43 GMC Completed as SAMBOSTON. 47: CITY OF ROCHESTER. 62: FOTINI XILAS. 64: RESOLUTE II. 68: Scrapped Taipei, Formosa.

2281 HUGH M. SMITH 12.43 GMC 11.69: Scrapped Portland, Ore.

2282 ROSS G. MARVIN 12.43 EMC Completed as SAMTROY. 47: EDENBANK. 60: HOPING SAN SHI WU (Hoping No. 35).

2283 J. FRED ESSARY 12.43 GMC Completed as SAGITTARIUS AKN 2, (USN). 1946: J. FRED ESSARY. USN Reserve Fleet, site 2.

2284 A.J. CERMAK 12.43 GMC 64: Scrapped Philadelphia.

2285 AMMLA 12.43 WPM Completed as SAM-VARD. 44: AMMLA. 47: BENARTY. 54: CREATOR. 60: TREIS IERARCHA. 63: CAPTAIN G. 68: Sold to Shanghai breakers but 21.8.68: In distress with machinery damage and flooding in typhoon 60 miles south of Hong Kong. Sank approx 22.24N 114.55E (voyage Kosseir/Shanghai).

2286 LOUIS KOSSUTH 12.43 GMC 9.59: Scrapped Baltimore.

2287 ISRAEL WHEELEN 12.43 GMC Completed as SAMPORT. 1948: ISRAEL WHEELEN. 11.62: Scrapped Panama City.

2288 HUGH L. KERWIN 12.43 GMC Completed as SAMYALE. 47: ZUNGON. 59: AEGINA. 66: IRINI. 10.6.67: In collision with tanker RUSSELL H.

GREEN (65/31,975 grt) 10 miles north of Cape Spartel. Later arrived Cadiz, seriously damaged.(Voyage Gdynia/Med, sulphate). 6.12.67: Towed Valencia and scrapped.

2289 JOSHUA B. LIPPINCOTT 12.43 WPM Reserve Fleet, site 1.

2290 ROBERT WICKLIFFE 12.43 GMC Completed as SAMBALT. 47: LILIAN MOLLER. 48: SPEAKER. 62: BYZANTION. 5.69: Scrapped Onomichi.

2291 FRANK R. STOCKTON 12.43 GMC 51: SOUTHWAVE. 51: AMERSEA. 56: OCEAN SKIPPER. 62: UNIVERSAL. 63: KINGSUN. 10.68: Scrapped Kaohsiung.

2292 BEN H. MILLER 12.43 WPM 47: CITY OF SHREWSBURY. 59: MARUCLA. 5.69: Scrapped Hong Kong.

2293 MARTHA C. THOMAS 12.43 GMC Completed as SAMHARLE. 47: TROILUS. 58: GREEN RIVER. 63: Scrapped Osaka.

2294 LOUIS C. TIFFANY 12.43: Caught fire and burned out whilst under construction. Scrapped.

2295 CARL THUSGAARD 12.43 EMC Completed as SAMKEY. 31.1.48: Reported by radio when in position 41.48N 24.00W on voyage London/Cuba in ballast. Untraced, presumed foundered. (See also Part Five, the 'Sam' Ships).

2296 BYRON DARNTON 12.43 GMC 16.3.46: Ashore on Sanda Island 55.17N 05.35W. Broke in two. Total loss. (Voyage Copenhagen/USA – ballast). 10.53: Scrapped 'in situ'.

2297 MELVIL DEWEY 12.43 GMC Completed as SAMSACOLA. 47: SILVER CEDAR. 49: BEN-WYVIS. 55: LINDA. 58: AGIA IRENE. 65: ANGELINA. 31.7.67: Afire in engine room 85 miles E.N.E. of Madras. Abandoned 14.00N 81.26E (Voyage Visakhapatnam/Madras – ballast). 4.8.67: Salved with machinery space and superstructure burnt out; towed to Madras, thence Singapore. CTL.

2298 FREDERICK BANTING 12.43 GMC 47: CITY OF ST. ALBANS. 60: MARINERI. 67: LIBERTAS. 3.69: Scrapped Onomichi.

2299 MARTIN VAN BUREN 12.43 GMC 14.1.45: Damaged by submarine (U.1232) torpedo off Halifax

NS, 44.28N 63.28W. Beached. CTL. 50: Scrapped 'in situ'.

2300 WILLIAM R. COX (I) 12.43 GMC Completed as SAMTWEED. 47: CITY OF NEWPORT. 61: ISTROS II. 4.67: Scrapped Trieste.

2301 SAMFORTH 1.44 GMC 48: Returned USA. Reserve Fleet, site 4.

2302 SAMCLYDE 1.44 GMC 46: Returned USA. 3.66: Scrapped Philadelphia.

2303 WILLIAM R. COX (II) 1.44 GMC 44: TUSCANA AKN 3 (USN). 46: WILLIAM R. COX. 5.67: Scrapped Wilmington, NC.

2304 SAMETTRICK 1.44 GMC 47: ELSTREE GRANGE. 60: KOPALNIA MIECHOWICE.

2305 SAMCREE 1.44 GMC 47: Returned USA. 3.70: Sold to Seoul shipbreakers.

2306 SAMFEUGH 1.44 EMC 47: Returned USA. 8.69: Scrapped Philadelphia.

2307 SAMEVERON 1.44 GMC 47: ERICBANK. 59: NAN HAI 146.

2308 SAMTAY 1.44 GMC 47: RUDBY. 52: THEKLA. 54: ADAMAS. 12.68: Scrapped Sakaide.

2309 SAMNID 1.44 WPM 47: PACIFIC STAR. 51: LALANDE. 51: NINFEA. 59: NAN HAI 147.

2310 SAMOUSE 1.44 GMC 47: MARABANK. 60: RUSCIN. 62: WHITEHORSE. 6.69: Scrapped Split.

2311 ELOY ALFARO 1.44 GMC 47: NORLUNA. 48: ELOY ALFARO. 50: NORLUNA. 51: AURORA. 18.5.66: Abandoned 300 miles east of Cape Race after developing leaks in holds and engine room. Presumed sunk. (Voyage Hamburg/Montreal – ballast).

2312 SAMCHESS 1.44 GMC 47: ALPHA MOOI. 48: PORLOCK HILL. 21.12.51: Ashore 2 miles south east of Famagusta in gale. 22.12.51: Broke in two. Total loss (Voyage Southampton/Port Said – army stores). 29.3.52: After part refloated and 29.4.52: Towed to Alexandria. 14.5.52: Towed Palermo and scrapped.

2313 VAN LEAR BLACK 1.44 EMC Completed as ALLEGAN AK 225. (USN). 45: VAN LEAR BLACK. 47: SAN LEONARDO. 51: WANDERER. 59:

The *USS Laertes* in April 1945. Launched on September 13, 1944, and intended for service with the Royal Navy, she was retained to serve with the US Navy. (Bethlehem, Yard no 2406)

War-damaged Liberty ships in a section of the 'Gooseberry' breakwater formed by a line of sunken ships off Omaha beach-head, Normandy, in June 1944. (Bethlehem, Yard no 2164; California, Yard no 95; Delta, Yard no 6, etc)

Ignace Paderewski (California, Yard no 181)

The *Panamolga,* built as the *Martin Johnson,* was the last Liberty ship constructed by the California yard. (Yard no 306)

The spectacular launching of the *Jonathan Grout,* illustrating the method of sideways-launchings from this yard. (Delta, Yard no 9)

VALIANT FORCE. 63: WANDERLUST. 64: AGATHOPOLIS. 10.69: Scrapped Onomichi.

2314 SAMESK 2.44 WPM 47: LEICESTER. 16.9.48: Abandoned sinking after shifting boards carried away and ballast shifted in hurricane in Atlantic 40.27N 55.10W. Vessel listed to 55 degrees and later to 70 degrees. 21.9.48: Resighted with 50 degree list in position 37.07N 52.14W. 27.9.48: Taken in tow by salvage tugs and 3.10.48: Arrived Bermuda. 7.10.48: Ashore (with salvage tug) in hurricane at Bermuda. 19.10.48: Refloated and 24.10.48: Towed New York and later to Baltimore. Repaired. 50: INAGUA. 58: SERAFIN TOPIC. 62: JELA TOPIC. 65: VIKING LIBERTY. 21.1.66: Aground off Trinidad (Voyage Recife/New York). 1.2.66: Refloated, towed New Orleans. Repair uneconomic; sold. 8.66: Scrapped Santander.

2315 BENJAMIN SCHLESINGER 2.44 GMC 47: JEANNETTE L. ROUTH. 48: BLACK POINT. 55: MARINE PIONEER. 7.63: Scrapped Veracruz, Mexico.

2316 MORRIS HILLQUIT 2.44 GMC 51: HILTON. 62: GOVIND JAYANTI. 3.66: Scrapped Hamburg.

2317 MEYER LONDON 2.44 GMC 16.4.44: Sunk by submarine (U.407) torpedo off Libya, 32.38N 23.08E (Voyage Philadelphia/Abadan).

2318 MORRIS SIGMAN 2.44 GMC 47: ARTHUR FRIBOURG. 56: LOSMAR. 68: Returned to US Govt under Ship Exchange Act. Sold 12.68: Towed Santander and scrapped.

2319 SAMLEVEN 2.44 GMC 47: BISHAM HILL. 52: NAUSICA. 56: PRAGLIA. 60: VASSILIKI.

2320 WILLIAM D. BYRON 2.44 GMC 15.8.44: Damaged by mine off Italian coast; towed to Savona. CTL. 6.48: Scrapped Savona.

2321 SAMLYTH 2.44 WPM 47: ST. ARVANS. 63: SAJANY.

2322 SAMSTRULE 2.44 GMC 47: ARTEMISIA. 56: ALLEGRA S. 66: MARINA.

2323 SAMINVER 2.44 EMC 48: Returned USA. 3.64: Scrapped New Orleans.

2324 THOMAS DONALDSON 2.44 GMC 20.3.45: Sunk by submarine (U.968) torpedo off Murmansk, Russia.

2325 SAMLOSSIE 2.44 WPM 47: BARN HILL. 51: PORTO ALEGRE. 54: STAVROS.

2326 JOHN L. ELLIOTT 2.44 GMC 47: SEA KING. 48: JALAMANJARI. 5.63: Scrapped Bombay.

2327 LEYTE 2.44 GMC Completed as LEYTE ARG 8, (USN). 45: MAUI ARG 8, (USN). USN Reserve Fleet, site 6.

2328 SAMGAUDIE 3.44 GMC 47: NORAH MOLLER. 48: STATESMAN. 62: AKTIS. 68: Scrapped Kaohsiung.

2329 WARREN DELANO 3.44 EMC 51: SEA-CHAMPION. 54: CHAMPION. 55: KONSTANTINOS V. 62: SILVANA. 64: KUO TAI. 6.66: Scrapped Kaohsiung.

2330 SAMAFFRIC 3.44 GMC 47: BENVRACKIE. 52: CITTA DI SALERNO. 64: NEWFOREST.

2331 SAMCONON 3.44 GMC 50: MODERATOR. 55: ANGELIKI II. 64: CONCHITA. 5.7.67: Sank after developing leaks 300 miles S.W. of Seychelles 06.20S 50.27E (Voyage Mormugao/Poland).

2332 SAMNETHY 3.44 GMC 48: Returned USA. 3.63: Scrapped Mobile.

2333 STEPHEN W. GAMBRILL 3.44 WPM 48: COLUMBIA TRADER. 54: SEABREEZE. 57: SEA MAIDEN. 60: NORA. 8.67: Scrapped Singapore.

2334 SAMEDEN 3.44 F & S 47: MILL HILL. 51: EDUCATOR. 61: KANARIS. 66: SPLENDID SKY.

2335 ROBERT ELLIS LEWIS 3.44 GMC 3.70: Towed Santander for scrapping.

2336 SAMCOLNE 3.44 GMC 47: MARY MOLLER. 48: SCULPTOR. 62: CAPE VENETICO. 12.67: Scrapped Hong Kong.

2337 SAMLEA 3.44 EMC 47: CITY OF COL-CHESTER. 59: SUNSET. 65: MARIA ELENI. 67: BLUE WAVE. 68: Scrapped Matsuyama.

2338 SAMSHEE 3.44 GMC 48: Returned USA. 8.64: Scrapped New Orleans.

2339 SAMJACK 4.44 GMC 47: TYDEUS. 50: GLENBEG. 58: ROAN. 60: JUCAR. 9.67: Scrapped Mihara.

2340 SAMSPELGA 4.44 GMC 47: SPRINGBANK. 58: NAN HAI 142.

2341 SAMDONARD 4.44 GMC 47: DAYBEAM. 52: KRIONERI. 52: ALBA. 61: ALBAMAR. 64: ALBARAN. 68: Scrapped Kaohsiung.

2342 SAMGALLION 4.44 WPM 47: MARIETTA DAL. 15.5.50: Ashore, broke in two on Smith Rock, 2 miles N.N.E. of Cape Moreton Lighthouse, Queensland. Total loss. (Voyage Galveston/Adelaide — sulphur and general).

2343 SAMNEAGH 4.44 EMC 47: STAMFORD HILL. 51: RIO MAR. 59: PRESIDENT BOSHOF. 61: RIO MAR. 65: AMON. 10.68: Scrapped Hsinkang.

2344 EDWARD B. HAINES 4.44 GMC 47: JOHN WEYERHAEUSER. 69: RELIANCE INTEGRITY.

2345 SAMHOPE 4.44 GMC 47: ROSALIE MOLLER. 48: SUCCESSOR. 63: ZELA M. 68: IGNACIO AGRAMONTE.

2346 JOHN H. MURPHY 4.44 NT 46: OLD DOMINION STATE. 54: HENRY ULLMAN. 57: OMNIUM EXPLORER. 58: VALIANT EXPLORER. 60: MOUNT McKINLEY. 62: Lengthened at Tokio to 511½ ft (8,584 grt). 63: VOLUSIA.

2347 SAMSTURDY 4.44 GMC 47: BALUCHISTAN. 53: LA LOMA. 58: ANGELIC FORCE. 59: DYNAMIS. 11.66: Scrapped Osaka.

2348 LAWRENCE J. BRENGLE 4.44 GMC 47: ARA J. PONCHELET. 48: MICHAEL J. GOULANDRIS. 53: MICHAEL G. 63: MICHELIN. 65: TAINAN. 68: Scrapped Kaohsiung.

2349 SAMDAUNTLESS 4.44 WPM 47: BENDORAN. 53: THALASSOPOROS. 59: PATERONISOS. 60: LAMYREFS. 6.67: Scrapped Kaohsiung.

2350 WILLIAM HODSON (I) 4.44 GMC Completed as SVERRE HELMERSEN. 23.4.45: Damaged by mine in position 51.19N 01.47E, (Voyage Antwerp/New York — ballast). Towed Dover, thence Falmouth. 46: Returned US Govt, CTL. 7.48: Scrapped Zeebrugge.

2351 SAMTRUSTY 4.44 WPM 47: LAKONIA. 61: SANGAETANO.

2352 DEBORAH GANNETT 4.44 EMC 62: Scrapped Baltimore.

2353 SAMCONSTANT 5.44 GMC 47: SKIPSEA. 48: RAMON DE LARRINAGA. 52: OKEANOPOROS.

62: KOSTIS A. GEORGILIS. 3.11.67: Fire and explosions in engine room, stranded Coco Islands. 4.11.67: Afire in all holds; abandoned, (Voyage Rangoon/Colombo — rice).

2354 FRANCIS D. CULKIN 4.44 GMC 47: THOMAS F. BAKER. 54: META D. 22.2.55: Aground during fog on Fuller Bank, 4 miles south of Selsey (Voyage Hampton Roads/Rotterdam — coal). 25.2.55: Refloated, towed Southampton. CTL. Sold. Repaired. 55: PERIOLOS. 20.10.67: Aground after anchors dragged in heavy weather 3 miles north of Colombo. Flooded and abandoned. Salvage not economic.

2355 SAMFAITHFUL 4.44 GMC 47: BALANTIA. 58: BETAMAR. 65: ACME. 4.69: Scrapped Shanghai.

2356 SAMWINGED 4.44 WPM 48: Returned USA. Reserve Fleet, site 4.

2357 SAMLOYAL 5.44 WPM 47: ST. HELENA. 1.63: Scrapped Tamise, Belgium.

2358 SAMFLEET 5.44 GMC 47: CORABANK. 59: SANTA GRANDA. 2.68: Scrapped Hong Kong.

2359 SAMGLORY 5.44 EMC 47: SERBISTAN. 62: CALYPSO. 3.69: Scrapped Hong Kong.

2360 JAMES KERNEY 5.44 NT 47: F.E. WEYERHAEUSER. 69: RELIANCE UNITY.

2361 SAMSOARING 5.44 GMC 47: FRASER RIVER. 52: NORTH PRINCESS. 59: GEORGIOS A. 60: IOANNIS K. 3.1.68: Grounded after steering gear damage at Vung Tau, 10.14N 107.05E. Damaged and tidal; abandoned.

2362 SAMCREST 5.44 GMC 47: CITY OF LEEDS. 60: GROSVENOR EXPLORER. 3.65: Scrapped Hong Kong.

2363 JAMES D. TRASK 5.44 GMC 48: ARKANSAN. 50: OREGONIAN. 54: EVILIZ. 55: Lengthened at Innoshima to 511½ ft, (8,370 grt). 68: Scrapped Mukaishima.

2364 SAMFREEDOM 5.44 WPM 47: FINNAMORE HILL. 48: WYE VALLEY. 51: CAVOPLATANOS. 52: LILIBET. 54: HELLESPONT. 63: ALICE.

2365 SAMTRUTH 5.44 F & S 50: ASPIRATOR. 60: PLOCE.

2366 MONA ISLAND 5.44 GMC Completed as MONA ISLAND ARG 9, (USN). USN Reserve Fleet, site 2.

2367 SAMTORCH 5.44 EMC 47: CITY OF STAFFORD. 61: KUNIANG. 66: PROSPECT. 4.67: Scrapped Kaohsiung.

2368 SAMLISTAR 6.44 GMC 47: HURWORTH. 54: SUERTE. 9.1.62: Aground off Shut-In Island, 15 miles east of Halifax, NS, (Voyage Brest/Halifax – ballast). CTL. 5.4.62: Pulled from rocks. 6.4.62: Towed to sea and sunk.

2369 DUMARAN 6.44 WPM Launched as DUMARAN ARG 14, (USN), but completed as CHOURRE ARV 1 (USN). USN Reserve Fleet, site 6.

2370 SAMSPEED 6.44 F & S 47: CAPE YORK. 52: PAESTUM. 7.66: Put into Charleston leaking in No 2 hold. Sailed for Norfolk for repairs but 10.7.66: Abandoned due to holds and engine room flooding. 11.7.66: Sank off Cape Hatteras 34.48N 75.17W (Voyage Boca Grande/Catania – phosphates).

2371 SAMLUZON 6.44 GMC 47: JERSEY MAY. 50: MIGUEL DE LARRINAGA. 56: TRITONIA. 7.69: Scrapped Hong Kong.

2372 SAMNEGROS 6.44 GMC 47: TITANBANK. 59: LUCINA. 62: CANDY. 66: YVONNE. 5.67: Scrapped Kaohsiung.

2373 SAMINDORO 6.44 F & S 47: SANDSEND. 12.67: Scrapped Kaohsiung.

2374 WILLIAM HODSON (II) 6.44 WPM Completed as CHUNG TUNG. 47: ARTHUR P. FAIRFIELD. 48: ADMIRAL ARTHUR P. FAIRFIELD. 50: SEA-CORONET. 54: TONSINA. 64: Converted into container ship (7,890 tdw) for 175 24-ft containers.

2375 SAMTANA 6.44 EMC 47: CAPE VERDE 57: AFRICAN NIGHT. 10.67: Scrapped Kaohsiung.

2376 SAMSKERN 6.44 WPM 47: STANTHORPE. 49: DOMINGO DE LARRINAGA. 55: VASSILIS. 59: KATINA. 64: ANASTASSIA. 6.1.69: Aground off Constanza in heavy weather. Abandoned. Total loss. (Voyage Alexandria/Constanza).

2377 SAMSYLARNA 6.44 WPM 4.8.44: Damaged by aircraft torpedo; stern blown off and engine room flooded. Abandoned when awash but reboarded and beached near Benghazi. Later refloated and towed Alexandria. Repaired. 51: TITO CAMPANELLA. 61: HUTA SOSNOWIEC.

2378 SAMLAMU 6.44 GMC 47: KINGSBURY. 60: HUTA BEDZIN. 69: Converted in Poland to non-seagoing floating warehouse, renamed MP–ZPGDY6.

2379 SAMUEL F.B. MORSE (II) 6.44 WPM 47: ALAMAR. 68: Returned to US Govt under Ship Exchange Act. Sold. 12.68: Towed Santander and scrapped.

2380 DEXTER W. FELLOWS 6.44 F & S 47: DIANA H. PONCHELET. 48: GEORGE S. LONG. 69: RELIANCE HARMONY.

2381 ASSISTANCE 6.44 WPM Completed as repair ship AR17 for USN but transferred to RN and re-named HMS ASSISTANCE, F.173 (repair ship). 8.46: Returned to USN. USN Reserve Fleet, site 2.

2382 OAKLEY WOOD 6.44 NT 46: KEYSTONE STATE. 55: GEORGES FRIBOURG. 57: MAGALLANES. 59: ALEXANDER S.M. 66: THIMAR S. 23.6.67: Aground and abandoned near Soehi Besar, North Sarawak, 02.58N 108.40E. Total loss. (Voyage Mormugao/Japan – ore).

2383 WILLIAM S. BAER 7.44 GMC 47: PENNMAR. 64: Returned US Govt (with five other Liberties) in exchange for six C.4 type ships. Reserve Fleet, site 2.

2384 SIDNEY WRIGHT 7.44 EMC 47: MORGAN H. GRACE. 49: SHAHROKH. 51: PANTANASSA. 53: EFTHALASSOS. 60: DOCTOR G. LEMOS. 5.67: Scrapped Hong Kong.

2385 WILLIAM HODSON (III) 7.44 GMC 48: OREGON TRADER. 62: Returned US Govt. 63: Scrapped Portland, Ore.

2386 MARY PICKERSGILL 7.44 F & S 47: OCEAN TRAVELLER. 48: W.H. PEABODY. 69: RELIANCE PROSPERITY.

2387 JOSEPH B. EASTMAN 7.44 GMC 47: PORTMAR. 64: Returned US Govt (with five other Liberties) in exchange for six C.4 type ships. Reserve Fleet, site 2.

2388 WALTER KIDDE 7.44 GMC 47: YORKMAR. 64: Returned US Govt (with five other Liberties) in exchange for six C.4 type ships. 2.66: Scrapped Tacoma.

2389 GEORGE R. HOLMES 7.44 WPM 51: JULES FRIBOURG. 56: KENMAR. 11.67: Sold for scrap but 3.68: resold for trading, renamed CORINNE S. YABUT. 9.69: Scrapped Kaohsiung.

2390 DILIGENCE 7.44 F & S Completed as AR 18 for USN but transferred to RN and renamed HMS DILIGENCE, F.174 (repair ship). 1.46: Returned USN. USN Reserve Fleet, site 6.

2391 FREDERIC A. KUMMER 7.44 EMC 10.67: Scrapped Philadelphia.

2392 EDWARD A. SAVOY 7.44 F & S 47: DAVID CLINCHFIELD 21. 48: MARY J. GOULANDRIS. 53: MARY J.G. 54: ESTORIL. 11.7.56: In collision in fog with ss DEA MAZZELLA (42/7,031 grt), sank 440 miles east of Boston, Mass., 42.50N 61.00W (Voyage Seven Islands/Baltimore — ore).

2393 VINCENT HARRINGTON 7.44 WPM 47: CALMAR. 63: Scrapped Richmond, Cal.

2394 A.J. CASSATT 7.44 GMC 44: APPANOOSE AK 226 (USN). 46: A.J. CASSATT. 47: SANTA ANA. 1.65: Scrapped Yokohama.

2395 S. WILEY WAKEMAN 8.44 GMC 13.9.46: Struck and grounded on wreck 12 miles south of Tobago Island, (Voyage Hampton Roads/Buenos Aires — coal). 22.9.46: Refloated, towed Port of Spain, thence Mobile. Laid up, damaged. 9.48: Scrapped New Orleans.

2396 HECLA 8.44 GMC Completed as naval repair ship and intended for transfer to RN as HMS HECLA, F.175, but retained by USN and renamed XANTHUS AR 9. USN Reserve Fleet, site 2.

2397 FREDERICK W. WOOD 8.44 EMC 47: GREENHAVEN TRAILS. 51: SEA CLOUD. 57: PACIFIC CLOUD. 58: WALDO. 60: SAN MARINO. 63: Returned US Govt. 63: Scrapped Tacoma.

2398 MASBATE 8.44 GMC Launched as MASBATE ARG 15, (USN), but completed as WEBSTER ARV 2 (USN). USN Reserve Fleet, site 2.

2399 S.M. SHOEMAKER 8.44 WPM 49: TADDEI. 55: VILLA MARION. 63: EVERLIFE. 6.67: Scrapped Kaohsiung.

2400 PALAWAN 8.44 GMC Completed as PALAWAN ARG 10, (USN). USN Reserve Fleet, site 6.

2401 ALEXANDER V. FRASER 8.44 GMC 47: MASSMAR. 64: Returned US Govt (with five other Liberties) in exchange for C.4 type troopship GENERAL H.L. SCOTT (and five other C.4's). Reserve Fleet, site 2.

2402 FREDERICK H. BAETJER 8.44 WPM 47: MARYMAR. 64: Returned US Govt (with five other Liberties) in exchange for six C.4 type ships. Reserve Fleet, site 2.

2403 JESSE COTTRELL 9.44 WPM 47: SEA QUEEN. 49: CARIBSEA. 50: HOLYSTAR. 54: SYMPHONY. 60: EKTOR. 9.66: Scrapped Bilbao.

2404 WILLIAM LIBBEY 9.44 NT 47: AMERICAN STARLING. 57: ATLANTIC STARLING. 63: BEAR CAT. 66: Scrapped Hong Kong.

2405 BENJAMIN PEIXOTTO 9.44 EMC Reported as a CTL in 1946 but no details. 48: Sold to China for scrap. 7.9.49: Grounded in Tola Harbour, Hong Kong during typhoon. 20.10.50: Refloated, damaged 11.50: Scrapped Hong Kong.

2406 DUTIFUL 9.44 GMC Completed as naval repair ship RELIANCE and intended for transfer to RN as HMS DUTIFUL, F.176., but retained by USN and renamed LAERTES AR 20. USN Reserve Fleet, site 6.

2407 GEORGE M. VERITY 9.44 NT 47: SEAMAR. 65: WILMAR. 11.67: Sold for scrap but 3.68: resold for trading, renamed IRENE YABUT. 3.69: Scrapped Hong Kong.

2408 CHARLES C. GLOVER 10.44 GMC 24.10.45: Ashore at entrance to river Loire. 20.11.45: Refloated towed St. Nazaire. CTL. 5.48: Towed Antwerp and scrapped.

2409 JOHN HANSON 10.44 NT 52: LIBERTY F. 56: MARINE RANGER. 1.65: Scrapped Aviles, Spain.

2410 CHARLES A. McCUE 10.44 GMC 47: JOSEPH FEUER. 50: OLYMPIC. 25.7.51: Ashore on Madh Fort, 15 miles north of Bombay. 18.8.51: Refloated, CTL. (Voyage Navalakhi/Bombay — ballast). Sold and repaired. 52: OCEAN LEADER. 54: NICOLAOS. 60: NICOLAOS P. 9.3.65: Dragged anchors in heavy weather, aground off Necochea. CTL (Voyage San Nicolas/Necochea — ballast). Sold for scrapping.

2411 MILAN R. STEFANIK 10.44 GMC 47: AMPAC LOS ANGELES. 49: MOHICAN. 56: WORLD LORE. 58: KALI L. 18.11.64: Aground at Nojima Saki, 34.53N 139.50E. 14.12.64: Refloated, towed Yokosuka. CTL. (Voyage Iloilo/New Orleans – sugar). 3.65: Scrapped Yokosuka.

2412 KERMIT ROOSEVELT 10.44 GMC Completed as DEAL ISLAND (USN) but renamed KERMIT ROOSEVELT ARG 16,(USN). 60: Scrapped Portland, Ore.

2413 FAITHFUL 10.44 GMC Completed as naval repair ship and intended for transfer to RN as HMS FAITHFUL F.177, but retained by USN and renamed DIONYSUS AR 21. USN Reserve Fleet, site 5.

2414 BERT McDOWELL 10.44 GMC Completed as HOOPER ISLAND ARG 17, (USN). USN Reserve Fleet, site 6.

2415 SAMAR 10.44 GMC Completed as SAMAR ARG 11, (USN). USN Reserve Fleet, site 6.

BUILT BY CALIFORNIA SHIPBUILDING CORPORATION

The California Shipbuilding Corporation at Terminal Island, Los Angeles, was another of the nine shipyards approved in early 1941 and from which it was estimated that 260 ships would flow from their 65 ways in two years.

This yard, generally known as 'Calship', was the third emergency yard on the West coast and was managed by Henry Kaiser and his associates. Situated on land owned by the local ports authority, it was originally planned with eight ways but this figure was soon raised to fourteen as the yard expanded along the Cerritos Channel – which connects the port of Los Angeles with the port of Long Beach.

Records for speed were achieved after the yard had expanded and was remodelled. The monthly quota of ship deliveries, set at twelve, was exceeded by June 1942 and substantially exceeded during every month of 1943. One of the vagaries of supply and demand was that whilst the contracts urged builders to deliver as many ships as possible, the Maritime Commission was endeavouring to impose restraint due to a ten per cent shortage of steel, this shortage in some measure being brought about by the commission's own revised figures of ship output which had already been lowered due to the earlier lack of steel.

In an effort to improve welding methods Calship developed special welding procedures, for although the sequence of welding plates and sections was difficult to plan, it was believed these sequences were connected with the 'locked-in' stresses – the possible cause of some fractures. However, the experts were to hold a very different theory to this a few years later.

This shipyard supplied the nucleus management required to establish the Marinship yard, and early fabrication for Marinship was performed at the Calship plant.

Suggestions from the personnel of all shipyards for improving efficiency gave large savings to the commission and Calship ranked third in the scale of total savings.

At the end of the war Calship was paid 2½ million dollars and given title to all its yard facilities which, in 1941 was estimated to cost 10 million dollars but which in actual fact cost some 27 million. In return they undertook to restore the property to the condition called for in the lease.

Liberty ship output: 306 vessels at an average cost of 1,858,000 dollars each, plus 30 Liberty tankers

USMC hull numbers: MCE 64– 94)
     277– 294) (Yard Nos 1– 49)
     295– 300 (" 50– 55)
     631– 739 (" 56–164)
     1632–1691 (" 165–224)
     1854–1879 (" 225–250)

2225–2230　(Yard Nos 251–256)
1910–1915　(　"　　257–262)
2538–2567)
2231–2244)　(　"　　263–306)

1 JOHN C. FREEMONT 3.42 GMC 31.3.45: Damaged by mine, taken Subic Bay, Philippines. CTL. 48: Sold Asia Development Co, Shanghai, for scrap but 52: still laid up in Manila. No further trace but presume later scrapped.

2 THOMAS PAINE 3.42 GMC 3.60: Scrapped Baltimore.

3 BENJAMIN FRANKLIN 3.42 JHIW 58: Scrapped Tacoma.

4 JOHN PAUL JONES 3.42 JHIW Reserve Fleet, site 4.

5 PAUL REVERE 4.42 JHIW 65: Scrapped New Orleans.

6 DANIEL BOONE 4.42 GMC 43: ARA AK 136, (USN). 45: DANIEL BOONE. USN Reserve Fleet, site 2.

7 ROBERT MORRIS 4.42 JHIW Reserve Fleet, site 2.

8 SAMUEL ADAMS 4.42 JHIW 11.66: Scrapped New Orleans.

9 ALBERT GALLATIN 4.42 GMC 28.7.43: Struck by three submarine (U.107?) torpedoes off Savannah – all of which failed to explode. 2.1.44: Sunk by Japanese submarine (I.26) torpedo in Arabian Sea, 21.21N 59.58E.

10 NATHAN HALE 5.42 JHIW 5.2.46: Damaged by mine 5 miles west of Gorgona; put into Leghorn, thence laid up at Genoa. CTL. 4.49: Scrapped Savona.

11 OLIVER HAZARD PERRY 5.42 JHIW Reserve Fleet, site 5.

12 ELBRIDGE GERRY 5.42 JHIW 6.66: Scrapped New Orleans.

13 ZEBULON PIKE 5.42 JHIW 7.61: Scrapped Panama City.

14 RUFUS KING 5.42 JHIW 7.7.42: Ashore outside Rake Passage, Moreton Island, Australia 27.12S 153.12E (Voyage Los/Angeles/Brisbane). Broke in two. Forepart later salved and rebuilt as a lighter.

15 ABIEL FOSTER 5.42 JHIW 61: Scrapped Philadelphia.

16 BENJAMIN GOODHUE 5.42 JHIW 10.61: Scrapped Staten Island, NY.

17 HENRY KNOX 6.42 JHIW 19.6.43: Sunk by Japanese submarine (I.37) torpedo off Maldive Islands, 00.01S 71.15E.

18 ABRAHAM CLARK 6.42 JHIW 47: GOVERNOR DIXON. 49: DOLLY G. 50: LIPARI. 23.10.59: Grounded off Grays Harbour, Wash., (Voyage Calcutta/Seattle). 31.10.59: Refloated, seriously damaged; taken to Portland, Ore. Later towed to Japan and 7.60: Scrapped Nagasaki.

19 WILLIAM FLOYD 5.42 JHIW Reserve Fleet, site 5.

20 JOHN LANGDON 6.42 JHIW 44: TBILISI.

21 CALEB STRONG 5.42 JHIW 2.66: Scrapped Panama City.

22 PAINE WINGATE 5.42 JHIW Reserve Fleet, site 2.

23 JAMES MONROE 6.42 JHIW Reserve Fleet, site 4.

24 JOHN HATHORN 6.42 JHIW Reserve Fleet, site 5.

25 EDWIN MARKHAM 6.42 JHIW 5.65: Scrapped Portland, Ore.

26 GEORGE MATTHEWS 6.42 GMC 7.67: Scrapped Oakland, Cal.

27 F.A.C. MUHLENBERG 6.42 JHIW 47: ROBERT ESPAGNE. 61: AGAPI. 1.7.66: Grounded Pussur river, 21.36N 89.31E (Voyage Chinwangtao/Chalna – coal). Forepart afire; extinguished but severely damaged. Refloated, towed Chalna. CTL. 10.66: Scrapped Osaka.

28 JOHN B. ASHE 6.42 JHIW 46: HAI HUANG. 6.62: Scrapped Keelung.

29 JOHN PAGE 6.42 GMC 11.59: Scrapped Richmond, Cal.

30 JAMES SCHUREMAN 6.42 JHIW 4.62: Scrapped Baltimore.

31 PETER SILVESTER 6.42 JHIW 6.2.45: Sunk by submarine (U.862) torpedo in Indian Ocean, 34.19S 99.37E. Note: The last vessel to be sunk by submarine in this area.

32 EGBERT BENSON 6.42 JHIW Reserve Fleet, site 1.

33 ISAAC COLES 6.42 JHIW 5.67: Scrapped Mobile.

34 STEPHEN JOHNSON FIELD 6.42 JHIW 47: MORTAIN. 63: MARATHA INDUSTRY. 65: ALEXANDROS. 7.68: Scrapped Whampoa.

35 JOSEPH McKENNA 6.42 JHIW 5.62: Scrapped Baltimore.

36 WILLIAM M. STEWART 7.42 GMC 9.61: Scrapped Baltimore.

37 WILLIS VAN DEVANTER 7.42 JHIW 9.67: Scrapped Kearny, NJ.

38 JOHN STEELE 7.42 JHIW 11.61: Scrapped Baltimore.

39 GEORGE THACHER 7.42 JHIW 1.11.42: Sunk by submarine (U.126) torpedo off French Equatorial Africa, approx. 01.50S 08.00E.

40 JUAN CABRILLO 7.42 JHIW 4.61: Scrapped Everett, Wash.

41 FRANCIS PARKMAN 7.42 JHIW 4.61: Scrapped Osaka.

42 JOHN FISKE 7.42 JHIW Reserve Fleet, site 1.

43 JUNIPERO SERRA 7.42 JHIW 2.59: Scrapped Seattle.

44 JOHN A. SUTTER 7.42 JHIW 11.69: Scrapped Mobile.

45 RICHARD HENRY DANA 8.42 GMC 66: Converted into crane barge at Portland, Ore.

46 GEORGE BANCROFT 8.42 GMC 2.60: Scrapped Baltimore.

47: JAMES FORD RHODES 8.42 JHIW 64: Scrapped Panama City.

48 WILLIAM H. PRESCOTT 8.42 JHIW 2.2.44: Reported severe cracks in hull and deck plating in Atlantic (voyage Cardiff/New York). Later arrived St Johns, NF. Repaired. Reserve Fleet, site 4.

49 HINTON R. HELPER 8.42 JHIW 3.61: Scrapped Baltimore.

50 WILLIAM F. CODY 8.42 JHIW 5.67: Scrapped Tacoma.

51 ROBERT F. STOCKTON 8.42 JHIW 63: Sold Alabama State Docks Dept for scrap, but used as a grain store. Later reported out of service as storeship — dismantled. Destined for scrap when finally disposed of.

52 STARR KING 8.42 JHIW 10.2.43: Sunk by Japanese submarine (I.21) torpedo in Pacific, 34.15S 154.20E (voyage Sydney/Noumea).

53 LELAND STANFORD 8.42 GMC 8.67: Scrapped Oakland, Cal.

54 FRANCIS DRAKE 8.42 JHIW Reserve Fleet, site 4.

55 PETER H. BURNETT 8.42 JHIW 23.1.43: Damaged by Japanese submarine (I.21) torpedo in Pacific, 32.54S 159.32E (voyage Newcastle NSW/San Francisco). 3.2.43: Arrived Sydney in tow. Temporarily repaired, acquired by USN, renamed P.H.BURNETT, IX 104. 8.46: PETER H. BURNETT. 59: Scrapped Terminal Island.

56 EWING YOUNG 8.42: JHIW 11.59: Scrapped Hirao.

57 PETER CARTWRIGHT 9.42 JHIW 61: Scrapped Galveston.

58 BRIGHAM YOUNG 9.42 GMC 43: MURZIM AK 95 (USN). 1947: Returned US Govt. USN Reserve Fleet, site 6.

59 HORACE MANN 9.42 JHIW 47: PETROS NOMIKOS. 60: ARETI.

60: JANE ADDAMS 9.42 JHIW 3.69: Sold for scrapping at Portland, Ore.

61 CLARA BARTON 9.42 JHIW Reserve Fleet, site 2.

62 WILLIAM ELLERY CHANNING 9.42 JHIW 10.69: Scrapped Portland, Ore.

63 WENDELL PHILLIPS 9.42 JHIW 10.59: Scrapped Wilmington, Del.

64 FELIPE DE NEVE 9.42 JHIW 66: Scrapped Kearny, NJ.

65 SAMUEL GOMPERS (I) 9.42 GMC 29.1.43: Sunk by aircraft torpedo off New Caledonia 24.21S 166.12E (voyage Noumea/Newcastle NSW).

66 HORACE GREELEY 9.42 GMC 66: Transferred to USN. Loaded with obsolete ammunition at Navy Ammunition Pier, Earle, NJ and 28.7.66: scuttled in Atlantic. Her cargo was detonated at 4,000 ft as a scientific experiment.

67 HENRY WARD BEECHER 9.42 JHIW 2.69: Scrapped Kearny, NJ.

68 JAMES GORDON BENNETT 9.42 JHIW 8.61: Scrapped Baltimore.

69 JOSEPH PULITZER 10.42 JHIW Reserve Fleet, site 2.

70 MALCOLM M. STEWART 10.42 JHIW Reserve Fleet, site 1.

71 GEORGE A. CUSTER 10.42 JHIW 61: Scrapped Seattle.

72 GEORGE G. MEADE 10.42 JHIW 9.3.43: Damaged by submarine (U.510) torpedo in Atlantic, 07.11S 52.30W (voyage Bahia/USA). Towed into Paramaribo. Repaired. 47: ROUEN. 53: GANNET. 5.69: Scrapped Kaohsiung.

73 BOOKER T. WASHINGTON 10.42 JHIW 7.69: Scrapped Portland, Ore.

74 FITZ-JOHN PORTER 10.42 JHIW 1.3.43: Sunk by submarine (U.518) torpedo in S.Atlantic, 12.20S 37.01W (voyage Bombay/Paramaribo – ballast).

75 JAMES B. McPHERSON 10.42 JHIW 3.62: Scrapped Baltimore.

76 SAMUEL HEINTZELMAN 10.42 JHIW 3.7.43: Shelled, torpedoed and sunk by Japanese surface raider in Indian Ocean, 28.30S 105.00E (voyage Charleston/Karachi). Note: German records claim this vessel to have been sunk by submarine (U.511) torpedo in the same position six days later.

77 JOHN SEDGWICK 10.42 JHIW 63: Scrapped Terminal Island.

78 WILLIAM LLOYD GARRISON 10.42 JHIW 59: Scrapped Terminal Island.

79 SMITH THOMPSON 10.42 JHIW 63: Scrapped Philadelphia.

80 JOSEPH STORY 11.42 GMC 63: Scrapped Kearny, NJ.

81 GABRIEL DUVAL 10.42 F & S 62: Scrapped Terminal Island.

82 HENRY BALDWIN 11.42 JHIW Reserve Fleet, site 1.

83 BROCKHOLST LIVINGSTON 11.42 GMC 9.10.45: Ashore and abandoned in typhoon at Okinawa. Total loss. Later reported scrapped by China Merchants & Engineers Inc, China.

84 THOMAS JOHNSON 11.42 JHIW 47: UNION SULPHUR. 55: CILCO LOGGER. 61: SPEED. 61: ALFA. 68: Scrapped Kaohsiung.

85 PHILIP P. BARBOUR 11.42 F & S Reserve Fleet, site 4.

86 PETER V. DANIEL 11.42 JHIW 63: Scrapped Philadelphia.

87 SAMUEL NELSON 11.42 JHIW 64: Scrapped Kearny, NJ.

88 ROBERT C. GRIER 11.42 JHIW 66: Scrapped Tacoma, Wash.

89 BENJAMIN R. CURTIS 11.42 JHIW 47: GRAND-CAMP. 16.4.47: Caught fire, exploded and sank at Texas City.

The GRANDCAMP was found to be on fire in Texas City docks early on the morning of 16 April 1947, whilst loading a cargo of ammonium nitrate fertiliser for Dunkirk and Bordeaux. Efforts to control the blaze proved abortive and the ship, burning fiercely, was towed into the stream. But before she could be taken to a place of greater safety a tremendous explosion tore the ship apart.

The blast set up a chain of other explosions which demolished many large warehouses on the waterfront and also reached the new buildings of a chemical plant which, in their turn, also exploded and the plant was completely wrecked. Many other buildings collapsed and huge piles of debris blocked the city streets. A further wave of fires and explosions at refineries and other chemical plants prevented access to the disaster area, and the entire town was evacuated due to the spreading of gas fumes from lethal chemicals.

The following morning fires still raged along a two mile stretch of oil tanks and five new, heavy, explosions during that day rocked the city again and caused considerably more damage. The force of these explosions was felt in Galveston — situated 15 miles away across the bay.

One blast was from the nitrate and sulphur-laden American steamer HIGHFLYER (44/6214 grt) which, after burning fiercely for some time, disintegrated with a shattering roar. Large pieces of the ship were blasted into the air and large sections were scattered far inland.

Alongside the HIGHFLYER when she exploded was the Liberty ship WILSON B.KEENE (qv) and this vessel was later found on her side, deep in the water, with her stern blown off and the ship 80 per cent demolished.

Still later more burning oil tanks exploded and even six days after the initial tragedy warehouses stored with nitrate burst into flames, until eventually all dockside structures were demolished.

Total death-roll in the disaster was well over 500 persons, and whilst the shipping losses involved the virtual demolition of one ship and the disintegration of another, the GRAND-CAMP had herself disappeared completely after the explosion.

90 MARION McKINLEY BOVARD 11.42 F & S 11.60: Scrapped Troon.

91 STEPHEN M. WHITE 11.42 GMC 67: Scrapped Portland, Ore.

92 WILLIAM EATON 12.42 JHIW 13.4.52: Ashore at Toshima, 34.34N 139.15E, (voyage Otaru/Pusan — coal). 26.4.52: Broke in two, abandoned. Total loss.

93 LINCOLN STEFFENS 12.42 JHIW Reserve Fleet, site 2.

94 HUBERT HOWE BANCROFT 11.42 JHIW 47: GLOBAL SPINNER. 48: VINJE. 49: VINSTRA. 53: NICOLAOS MICHALOS III. 5.67: Scrapped Whampoa.

95 JAMES W. MARSHALL 12.42 GMC 15.9.43: Damaged by aircraft guided bomb off Salerno. Towed Bizerta thence UK. 8.6.44: Sunk as 'Gooseberry 2' breakwater blockship at Mulberry Harbour A beach-head, St Laurent, Normandy. 16.7.44: Officially abandoned (foundered) after harbour was destroyed by the storms of 19—22.6.44.

96 GEORGE CHAFFEY 12.42 GMC 12.55: Converted to YAG, (same name, USN). (Conversion type EC2-S-22a). USN Reserve Fleet, site 4.

97 FRANK JOSEPH IRWIN 12.42 GMC 3.70: Sold to Bilbao shipbreakers.

98 HELEN HUNT JACKSON 12.42 F & S Reserve Fleet, site 2.

99 ABEL STEARNS 12.42 GMC 6.66: Scrapped Portland, Ore.

100 BENJAMIN IDE WHEELER 12.42 F & S 10.44: Sank in shallow water after attack by Kamikaze suicide aircraft near Leyte. Refloated, used as depot ship. Received further battle and storm damage in Leyte Gulf, taken to Suisun Bay, Cal, and laid up. 48: Scrapped USA.

101 AMOS G. THROOP 12.42 JHIW 2.68: Scrapped Oakland, Calf.

102 WILLIAM MULHOLLAND 12.42 JHIW 5.62: Scrapped Chickasaw, Ala.

103 GASPAR DE PORTOLA 12.42 JHIW 7.6.43: Aground on Quita Sueno Reef, Caribbean, (voyage Panama/Key West). 31.7.43: Refloated, towed Savannah. CTL. 12.46: Towed Baltimore and used as fire prevention training hulk by USCG. 48: Scrapped USA.

104 LUIS ARGUELLO 12.42 GMC 10.60: Scrapped Kure.

105 SEBASTIAN VIZCAINO 12.42 GMC 3.61: Scrapped Everett, Wash.

106 KING S. WOOLSEY 12.42 JHIW 51: AMPAC NEVADA. 56: MUSKEGON. 56: WORLD LUCK. 64: LINDA. 4.69: Scrapped Kaohsiung.

107 ARCHBISHOP LAMY 12.42 F & S 4.64: Scrapped Mobile.

108 JOHN BIDWELL 12.42 JHIW 8.60: Scrapped Philadelphia.

109 LOUIS McLANE 12.42 JHIW 66: Scrapped New Orleans.

110 HUGH S. LEGARE 1.43 JHIW 9.59: Scrapped Baltimore.

111 JAMES BUCHANAN 1.43 JHIW 47: SAINT LO. 63: ATHENIAN. 67: GLEE. 7.69: Scrapped Shanghai.

112 JOHN M. CLAYTON 1.43 JHIW 1.1.45: Damaged by aircraft bombs in Pacific (voyage Leyte/Mangarin Bay). Beached, refloated but beached again. 25.4.45: Refloated, towed Leyte. 6.45: HARCOURT IX 225 (USN). 5.46: JOHN M. CLAYTON. 11.62: Scrapped Portland, Ore.

113 WILLIAM L. MARCY 1.43 JHIW 7.8.44:
Damaged by E boat torpedo in English Channel
49.25N 00.27W. 11.8.44: Towed to St Helens
Roads. 18.8.44: Towed Mumbles, beached. 27.8.45:
Refloated, towed Swansea. CTL. 25.9.45: Towed
River Blackwater and laid up. 48: Towed Bremer-
haven, loaded with surplus ammunition, towed to sea
and scuttled in North Sea.

114 LEWIS CASS 1.43 JHIW 26.1.43: Ashore and
wrecked at Guadalupe Island, Mexico (voyage Los
Angeles/Balboa).

115 JEREMIAH S. BLACK 1.43 JHIW 63: Scrapped
Tacoma, Wash.

116 ELIHU B. WASHBURNE 1.43 JHIW 3.7.43: Sunk
by submarine (U.513) torpedo off Brazil, 24.05S
45.23W (voyage Lourenco Marques/Rio de Janeiro).

117 HARRISON GRAY OTIS 1.43 JHIW 4.8.43:
Damaged by Italian limpet mine at Gibraltar. Beached.
49: Cut in two and 5.7.49: bow part towed Cadiz for
scrap. 28.9.50: Afterpart towed Carthagena for scrap.

118 JOSEPH H. HOLLISTER 1.43 JHIW 4.66: Scrapped
Panama City.

119 PHOEBE A. HEARST 1.43 JHIW 30.4.43: Sunk
by Japanese submarine (I.19) torpedo north of Fiji
Islands, 20.07S 177.33E.

120 ZANE GREY 1.43 JHIW Reserve Fleet, site 2.

121 PIO PICO 1.43 JHIW 10.60: Scrapped Hirao.

122 JOHN DRAKE SLOAT 1.43 JHIW 8.60: Scrapped
Terminal Island.

123 CARLOS CARRILLO 1.43 JHIW 2.63: Scrapped
Portland, Ore.

124 WILLIAM S. YOUNG 2.43 JHIW 47: NANTES.
60: TAJO. 28.3.64: Aground 30 miles North West of
Las Palmas. Total loss. (Voyage Takoradi/Rotterdam
– iron ore). Salvage operations undertaken but
abandoned.

125 GEORGE E. HALE 2.43 JHIW 9.61: Scrapped
Bellingham, Wash.

126 THOMAS NAST 2.43 JHIW 43: JEAN JAURES.

127 SAMUEL P. LANGLEY 2.43 JHIW 43: VOIKOV.

128 JAMES ROBERTSON 2.43 JHIW 7.7.43: Sunk
by submarine (U.185) torpedo off Brazil, 04.05S 35.58W.

129 WILLIAM J. WORTH 2.43 JHIW 1.67: Scrapped
Mobile.

130 HOWARD STANSBURY 2.43 JHIW 8.61:
Scrapped Everett, Wash.

131 ROBERT STUART 2.43 JHIW 61: Scrapped
Philadelphia.

132 WILLIAM DUNBAR 2.43 JHIW 47: FLOREN-
TINE. 20.2.51: Abandoned, sank, after cargo shifted
in heavy weather 22.04N 140.30E (voyage Manila/
Tacoma – copper concentrates).

133 GEORGE C. YOUNT 2.43 JHIW Completed as
ASCELLA AK 137 (USN). 47: GEORGE C. YOUNT.
64: Scrapped Terminal Island.

134 SOLOMON JUNEAU 2.43 JHIW 9.4.45:
Damaged by submarine (midget?) torpedo in English
Channel (voyage Deal/Cherbourg). Salved and later
towed Gravesend. Repaired. 62: Scrapped Panama
City.

135 EDMUND FANNING 2.43 JHIW 13.3.47: Afire
and exploded whilst discharging petrol at Genoa.
Beached. Refloated but CTL. (Voyage Bremen/Fusan
– nitrate, petrol and general). 48: Scrapped Genoa.

136 PHINEAS BANNING 2.43 JHIW 5.67:
Scrapped San Francisco.

137 EDMUND RANDOLPH 2.43 JHIW 12.66:
Scrapped Portland, Ore.

138 EDWARD LIVINGSTON 3.43 JHIW 66:
Scrapped Kearny, NJ.

139 JOSIAH ROYCE 3.43 JHIW 9.66: Scrapped
New Orleans.

140 DANIEL DRAKE 3.43 JHIW 12.59: Scrapped
Portland, Maine.

141 BENJAMIN LUNDY 3.43 JHIW 62: Scrapped
Philadelphia.

142 THEODORE DWIGHT WELD 3.43 JHIW
20.9.43: Sunk by submarine (U.238) torpedo in
N.W.Atlantic, 57.03N 28.08W.

143 THEODORE PARKER 3.43 JHIW Reserve
Fleet, site 2.

144 JAMES G. BIRNEY 3.43 JHIW 1.67: Scrapped
Panama City.

145 LYDIA M. CHILD 3.43 JHIW 27.4.43: Sunk by Japanese submarine (I.178) torpedo off Australia, 33.08S 153.24E.

146 RACHEL JACKSON 3.43 JHIW Reserve Fleet, site 5.

147 MARIA MITCHELL 3.43 JHIW Reserve Fleet, site 2.

148 MARGARET FULLER 3.43 JHIW 2.67: Scrapped Coos Bay, Ore.

149 WILLIAM B. ALLISON 3.43 JHIW 25.5.45: Damaged by aircraft torpedo in Pacific. Towed Okinawa. CTL, but 7.45: GAMAGE IX 227 (USN). 4.46: WILLIAM B.ALLISON. 49: Reported scrapped by China Merchants & Engineers Inc, China.

150 ANSEL BRIGGS 3.43 JHIW Completed as MINTAKA AK 94, (USN). 46: ANSEL BRIGGS. 4.68: Scrapped Oakland, Cal.

151 ALICE F. PALMER 3.43 JHIW 10.7.43: Sunk by submarine (U.177) torpedo and gunfire in Mozambique Channel, 26.30S 44.20E.

152 JAMES M. GOODHUE 3.43 JHIW 47: CAPTAIN FARMAKIDES. 61: PYTHEAS. 2.1.66: Beached at Aghios Minas, Rhodes Island, after developing leaks in heavy weather. Abandoned. Total loss (voyage Gocek/Baltimore).

153 HENRY H. SIBLEY 3.43 JHIW 47: ASTERIS. 65: PERICLES G.C. 10.68: Scrapped Hong Kong.

154 HENRY M. RICE 3.43 JHIW 7.63: Scrapped Panama City.

155 JOHN S. PILLSBURY 4.43 JHIW 3.68: Scrapped Panama City.

156 KNUTE NELSON 4.43 JHIW 7.69: Sold to New York shipbreakers.

157 JAMES B. WEAVER 4.43 JHIW 65: Scrapped Portland, Ore.

158 SIMON NEWCOMB 4.43 JHIW 11.59: Scrapped Hirao.

159 AMY LOWELL 4.43 JHIW 47: NEVADA. 59: WHITE SEA. 67: Scrapped Kaohsiung.

160 WILLIAM G. FARGO 4.43 JHIW 47: JACOB CATS. 50: AGIOI VICTORES. 60: EFFIE II. 62: AYIOS DIMITRIS. 65: KUO FU. 65: THAI HSING. 67: Scrapped Kaohsiung.

161 WILLIAM JAMES 4.43 JHIW 4.63: Scrapped Bordentown, NJ.

162 JACQUES CARTIER 4.43 JHIW 4.62: Scrapped Baltimore.

163 STANFORD WHITE 4.43 JHIW 43: POPPY (assigned name of hospital ship — not used). 11.43: Converted at Hoboken, New York, and renamed BLANCHE F.SIGMAN US Army Hospital ship, 7,933 grt). 4.46: Returned to US Govt. US Army Reserve Fleet, site 2.

164 BENJAMIN N. CARDOZO 4.43 JHIW Completed as SERPENS AK 97 (USN). 29.1.45: Exploded whilst loading depth charges off Lunga Beach, Guadalcanal. Total loss. Note: Some sources list this vessel as having been sunk in error by a US submarine.

165 WILLIAM CARSON 4.43 JHIW Reserve Fleet, site 8.

166 CHARLES H. WINDHAM 4.43 JHIW 3.60: Scrapped Baltimore.

167 JUAN FLACO BROWN 4.43 JHIW 7.61: Scrapped Everett, Wash.

168 THADDEUS S.C. LOWE 4.43 JHIW (date and place?) Damaged whilst discharging cargo into landing craft in heavy seas. CTL, towed USA and laid up Suisun Bay, Cal. 6.59: Scrapped Oakland, Cal.

169 MIGUEL HIDALGO 4.43 JHIW 58: Scrapped Terminal Island.

170 JOSIAH D. WHITNEY 4.43 JHIW Completed as LIVINGSTON AP 163 (USN). 1945: LIVINGSTON AK 222 (USN). 46: JOSIAH D. WHITNEY. Reserve Fleet, site 6.

171 WILLIAM M. GWIN 4.43 JHIW Completed as LESUTH AK 125 (USN). 46: WILLIAM M. GWIN. 64: Scrapped Richmond, Cal.

172 MARK KEPPEL 4.43 JHIW 4.63: Scrapped Terminal Island.

173 WILEY POST 4.43 JHIW 12.59: Scrapped Portland, Maine.

174 GEORGE GERSHWIN 5.43 JHIW Reserve Fleet, site 4.

175 GENERAL VALLEJO 5.43 JHIW Completed as
MEGREZ AK 126 (USN). 46: Returned US Govt
(same name). USN Reserve Fleet, site 6.

176 ANDREW ROWAN 5.43 JHIW Completed as
RUTILICUS AK 113 (USN). 46: ANDREW ROWAN.
USN Reserve Fleet, site 2.

177 THOMAS HILL 5.43 JHIW 46: LORIENT. 61:
YANIX. 5.2.62: Sprung leak and sank 50 miles North
of Luzon Island, 19.00N 120.00E (voyage Madras/
Kobe).

178 EDWARD W. SCRIPPS 5.43 JHIW Reserve
Fleet, site 5.

179 BENJAMIN D. WILSON 5.43 WISC 2.62:
Scrapped Baltimore.

180 JOSE SEPULVEDA 5.43 JHIW 43: SUCHAN.

181 IGNACE PADEREWSKI 5.43 JHIW 45: Reported
as severely damaged by stranding in typhoon (no
further details). CTL, returned USA and laid up in
James River. 9.47: Scrapped Baltimore.

182 CHARLES LUMMIS 5.43 WISC 5.65: Scrapped
Portland, Ore.

183 JEDEDIAH S. SMITH 5.43 WISC 10.64:
Scrapped Oakland, Cal.

184 JOSIAH NELSON CUSHING 5.43 JHIW 12.67:
Scrapped Portland, Ore.

185 JOHN BURROUGHS 5.43 WISC 11.62:
Scrapped Tacoma, Wash.

186 CHARLES CROCKER 5.43 JHIW 1.65: Scrapped
Portland, Ore.

187 JOHN S. CASEMENT 5.43 JHIW 47: LETO.
48: NORITA. 51: SEATREASURE. 51: TRANS-
PORTER. 54: PEARL ISLAND. 63: MPARMPA-
MARCOS. 14.6.67: Damaged in collision with
GEM PET (52/21,958 grt) in Shimonoseki Strait
(voyage Media Luna/North Korea). Sold. 12.67:
Scrapped Kaohsiung.

188 P.T. BARNUM 5.43 JHIW 6.61: Scrapped
Osaka.

189 THOMAS OLIVER LARKIN 5.43 JHIW 43:
BOOTES AK 99 (USN). 47: Returned to US Govt
(same name). 67: Scrapped Hong Kong.

190 JUAN BAUTISTA DE ANZA 5.43 JHIW 43:
LYNX AK 100 (USN). 46: JUAN BAUTISTA DE
ANZA. USN Reserve Fleet, site 6.

191 LYMAN STEWART 5.43 JHIW 1.69: Sold to
New York shipbreakers.

192 JOHN ALDEN 6.43 JHIW 59: Scrapped
Oakland, Cal.

193 CLARENCE DARROW 6.43 JHIW 47:
OREGON. 59: WHITE CROSS. 64: DON RAMON.
65: SAFE PHILIPPINE ANCHORAGE. 68:
Scrapped Kaohsiung.

194 CHARLES D. POSTON 6.43 JHIW Reserve
Fleet, site 4.

195 JOSIAH EARL 6.43 JHIW 47: GREGORS
GRAM. 53: New oil engine at Spezia by Fiat. 60:
THALIS. 68: TAISHUNHONG. 1.69: Damaged by
boiler fire whilst at Dairen. Repairs uneconomic.
6.69: Scrapped Hirao.

196 FRANKLIN K. LANE 6.43 WISC 10.65:
Scrapped Panama City.

197 JAMES H. McCLINTOCK 6.43 JHIW
Completed as KENMORE AP 162 (USN). 1945:
KENMORE AK 221 (USN). 46: JAMES H.
McCLINTOCK. USN Reserve Fleet, site 6.

198 JACOB S. MANSFELD 6.43 JHIW Reserve
Fleet, site 4.

199 DAVID E. HUGHES 6.43 JHIW Reserve
Fleet, site 1.

200 BILLY MITCHELL 6.43 JHIW 65: Scrapped
Kearny, NJ.

201 JAMES SHIELDS 6.43 JHIW Reserve Fleet,
site 2.

202 EUGENE B. DASKAM 6.43 JHIW 43:
TRIANGULUM AK 102 (USN). 47: EUGENE B.
DASKAM. USN Reserve Fleet, site 6.

203 ANDREW T. HUNTINGTON 6.43 JHIW 47:
LORENTZ. 47: LINDEKERK. 61: MARITSA. 66:
EFDROMOS.

204 D.W. HARRINGTON 6.43 IFM 43:
SCULPTOR AK 103 (USN). 46: D.W.HARRING-
TON. 47: DIMOSTHENIS PANTALEON.
9.69: Scrapped Trieste.

205 WILLIAM F. MACLENNAN 6.43 JHIW 6.63: Scrapped Baltimore.

206 WILFRED GRENFELL 6.43 JHIW Reserve Fleet, site 1.

207 FLORENCE CRITTENTON 6.43 JHIW 1.67: Scrapped Panama City.

208 JOSEPH PRIESTLEY 6.43 JHIW Reserve Fleet, site 8.

209 STEPHEN T. MATHER 6.43 JHIW 11.66: Scrapped Portland, Ore.

210 FRANK SPRINGER 6.43 JHIW 10.67: Scrapped Wilmington, NC.

211 FINLEY PETER DUNNE 6.43 JHIW 47: VASSILIOS E. KULUKUNDIS. 50: EVROTAS. 53: EPIDAVROS. 65: IONIC BAY. 4.67: Scrapped Tsuneishi.

212 MARINA RASKOVA 7.43 JHIW 3.62: Scrapped Baltimore.

213 CHARLES A. WARFIELD 7.43 JHIW 4.69: Scrapped Mobile.

214 STEPHEN VINCENT BENET 7.43 JHIW 11.67: Scrapped Portland, Ore.

215 STEPHEN H. LONG 7.43 JHIW 46: HAI YU. 12.67: Scrapped Kaohsiung.

216 ANSON P.K. SAFFORD 7.43 JHIW 12.65: Scrapped Kearny, NJ.

217 WILLIAM R. NELSON 7.43 JHIW 43: NAOS AK 105 (USN). 45: WILLIAM R.NELSON. 7.69: Sold to New York shipbreakers.

218 JACOB RIIS 7.43 JHIW Completed as SAMHOLT. 48: JACOB RIIS. 10.59: Scrapped Baltimore.

219 JOHN J. INGALLS 7.43 JHIW Completed as SAMSON. 48: Returned to US Govt. 6.61: Scrapped Orange, Texas.

220 BILLY SUNDAY 7.43 WISC 47: EURYVIADES. 61: PROTOKLITOS. 18.3.63: Aground on Estelas Rocks, Portugal. 39.30N 09.35W. Abandoned. Drifted off rocks and 19.3.63: Taken in tow but 20.3.63: Sank 4 miles north of Cabo Roca (voyage Bremerhaven/ Hong Kong – fertiliser).

221 GRANVILLE STUART 7.43 JHIW Completed as SAMARITAN. 47: VANDALIA. 54: SIDERIS.

222 ZONA GALE 7.43 WISC 64: Scrapped Kearny, NJ.

223 BRAND WHITLOCK 7.43 JHIW 47: NAVIGATOR. 60: KORNAT. 6.67: Scrapped Split.

224 VERNON L. KELLOGG 7.43 JHIW 47: WILFRED. 49: FOLKE BERNADOTTE. 54: ARCHON GABRIEL. 59: ERNST MORITZ ARNDT. 68: KYPROS.

225 HOWARD T. RICKETTS 7.43 JHIW 51: AMPAC IDAHO. 56: MODOC. 56: WORLD LEGION. 63: ELEANOR. 64: CHEE LEE. 64: ELEANOR. 68: Scrapped Kaohsiung.

226 ROBERT G. INGERSOLL 7.43 JHIW 2.61: Scrapped Terminal Island.

227 INA COOLBRITH 7.43 JHIW Reserve Fleet, site 2.

228 CORNELIUS COLE 8.43 WISC Completed as SAMSURF. 48: CORNELIUS COLE. 4.61: Scrapped Mobile as SAMSURF.

229 ARTHUR P. DAVIS 8.43 JHIW 47: NORTH VALLEY. 50: ANDRE 60: CAPTAIN LEMOS. 5.68: Scrapped Shanghai.

230 AUGUSTUS H. GARLAND 8.43 JHIW Completed as SAMBLADE. 48: AUGUSTUS H. GARLAND. 10.59: Reported scrapped Baltimore.

231 WYATT EARP 8.43 JHIW 43: CAELUM AK 106 (USN). 46: WYATT EARP. 8.61: Scrapped Everett, Wash.

232 EDWIN JOSEPH O'HARA 8.43 WISC Completed as SAMBO. 10.11.43: Sunk by Japanese submarine (I.27) torpedo in Gulf of Aden, 12.28N 43.31E.

233 JAMES H. ROBINSON 8.43 IFM Completed as SAMSTEEL. 47: JAMES H.ROBINSON. 12.61: Scrapped Panama City.

234 WILLIAM I. KIP 8.43 JHIW Completed as SAMPAN. 50: WILLIAM I.KIP. 5.62: Scrapped New Orleans.

235 EDWIN ABBEY 8.43 JHIW 51: GREENSTAR. 54: VALOR. 60: ORMOS. 2.67: Scrapped Moji.

236 HENRY M. ROBINSON 8.43 IFM Completed as SAMAROVSK. 47: HENRY M.ROBINSON.

60: Scrapped Philadelphia.

237 GEORGE KENNY 8.43 JHIW 7.60: Scrapped Baltimore.

238 DAVID R. FRANCIS 8.43 WISC 5.60: Scrapped Baltimore.

239 THOMAS G. MASARYK 8.43 JHIW 16.4.44: Damaged by aircraft torpedo off Libya, 32.51N 23.00E. Caught fire, beached and abandoned, (voyage New York/Abadan — planes and general). Refloated and 28.8.44: Towed Alexandria. CTL. 2.48: Sold for scrap. 18.8.51: Towed Malaga and scrapped following month.

240 GUTZON BORGLUM 8.43 JHIW 1945: Damaged in typhoon; grounded. Refloated and collided with USN tug 'in Pacific'. CTL, towed USA and laid up in James River. 59: Transferred USN and reported disposed of.

241 JOSEPH REYNOLDS 8.43 JHIW 5.59: Scrapped Portland, Ore.

242 VICTOR F. LAWSON 8.43 JHIW Completed as SAMPEP. 48: Returned to US Govt. 4.69: Scrapped Portland, Ore.

243 WILLIAM KELLY 9.43 JHIW Completed as ROTANIN AK 108, USN. 46: WILLIAM KELLY. 9.66: Scrapped Richmond, Cal.

244 FRANK WIGGINS 9.43 IFM 47: DIRPHYS. 10.67: Scrapped Shanghai.

245 DON MARQUIS 9.43 JHIW 26.9.44: Afire and beached after collision with MISSIONARY RIDGE (43/10,195 grt) north of New Guinea, 02.10S 147.32E, (voyage Langemak Bay/Seeadler Harbour — military stores and personnel). 28.9.44: Refloated and towed Seeadler Harbour. CTL, but 5.45: DON MARQUIS IX 215, USN, hulk. 11.45: Returned US Govt. 49: Scrapped Manus Island.

246 JOSEPH FRANCIS 9.43 JHIW 5.60: Scrapped Portland, Ore.

247 DWIGHT B. HEARD 9.43 IFM Completed as SAMBUR. 44: SAMWHARFE. 47: Returned US Govt. 60: Scrapped Philadelphia.

248 ALBERT P. RYDER 9.43 JHIW 47: LEONIDAS MICHALOS. 3.66: Scrapped Hamburg.

249 SAMSON OCCUM 9.43 JHIW Completed as SAMARINDA. 47: STUDENT. 63: PARTHENON. 64: AL AMIN. 66: FORTUNE SEA. 4.67: Scrapped Kaohsiung.

250 ALBINO PEREZ 9.43 JHIW 1.61: Scrapped Baltimore.

251 JOHN TIPTON 9.43 JHIW Completed as SAMTREDY. 47: PACIFIC IMPORTER. 53: AQUITANIA. 65: AYIA MARINA.

252 LORRIN A. THURSTON 9.43 JHIW Completed as SAMCALIA. 47: PACIFIC LIBERTY. 54: PHOEBUS. 63: BAYHORSE. 70: SAN GABRIEL.

253 ANNIE OAKLEY 9.43 JHIW Completed as SAMIDA. 9.4.45: Sunk by submarine (midget?) torpedo in English Channel, 3 miles off Dungeness, (voyage Antwerp/Barry). Wreck dispersed with explosives.

254 HENRY M. STANLEY 9.43 JHIW Completed as SAMNEVA. 24.7.44: Damaged by submarine (U.309) torpedo in English Channel, 50.14N 00.47W. Beached Southampton. Broke in two. Stern part later salved and 6.48: scrapped Briton Ferry. Bow part scrapped on beach at Netley, Hants.

255 E.H. SOTHERN 9.43 JHIW Completed as SAMMONT. 47: SALMONIER. 49: BENMHOR. 51: ARMAR. 61: Lengthened at Maizuru to 511½ ft (8,527 grt). 67: CAPTAIN GEORGE K. 25.6.69: plates fractured, leaking and holds flooded off Somaliland coast, 10.03N 54.60E, (voyage Vancouver/Eilat — sulphur). Later arrived at Djibouti for temporary repairs. 11.69: Scrapped Kaohsiung.

256 PAUL CHANDLER 10.43 IFM 47: JEROEN BOSCH. 47: OOTMARSUM. 49: JOOST VAN DEN VONDEL. 50: SPARTO. 63: IRENA.

257 RALPH A. CRAM 12.43 JHIW 47: ATLANTICC 63: HUTA OSTROWIEC.

258 JOHN A. ROEBLING 12.43 JHIW 47: GRIFONE. 61: SETTEMARI. 2.68: Scrapped Trieste.

259 ORLAND LOOMIS 12.43 JHIW Reserve Fleet, site 2.

260 EDWARD PAINE 12.43 JHIW 1.61: Scrapped Mobile.

261 SYLVESTER PATTIE 12.43 JHIW 10.67: Scrapped Wilmington, NC.

262 LEOPOLD DAMROSCH 12.43 JHIW 9.61: Scrapped Baltimore.

263 HENRY MILLER 12.43 JHIW 3.1.45: Damaged by submarine (U.870) torpedo off Morocco, 35.51N 06.24W (voyage Leghorn/Hampton Roads). 4.1.45: Arrived Gibraltar. CTL, sold. 30.8.48: Towed Malaga and scrapped.

264 JOHN DAVEY 12.43 JHIW 61: Scrapped Seattle.

265 JOHN W. SEARLES 12.43 JHIW 47: NORNESS. 50: LEONIDAS D. 53: EUROPEAN TRADER. 63: MARATHA TRADER. 67: SAMUDRA JIT.

266 MEYER LISSNER 12.43 JHIW 47: TRUN. 61: ARMONIA. 10.68: Scrapped Yokosuka.

267 FRANKLIN H. KING 12.43 JHIW 7.67: Scrapped Kearny, NJ.

268 BEN B. LINDSEY 12.43 JHIW 47: GIAMBATT-ISTA. 64: DR. ANTONIS LEMOS. 66: OINOUSSIAN SEA. 67: EGNOUSA. 6.68: Scrapped Shanghai.

269 SHERWOOD ANDERSON 12.43 IFM 47: MARSEILLE. 60: ELIAS X. 4.8.62: Lost rudder in Arabian Sea, 12.40N 63.59E. 22.8.62: Arrived Bombay in tow. 24.9.62: Towed Trieste thence Naples, laid up. CTL, (voyage Mormugao/Italy — iron ore). 4.64: Scrapped Valencia.

270 PHILIP C. SHERA 12.43 IFM 47: IGOR. 60: VAN FU. 2.69: Scrapped Kaohsiung.

271 JAMES W. JOHNSON 12.43 JHIW Reserve Fleet, site 1.

272 JOHN H. QUICK 12.43 JHIW 11.69: Scrapped Portland, Ore.

273 CHARLES FORT 12.43 JHIW 47: EMANCIPA-TOR. 61: STEFANIOS. 12.10.64: Aground 5 miles north west of Tarifa Light, 36.01N 05.43W., (voyage Mormugao/Emden — iron ore). 21.10.64: Refloated, taken Gibraltar. CTL, sold. 4.65: Scrapped Santander.

274 JOHN DREW 12.43 JHIW 47: MICHAEL. 60: KORAIS. 66: UNITED ONWARD. 5.67: Scrapped Kaohsiung.

275 WILLIAM WOLFSKILL 12.43 JHIW 47: LELY. 47: ALDERAMIN. 58: APATOURIA.

276 HART CRANE 1.44 JHIW 46: VALOGNES. 54: RICHETTO PARODI. 1.66: Scrapped Savona.

277 JACK SINGER 1.44 JHIW 10.8.45: Damaged by aircraft torpedo at Naha, Okinawa. Beached. Refloated. 9.10.45: Grounded in typhoon at Naha. Abandoned. Total loss. Later reported scrapped by China Merchants & Engineers Inc, China.

278 CHARLES PADDOCK 1.44 JHIW 51: KENNETH H.STEVENSON. 62: SKIATHOS. 66: DEMITRIOS. 12.7.67: Abandoned after developing leaks off Diego Suarez 09.20S 48.30E. Sank. (Voyage Bombay/Poland).

279 EDWARD J. O'BRIEN 1.44 JHIW 47: DEMOS-THENES. 6.67: Scrapped Bilbao.

280 HENRY L. GANTT 1.44 JHIW 47: GERARD-MER. 63: GERARDMERE. 12.63: Scrapped Bruges.

281 WILLIAM GLACKENS 1.44 JHIW 51: OCEAN SKIPPER. 55: WHITE STAR. 63: LOYAL ALLIES. 2.67: Scrapped Kaohsiung.

282 AUGUSTIN STAHL 1.44 JHIW 47: VAN'T HOFF. 50: TOMORI. 60: THETIS. 63: MARMARON. 9.69: Scrapped Split.

283 JULIAN W. MACK 1.44 JHIW 47: ANDREAS. 55: DESPO. 67: DANTE. 2.69: Scrapped Sakaide.

284 CLARENCE H. MATSON 1.44 JHIW 10.69: Sold for scrapping at Portland, Ore.

285 JAMES A. WILDER 1.44 JHIW 47: FIDES. 20.1.62: Aground Grosser Vogelsand, Elbe Estuary. Broke in two. Total loss (voyage Corpus Christi/Gdynia — iron ore).

286 CAROLE LOMBARD 1.44 JHIW 8.59: Scrapped Hirao.

287 ALLEN C. BALCH 2.44 JHIW 51: OCEAN SEAMAN. 60: THEIA MARIA. 14.4.61: Aground near Punta Galera, Mexico, 15.57N 97.46W. Broke in two, CTL, (Voyage Demerara/Japan — scrap). 61: Sold Mexican shipbreakers and scrapped 'in situ'.

288 RAYMOND T. BAKER 2.44 JHIW 47: NICOLAOU ZOGRAFIA. 60: DESPO.

289 A.B. HAMMOND 2.44 JHIW 47: MARIO II. 48: ENSENADA. 59: CESTOS. 61: NICOLAOS TSAVLIRIS. 25.1.63: Aground, refloated and again

aground in heavy seas at Kilyos (voyage Bougas/
Piraeus). Sold. 63: Scrapped Kilyos Beach, Turkey.

290 ELINOR WYLIE 2.44 JHIW 10.44: Damaged by
mine in Mediterranean (voyage Marseilles/Toulon).
Towed into port. CTL, but 5.45: TRIANA IX 223,
(USN). 46: Returned to USA, renamed ELINOR
WYLIE. 10.58: Scrapped Oakland, Cal.

291 HENRY E. HUNTINGTON 2.44 JHIW 10.61:
Scrapped Tacoma.

292 JOHN DOCKWEILER 2.44 JHIW
2.70: Sold for scrapping at Portland, Ore.

293 DAVID A. CURRY 2.44 JHIW 47: VIRE. 63:
APOLLONIAN. 9.69: Scrapped Shanghai.

294 SHERMAN O. HOUGHTON 2.44 JHIW Reserve
Fleet, site 2.

295 OSCAR UNDERWOOD 2.44 JHIW 47:
HELLENIC BEACH.

296 HORATIO ALLEN 2.44 JHIW 47: GREEN
WAVE. 52: SEAGATE. 56: Lengthened in Japan
to 511½ ft (8,384 grt). 6.9.56: Aground on Sonora
Reef near Aberdeen, Wash. 9.9.56: Washed off reef
in storm and grounded Quinault River. (Voyage
Muroran/Vancouver – ballast). 21.9.56: Broke in
two. CTL. 58: Scrapped on beach at Point Greenville.

297 RUSSELL H. CHITTENDEN 3.44 JHIW 13.3.45:
Ashore and wrecked off New Guinea, 05.55S 149.10E
(voyage Hollandia/Langemak).

298 J. FRANK COOPER 3.44 JHIW 47: CICLOPE.
62: MARIA LAURETANA. 63: AMALIA. 2.69:
Scrapped Sakaide.

299 ROBERT L. HAGUE 3.44 JHIW 47: PINIOS.
64: ATLANTIC MASTER. 65: FORWARD. 68:
Scrapped Kaohsiung.

300 I.N. VAN NUYS 3.44 JHIW 47: ALEXANDROS
KORYZIS.

301 IDA M. TARBELL 3.44 JHIW 47: TRITON.
1.68: Scrapped Hirao.

302 FREDERICK C. HICKS 3.44 JHIW 47: NIDAR-
LAND. 49: TRYA. 52: BENITA. 58: DESPINA K.
19.5.67: Aground and wrecked 5 miles north east of
San Lazaro Light, 24.52N 112.16W (voyage Tokio/
Ecuador). 6.67: Broke in two. Total loss.

303 JOE FELLOWS 3.44 JHIW 47: NORLAGO. 50:
SYRA. 57: LONDREDAM L.S. 57: ANTIBES. 65:
ELIAS D. 65: ARCHANGEL MICHAEL. 28.7.66:
Aground on Bural reef, near Port Okha, Gulf of
Kutch, 22.27N 68.59E. Abandoned, broke in two.
Total loss, (voyage Tampa/Kandla – fertiliser). 11.66:
Wreck reported afire and burnt out.

304 C.K. McCLATCHY 4.44 JHIW 47: AMBRA.
63: ANDARIN. 8.68: Scrapped Hirao.

305 PETER LASSEN 4.44 JHIW 47: BONDE.
61: CHEPO. 64: GOLDEN ROSE. 68: Scrapped
Kaohsiung.

306 MARTIN JOHNSON 5.44 JHIW 47:
PANAMOLGA. 65: SEVILLIANA. 66: EUREKA.
7.69: Scrapped Spezia.

BUILT BY DELTA SHIPBUILDING COMPANY

This shipyard, with six slipways, was one of the nine new yards for which building approval was given early in
1941.

Of prime importance when the emergency shipbuilding programme was launched was the necessity of enlisting
the skills and the 'know-how' of the leaders of the shipbuilding industry. To this end one of the 'big five' builders,
Federal Shipbuilding & Dry Dock Co. was considered as possible suppliers of management for this new yard at
New Orleans. But Navy and C-type contracts and anticipated future expansion were already stretching its talent
and resources to the limit and the company was simply unable to undertake any further tasks. Instead the Maritime Commission turned for aid to the American Shipbuilding Company, a leading shipbuilder on the Great Lakes,
and it somewhat reluctantly agreed to operate the new yard.

Accordingly, a subsidiary company, Delta Shipbuilding, was formed to control the new establishment. The nucleus
of its labour force was a few craftsmen from the operating company's own Lakes yards and some others found

The US Navy's stores issuing ship *Hesperia* in April 1945. (Delta, Yard no 151)

The *Helena Modjeska*. The ship grounded on the Goodwins after leaving her anchorage at Deal on September 12, 1946, bound for Bremerhaven. Four days later she broke her back as eight tugs pulled on her, and this illustration shows the effect of subsequent heavy weather which tore the pieces apart and, still aground, swung them at right-angles to each other. (Delta, Yard no 152)

The Brocklebank Line's *Malabar* undocking in London
River. (Jones, Brunswick, Yard no 123)

The *Granville S. Hall* after overhaul at San Francisco
Naval Yard. Note the atomic fall-out 'bird-bath'
collecting tub on the mast. (Jones, Panama City,
Yard no 66)

Susan Colby as the Greek *Olga*. (New England, East
yard, Yard no 2213)

locally, and by June 1942 this force had grown to a total of more than 13,000 employees.

Many of the new shipyards formed throughout the nation developed, up to a limit, their own techniques and methods and also their own special features, this often being due to the nature of the local terrain. With Delta they decided to weld 100 per cent, influenced by the fact that the yard was entirely new and therefore could be organised to best advantage. With the yard so constructed that launchings were into a narrow channel, the sideways launching method was adopted.

Soon the third wave of shipyard expansions caused two more slips to be added to the layout of the yard. Later, as the demands for specialised types of shipping increased, the company was given the task of designing the Liberty tankers. Still later it was requested to produce plans for the Liberty collier and subsequently it was to build thirty two of the former and twenty four of the latter. The construction of all these differing vessels gave sufficient break in the production flow to cause the yard, at one time, to be the slowest of all the yards established during 1941.

At the end of 1943 the US President, in a directive to all shipyards, called for an intense drive to secure a record number of deliveries before the year's end. Special efforts gave delivery of more ships in the December than in any previous month, but this was at the cost of delivering far fewer than usual in the following month.

Delta's share of these figures were nine deliveries in December 1943 but only three in January 1944.

The delivery dates of the twenty four Liberty colliers ranged over an eight month period from early 1945, and shipbuilding at the Delta yard ceased towards the end of the same year with the completion of the last vessel of the class.

Liberty ship output: 132 vessels, plus 32 Liberty tankers and 24 Liberty colliers.

USMC hull numbers: MCE

120– 144	(Yard Nos	1– 25)
313– 320	(" "	26– 33)
1023–1050	(" "	34– 61)
1732–1733	(" "	62– 63)
1935	(" "	96)
2448–2466	(" "	97–115)
2790–2815	(" "	116–141)
2817–2823	(" "	143–149)
2825–2831	(" "	151–157)
2833–2835	(" "	159–161)
2837–2839	(" "	163–165)
2841	(" "	167)
2843	(" "	169)
2845	(" "	171)

1 WILLIAM C.C. CLAIBORNE 5.42 ASB 61: Scrapped Seattle.

2 T.J. JACKSON 6.42 GMC 60: Scrapped Boston.

3 THOMAS B. ROBERTSON 7.42 ASB 10.69: Sold for scrapping at New Orleans.

4 ABRAHAM BALDWIN 7.42 ASB Reserve Fleet, site 4.

5 THEODORIC BLAND 7.42 ASB 6.63: Scrapped New Orleans.

6 BENJAMIN CONTEE 8.42 ASB 16.8.43: Damaged by aircraft torpedo 16 miles off Cape de Gardia, 37.07N 07.50E (voyage Bona/Oran – 1,800 Italian POWs). Later towed Gibraltar, thence proceeded UK. 8.6.44: Sunk as Gooseberry 1 breakwater blockship at Mulberry Harbour A beach-head, Verreville, Normandy. 16.7.44: Officially abandoned (foundered and destroyed) after harbour was destroyed in storms of 19–22.6.44.

7 GEORGE GALE 8.42 ASB Reserve Fleet, site 8.

8 WILLIAM B. GILES 8.42 ASB 47: BOULOGNE SUR MER. 66: BOULOGNE. 12.68: Scrapped Kaohsiung.

9 JONATHAN GROUT 9.42 ASB Reserve Fleet, site 4.

10 DANIEL HUGER 9.42 ASB Reserve Fleet, site 4.

11 GEORGE LEONARD 9.42 F & S 2.64: Scrapped New Orleans.

12 ANDREW MOORE 10.42 ASB 3.63: Scrapped Philadelphia.

13 JOSIAH PARKER 10.42 ASB 47: EPINAL. 64: Renamed DEKA for delivery trip to shipbreakers. 5.64: Scrapped Aioi.

14 THOMAS SCOTT 10.42 GMC 17.2.45: Sunk by aircraft bombs at Kola Inlet, North Russia.

15 JOSHUA SENEY 10.42 GMC 5.62: Scrapped New Orleans.

16 THOMAS SINNICKSON 11.42 GMC 7.7.43: Sunk by submarine (U.185) torpedo off Natal, Brazil, 03.51S 36.22W.

17 JONATHAN STURGES 11.42 AME 23.2.43: Sunk by submarine (U.707) torpedo in N.W.Atlantic, 46.15N 38.11W.

18 JONATHAN TRUMBULL 11.42 WPM Reserve Fleet, site 4.

19 JOHN VINING 11.42 AME 60: Scrapped Baltimore.

20 ALEXANDER WHITE 12.42 GMC 8.64: Scrapped Portland, Ore.

21 HENRY WYNKOOP 12.42 ASB 58: Reported scrapped Baltimore.

22 SAMUEL JORDAN KIRKWOOD 12.42 ASB 7.5.43: Sunk by submarine (U.195) torpedo in S.Atlantic, approx. 15.00S 07.00W.

23 ABRAHAM LINCOLN 12.42 CB 10.67: Scrapped Mobile.

24 PAT HARRISON 1.43 GMC 8.5.43: Damaged by Italian limpet mine at Gibraltar; beached. CTL. Sold and 49: vessel cut in two. 50: Both parts towed separately to Spain. 5.51: Scrapped Cadiz.

25 LEONIDAS POLK 1.43 ASB 2.65: Scrapped New Orleans.

26 CHARLES BRANTLEY AYCOCK 9.42 ASB 8.62: Scrapped Tacoma.

27 WILLIAM BLOUNT 9.42 ASB Reserve Fleet, site 5.

28 WADE HAMPTON 12.42 CB 28.2.43: Sunk by submarine (U.405) torpedo in N.Atlantic, 59.49N 34.43W (voyage New York/N.Russia — war supplies).

29 RICHMOND MUMFORD PEARSON 11.42 CB 10.63: Scrapped Tacoma.

30 DAVID G. FARRAGUT 1.43 CB Reserve Fleet, site 2.

31 MAYO BROTHERS 12.42 GMC 1.65: Scrapped Panama City.

32 WILLIAM HARPER 2.43 JHIW Reserve Fleet, site 4.

33 PIERRE SOULE 2.43 ASB 12.69: Scrapped Mobile.

34 BLACK HAWK 2.43 GMC 29.12.44: Damaged by submarine (U.772) torpedo in English Channel, stern blown off and sank. Forepart later beached Warbarrow Bay (voyage Cherbourg/Fowey). CTL. 48: Forepart reported scrapped.

35 ROBERT M. LA FOLLETTE 2.43 GMC 47: TROARN. 64: Used as storeship at Havre. 65: Sold for further trading (same name).

36 WALTER Q. GRESHAM 2.43 ASB 18.3.43: Sunk by submarine (U.221) torpedo in N.W.Atlantic, 53.35N 28.05W.

37 RICHARD OLNEY 2.43 GMC 22.9.43: Damaged by mine in Mediterranean, 37.25N 09.54E. Towed Bizerta. Total loss. 48: Wreck sold Italian shipbreakers and scrapped.

38 ROBERT BACON 3.43 JHIW 14.7.43: Sunk by submarine (U.178) torpedo off Mozambique, 15.02S 41.13E (voyage Suez/Bahia — general).

39 PHILANDER C. KNOX 3.43 GMC 3.61: Scrapped Hamburg.

40 LUCIUS Q.C. LAMAR 3.43 F & S 4.67: Scrapped Tacoma.

41 JAMES McHENRY 3.43 F & S Reserve Fleet, site 8.

42 SAMUEL DEXTER 3.43 F & S 24.1.44: Abandoned after developing cracks in hull and deck, 56.19N 11.43W. Drifted ashore 3 miles north east of Greian Head, Barra Island. Broke in two. Total loss. (Voyage Cardiff/New York — ballast).

43 ROGER GRISWOLD 3.43 JHIW Reserve Fleet, site 2.

44 TIMOTHY BLOODWORTH 4.43 GMC 11.63: Scrapped Portland, Ore.

45 ELIAS BOUDINOT 3.43 GMC 3.62: Scrapped Baltimore.

46 AEDANUS BURKE 4.43 F & S 4.64: Scrapped New Orleans.

47 THOMAS FITZSIMONS 4.43 JHIW 8.64: Scrapped Portland, Ore.

48 HENRY GROVES CONNOR 4.43 WISC 47: ARISTIDIS. 10.69: Scrapped Hong Kong.

49 WILLIAM M. EVARTS 5.43 F & S 10.61: Scrapped Baltimore.

50 F.T. FRELINGHUYSEN 5.43 ASB 6.60: Scrapped Baltimore.

51 TARLETON BROWN 4.43 ASB 5.67: Converted in USA to crane barge, (at Tacoma).

52 HENRY S. FOOTE 5.43 F & S 10.60: Scrapped Nagasaki

53 JAMES E. HOWARD 5.43 F & S Reserve Fleet, site 1.

54 CHARLES HENDERSON 5.43 AME 9.4.45: Exploded and sank whilst discharging at Bari. Total loss. 48: Sold Genoa shipbreakers for scrapping.

55 ROBERT LOWRY 5.43 F & S 11.69: Scrapped Portland, Ore.

56 GEORGE POINDEXTER 5.43 F & S 5.67: Scrapped Tacoma.

57 JOHN A. QUITMAN 6.43 WISC Reserve Fleet, site 2.

58 JOHN SHARP WILLIAMS 6.43 WISC 8.61: Scrapped Panama City.

59 JULIEN POYDRAS 5.43 F & S Reserve Fleet, site 2.

60 RICHARD M. JOHNSON 6.43 WISC Reserve Fleet, site 5.

61 JOSEPH N. NICOLLET 6.43 ASB 59: Scrapped Baltimore.

62 EDWARD SPARROW 6.43 IFM Reserve Fleet, site 2.

63 JOHN McDONOGH 7.43 IFM 51: GULFWATER. 62: ORSA. 63: KIMISIS. 5.69: Scrapped Kaohsiung.

96 JEAN LOUIS 2.44 IFM Completed as ACUBENS AKS 5, (USN). 46: Returned US Govt. 65: Reported scrapped Portland, Ore.

97 LINN BOYD 3.44 IFM 12.67: Scrapped Mobile.

98 WARREN STONE 2.44 IFM 44: ARKAB AK 130, (USN). 46: WARREN STONE. Reserve Fleet, site 2.

99 JAMES B. ASWELL 3.44 ASB 47: LIBERATOR. 63: THIOS COSTAS.

100 RUFUS E. FOSTER 3.44 ASB 47: LEEGHWATER. 47: LIEVE VROUWEKERK. 20.1.60: Aground in storm on Vlieland Island, (voyage Hamburg/Antwerp — ballast). 26.2.60: Refloated. Sold. 4.60: Scrapped Dunston-upon-Tyne.

101 R.S. WILSON 3.44 IFM 31.12.45: Grounded at entrance to Boston, Mass., harbour (voyage Newport News/Boston — coal). Later refloated, damaged. CTL, laid up in James River. 1.59: Scrapped Baltimore.

102 HARRY TOULMIN 4.44 IFM Completed as SEGINUS AK 133, USN. 46: HARRY TOULMIN. 47: KEHREA. 10.67: Scrapped Shanghai.

103 GEORGE A. MARR 3.44 IFM 47: STATHES J. YANNAGHAS. 51: ANIA. 59: GRAMMATIKI. 7.2.65: Sprang leak in heavy weather in Pacific. 8.2.65: Abandoned, sank 40.38N 159.31W (voyage Tacoma/Formosa — scrap).

104 ANDRES ALMONASTER 3.44 ASB Completed as SYRMA AK 134, (USN). 46: ANDRES ALMONASTER. 48: SAN JORGE. 54: ST JOHN. 1.68: Scrapped Shanghai.

105 JOHN M. PARKER 4.44 IFM 58: Scrapped Oakland, Cal.

106 CECIL N. BEAN 4.44 IFM 49: Sold commercial (same name). 57: PENN VOYAGER. 61: DELOS PIONEER. 65: RENA. 5.67: Scrapped Utsumi.

107 MOLLIE MOORE DAVIS 4.44 IFM Completed as BURIAS ARG 13, (USN). 45: BURIAS AG 69, (USN). 47: Returned to US Govt. USN Reserve Fleet, site 6.

108 KOCHAB 4.44 IFM Completed as KOCHAB AKS 6, (USN). 47: Returned to US Govt. 4.65: Scrapped Richmond, Cal.

109 JACQUES PHILLIPE VILLERE 4.44 IFM Completed as BASILAN ARG 12, (USN). 45: BASILAN AG 68, (USN). 47: Returned to US Govt. USN Reserve Fleet, site 6.

110 CHARLES W. WOOSTER 5.44 IFM 12.69: Scrapped Brownsville, Texas.

111 W.C. LATTA 5.44 IFM 61: Scrapped Wilmington.

112 ANDREW STEVENSON 5.44 IFM Reserve Fleet, site 5.

113 WILLIAM WHEELWRIGHT 6.44 ASB Reserve Fleet, site 5.

114 EDWIN A. STEVENS 6.44 IFM 47: IOANNIS G.KULUKUNDIS. 11.7.49: Ashore in fog at Point Arguello, Cal. Total loss. (Voyage Vancouver/Cape Town – wheat).

115 ALEXANDER W. DONIPHAN 7.44 WISC 64: Scrapped Philadelphia.

116 AMASA DELANO 7.44 IFM 51: STRATH-PORT. 54: ELPIS. 56: Lengthened at Kobe to 511½ ft (8,541 grt). 66: ELPIS II. 67: ARI K. 12.68: Scrapped Onomichi.

117 FRANK ADAIR MONROE 7.44 WISC 51: SKYSTAR. 52: CHRISTOS M. 54: CHRISTOS. 4.6.60: Aground on Serrana Bank, Caribbean, (voyage Tampa/Yokohama – phosphate rock). 12.6.60: Refloated, CTL. Repurchased by owner (same name). 61: AGIOS NICOLAS. 1.68: Scrapped Kaohsiung.

118 CYRUS ADLER 7.44 JHIW 1.60: Scrapped Baltimore.

119 GEORGE W. ALTHER 7.44 IFM 51: ANNIOC. 56: VENETIA. 59: AUROMAR. 64: COSMOS CAPELLA. 6.68: Scrapped Kaohsiung.

120 ROBERT W. BINGHAM 7.44 IFM Completed as BRIGADIER GENERAL CLINTON W.RUSSELL (US Army aircraft repair ship). 47: ROBERT W.BINGHAM 59: Scrapped New Orleans.

121 COLLIN McKINNEY 8.44 IFM 1.67: Scrapped Portland, Ore.

122 WALKER D. HINES 7.44 JHIW Reserve Fleet, site 1.

123 ALCEE FORTIER 8.44 IFM 64: Scrapped New Orleans.

124 MILTON B. MEDARY 8.44 IFM 11.66: Scrapped Philadelphia.

125 FERDINAND R. HASSLER 8.44 IFM Reserve Fleet, site 4.

126 O.L. BODENHAMER 8.44 JHIW Reserve Fleet, site 4.

127 FREDERICK VON STEUBEN 8.44 WISC 3.61: Scrapped Hamburg.

128 FLOYD W. SPENCER 9.44 IFM 53: Converted at Yokosuka to experimental minefield sweeper YAG 36, (no name, USN). 60: Sold Japan, presume scrapped

129 MILTON H. SMITH 9.44 WISC Reserve Fleet, site 2.

130 E.G. HALL 9.44 JHIW 1.60: Scrapped Baltimore.

131 ROBERT F. BROUSSARD 9.44 WISC 65: Scrapped Philadelphia.

132 ANCIL F. HAINES 10.44 F & S 46: HAI SIU. 28.4.61: Abandoned, listing, after cargo shifted in heavy weather off Chiba Prefecture, 34.57N 142.55E (voyage Keelung/Los Angeles). 30.4.61: Taken in tow to Yokosuka. Repaired and proceeded on voyage. 64: WUCHANG. 5.67: Scrapped Kaohsiung.

133 GEORGE POMUTZ 9.44 WISC Reserve Fleet, site 2.

134 AM–MER–MAR 9.44 GMC 27.12.46: Ashore near Lindesnaes (voyage New Orleans/Larvik – soya beans). 1.1.47: Dislodged from reef in storm and sank. 3.48: Wreck purchased by Stavanger Ship-breaking Co. for scrapping.

135 SIEUR DE LA SALLE 10.44 WISC 66: Scrapped Panama City.

136 ISAAC DELGADO 9.44 F & S
4.69: Scrapped Panama City.

137 CHRISTIAN BERGH 10.44 GMC 48: Sold
commercial (same name). 52: SEAVIGIL. 53: OCEAN
NIMET. 61: EVICYNTHIA. 64: LOYAL DEFENDERS.
1.67: Scrapped Aioi.

138 ALFRED J. EVANS 10.44 WISC Reserve Fleet,
site 5.

139 KATHARINE B. SHERWOOD 10.44 GMC 4.66:
Scrapped Terminal Island.

140 J. RUFINO BARRIOS 11.44 GMC 11.67:
Scrapped Portland, Ore.

141 THOMAS P. LEATHERS 10.44 GMC 10.68:
Scrapped Kearny, NJ.

143 ALES HRDLICKA 11.44 GMC 47: HAWAIIAN
LOGGER. 61: ARTEMISION. 25.1.64: Stranded at
Gaidhouronisi Island, near Crete. 29.1.64: Driven
further ashore in gale. (Voyage Port Sudan/Venezuela
– sesame seeds). 17.2.64: Refloated, towed Piraeus
thence Ambeliki Bay. CTL. 6.65: Scrapped Split.

144 BENJAMIN SILLIMAN 10.44 GMC Reserve
Fleet, site 2.

145 KING HATHAWAY 11.44 GMC Reserve Fleet,
site 1.

146 WILLIAM HACKETT 11.44 GMC Completed
as CYBELE AKS 10, (USN). 46: WILLIAM HACKETT.
8.65: Scrapped Portland, Ore.

147 GEORGE W. CABLE 11.44 JHIW Completed
as HECUBA AKS 12, (USN). 46: Returned to US
Govt. 65: Reported scrapped Portland, Ore.

148 JOSEPH WEYDEMEYER 11.44 JHIW 11.61:
Scrapped New Orleans.

149 JOHN W. DRAPER 11.44 GMC Completed as
GRATIA AKS 11, (USN). 46: Returned to US Govt.
4.65: Scrapped Richmond, Cal.

151 SAM DALE 12.44 JHIW Completed as
HESPERIA AKS 13, (USN). 46: Returned US Govt.
USN Reserve Fleet, site 6.

152 HELENA MODJESKA 12.44 GMC 12.9.46:
Aground on Goodwin Sands. Broke in two, total loss.
(Voyage Marseilles/Bremerhaven – vehicles and
general). 23.10.46: After part refloated, beached

Sandwich Bay. 28.10.46: Forepart refloated, moored
Deal. 10.1.47: Forepart towed River Blackwater.
10.6.47: Afterpart towed River Blackwater, moored
alongside bow. Both parts later sold and scrapped
Grays, Essex.

153 MARTIN BEHRMAN 12.44 JHIW 6.65:
Scrapped Portland, Ore.

154 WILLIAM H. KENDRICK 12.44 JHIW 49:
JUDGE BLAND. 54: ATHENIAN. 57: ANDROS
CITADEL. 63: SAN NICOLA. 21.1.65: Abandoned
damaged and breaking up 30.13N 168.52W (voyage
San Francisco/Formosa – scrap). 23.1.65: Sank
about 750 miles north west of Honolulu.

155 ANDREAS HONCHARENKO 12.44 JHIW 47:
ALABAMAN. 52: SEACLIFF. 56: JOSEFINA. 65:
FAIRWIND. 66: CINDY. 7.12.66: On fire near Kobe,
towed Sumoto, Awaji Island; beached. (Voyage
Mormugao/Amagasaki – ore). 16.12.66: Refloated,
towed Amagasaki. CTL. Sold 3.67: Scrapped Hirao.

156 NACHMAN SYRKIN 1.45 JHIW 51: SEA-
MYSTERY. 53: KATINA. 59: THEOMANNA. 3.67:
Scrapped Hong Kong.

157 JAMES EAGAN LAYNE 12.44 JHIW 21.3.45:
Damaged by submarine (U.1195) torpedo off
Plymouth, 50.13N 04.05W. Beached Whitesand Bay.
Total loss. 48: Wreck sold and reported scrapped 'in
situ'.

159 CARL ZACHARY WEBB 1.45 JHIW 63:
Scrapped Panama City.

160 BENJAMIN A. FISHER 12.44 JHIW 1.66:
Scrapped Portland, Ore.

161 WILLIAM W. McKEE 1.45 JHIW 51: SUN-
WAVE. 52: SEAGLOBE. 53: YPSILOU. 57:
ANDROS HEIGHTS. 60: GEORGIA S.M. 66:
GRAND VIRTUE. 2.68: Scrapped Kaohsiung.

163 JOHN C. PRESTON 1.45 JHIW Completed as
HYDRA. 46: COSTAS MICHALOS. 26.10.62:
Aground on Banc les Quenocs, between Calais and
Cap Griz Nez, (voyage Archangel/Calais – wood
pulp). 19.11.62: Broke in two, sank. Total loss.

164 DAREL M. RITTER 2.45 JHIW 51: SEA-
MANOR. 53: PITROFOS. 54: FARALIS. 3.68:
Scrapped Keelung.

165 FRANK E. SPENCER 1.45 JHIW 51: ANNE BUTLER. 54: ARTEMIDI. 57: MYRIAM III. 61: HARI. 65: GEORGIA. 9.67: Scrapped Hirao.

167 ROY K. JOHNSON 2.45 JHIW 51: SEA-GALLANT. 53: ADMIRAL DEWEY. 54: NATIONAL LEADER. 61: ARIE H. 62: ARISTEA. 66: BEATA. 7.68: Scrapped Kaohsiung.

169 DONALD S. WRIGHT 3.45 JHIW 49: STRATH-CAPE. 52: TROJAN SEAMAN. 54: GEORGEL. 8.68: Scrapped Hirao.

171 LAURENCE J. GALLAGHER 5.45 JHIW 51: NIGEL. 58: RUSSELL L. 65: U.S. RED RIVER. 66: Returned US Govt under Ship Exchange Act. 9.66: Scrapped Kaohsiung.

BUILT BY J.A. JONES CONSTRUCTION CO, BRUNSWICK YARD, BRUNSWICK, GA

In January 1942 the Maritime Commission deemed that a sufficiency of ships was then building or planned for and considered that any additional ones would be in excess of the available shipyard capacity. They therefore decided not to undertake any further expansion unless so ordered by a further decree from the President.

They were, in fact, so ordered. Shipping losses were running at a high level and needed constant replacement, and at the same time the military authorities were demanding an increase in the shipbuilding tempo, this to enable them to meet and maintain the ever expanding requirements of overseas forces.

So a new six-slipway shipyard was commenced at Brunswick, Georgia. But by January 1943 the commission concluded that the Brunswick Marine Construction Corporation, although it had almost completed the yard, had not made sufficient progress in actual shipbuilding. The corporation therefore agreed to transfer the yard and its contracts to the J.A.Jones Construction Co, and it was awarded compensation for the plant and equipment. The Jones Company had no shipbuilding experience; they were construction engineers from North Carolina and had been recommended to the commission as 'good management'. In keeping with many other yard operators when entering shipbuilding for the first time they were disposed to try new methods. The company soon proved that ordinary industrial efficiency could improve shipyard efficiency, and that 'shipbuilding brains' were not really special or mysterious, nor did it take a lifetime to acquire them. Nevertheless, both here and at the yard in Panama City the Jones Company experienced some difficulty in meeting all the demands, but it was a large concern and was able to strengthen its force with both new management and labour diverted from other projects. However, shipbuilding always remained a minor part of the firm's operations.

At this yard most of the workers came from towns and farms in Georgia and the other Southern states, but not all were of the farming fraternity, for the employees included prize-fighters, professional golfers and jockeys, an investment banker and thirteen clergymen!

During 1944 the yard was given contracts for the construction of vessels of the C1-M type.

Liberty ship output: 85 vessels at an average cost of 1,992,000 dollars each.

USMC hull numbers: MCE 1489–1518   (Yard Nos 105–134)
                                    2350–2404   (”   ” 135–189)

105 JAMES M. WAYNE 5.43 GMC 6.67: Scrapped Kearny, NJ.

106 WILLIAM B. WOODS 6.43 GMC 10.3.44: Damaged by submarine (U.952) torpedo north east of Palermo, Italy, 38.43N 13.50E. Abandoned. 15.3.44: Sank (voyage Palermo/Naples — troops and stores).

107 JOSEPH R. LAMAR 6.43 GMC 3.61: Scrapped Mobile.

108 THOMAS TODD 6.43 HMC Reserve Fleet, site 1.

109 ROBERT TRIMBLE 7.43 GMC 47: ANDREA. 6.63: Scrapped Spezia.

110 JOHN CATRON 7.43 GMC Reserve Fleet, site 5.

111 JOHN McKINLEY 8.43 GMC 67: Scrapped Richmond, Cal.

112 JOHN A. CAMPBELL 8.43 F & S 68: Scrapped Portland, Ore.

113 JOHN M. HARLAN 9.43 F & S 6.66: Scrapped New Orleans.

114 HOWELL E. JACKSON 9.43 GMC 9.62: Scrapped Bordentown, NJ.

115 EDWARD D. WHITE 9.43 F & S Reserve Fleet, site 1.

116 HORACE H. LURTON 10.43 F & S 46: ROYAN. 3.68: renamed ROY for delivery trip to breakers. 6.68: Scrapped Shanghai.

117 HENRY W. GRADY 10.43 GMC Reserve Fleet, site 5.

118 JAMES A. WETMORE 11.43 GMC 8.67: Scrapped Philadelphia.

119 FREDERICK BARTHOLDI 11.43 GMC 25.12.43: Ashore on Fladda Chuain rocks, north coast of Skye, 57.44N 06.26W. Total loss. (Voyage Jacksonville/London — general). 22.6.44: Refloated, beached. Later towed River Clyde and 9.44: Scrapped on beach at Kames Bay.

120 JOHN B. GORDON 11.43 GMC 1.61: Scrapped Baltimore.

121 EDWARD P. ALEXANDER 11.43 GMC 47: ORIZIA. 20.1.63: Aground on southern breakwater at Veracruz harbour. Total loss. (Voyage Genoa/Houston — general). Wreck reported sold for scrap, but at March 1970 still lying aground.

122 ROBERT BATTEY 12.43 GMC 6.9.45: Aground at Bilaa Point, Mindanao (voyage Batangas/San Francisco). Refloated, severely damaged. Later returned to USA and laid up. Circa 65: Reported transferred USN and disposed of.

123 PATRICK H. MORRISSEY 12.43 F & S Completed as SAMDEE. 47: MALABAR. 61: OMONIA. 67: Scrapped Hirao.

124 JOE C.S. BLACKBURN 12.43 GMC 68: Converted at Portland, Ore.for use as floating dock.

125 JOHN B. LENNON 12.43 GMC 47: STRASBOURG. 59: MANTRIC. 10.68: Scrapped Onomichi.

126 GEORGE G. CRAWFORD 1.44 GMC 47: MEGALOHARI. 57: CALLIOPI MICHALOS.

127 DAVID B. JOHNSON 1.44 GMC 2.68: Scrapped Oakland, Cal.

128 HOWARD E. COFFIN 1.44 GMC 47: PATRIZIA FASSIO. 10.62: Scrapped Trieste.

129 R. NEY McNEELY 2.44 F & S 55: Converted to YAG, (same name, USN). (Conversion type EC2-S-22a). USN Reserve Fleet, site 2.

130 BENJAMIN H. HILL 2.44 F & S Reserve Fleet, site 2.

131 JOSEPH M. TERRELL 2.44 GMC 6.66: Scrapped Panama City.

132 ROBERT R. LIVINGSTON 2.44 F & S 4.62: Scrapped Tacoma.

133 SAMALNESS 3.44 F & S 47: CASTLEDORE. 27.1.51: Lost propeller in Bay of Biscay. 28.1.51: Abandoned; aground on north coast of Spain 43.44N 07.31W. Broke in two. 5.2.51: Sank. Total loss. (Voyage Hull/Torrevieja — ballast).

134 ISAAC SHELBY 2.44 F & S 6.1.45: Damaged by mine 50 miles south west of Rome, 41.12N 13.30E, beached Cape Circeo. Broke in two, total loss. (Voyage Leghorn/Naples). Stern later refloated and 8.48: Scrapped Naples.

135 SAMFAIRY 3.44 GMC 47: ADMIRAL CUNNINGHAM. 52: AELLO. 55: KYMO. 65: EUTHALIA. 2.69: Scrapped Onomichi.

136 SAMFOYLE 3.44 F & S 47: VARDULIA. 54: VALENCIA. 57: SEACOB. 12.68: Scrapped Hong Kong.

137 SAMFINN 4.44 GMC 47: Returned to US Govt. 1.62: Scrapped Mobile.

138 SAMVIGNA 4.44 GMC 48: Returned to US Govt. 5.60: Scrapped Mobile.

139 SAMSELBU 4.44 HEW 19.3.45: Mined and sunk off Belgian coast, 51.23N 03.06E.

140 SAMLEYTE 4.44 F & S 47: Returned to US Govt. 11.60: Scrapped Baltimore.

141 SAMAUSTRAL 5.44 GMC 47: HARPATHIAN. 56: SUNCAMPANELLA. 63: CALIOPI A. 66: MARACH.

142 SAMINGOY 5.44 GMC 47: STAFFORD. 50:

BIMINI. 61: HERNAN CORTES. 15.10.66: Stranded on Alacran reef, Yucatan (voyage Tampa/Montevideo – fertiliser). 4.11.66: Blown further on to reef in storm, abandoned. 11.2.67: Refloated, towed Coatzacoalcos. CTL. 8.67: Scrapped Veracruz, PR.

143 SAMLORIAN 5.44 JHIW 47: HELMSPEY. 49: LLANOVER. 51: CAPESTAR. 60: ATHLOS. 12.66: Scrapped Sakai.

144 SAMOLAND 6.44 F & S 47: SEA TRIUMPH. 48: ASUNCION DE LARRINAGA. 51: KATINGO. 22.12.54: Aground in gale off Bergen-au-Zee, near Ymuiden. (Voyage Rotterdam/Hamburg – ballast). 19.2.55: Refloated, towed Rotterdam. CTL. Sold and repaired. 55: VIRGINIA G. 60: KAPETANISSA. 64: NATIONAL STRENGTH. 67: GOOD EDDIE. 4.67: Arrived Taiwan for scrap but sold for further trade, renamed ESCOMDIDO. 29.6.67: Broke adrift whilst anchored outside Keelung (completing registration formalities), struck breakwater and severely damaged stern. Registration not proceeded with and purchase cancelled. Name reverted, vessel towed to shallow water and laid up.

145 DONALD W. BAIN 6.44 GMC 49: LILICA. 25.12.51: Ashore off Civitavecchia (voyage Hampton Roads/Civitavecchia – coal). 30.12.51: Refloated. CTL. Sold and repaired. 55: Re-engined at Genoa with oil engine by Fiat, renamed ELISA CAMPANELLA. 6.69: Scrapped Vado.

146 AUGUSTINE B. McMANUS 6.44 NT Reserve Fleet, site 1.

147 JAMES B. DUKE 6.44 JHIW Reserve Fleet, site 5.

148 W.P. FEW 7.44 GMC 1945: Stranded and severely damaged 'on a beach' (no further details). Later refloated but CTL. Towed to USA and laid up at Mobile. 59: Scrapped Baltimore.

149 ALEXANDER S. CLAY 7.44 JHIW 11.69: Sold for scrapping at New Orleans.

150 F. SOUTHALL FARRAR 7.44 GMC 66: Scrapped Beaumont, Texas.

151 JAMES W. CANNON 7.44 GMC 51: TRANS-OCEANIC. 54: NATIONAL MARINER. 61: VORIOS IPIROS. 3.63: Scrapped Yokosuka.

152 FRANK PARK 8.44 JHIW 7.62: Scrapped Philadelphia.

153 EUGENE T. CHAMBERLAIN 8.44 GMC 66: Towed Philadelphia for scrap, but scrapping delayed 'due to Vietnam situation'.

154 THOMAS B. KING 8.44 JHIW Reserve Fleet, site 1.

155 R. WALTON MOORE 8.44 GMC 5.61: Scrapped Tacoma.

156 NIELS POULSON 8.44 GMC 14.9.46: Damaged by mine off Gorgona, Italy. Towed to Leghorn, CTL. (Voyage Baltimore/Leghorn). 11.48: Scrapped Genoa.

157 ARTHUR J. TYRER 8.44 GMC Reserve Fleet, site 2.

158 CASSIUS HUDSON 9.44 GMC 16.10.46: Damaged by mine in Gulf of Trieste, 45.32N 13.12E. Taken in tow but struck another mine and sank, (voyage Hampton Roads/Venice).

159 LUNSFORD RICHARDSON 9.44 GMC 61: Scrapped Philadelphia.

160 JOHAN PRINTZ 9.44 GMC Reserve Fleet, site 2.

161 CHARLES S. HAIGHT 10.44 GMC 2.4.46: Ashore on Avery Ledge, off Cape Ann, Mass, (voyage Newport/Boston – ballast). Total loss. 17.8.46: Caught fire and burnt out whilst being stripped of removable equipment. Winches, masts, derricks and chains later salved for scrap.

162 R.J. REYNOLDS 10.44 GMC 3.58: Scrapped Baltimore.

163 DUNCAN L. CLINCH 10.44 GMC 23.12.45: Damaged by mine in Havre Roads (voyage Buenos Aires/Rouen). 27.12.45: Bow sank to sea bed, leaving stern in air. 28.12.45: Broke in two, total loss.

164 ABIGAIL GIBBONS 10.44 GMC Reserve Fleet, site 4.

165 CHARLES W. STILES 10.44 GMC 47: GLOBAL SHIPPER. 48: BYGDIN. 49: AURA. 59: FLORENTIA. 64: METAMORFOSIS. 3.69: Scrapped China.

166 MURRAY M. BLUM 11.44 GMC Reserve Fleet, site 4.

167 LAURA BRIDGMAN 11.44 GMC 51: CATHERINE. 58: PENN EXPLORER. 61: GRAND EXPLORER. 2.68: Scrapped Kaohsiung.

168 RICHARD RANDALL 11.44 GMC 12.64: Scrapped Mobile.

169 EDWARD R. SQUIBB 11.44 GMC Reserve Fleet, site 5.

170 JOHN H. HAMMOND 11.44 GMC 17.7.45: Damaged by mine off Elba. 23.7.45: Towed to Piombino, thence Naples. (Voyage Baltimore/Leghorn). CTL. 7.48: Scrapped Savona.

171 ALBERT K. SMILEY 11.44 GMC 10.65: Scrapped Panama City.

172 IRA NELSON MORRIS 12.44 GMC 11.65: Scrapped Terminal Island.

173 GEORGE W. NORRIS 12.44 GMC 6.3.46: Grounded and wrecked at Tenega Shima, Japan. Total loss.

174 ARTHUR M. HULBERT 12.44 GMC 67: Scrapped New Orleans.

175 M.E. COMERFORD 12.44 GMC 2.70: Sold for scrapping at Portland, Ore.

176 FELIX RIESENBERG 12.44 GMC 51: TRANS-ATLANTIC. 59: NENANA.

177 ROBERT J. BANKS 12.44 GMC Completed as VADSO. 46: LIBREVILLE. 52: AFROS. 62: THEODOROS LEMOS. 6.67: Scrapped Shanghai.

178 WILLIAM F. JERMAN 12.44 GMC 6.60: Scrapped Baltimore.

179 WILLIAM COX 1.45 GMC 68: Scrapped Wilmington, NC.

180 GEORGE R. POOLE 1.45 GMC 3.58: Scrapped Baltimore.

181 HAROLD O. WILSON 1.45 GMC 47: NORTH BEACON. 55: TEXMAR. 30.12.60: Broke in two and abandoned after grounding off Grays Harbour, Wash. Total loss (voyage Seattle/New York – pulp). 10.61: Both parts refloated, towed to and scrapped at Aberdeen, Wash.

182 JAMES BENNETT MOORE 1.45 GMC Reserve Fleet, site 4.

183 HALTON R. CAREY 2.45 GMC 63: Scrapped Philadelphia.

184 HAROLD DOSSETT 2.45 GMC Reserve Fleet, site 1.

185 PATRICK S. MAHONY 2.45 GMC 2.60: Scrapped Baltimore.

186 RICHARD A VAN PELT 2.45 GMC Completed as BELGIAN EQUALITY. 47: CAPITAINE HEUSERS. 62: ST.DEMETRIUS.

187 CHARLES C. RANDLEMAN 3.45 GMC 31.8.45: Ashore and wrecked Apo Reef, Philippine Islands, (voyage Liverpool/Manila/San Jose).

188 ROY JAMES COLE 3.45 GMC 51: NORTH HEAVEN. 54: DELPHI. 64: EVER STRENGTH. 67: GRAND DOLPHIN.

189 PATRICK B. WHALEN 3.45 GMC 49: CHRISTAM. 50: BOSTONIAN. 51: CHRISTAM. 52: MANHATTAN. 53: SEADRAGON. 53: CHARLES C. DUNAIF. 61: WILDERNESS. 62: Lengthened at Cadiz to 511½ ft (8,457 grt). 67: DEBBIE MAE. 5.67: Scrapped Kaohsiung.

BUILT BY J.A.JONES CONSTRUCTION CO, WAINWRIGHT YARD, PANAMA CITY, FLA.

This yard – another one with six slipways – was established under similar circumstances to the Brunswick yard, but here the Jones Company had, in the first instance, wished to set up its facilities in South Carolina. It was 'persuaded' by the Maritime Commission that Panama City offered the better site.

In 1940, and before the advent of the shipyard, the whole of the Panama City community numbered some 20,000 persons. By 1943 wartime expansion had increased this figure threefold. The company built not only the shipyard and the ships, but also constructed essential houses, restaurants and other facilities with which to attract the workers. It also delivered the milk to the community and supplied to them tools, trucks and furniture – on credit. Any losses so incurred whilst performing these services were permitted to be offset against profits from the company's other activities.

In October 1943 the yard interrupted its standard Liberty ship programme and commenced the construction of a special type of Liberty for the carriage of army tanks, (Z-EC2-S-C2 type). Later it reverted to its normal programme with Yard No 24.

Fifteen months later it turned to the production of a further special Liberty type, that for the transport of boxed aircraft, (Z-EC2-S-C5 type), but even this new programme was itself interrupted in May 1945 by the building of six T1 type tankers.

The Wainwright yard is now used by a firm of shipbreakers (see Part Seven, The 'Mothball' Fleet) and it is here that work is now carried out in the rolling and reshaping of plates taken from 'scrapped' Liberties, for their inclusion in new barge construction.

Liberty ship output: 66 vessels at an average cost of 2,020,000 dollars each, plus 8 for the transport of army tanks and 28 for the transport of boxed aircraft.

USMC hull numbers: MCE 1519–1533 (Yard Nos 1–15)
1542–1551 (” ” 24–33)
2293–2333 (” ” 34–74)

1 E. KIRBY SMITH 3.43 AME 56: Scrapped Baltimore.

2 NEWTON D. BAKER 4.43 GMC 11.68: Scrapped Panama City.

3 JOHN BASCOM 4.43 AME 2.12.43: Sunk during German air attack on Bari Harbour, Italy. 48: Wreck sold to Genoa shipbreakers.

4 WILLIAM J. BRYAN 5.43 GMC 8.65: Scrapped Kearny, NJ.

5 JOSEPH M. MEDILL 5.43 GMC 6.60: Scrapped Baltimore.

6 ELIHU ROOT 6.43 GMC Reserve Fleet, site 1.

7 JOHN HAY 6.43 AME 2.61: Scrapped Seattle.

8 DWIGHT L. MOODY 7.43 VIW Reserve Fleet, site 5.

9 PETER ZENGER 7.43 VIW 8.66: Scrapped Portland, Ore.

10 HARRIET HOSMER 10.43 F & S 43: LUNA AKS 7 (USN). 46: HARRIET HOSMER. 5.65: Scrapped Richmond, Cal.

11 DUNCAN U. FLETCHER 8.43 VIW 47: PERICLES. 19.4.66: Aground on Ajax Reef, 23 miles south of Miami, 25.25N 80.07W (voyage Swansea/Tampa – ballast). 28.4.66: Refloated, damaged, towed Turtle Cay thence New Orleans. Later proceeded on voyage to Far East. 9.66: Sold for scrap, renamed TUNG HO for delivery trip from Kobe. 12.66: Scrapped Kaohsiung.

12 DOLLY MADISON 10.43 F & S 50: ARCH-ANGELOS. 15.11.64: Sprung leak, sank off Baja California, 24.10N 111.50W (voyage Philadelphia/

Tokio – scrap iron).

13 ROBERT LANSING 8.43 F & S 2.68: Scrapped Green Cove Springs, Fla.

14 VICTOR HERBERT 9.43 GMC 47: LE VERDON. 11.63: Scrapped Bremerhaven.

15 JULIUS ROSENWALD 9.43 F & S 46: ASSIRIA. 54: ROBERTO PARODI. 9.7.62: Aground on Colorado Reefs, Cuba. 17.7.62: Refloated, damaged, proceeded Havana. Later completed voyage Tampa/Tokio with scrap iron. 3.63: Scrapped Yokosuka.

24 WALTER L. FLEMING 1.44 F & S 1.61: Scrapped Baltimore.

25 SALVADOR BRAU 1.44 GMC 3.67: Scrapped New Orleans.

26 HAROLD T. ANDREWS 2.44 F & S 50: Sold commercial (same name). 57: BASSA. 58: SPIROS MAKRIS. 58: ROBERTVILLE. 59: VALIANT ENTERPRISE. 60: Arrived Colombo, disclaimed by owners and abandoned. 12.2.60: Placed under arrest. During the following six years frequently became danger to navigation in harbour, repeatedly breaking adrift and often listing dangerously due to water in holds. 66: Sold to Japanese shipbreakers but enforced to stay in port due to outstanding Port Dues of over Rs.400,000. 11.66: Reported sold to Hong Kong shipbreakers, but 2.67: Again in imminent danger of sinking. 23.2.67: Towed to a position 6 miles north of harbour and allowed to sink in position clear of navigational areas.

27 RUSSELL SAGE 2.44 F & S 47: GLEN I. 54: MARIA DOLORES. 66: NIKOLIS M. 16.2.67:

Grounded Catalina Shallow, Isabela de Sagua, Cuba, 23.00N 79.58W. 23.2.67: Refloated, proceeded Sagua, laid up. Compromised total loss.

28 WILLIAM W. LORING 3.44 GMC 2.62: Scrapped Baltimore.

29 MINNIE M. FISKE 3.44 F & S 6.66: Scrapped Portland, Ore.

30 JOHN W. GRIFFITHS 3.44 IFM 47: DINO. 64: IMERA. 5.65: Scrapped Spezia.

31 AUGUSTUS SAINT-GAUDENS 3.44 GMC 47: NAZARENO. 2.67: Scrapped Spezia.

32 JOHN M. BROOKE 3.44 GMC 47: STAVROS COUMANTAROS. 60: SPETSAI. 4.68: Scrapped Kaohsiung.

33 REBECCA LUKENS 4.44 IFM 44: MAJOR GENERAL HERBERT A.DARGUE (US Army aircraft repair ship). 1946: REBECCA LUKENS. Reserve Fleet, site 2.

34 ALANSON B. HOUGHTON 4.44 GMC Reserve Fleet, site 4.

35 SAMUEL G. FRENCH 4.44 IFM 47: EGMOND. 47: ALCYONE. 58: NICOS S.

36 THOMAS LE VALLEY 4.44 IFM 44: MAJOR GENERAL WALTER R.WEAVER (US Army aircraft repair ship). 1946: THOMAS LE VALLEY. 3.70: Sold to Genoa shipbreakers.

37 JOSEPHINE SHAW LOWELL 4.44 IFM 46: ALBARO. 60: Reported sold for scrap, but afterpart joined at Genoa to forepart of PRIARUGGIA (ex SAMDARING, qv), length 511½ ft (8,481 grt) and resultant vessel named ALBARO. 63: AIGAION. 9.68: Scrapped Osaka.
Note: The owner of ALBARO and PRIARUGGIA (Porto Figari of Genoa) operated another Liberty ship, the BOCCADASSE, which was also constructed from halves of two different ships (NATHANIEL BACON/BERT WILLIAMS II, qv).

38 RICHARD V. OULAHAN 5.44 IFM 16.9.45: Ashore and wrecked in Buckner Bay, Okinawa, during typhoon. (Voyage Seattle/Okinawa — army stores). Later reported scrapped by China Merchants & Engineers Inc, China.

39 JAMES H. KIMBALL 5.44 IFM 47: AZUERO.

24.12.68: Engine trouble during heavy weather, grounded in Gironde Estuary. Broke in two, sank. (Voyage Recife/Bordeaux — sugar).

40 STEPHEN FURDEK 5.44 IFM Reserve Fleet, site 4.

41 JEAN RIBAUT 5.44 IFM Reserve Fleet, site 1.

42 LE BARON RUSSELL BRIGGS 5.44 IFM Reserve Fleet, site 1.

43 HOWARD GRAY 6.44 GMC 47: ITALICO. 59: AZAHAR. 69: Scrapped Shanghai.

44 H.H. RAYMOND 6.44 GMC Reserve Fleet, site 1.

45R T.A. JOHNSTON 12.44 F & S Reserve Fleet, site 1.
Note: This ship was the replacement of a previous one which was damaged by fire on the stocks and subsequently dismantled.

46 M. MICHAEL EDELSTEIN 6.44 GMC 47: MILANO. 53: MILANO II. 54: MERIT. 63: MARIA BOTTIGLIERI.

47 WILLIAM D. BLOXHAM 6.44 GMC 47: SISTIANA. 63: SOCLYVE.

48 NICK STONER 6.44 GMC 7.64: Scrapped Panama City.

49 WILLIAM E. DODD 7.44 GMC 47: MILBANK. 58: THANKSGIVING. 2.67: Scrapped Hirao.

50 J.H. DRUMMOND 7.44 WISC 47: HUGO DE GROOT. 50: AMSTELPARK. 59: SEVERN RIVER. 65: ANGELIC. 25.7.66: Grounded in fog off Nojima Saki, Chiba, 35.02N 140.01E (voyage Vancouver, Wash./India — grain). 26.7.66: Abandoned. 6.8.66: Refloated, towed Tateyama. Sold. 12.66: Scrapped Yokosuka.

51 WILLIAM L. WATSON 7.44 GMC 47: PANORMUS. 62: AL KHEIR. 22.7.66: Put back to Bombay with cracks in hull (voyage Bombay/Baltimore — ore). Temporary repairs only, and 13.9.66: Proceeded on voyage. Sold. 2.67: Scrapped Spezia.

52 JOHN R. McQUIGG 7.44 GMC 46: VILLA DI BRUGINE. 56: BRUGINE. 59: PLATE EXPORTER. 67: PANEXPORTER. 12.68: Scrapped Whampoa.

53 CARL E. LADD 8.44 WISC 12.67: Scrapped Portland, Ore.

54 PEDRO MENENDEZ 8.44 GMC 11.66: Scrapped New Orleans.

55 GEORGE ADE 8.44 GMC 9.68: Scrapped Panama City.

56 EDWARD K. COLLINS 8.44 GMC 47: CHELA-TROS. 61: SOULIOTIS II. 63: UNIVERSAL TRADER. 9.3.68: Afire, grounded Ceylon, 06.24N 81.47E (voyage Gdynia/Chittagong – grain). Abandoned. 18.3.68: Broke in two, submerged. Total loss.

57 C. FRANCIS JENKINS 9.44 F & S 47: IONIAN LEADER. 11.66: Scrapped Kaohsiung.

58 RAYMOND V. INGERSOLL 9.44 GMC 47: SNELAND I. 59: KOPALNIA ZABRZE.

59 BENJAMIN F. COSTON 9.44 GMC 10.64: Scrapped New York.

60 WILLIAM P. DUVAL 9.44 GMC 47: VESUVIO.

61 STEPAS DARIUS 10.44 GMC 47: MANDO. 21.1.55: Aground and wrecked in fog between Men-A-Vaur and Golden Ball, Scilly Isles (voyage Hampton Roads/Ymuiden – coal).

62 ALEXANDER E. BROWN 10.44 F & S 47: MICHALAKIS. 63: GEORGAKIS. 64: HUMBOLDT. 11.66: Sold to Spanish shipbreakers. 2.12.66: Broke adrift from tug during heavy weather whilst on voyage to scrap-yard, grounded off Banjaard, Holland, 51.41N 03.32W. 4.12.66: Refloated, towed Flushing. 9.12.66: Voyage in tow recommenced. 1.67: Scrapped Santander.

63 CHIEF OSCEOLA 10.44 F & S 47: GEORGE D. GRATSOS. 26.7.65: Grounded in Chacao Channel, Chile. Refloated, severely damaged. Later proceeded Piraeus and laid up. 5.67: Scrapped Valencia.

64 RICHARD HALLIBURTON 10.44 F & S 61: Scrapped Kearny, NJ.

65 SAMUEL G. HOWE 10.44 F & S 7.69: Sold to New York shipbreakers.

66 GRANVILLE S. HALL 11.44 F & S 53: Converted to experimental minesweeper YAG 40 (same name, USN). Served as atomic fall-out sampling ship during Pacific tests, being fitted with 'bird-bath' collecting tubs on masts. Engines and steering were remotely controlled from a shielded interior compartment to permit entry of ship into dangerous radiation zones. Later used as storeship. 62: Reported in service as research ship. 7.68: Still in service.

67 STEPHEN SMITH 11.44 F & S 6.60: Scrapped Baltimore.

68 CHARLES D. WALCOTT 11.44 F & S 8.61: Scrapped Wilmington, NC.

69 ART YOUNG 11.44 F & S Reserve Fleet, site 5.

70 CHARLES H. MARSHALL 11.44 F & S 49: POLARUS PIONEER. 51: TRANSAMERICAN. 54: GERTRUD THERESE. 59: PACIFIC THUNDER. 60: TRANSMARINER. 61: SANTA EMILIA. 63: Returned to US Govt. Reserve Fleet, site 2.

71 RANSOM A. MOORE 11.44 F & S Reserve Fleet, site 5.

72 SOTER ORTYNSKY 12.44 F & S 1.60: Scrapped Baltimore.

73 BJARNE A. LIA 12.44 F & S 49: FREDERIC C. COLLIN. 58: PENN TRADER. 64: HANOVER. 66: SANTA SOPHIA. 66: SIGALPHA. 7.68: Scrapped Split.

74 WENDELL L. WILLKIE 12.44 F & S 2.70: Sold for scrapping at Mobile.

BUILT BY KAISER COMPANY

In the United States, in January 1942, there occurred a sudden need for additional shipyards for the construction of major types of ships to meet an increase of one third in the previous objectives.

One of these new yards was set up by the Kaiser group at Vancouver, across the Columbia River from Portland, Oregon, and in the following month the decision was taken to increase the original plans to a total of twelve slipways.

The yard was constructed on land owned by the local ports authority; it was leased at the nominal fee of 300 dollars per year, and the final terms of leasing required the premises to be restored to 'as good a condition as before'.

In mid-1942, with the yard itself still under construction, the first ship on the stocks and the local labour supply almost exhausted, a big recruiting drive was directed not only to the mid-West and to the mountain states, but even to places as distant as New York. The subsequent influx of personnel tended, at first, to outstrip the available facilities and one service the commission was forced to provide was a private railway to carry workers to the shipyard.

The yard was awarded a large contract for Liberty ships, but soon this was changed to one for military types. More than a hundred Liberty contracts were cancelled and this gave a large surplus of Liberty material, which was transferred to the Oregon shipyard. Nevertheless, included in the yard's facilities was a 'deckhouse' slip, situated between the slipways and the outfitting dock. Thus, whilst in transit between these two points ships would pause to have previously-completed 210 ton deckhouses installed. The deckhouses were complete, even to the installation of the funnel, before they emerged for fitting. This system, in fact, set another trend in assembly line methods, but was of no real importance to the Liberty programme, being mainly used on military constructions. It also gained unfavourable publicity when, in October 1942, the first 210 ton assembly was accidentally dropped twenty feet on to a waiting hull!

The first of the military types, (LST's) were ordered in May 1942 and for these newbuildings the yard ceased work on Liberties after launching and completing only two and clearing away two more which were only half-built. Immediately afterwards fifty escort carriers were ordered, yard facilities were again improved and it became one of the best emergency yards in both its equipment and its layout.

In early 1943 the yard was able to revert to Liberty building long enough to construct eight more vessels, but with these ships the propelling machinery was installed at Portland by the Oregon Shipbuilding Corporation. Later still the yard turned its production to military transports.

After the war the leasing arrangements were revised and the yard became one of the commission's four stand-by yards for use in future emergency. In 1960 it was sold to the Gilmore Steel Corporation for some 3¼ million dollars.

Liberty ship output: 10 vessels.

USMC hull numbers: MCE 353– 356 (Yard Nos 1 – 4)
    357– 392 cancelled.
    393– 400 (Yard Nos 41–48)
    401– 417 cancelled.
    1075–1098 cancelled.
    1123–1152 cancelled.

1 GEORGE VANCOUVER 7.42 GMC Reserve Fleet, site 5.

2 ELIAS HOWE 7.42 WISC 24.9.43: Sunk by Japanese submarine (I.10) torpedo in Arabian Sea, 11.35N 45.50E.

3 – – – Construction of hull not completed; scrapped whilst still on stocks.

4 – – – Construction of hull not completed; scrapped whilst still on stocks.

41 JUAN DE FUCA 1.43 GMC 9.12.44: Damaged by Japanese air attack in Pacific. 30.12.44: Further damaged by aerial torpedo, run aground. 4.45: Again damaged during air attacks. Later refloated, towed to Subic Bay, Philippines, and 9.45: ARANER IX 226 (USN). 10.46: JUAN DE FUCA. 1950: Sold to Shanghai shipbreakers but 26.9.50: Intercepted by Chinese Nationalist warships in international waters 180 miles north of Keelung when in tow of tug MARGARET MOLLER (voyage Hong Kong/ Shanghai). Tug ordered to cut loose tow; vessel cast adrift in position 28.05N 123.00E. Later reported drifting off Chinese coast north of Formosa, but

no further trace and presumed sunk in Formosa Strait.

42 FRANCISCO CORONADO 1.43 GMC 3.62: Scrapped Baltimore.

43 JOHN CABOT 1.43 GMC 12.59 Scrapped Portland, Maine.

44 MOSES CLEAVELAND 2.43 OWI 4.61: Scrapped Everett, Wash.

45 JOSEPH HENRY 2.43 OWI 3.60: Scrapped San Francisco.

46 LAURA KEENE 2.43 OWI Reserve Fleet, site 2.

47 WALTER REED 2.43 IFM 7.67: Scrapped Mobile.

48 RUSSELL A. ALGER 3.43 IFM Reserve Fleet, site 5.

BUILT BY MARINSHIP CORPORATION

In February 1942 a directive from President Roosevelt demanded the 'impossible' task of increasing the tempo of shipbuilding; and the previous objective of 18 million tons of new shipping during 1942-1943 was raised to 24 million, this being 9 million tons in 1942 and 15 million in 1943.

The shipways planned and those already in operation were quite unable to increase their schedules to this great extent and it became necessary to add further slips to these existing yards and to create new yards in new locations. On the East Coast the first few Liberties had been launched; on the Gulf the yards were only just commencing, and on the West Coast, Liberties were ready for launching and British 'Ocean' type vessels were under rapid construction. So it was to this latter area that the Maritime Commission turned for the siting of another yard and, due to its outstanding record, they again looked to the Kaiser organisation for assistance.

Each company within Kaiser's Six Services group was invited to submit proposals for a new yard which would produce ships during 1942.

The initial contract for the yard and for Liberty ships was given to the W.A. Bechtel partnership. Management and workers were enlisted from allied companies, steel for the first ships was fabricated more than 400 miles away at the associated Calship plant and the venture, under the name of the Marinship Corporation, was successful in getting ship construction under way very rapidly.

The yard was located at Sausalito, Marin County, California, on the north west side of San Francisco Bay and was situated so as to attract labour which could not easily reach other shipyards across the bay. It was commenced as a six-way yard, this number then being presumed to be adequate for maintaining a steady production flow.

In accordance with the terms of the contract the first delivery was made in the latter part of 1942, and before the end of this same year five vessels had been completed.

At sea at around this same time shipping losses had reached a high peak and attacks by the enemy on oil tankers had proved so successful that there was a dire need of further tanker tonnage. Accordingly, the Marinship yard, designed to produce a relatively simple ship, was given large additions to its facilities and had its remaining Liberty contracts cancelled. These were replaced by ones which authorised construction of various types of tankers.

Liberty ship output: 15 vessels

USMC hull numbers: MCE 1223—1234   (Yard Nos 1—12)
1235—1237   (”   ”   16—18)
1238—1272   cancelled.

1 WILLIAM A. RICHARDSON 10.42 JHIW 10.69: Scrapped Panama City.

2 WILLIAM T. COLEMAN 11.42 JHIW Reserve Fleet, site 2.

3 WILLIAM KENT 12.42 JHIW 12.64: Scrapped Oakland, Cal.

4 JOHN MUIR 12.42 JHIW 5.66: Scrapped Portland, Ore.

5 PHILIP KEARNY 1.43 JHIW
7.69: Scrapped Tacoma.

6 THOMAS HART BENTON 1.43 JHIW
6.69: Scrapped Kearny, NJ.

7 LYMAN BEECHER 12.42 JHIW 46: HAI CHEN.
51: ASIAN. 11.67: Scrapped Kaohsiung.

8 FRANCIS PRESTON BLAIR 1.43 GMC 15.7.45:
Ashore and wrecked (reportedly whilst avoiding a
Japanese submarine) on Saumarez Reef, off Queens-
land, 21.49S 153.39E (voyage Manila/Sydney — ballast).

9 MARK HOPKINS 2.43 JHIW 7.68: Scrapped
Terminal Island.

10 ANDREW D. WHITE 2.43 JHIW 62: Scrapped
Portland, Ore.

11 SEBASTIAN CERMENO 3.43 JHIW 27.6.43:
Sunk by submarine (U.511) torpedo in Indian
Ocean, 28.50S 50.20E.

12 PETER DONAHUE 3.43 JHIW 9.63: Scrapped
Oakland, Cal.

16 SUN YAT-SEN 4.43 JHIW 47: LIVIA. 50:
TELAMON. 58: POLIKOS. 60: POLICOS. 9.68:
Scrapped Hirao.

17 HENRY DURANT 7.43 JHIW 3.63: Scrapped
Portland, Ore.

18 JACK LONDON 8.43 JHIW 47:
CHRISTOSTOMIS. 48: NORA. 58: BELLATRIX.
4.68: Scrapped Spezia.

BUILT BY NEW ENGLAND SHIPBUILDING CORPORATION

The two yards of the New England Shipbuilding Corporation — the East and the West — commenced operations under different titles and until early 1942 were separated by rigid legal conditions.

The origins of the east yard date from 1941, for in that year two American concerns contracted to build 'Ocean' type ships for British account. One such concern was the Todd-Bath Iron Shipbuilding Corpn, whose new yard of the dry dock (or basin) type was situated on the edge of a residential community to the east of Cushing Point, South Portland, Maine. Here, launchings were not down slipways; instead the basins were flooded and the ships were floated out.

Whilst this yard was still under construction the management was instructed by the Maritime Commission to build another new yard next to it. Situated to the west of Cushing Point, it was to be operated by the South Port-land Shipbuilding Corporation and became known as the West yard.

After Pearl Harbour the restrictive legalities of the separate yards were swept aside and both yards were operated as one enterprise by this corporation.

The Todd-Bath Corporation, when building the 'Ocean' ships carried out much of the steel fabrication at the new plant of the Bath Iron Works (the parent company of both these South Portland yards) and which, owing to the lack of local expansion facilities, was situated some 30 miles away from the shipyard. The East yard, therefore, was given no great fabricating or assembling areas.

The construction of the four-way West yard was more orthodox, the ships being launched from normal slipways. As a four-way yard it seemed ideal but the increase to six slips was really more of a contraction than expansion, for there was then no additional space and the extra slips just had to be fitted in with the others. However, all the materials for their construction had to be taken across the four original ways, and this greatly interfered with the shipbuilding activities.

Here also, the layout failed to include fabricating shops, the intention again being to have this work carried out by Bath Iron Works and thence carried by road from the nearest railhead, some three miles away. But production by this method was too slow and when the call came for an all-out effort these plans were of little use. In March 1942 the commission took an active part in providing the facilities to enable ships to be pre-assembled in large units instead of being put together piece by piece.

Soon the inhabitants of Cushing Point found the two shipyards encroaching into their community and con-demnation of property became commonplace as expansion demanded fabricating shops, housing for the workers and even a railroad. During the summer of 1942 eviction and demolition proceeded rapidly but long disputes and troubles over construction, supervision, facilities, fees and management all ensured that the deliveries of ships from the first contract were very much delayed. In fact, after the first Liberty keel was laid in September 1942 the East yard found itself building in some of its basins for British account and in the others for the Maritime Commission.

Collectively however, the delays were so great that the commission contemplated termination of the agreements by default, but their bitter experiences at Savannah (see Southeastern Shipbuilding Corpn) indicated the wiser course of a negotiated settlement. So, in early 1943 – at which time the yards had been without a clear authority for nearly a year – Todd Shipyards Corporation took over control from Bath Iron Works and installed new management 'on trial' for a period of sixty days.

During this time the two yards, now with the New England title, were expected to fabricate and erect 36,000 tons of steel and to deliver twelve vessels.

By March 1943 their performances were considered by the commission to be satisfactory, and soon after further expansion occurred with the acquisition from the USN of land to the north of the area.

These new shipbuilders, who failed to become one of the fastest yards and were in fact one of the two slowest, nevertheless considerably reduced their total number of manhours per ship. Over a two-year period commencing in May 1943 the figure dropped from 760,000 to 410,000, and after many early troubles the yard finally constructed an excellent number of vessels.

Liberty ship output (both yards) :　236 vessels at an average cost of 1,892,000 dollars each,
plus 8 for the transport of boxed aircraft.

Vessels built at the East Yard:

USMC hull numbers :

Built by South Portland Shipbuilding Corpn,	MCE	768–792	(Yard Nos 252–276, varied order).
		814–815	(” ” 238–239)
		820–821	(” ” 244–245)
		823–824	(” ” 247–248)
		827	(” ” 251)
Built by New England Shipbuilding Corpn,	MCE	793–800	(” ” 277–284)

For the remaining constructions at this yard the MCE number was used as the yard number.

238 FERDINANDO GORGES 8.43 WPM 1.65: Scrapped Panama City.

239 JOHN MASON 8.43 HMC 47: VIKDAL. 47: MATHEOS. 65: FOSMING. 3.11.65: Aground on Castle Island, Bahamas, 22.06N 74.19W (voyage Japan/Philadelphia – steel). 8.11.65: Refloated, towed Philadelphia. CTL. Sold 3.66: Scrapped Valencia.

244 CYRUS H.K. CURTIS 9.43 GMC 58: Scrapped Baltimore.

245 WILLIAM DE WITT HYDE 9.43 HMC Completed as HELLAS. 11.68: Scrapped Hirao.

247 PARK HOLLAND 9.43 VIW 47: OCEAN LIBERTY. 28.7.47: Caught fire whilst discharging at Brest. Towed to shallow water of St.Marc Banks and abandoned. French gunboat attempted to sink ship by gunfire before cargo exploded, but after 8th shell the vessel blew up. Wreckage strewn over wide area of port and vessel almost completely destroyed, except extreme afterpart from No 5 hold which remained on its side sunk into the mud. (Voyage Baltimore/Antwerp – nitrate and general).

248 PEREGRINE WHITE 9.43 HMC 47: LIGURIA. 49: MATTEO MARSANO. 57: GOLFO DI NAPOLI.

The US Navy's electronics repair ship *Belle Isle* in July 1945, shown with a pontoon barge and a tug alongside. (New England, East yard, Yard no 3070)

The *Charles A. Young* as the *African Monarch*, departing from Hampton Roads in March 1969. (New England, West yard, Yard no 2202)

Zebulon B. Vance as a military transport at New York in 1947. (North Carolina, Yard no 1)

The Yugoslav *Trebisnjica* discharging in the river Thames prior to her ill-fated voyage to the West Indies. (North Carolina, Yard no 178)

251 JOHN FAIRFIELD 10.43 VIW 1.68: Scrapped Portland, Ore.

252 WILLIAM P. FESSENDEN 12.42 HMC 2.59: Scrapped Portland, Ore.

253 WINSLOW HOMER 12.42 EMC Reserve Fleet, site 8.

254 JOHN MURRAY FORBES 1.43 VIW 4.67: Scrapped Portland, Ore.

255 AUGUSTINE HEARD 1.43 WPM 47: HERVA. 52: MODENA. 56: ALASKA. 4.68: Scrapped Hong Kong.

256 EDWARD PREBLE 1.43 HMC 43: VOLANS AKS 9 (USN). 1947: EDWARD PREBLE. 2.65: Scrapped Oakland, Cal, as VOLANS.

257 CALVIN COOLIDGE 2.43 GMC 1.65: Scrapped Wilmington, Del.

258 JOHN A. DIX 2.43 HMC 47: SAINT TROPEZ. 61: MARIASMI. 6.68: Scrapped Kaohsiung.

259 WALTER E. RANGER 2.43 HMC Reserve Fleet, site 2.

260 NOAH WEBSTER 2.43 DEW Reserve Fleet, site 4.

261 ELIPHALET NOTT 2.43 DEW 54: Scrapped Baltimore.

262 ISAAC SHARPLESS 3.43 VIW Reserve Fleet, site 2.

263 TIMOTHY DWIGHT 3.43 CAC 10.69: Scrapped Kearny, NJ.

264 EZRA CORNELL 3.43 DEW 47: ISIGNY. 65: ODYSION. 22.12.67: Abandoned sinking after developing leaks 200 miles west of Luderitz. 23.12.67: Sank south of Walvis Bay, approx. 25.49S 11.13E (voyage Ancona/Shanghai).

265 FRANCIS AMASA WALKER 4.43 JIC 65: Scrapped Panama City.

266 JOSEPH WARREN 4.43 JIC 47: MARIA STATHATOS. 65: ALBATROS.

267 EMMA WILLARD 4.43 DEW 47: SAINT NAZAIRE. 61: AGHIA SOPHIA. 3.68: Scrapped Hong Kong.

268 WILLIAM PHIPS 4.43 HMC Reserve Fleet, site 4.

269 CHARLES SUMNER 4.43 HMC 62: Scrapped Philadelphia.

270 ASA GRAY 5.43 WPM 9.67: Scrapped Kearny, NJ.

271 MARY LYON 5.43 HMC 47: NESTOS. 61: KASTELA. 3.8.63: Developed leaks after sailing in pack ice; abandoned in Hudson Strait, 63.39N 77.20W. 4.8.63: Sank off Cape Wolstenholme, 500 miles NNE of Churchill (voyage Churchill/UK — grain).

272 HENRY WILSON 5.43 GMC 5.62: Scrapped Wilmington, NC.

The builders nameplate from this vessel was presented to the town of Natick on behalf of the Liberty Ship Memorial Programme.

Known as the 'Natick Cobbler', Henry Wilson, was prominent in Massachusetts and in national politics from 1840 until his death in 1873. A strong opponent of slavery, he was active in the formation of the Republican Party. Elected to the Senate for four consecutive terms, he resigned from that body in 1872, upon his election as Vice President of the United States, to serve with General U.S. Grant.

He died in office the following year, whilst still engaged on writing the final volume of his history of the Rise and Fall of Slave Power in America.

273 CHARLES W. ELIOT 5.43 HMC 28.6.44: Struck mine and sunk off Juno beach, Normandy.

274 HARRIET BEECHER STOWE 6.43 VIW 10.67: Scrapped Panama City.

275 EUGENE HALE 6.43 WPM 2.68: Scrapped Panama City.

276 ROBERT TREAT 6.43 HMC 67: Scrapped New Orleans.

277 GEORGE CLEEVE 6.43 HMC 22.2.44: Damaged by submarine (U.969) torpedo off Bona. Beached. Total loss. Later salved and 2.52: Scrapped Savona.

278 JACOB H. GALLINGER 6.43 HMC 46: CERNAY. 60: LEFTRIC. 1.7.67: Engine trouble when leaving Mormugao, grounded in harbour. Re-floated, drifted on to breakwater, broke in two, sank. (Voyage Mormugao/Europe — ore). 5.69: Sold Bombay shipbreakers and scrapped 'in situ'.

279 SILVESTER GARDINER 7.43 WPM 47: JANE STOVE. 56: CAPETAN PETROS. 65: KYRAMARTHA. 8.69: Scrapped Hirao.

280 ROBERT JORDAN 7.43 WPM 47: PLOUHAR-NEL. 14.6.59: On fire in holds when near Newport Rock; put back to Suez, (voyage Havre/Djibouti — phosphate and chemicals). Later proceeded to destination, still with traces of fire. 26.6.59: Fire extinguished. Vessel later laid up in damaged condition at Nantes. 11.63: Scrapped Aviles.

281 ROBERT ROGERS 7.43 WPM Reserve Fleet, site 2.

282 EZRA WESTON 8.43 HMC 8.8.44: Sunk by submarine (U.667) torpedo in English Channel, 50.47N 05.03W.

283 JOSIAH QUINCY 8.43 WPM Reserve Fleet, site 2.

284 WILLIAM STURGIS 8.43 HMC 10.69: Scrapped Kearny, NJ.

2188 SUMNER I. KIMBALL 9.43 HMC 16.1.44: Sunk by submarine (U.960) torpedo in N.Atlantic, approx. 52.35N 35.00W (voyage Loch Ewe/New York).

2189 ROBERT L. VANN 9.43 VIW 1.3.45: Struck mine and sank near Ostend, 51.23N 02.51E.

2193 OMAR E. CHAPMAN 10.43 HMC Reserve Fleet, site 2.

2194 GEORGE POPHAM 11.43 GMC 67: Scrapped Philadelphia.

2196 BARRETT WENDELL 11.43 SMF Completed as SAMPHILL. 47: BERBICE. 58: NIKOLAS S. 3.67: Scrapped Kaohsiung.

2197 WILLIAM PITT PREBLE 11.43 SMF Completed as SAMRICH. 47: CUFIC. 53: SANTA ELISABETTA. 67: STAR. 5.68: Scrapped Kaohsiung.

2199 PERCY D. HAUGHTON 11.43 HMC Completed as SAMTRENT. 47: Returned to US Govt. 4.62: Scrapped Mobile.

2200 ROBERT R. RANDALL 12.43 VIW 47: OUISTREHAM. 68: Renamed JUPITER for voyage to Shanghai breakers, but resold for further trading, renamed AVIAN. 5.69: Scrapped Shanghai.

2201 MERCY WARREN 12.43 HMC Reserve Fleet, site 1.

2205 WEBB MILLER 12.43 HMC 47: STUGARD. 61: LILY C.MICHALOS. 3.69: Scrapped Whampoa.

2206 GEORGE S. WASSON 12.43 HMC 31.1.44: Damaged by British mine 5 miles from Smalls; arrived Milford Haven same day (voyage Portland, Me./Avonmouth — general). 8.6.44: Sunk as 'Gooseberry I' breakwater blockship at Mulberry Harbour A beach-head, Verreville, Normandy. 16.7.44: Officially abandoned (foundered) after harbour was destroyed by the storms of 19–22.6.44.

2209 EUGENE E. O'DONNELL 12.43 HMC 47: SPINOZA. 47: LOENERKERK. 61: MARIKA.

2210 SAMDON 12.43 HMC 46: Returned to US Govt. 10.61: Scrapped Philadelphia.

2212 SAMYTHIAN 1.44 HMC 47: Returned to US Govt. 11.61: Scrapped Panama City.

2213 SUSAN COLBY 1.44 HMC 47: OLGA. 8.68: Scrapped Kaohsiung.

2214 SAMEARN 1.44 GMC 47: CLAREPARK. 50: ARGOLIB. 56: AFRICAN PRINCESS. 8.68: Scrapped Kaohsiung.

2218 SAMTEVIOT 2.44 HMC 47: Returned to US Govt. 2.61: Scrapped Baltimore.

2219 SARAH ORNE JEWETT 2.44 HMC 49: Sold commercial (same name). 51: NIKOS. 53: JOHN PAUL JONES. 54: NATIONAL LIBERTY. 59: MOUNT EVANS. 63: WYOMING. 63: YUCATAN. 65: EASTERN ARGO. 20.11.66: Stranded off Mapingil, Philippines. Refloated, damaged, towed to Jose Panganiban and later to Kaohsiung to complete voyage. 7.2.67: Arrived Keelung and laid up. 9.67: Scrapped Keelung.

2222 SAMTYNE 2.44 SMF 47: ARGENTINE TRANSPORT. 58: ARCHANDROS. 67: ZEPHYR. 12.68: Scrapped Hirao.

2223 SAMSTRAE 2.44 GMC 47: SNEATON. 8.67: Scrapped Shanghai.

2224 SAMDERWENT 3.44 SMF 47: CLAN MAC-FADYAN. 58: BETAVISTA. 68: VARUNA DEVI.

3005 SAMSPERRIN 3.44 HMC 47: Returned to US Govt. 11.61: Scrapped Panama City.

3006 ARTHUR SEWALL 3.44 HMC 29.12.44:
Damaged by submarine (U.772) torpedo in English
Channel; reached anchorage in Weymouth Bay
(voyage Seine/Mumbles). Later towed Portland,
Dorset; temporarily repaired. 11.5.46: Towed to
Bremerhaven. Loaded with obsolete chemical
ammunition and 12.10.46: Towed to sea and scuttled.

3008 PARK BENJAMIN 3.44 HMC 7.59: Scrapped
Seattle.

3009 SAMDERRY 3.44 GMC 47: HARPAGON. 58:
MARIA XILAS. 6.67: Scrapped Hirao.

3012 ELIJAH KELLOGG 4.44 HMC 47: OTHON.
27.6.52: Grounded outside Karachi harbour. 28.6.52:
Broke in two, sank. Total loss. (Voyage Philadelphia/
Karachi – coal).

3013 CHARLES DAURAY 4.44 HMC 47: EDWARD
O. McDONNELL JR. 47: ENTERPRISE. 54: SILVER
WAKE. 56: SILVER FISH. 56: ARENELLA. 1.69:
Sold for scrapping at Spezia.

3016 RAYMOND B. STEVENS 4.44 GMC 61:
Scrapped Philadelphia.

3017 SAMWAKE 4.44 HMC 30.7.44: Sunk by E-boat
torpedo in English Channel, approx. 50.40N 00.31E.

3018 SAMORESBY 4.44 HMC 48: Returned to US
Govt. 1.60: Scrapped Baltimore.

An international tribute to Liberty ships was launched in
New York with the presentation to the Consul-General of
the Commonwealth of Australia of the builder's nameplate
from this vessel at the time of her scrapping. Ultimate
recipient of the nameplate was the Museum and Record of
Australian-built Merchant Ships, at Largs Bay, South
Australia. At this Museum the plate became a central item
in a special Liberty Ship display.

3021 SAMSUVA 5.44 VIW 29.9.44: Sunk by
submarine (U.310) torpedo off North Cape, 72.58N
23.59E. (Voyage Kola Inlet/Loch Ewe).

3022 SAMIDWAY 5.44 HMC 47: SCHOLAR. 64:
KOSTANTIS YEMELOS. 3.69: Scrapped Mihara.

3024 SAMSMOLA 5.44 GMC 47: Returned to US
Govt. 1.68: Scrapped Oakland, Cal.

3025 GEORGE HAWLEY 5.44 GMC 22.1.45:
Damaged by submarine (U.1199) torpedo near
Lizard, towed to Falmouth and beached, (voyage
Cherbourg/Mumbles). Later refloated and 14.6.46:

Towed to Bremerhaven. Loaded with obsolete
chemical ammunition and 10.46: Towed to sea and
scuttled.

3029 JOSEPH-AUGUSTIN CHEVALIER 6.44 GMC
47: MARINE MERCHANT. 14.4.61: Broke in two
in heavy seas and sank 40 miles south east of Portland,
Maine (voyage Port Sulphur/Portland – sulphur).

3030 WILLIAM LEAVITT 6.44 GMC 10.64:
Scrapped New Orleans.

3031 LOT MORRILL 6.44 VIW Completed as
MIAOULIS. 47: MARIAM. 60: ARISTON. 10.67:
Scrapped Sakai.

3034 THOMAS H. SUMNER 6.44 GMC 47: SJOA.
51: ASTRID NAESS. 53: FLISVOS II. 63: MARIELY.
65: OMEGA. 13.11.66: Developed cracks in hull,
abandoned 2,000 miles south east of Honolulu,
06.57N 125.53E (voyage Philippines/Venezuela –
ore). Presumed foundered.

3035 JOSEPH C. LINCOLN 7.44 GMC 51: PURPLE-
STAR. 54: EPOS. 60: REA. 66: PELIKAN. 10.66:
Scrapped Kaohsiung.

3037 GEORGE L. FARLEY 7.44 HMC Reserve
Fleet, site 5.

3038 ANDREW J. NEWBURY 7.44 HMC 12.55:
Converted to YAG (same name, USN). (Conversion
type EC2-S-22a). USN Reserve Fleet, site 4.

3042 LOT M. MORRILL 8.44 HMC 5.67: Scrapped
Portland, Ore.

3043 JOSEPH N. DINAND 8.44 GMC 47: WOLVE-
RINE STATE. 54: OMNIUM TRADER. 58: DANA.
59: PACIFIC VENTURE. 60: VILLAGE. 63:
Returned to US Govt under Ship Exchange Act, in
exchange for the Victory ship BARTLESVILLE
VICTORY. Later transferred to USN for disposal,
and scuttled.

After transfer to the USN this vessel was loaded at the US
Naval Ammunition Pier at Earle, New Jersey, with 7,348
tons of obsolete ammunition and other assorted cargo.
Towed to the deep water dumping site on September 17,
1964, she sank some 3½ hours after her seacocks were
opened. Five minutes after she sank three violent explosions
were heard and felt and an oil slick and debris came to the
surface, and it was obvious that her cargo had detonated as
a result of pressure or from impact. These explosions were
sufficient to make seismic recordings all over the world and
as a result the US Naval Research Office decided that certain
future scuttlings would be used as scientific experiments.

3044 HAROLD I. PRATT 8.44 VIW Reserve Fleet, site 5.

3047 THOMAS BRADLEE 8.44 VIW 65: Scrapped New Orleans.

3048 WILLIAM TYLER 8.44 HMC Reserve Fleet, site 2.

3051 ARCHIBALD R. MANSFIELD 9.44 VIW 6.66: Scrapped Wilmington, NC.

3052 GALEN L. STONE 9.44 HMC 48: YANKEE STAR. 49: DEMOSTAR. 50: OCEANSTAR. 60: PYRGOS. 2.67: Scrapped Kaohsiung.

3056 ROBERT B. FORBES 9.44 VIW 11.65: Scrapped Portland, Ore.

3057 FRANK P. REED 9.44 HMC 8.69: Sold to Philadelphia shipbreakers.

3058 MICHAEL ANAGNOS 10.44 HMC 47: GRIGORIOS C. III.

3060 LOAMMI BALDWIN 10.44 GMC 65: Scrapped Philadelphia.

3061 JAMES T. FIELDS 10.44 VIW 3.70: Sold for scrapping at Portland, Ore.

3064 CHARLES TUFTS 10.44 GMC 51: MARINER. 55: CONFIANZA. 56: TIRYNS. 64: ROSSANA. 65: DEMETRA. 67: BLUE PENNANT. 9.68: Scrapped Sakaide.

3065 KENYON L. BUTTERFIELD 10.44 WPM Reserve Fleet, site 1.

3069 WINTHROP L. MARVIN 11.44 GMC 51: JOHN B.KULUKUNDIS. 60: PRINCIE. 63: LOYAL BREAKERS. 5.67: Arrived Kaohsiung for scrap, but 8.67: renamed PACMERCHANT for one voyage only. 10.67: Scrapped Kaohsiung.

3070 BELLE ISLE 11.44 WPM Completed as BELLE ISLE AG 73 (USN). 51: BELLE ISLE AKS 21 (USN). 4.60: Stricken from USN, no further trace, presumed scrapped USA.

3071 LIGURIA 11.44 VIW Completed as LIGURIA AKS 15 (USN). 47: Returned to USMC. USN Reserve Fleet, site 6.

3073 COASTERS HARBOR 11.44 GMC Completed as COASTERS HARBOR AG 74 (USN). 51: COASTERS HARBOR AKS 22 (USN). 3.61: Scrapped Sakai.

3074 EDMOND MALLET 11.44 GMC 51: ILIAMNA.

3077 THOMAS F. MEAGHER 12.44 VIW 8.69: Sold to Philadelphia shipbreakers.

3078 JOSEPH LEE 12.44 GMC 10.64: Scrapped Portland, Ore.

3082 JOSHUA SLOCUM 12.44 VIW 8.65: Scrapped Portland, Ore.

3083 JULIA P. SHAW 12.44 WPM 8.64: Scrapped Mobile.

3084 PAUL BUCK 12.44 GMC 3.66: Scrapped Mobile.

3086 F. SCOTT FITZGERALD 1.45 GMC 5.62: Scrapped Panama City.

3087 EZRA MEECH 1.45 GMC 51: LIBERTY FLAG. 56: RION. 58: MAURICE GEORGE. 58: PACIFIC CARRIER. 60: MONTEGO SKY. 61: ASPIS. 63: HELEN K. 9.67: Scrapped Hirao.

3090 LEON S. MERRILL 2.45 WPM 10.65: Sold to New Orleans shipbreakers. Vessel cut in two; stern portion scrapped by 7.67. Bow portion converted into a derrick barge.

3091 FRANCIS A. RETKA 2.45 GMC 51: LIBERTY BELL. 56: I.R.LASHINS. 57: SOUTHPORT. 64: Converted into partial container ship, renamed ODUNA. 26.11.65: Aground and abandoned at Cape Pankor, Unimak Isle, Alaska. Total loss. (Voyage Adak/Seattle — army equipment and containers).

3095 WILLIAM BEVAN 2.45 VIW Reserve Fleet, site 2.

3096 CHARLES N. COLE 3.45 GMC 51: AUDREY II. 55: PACIFIC TRADER. 63: WARM SPRINGS. 66: BARBARA. 8.67: Scrapped Hong Kong.

3097 GEORGE A. LAWSON 3.45 WPM 51: Sold commercial (same name). 57: PENN MARINER. 61: UNION ATLANTIC. 20.6.64: Sprung leak 270 miles north east of Ceylon, 12.07N 85.38E. 21.6.64: Abandoned and sank, (voyage Calcutta/Kobe — iron ore).

3099 RICHARD D. LYONS 3.45 GMC 46: Sold commercial (same name). 2.68: Scrapped Hirao.

3100 GEORGE N. DRAKE 3.45 GMC Completed as CARL OFTEDAL. 47: BRANT COUNTY. 54: MATANG. 56: HEDWIGSHUTTE. 60: SARONIS. 1.68: Scrapped Kaohsiung.

3102 LAWRENCE T. SULLIVAN 4.45 WPM Completed as BELGIAN AMITY. 47: CAPITAINE LIMBOR. 62: CAPITAINE. 62: NEVADA.

3103 JOSEPH CARRIGAN 4.45 VIW 10.9.45: Damaged by mine off Labuan; reached anchorage at Manila (voyage Morotai/Labuan). CTL. Sold 5.48: Scrapped Shanghai.

3107 ELWIN F. KNOWLES 4.45 GMC 47: PEACH TREE STATE. 55: ZUIDER ZEE. 61: WEST-CHESTER. 64: MERCANTILE WAVE. 64: GRAND STAR. 68: Scrapped Kaohsiung.

3108 ERNEST L. DAWSON 5.45 GMC 46: PONT L'EVEQUE.

3109 OLIVER WESTOVER 5.45 GMC 47: SETE. 68: Renamed ALLISON for delivery trip to breakers. 6.68: Scrapped Hirao.

3112 ALLEN G. COLLINS 6.45 GMC 47: LYON. 54: BASIL II. 63: EVER PROSPERITY. 26.2.65: Aground on Isie Reef, west coast of New Caledonia (voyage Miike/New Caledonia – ballast). Total loss.

3113 JOHN ROBERT GORDON 6.45 GMC 47: SAINT MARCOUF. 60: SPRINGWATER. 61: SEA-CREST. 5.6.63: Aground near Barcelona (voyage Boston/Genoa – scrap). 6.7.63: Refloated, seriously damaged; towed to destination. Sold 10.63: Scrapped Spezia.

3115 HAROLD H. BROWN 6.45 GMC 47: PONT AUDEMER. 64: VALFER. 65: VESPER. 13.12.65: Explosion in engine room, caught fire and abandoned in Mediterranean, 37.00N 01.38W (voyage Marseilles/Abidjan). 15.12.65: Salved, towed in to Carthagena. CTL. Sold. 5.66: Scrapped Carthagena, Spain.

3116 STANLEY R. FISHER 6.45 WPM 47: MARINE COURIER (bulk carrier, 6,625 grt). 8.65: Scrapped Castellon.

3118 FREDERICK AUSTIN 5.45 WPM Completed as DODEKANISOS. 47: AUDREY.

Vessels built at the West Yard:

USMC hull numbers:

Built by South Portland Shipbuilding Corporation,

Built by New England Shipbuilding Corporation,

MCE 201–213	(Yard Nos 201–213)	
333–338	(” ” 217–222)	
MCE 214–216	(” ” 214–216)	
339–340	(” ” 223–224)	
801–813	(” ” 225–237)	
816–819	(” ” 240–243)	
822	(” ” 246)	
825–826	(” ” 249–250)	

For the remaining constructions at this yard the MCE number was used as the yard number.

201 JOHN DAVENPORT 6.42 CB 7.60: Scrapped Philadelphia.

202 JOHN WINTHROP 7.42 CB 24.9.42: Sunk by submarine (U.619) torpedo in N.Atlantic, approx. 56.00N 31.00W (voyage Clyde/New York).

203 THOMAS HOOKER 7.42 CB 5.3.43: Abandoned after heavy weather damage; broke in two and foundered in N.Atlantic 53.20N 47.00W.

204 ETHAN ALLEN 8.42 CB 3.60: Scrapped Baltimore.

205 JOSIAH BARTLETT 10.42 CB 10.67: Scrapped Terminal Island.

206 WILLIAM KING 10.42 GMC 6.6.43: Sunk by submarine (U.198) torpedo off South Africa, 30.25S 34.15E.

207 JOHN CARVER 11.42 CB 23.4.45: Fuel tank exploded whilst vessel under repair at Philadelphia; sank. Refloated, towed Baltimore and laid up. 49: Scrapped Hoboken, NJ.

208 WILLIAM BRADFORD 12.42 HMC 6.60: Scrapped Philadelphia.

209 WILLIAM BREWSTER 12.42 HMC 63: Scrapped Kearny, NJ.

210 LOU GEHRIG 1.43 GMC 66: Scrapped Kearny, NJ.

211 DANIEL WEBSTER 1.43 GMC 10.1.44: Damaged by aircraft torpedo off Oran; towed in and beached. (Voyage Hampton Roads/Naples). CTL. Sold. Later salved and 9.48: Scrapped Carthagena.

212 WILLIAM PIERCE FRYE 2.43 HMC 29.3.43: Sunk by submarine (U.610) torpedo in N.Atlantic, 56.56N 24.15W,(voyage Halifax/UK).

213 HANNIBAL HAMLIN 3.43 GMC Reserve Fleet, site 5.

214 JOHN SULLIVAN 4.43 GMC 6.63: Scrapped Baltimore.

215 JOHN CHANDLER 4.43 HMC 47: ROCHEFORT.

216 JOHN HOLMES 4.43 DEW 47: NIDARHOLM. 50: TISTA. 53: SUHAE-HO. 58: SUHAE. 1.69: Scrapped Pusan.

217 JAMES G. BLAINE 9.42 CB 12.69: Scrapped Kearny, NJ.

218 HERMAN MELVILLE 10.42 CB 4.60: Scrapped Jersey City.

219 JULIA WARD HOWE 12.42 CB 27.1.43: Sunk by submarine (U.442) torpedo off Azores, 35.29N 29.10W (voyage USA/Gibraltar).

220 ANNE BRADSTREET 1.43 HMC 47: LA PALLICE. 5.69: Scrapped Hamburg.

221 JOHN TRUMBULL 3.43 GMC 47: ABBEVILLE. 60: FEDE. 61: Re-engined at Nantes to oil engine by

At. & Ch. de Bretagne, renamed PAGAN.

222 RICHARD HOVEY 4.43 GMC 29.3.44: Sunk by Japanese submarine (I.26) torpedo and gunfire in Indian Ocean, 16.40N 64.30E.

223 EMILY DICKINSON 5.43 DEW 1.69: Sold for scrapping at Kearny, NJ.

224 EUGENE FIELD 5.43 WPM 60: Scrapped Baltimore.

225 THOMAS W. HYDE 5.43 GMC 10.64: Scrapped New Orleans.

226 GEORGE F. PATTEN 5.43 GMC 3.70: Sold to Seoul, Korea shipbreakers.

227 WILLIAM PEPPERELL 6.43 HMC 12.69: Scrapped Portland, Ore.

228 THOMAS B. REED 6.43 GMC 66: Scrapped Kearny, NJ.

229 JOSHUA L. CHAMBERLAIN 6.43 GMC 11.66: Scrapped New Orleans.

230 JEREMIAH O'BRIEN 6.43 GMC Reserve Fleet, site 6.

231 JOHN A. POOR 6.43 HMC 19.3.44: Sunk by submarine (U.510) torpedo in Indian Ocean, 13.58N 70.30E. (Voyage Karachi/USA — Ilmenite sand).

232 HARRY A. GARFIELD 7.43 HMC 45: BELGIAN'DYNASTY. 47: CAPITAINE FRANKIGNOUL. 59: HONESTAS. 64: MASTER ELIAS. 11.3.65: Aground on Burias Island, Philippines, 12.49N 123.17E. (Voyage Japan/Manila). 15.3.65: Refloated, damaged; towed Manila. Sold. 8.65: Scrapped Hirao.

233 ARTHUR L. PERRY 7.43 GMC 57: Scrapped Seattle.

234 NELSON DINGLEY 7.43 VIW 47: ITALTERRA 53: Re-engined at Taranto to oil engine by Fiat. 66: BAYPORT.

235 JAMES BOWDOIN 8.43 WPM Reserve Fleet, site 2.

236 HENRY JOCELYN 8.43 GMC Reserve Fleet, site 2.

237 BARTHOLOMEW GOSNOLD 9.43 HMC 47: SEABREEZE. 59: SKJELNES. 61: JOHN G.L.

64: SWIFT RIVER. 65: KALLITHEA. 10.66: Scrapped Sakai.

240 ANNA HOWARD SHAW 9.43 GMC 5.67: Scrapped Tacoma, Wash.

241 TOBIAS LEAR 9.43 WPM Completed as FORT ORANGE. 47: BLYDENDYK. 57: TRANSILVANIA. 65: MOUNT ATHOS. 11.3.67: Grounded on coast of Rio Grande do Sul, 30.31S 50.20W (voyage Tampa/ Port Alegre). Salvage improbable, compromised TL.

242 WILLIAM H. TODD 9.43 HMC Completed as AMERIKI. 56: ELLINIS. 67: Scrapped Sakai.

243 JOHN N. ROBINS 10.43 HMC 47: LE LAVAN-DOU. 63: KETTARA VIII. 64: Scrapped Osaka.

246 THOMAS CLYDE 10.43 GMC 47: GIEN. 61: MARNIPO. 12.1.63: Aground on Zincirbozan Bank, Dardanelles. Broke in two. Total loss. (Voyage Constantza/Alexandria — şugar).

249 ENOCH TRAIN 10.43 GMC 66: Scrapped New Orleans.

250 WILLIAM BLACKSTONE 10.43 HMC Completed as SAMTUCKY. 48: WILLIAM BLACK-STONE. 2.62: Scrapped Panama City.

2190 JEREMIAH L. CHAPLIN 11.43 GMC Completed as SAMAKRON. 47: JEREMIAH L.CHAPLIN. 59: Reported scrapped Baltimore.

2191 ELIAS H. DERBY 11.43 SMF Completed as SAMLONG. 3.8.44: Damaged by (E-boat?) torpedo in approaches to Thames Estuary, towed into Gravesend. CTL. Later towed River Blackwater; laid up. Sold. 1.49: Scrapped Hendrik Ido Ambacht.

2192 MARY WILKINS FREEMAN 11.43 HMC 47: ORIONE. 2.66: Scrapped Spezia.

2195 J. WILLARD GIBBS 11.43 HMC 8.67: Scrapped Portland, Ore.

2198 JAMES MANNING 12.43 HMC 3.61: Scrapped Beaumont, Texas.

2202 CHARLES A. YOUNG 12.43 GMC Completed as SAMSPRING. 47: BERESINA. 56: AFRICAN MONARCH. 11.69: Scrapped Split.

2203 PELEG WADSWORTH 12.43 SMF Completed as SAMTAMPA. 23.4.47: Aground and wrecked on Sker Point, near Port Talbot, Glamorganshire, after dragging anchors in gale (voyage Middlesborough/ Newport — ballast). Total loss.

2204 BRONSON ALCOTT 12.43 VIW Completed as SAMAVON. 47: PACIFIC NOMAD. 54: NIKOLOS. 60: STAMATIS. 3.11.66: Grounded 4 miles south of Madras harbour in typhoon. 10.11.66: Wrecked during a further typhoon. Total loss. (Voyage Madras/Calcutta — wheat).

2207 EDWARD KAVANAGH 1.44 GMC 53: Converted at Yokosuka to experimental minefield sweeper YAG 38 (no name, USN). 60: Sold to US buyers, presumed scrapped.

2208 GEORGE T. ANGELL 1.44 HMC 46: FIRENZE. 57: SILENO. 60: IRIS. 4.69: Scrapped Spezia.

2211 EDWARD H. CROCKETT 1.44 GMC 29.9.44: Sunk by submarine (U.310) torpedo in Barents Sea, 72.59N 24.26E (voyage Kola Inlet/ Loch Ewe).

2215 RENALD FERNALD 2.44 HMC 51: AMEROCEAN. 56: MARINE PROGRESS. 26.4.63: Stranded Puerto Rico. Later refloated, damaged; towed San Juan. (Voyage Guanica/Philadelphia). Sold. 9.63: Scrapped Bordentown, NJ.

2216 SAMANNAN 2.44 HMC 47: OREGON STAR. 52: LAPLACE. 53: SAN PANTELEIMON. 27.3.67: Adrift in storm at Kobe; struck tower and buoy; severely damaged. Sold. 5.67: Scrapped Yokosuka.

2217 WASHINGTON ALLSTON 2.44 HMC 46: THORSBECKE. 47: LUTTERKERK. 62: MARIA DESPINA. 18.3.66: Aground outside Alexandria during storm. 20.3.66: Broke in two. Total loss. (Voyage Shanghai/Alexandria). Forepart (225 ft) later refloated, and 68: converted by Timsah SB Co, Alexandria, into a 2-deck derrick barge by addition of longitudinal bulkheads and one aft to form a square stern, renamed EL ALAMEIN (5,488 grt).

2220 FREDERICK W. TAYLOR 2.44 HMC 1.65: Scrapped Panama City.

2221 SAMWYE 3.44 SMF 47: WILLOWBANK. 56: CAVALA. 57: TRANSKIPPER. 62: CONSTRUC-TOR. 64: KIMON. 66: COSTOULA. 2.8.67:

Aground on North Reef, Malindi, 65 miles north of Mombasa, 03.16S 40.10E (voyage Bombay/Durban — ballast). Abandoned but 6.10.67: Refloated and towed Mombasa. CTL. 5.69: Towed Hong Kong and scrapped.

3004 STANTON H. KING 3.44 HMC 12.64: Scrapped Panama City.

3007 SAMDARING. 3.44 HMC 47: PACIFIC RANGER. 52: SAN DIMITRIS. 58: PRIARUGGIA. 60: Forepart joined at Genoa to afterpart of ALBARO (ex JOSEPHINE SHAW LOWELL, qv); resultant vessel with a length of 511 ft (8,481 grt) and named ALBARO. 63: AIGAION. 9.68: Scrapped Osaka.

3010 LILLIAN NORDICA 3.44 HMC 9.65: Scrapped Wilmington, NC.

3011 BELGIAN TENACITY 4.44 HMC 47: CAPITAINE COSTERMANS. 60: SUDALISEO. 6.68: Scrapped Vado.

3014 SAMADRE 4.44 GMC 47: MARIA DE LARRINAGA. 64: MELETIOS.
7.69: Scrapped Sakaide.

3015 SAMBANKA 4.44 HMC 47: Returned to US Govt. 67: Scrapped Philadelphia.

3019 GEORGE ELDRIDGE 4.44 HMC 58: Scrapped Baltimore.

3020 SAMADANG 4.44 HMC 48: Returned to US Govt. 9.68: Scrapped New Orleans.

3023 HADLEY F. BROWN 5.44 VIW 20.3.45: Damaged by mine in North Sea (voyage Barry/Ghent). Towed into River Scheldt; repaired. Reserve Fleet, site 2.

3026 JOHN CHESTER KENDALL 5.44 HMC Reserve Fleet, site 2.

3027 JOSEPH I. KEMP 5.44 GMC 49: SEA LEADER. 56: CHELSEA. 56: ADOLPH SPERLING. 61: Lengthened at Tokio to 511½ ft (8,508 grt) re-named CYCLONE. 66: MYSTRAS. 29.6.66: Grounded at full speed near Elbe L.V. Refloated, severely damaged; towed Cuxhaven thence Rostock (voyage Chimbote/Rostock — fishmeal). CTL. Sold. 10.66: Scrapped Santander.

3028 JOSEPH SQUIRES 5.44 HMC Reserve Fleet, site 6.

3032 HARRIET TUBMAN 6.44 GMC Reserve Fleet, site 5.

3033 ERNEST W. GIBSON 7.44 GMC 51: WEST-CHESTER. 53: NORTH PILOT. 57: PILOT. 57: KORTHI. 60: ROGO. 66: KORTHI.

3036 ARAM J. POTHIER 6.44 VIW Reserve Fleet, site 5.

3039 AUGUSTUS P. LORING 7.44 HMC Reserve Fleet, site 2.

3040 B. CHARNEY VLADECK 7.44 VIW 47: SARAYA. 49: RIO GRANDE. 56: ARCHON RAPHAEL. 23.5.67: Aground Musha Island, near Djibouti, 11.44N 43.11E. (Voyage Sunderland/Shanghai). 17.6.67: Refloated, towed Djibouti. 27.2.68: Broke adrift from moorings 3 miles from Musha Island Lighthouse, sank. 1.69: Reported to have broken in two.

3041 JAMES SULLIVAN 7.44 HMC 8.65: Scrapped Kearny, NJ.

3045 EDWARD E. SPAFFORD 7.44 HMC Reserve Fleet, site 5.

3046 MARCUS H. TRACY 8.44 HMC Reserve Fleet, site 4.

3049 GEORGE N. SEGER 8.44 HMC 11.67: Scrapped Portland, Ore.

3050 MICHAEL MORAN 8.44 HMC Circa 62: Presumed scrapped. No further trace.

3053 WILLIAM LYON PHELPS 8.44 HMC 64: Scrapped Philadelphia.

3054 C.H.M. JONES 9.44 VIW 61: Scrapped Kearny, NJ.

3055 FERDINAND GAGNON 9.44 HMC 63: Scrapped New Orleans.

3059 ELIJAH COBB 9.44 GMC 11.69: Scrapped Philadelphia.

3062 ROBERT R. McBURNEY 9.44 HMC 11.62: Scrapped Panama City.

3063 EDWARD L. LOGAN 10.44 VIW 47: AMERICAN EAGLE. 57: ATLANTIC ROBIN. 63: DIAMANTIS GAFOS. 4.12.67: Abandoned, sinking, in heavy weather off Trinidad, 00.45S 41.53W.

Presumed sank. (Voyage Tampa/Bombay — fertiliser).

3066 ABRAHAM ROSENBERG 10.44 GMC 51:
WESTERN OCEAN. 55: TRANSWESTERN. 55:
SANTA MADRE. 61: TUSCANY. 2.12.62: Aground
on Ladd Reef, 08.40N 111.40E. CTL. Salvage attempts
abandoned. (Voyage Hong Kong/Borneo — ballast).

3067 WILSON B. KEENE 10.44 WPM 16.4.47:
Wrecked in Texas City docks in explosions caused by
Liberty ship GRANDCAMP (ex BENJAMIN R.
CURTIS, qv) and other vessels.

3068 WILLIAM A. DOBSON (I) 10.44 GMC
Completed as IOLANDA AKS 14 (USN). 47:
Returned to US Govt. USN Reserve Fleet, site 6.

3072 BERT WILLIAMS (I) 11.44 GMC Completed
as BELGIAN UNITY. 46: EARL A.BLOOMQUIST.
Reserve Fleet, site 1.

3075 MATTHEW SHEEHAN 11.44 VIW Reserve
Fleet, site 2.

3076 FREDERICK BOUCHARD 11.44 GMC 1.64:
Scrapped Tacoma, Wash.

3079 BERT WILLIAMS (II) 11.44 WPM 10.4.48:
Ashore 8 miles off Al Ashrafi Lighthouse, Gulf of
Suez. (Voyage Fremantle/Cobh — wheat). 18.4.48:
Refloated, towed Suez. Sold. 7.48: Broke loose
from tug whilst in tow to Venice; broke in two and
drifted ashore near Mersa Matruh. CTL. Forepart
later salved and towed to Genoa and 51: joined to
stern part of Liberty ship NATHANIEL BACON (qv)
and renamed BOCCADASSE (length 471½ ft, 7,740
grt). 1.63: Scrapped Spezia.

3080 CUTTYHUNK ISLAND 11.44 VIW
Completed as CUTTYHUNK ISLAND AG 75 (USN).
51: CUTTYHUNK ISLAND AKS 23 (USN). 9.60:
Scrapped Mobile.

3081 CALVIN AUSTIN 12.44 GMC
9.69: Scrapped Panama City.

3085 AVERY ISLAND 12.44 GMC Completed as
AVERY ISLAND AG 76 (USN). 51: AVERY ISLAND
AKS 24 (USN). 3.61: Scrapped Sakai.

3088 INDIAN ISLAND 12.44 WPM Completed as
INDIAN ISLAND AG 77 (USN). 51: INDIAN ISLAND
AKS 25 (USN). 61: Scrapped New Orleans.

3089 WILLIAM A. DOBSON (II) 12.44 GMC 49:

SEA WIND. 57: PACIFIC WIND. 59: PACIFIC
TIDE. 60: SEAMIST. 61: YAU LIN. 65: NATIONAL
SUCCESS. 67: GOOD WILLIE. 9.67: Scrapped
Keelung.

3092 KENT ISLAND 1.45 VIW   Completed as
KENT ISLAND AG 78 (USN). 51: KENT ISLAND
AKS 26 (USN). 11.61: Scrapped New Orleans.

3093 ALFRED E. SMITH 1.45 WPM 49: MOTHER
M.L. 55: CAPTAIN LYRAS. 57: OCEAN CHIEF.
63: UNION TRANSPORT.

3094 T.S. GOLD 2.45 GMC 51: CHIAN BREEZE.
54: DELPHIN. 64: EVER BLESSING. 19.4.67:
Grounded Saishu To, near Inchon, 33.21N 126.11E
(voyage Inchon/Keelung — ballast). 29.4.67: Refloated, severely damaged. Towed Shimonoseki,
thence Kure. Sold. 8.67: Scrapped Hirao.

3098 JAMES A. BUTTS 2.45 GMC 47: LONESTAR
STATE. 51: LONE STAR STATE. 55: ANNISTON.
57: CALDWELL. 58: RIDGEFIELD. 18.12.62:
Aground on Grand Cayman, 19.18N 81.50W (voyage
Maracaibo/US Gulf — ballast). Later broke in two.
Total loss.

3101 CLARENCE F. PECK 2.45 GMC 47: EURY-
STHEUS. 61: ESFAHAN. 61: FOTINI P. 6.67:
Scrapped Shodoshima, Japan.

3104 DONALD H. HOLLAND 3.45 GMC 51: Sold
commercial (same name). 52: SEADARING. 53:
IKE. 28.11.62: Struck reef off Jabal Zuqar Island,
Red Sea, 14.40N 42.49E. 29.11.62: Beached north
of East Point. Abandoned. CTL. (Voyage Sfax/Saigon
— phosphates).

3105 WILFRED R. BELLEVUE 3.45 GMC 47:
EDISON MARINER. 61: IOANNIS DASKALELIS.
64: ROCKPORT. 1.2.66: Abandoned in Pacific after
springing leak in heavy weather. Taken in tow but
5.2.66: Sank in tow 600 miles from Midway Island,
30.46N 168.23W (voyage Vancouver/Japan — ore).

3106 FRED E. JOYCE 3.45 GMC 51: GEORGE L.
DUVAL. 54: NATIONAL FREEDOM. 58: VALIANT
FREEDOM. 20.11.59: Aground off Isla de Pinos,
Cuba, (voyage Trinidad/Mobile). 19.12.59: Refloated,
towed in. Sold and 60: renamed MOUNT HOOD for
delivery to shipbreakers. 5.61: Scrapped Hirao.

3110 ELIAS REISBERG 3.45 GMC 47: TURCK-
HEIM. 5.68: Scrapped Hamburg.

3111 WILLIAM H. LANE 4.45 GMC 47: PORT-EN-BESSIN. 63: ISLAY. 63: PORT-EN-BESSIN. 68: Scrapped Shanghai.

3114 LEIF M. OLSEN 4.45 GMC Reserve Fleet, site 4.

3117 CHARLES H. SHAW 5.45 GMC Completed as LESVOS. 46: MEANDROS. 64: ALFIOS. 64: ATLANTIC SAILOR. 4.67: Scrapped Kaohsiung.

BUILT BY NORTH CAROLINA SHIPBUILDING COMPANY

On the East Coast of the USA, Baltimore was so well situated that it was included on every shipyard expansion-list issued by the Planning Board of the Maritime Commission, although in early times it was doubtful who would finally develop the new site there. At the same time and further south, potential sites in North Carolina were under consideration. In Virginia the Newport News Shipbuilding Company, one of the nation's leading builders, were fully engaged on navy contracts and there was no possibility of merchantmen being built on their slips.

Even as late as December 1940 this company still refused to be interested in handling a new shipyard, but in the following month it relented and reluctantly agreed to develop a yard at Wilmington, North Carolina.

Subsequent and rapid development enabled this, the third of three East Coast emergency yards, to sign its first Liberty contracts during the same month.

The parent company transferred some of its own personnel to the new yard, these ranging from management to apprentices, but many of the new executives appointed had no shipbuilding knowledge. Skilled labour was recruited locally and later, more workers were drawn from the surrounding farmlands. This latter labour force became renowned for its 'permitted' absenteeism, although it was usually proved that these workers were still assisting the war effort elsewhere, for at certain seasons they stayed at home to help on the farms. Nevertheless, on the whole the yard operated with a fairly stable labour force and it was considered to have done the best 'new-yard' job of the established shipbuilders.

The first ships constructed were dependent upon the parent company for the fabrication of their steel, thus the yard was originally equipped with only a small fabricating shop of its own. Later expansion of the facilities and an increase from six to nine slipways sharply increased the production rate but also increased the original anticipated cost of the yard from 7½ million dollars to a total in excess of 20 million.

The building time of the ships was very much more rapid than the contracts stipulated, the mild climate of the area allowing the pre-assembly of large sections in the open, and for each day saved the shipyard received the usual bonus payment. The contracts allowed an estimated 640,700 man-hours per ship, but deliveries were made in an average of only 403,400 hours, and this established a record for low costs in Liberty building, although it must be remembered that wages in this state were lower than in many other areas. The yard earned no large bonuses for sheer speed alone, but earned them by this massive saving in man-hours.

During 1943 the Maritime Commission had tried to induce various shipbuilders to change from the cost-plus contracts to fixed price contracts in an effort to get the yards to use their manpower more efficiently, but during that year only this North Carolina yard was persuaded so to do.

Also in the same year a prime factor in the reduced Liberty ship output was the award to the yard of a contract for sixty C2 type cargo ships, for which it began laying keels in mid-1943. Its Liberty ship construction ceased altogether in August 1943 and from this date the yard directed its attentions to even more vessels of the C2 type.

After the war this North Carolina yard was retained by the Maritime Commission as a stand-by yard for use in any future emergency.

Liberty ship output : 126 vessels at an average cost of 1,543,600 dollars each

USMC hull numbers : MCE 145– 169 (Yard Nos 1– 25)
217– 228 (" " 26– 37)

USMC hull numbers: MCE 860– 912 (Yard Nos 38– 90)
1967–2002 (”   ” 151–186)

1 ZEBULON B. VANCE 2.42 F & S 43: ZINNIA (Assigned name of hospital ship – not used). 11.43: Converted at Boston to US Army hospital ship (7,933 grt) and renamed JOHN L.MEANY. 1.46: Converted at New York to transport for war brides, military dependents and children with capacity for 476 persons; name reverted to ZEBULON B.VANCE. US Army Reserve Fleet, site 2.

2 NATHANAEL GREENE 2.42 F & S 23.2.43: Sunk by submarine (U.565) torpedo 40 miles off Oran, Algeria.

3 VIRGINIA DARE 3.42 GMC 12.3.44: Damaged by mine, towed to Tunis Bay. Broke in two. Total loss, (voyage New York/Suez). Later sold and salved and 10.48: Scrapped Barcelona.

4 WILLIAM HOOPER 3.42 GMC 4.7.42: Disabled by aircraft torpedo in Barents Sea. Abandoned. Shelled by naval escort but remained afloat. Sunk by submarine (U.334) torpedo 75.55N 27.14E (voyage Reykjavik/N.Russia – tanks and ammunition).

5 DANIEL MORGAN 3.42 GMC 5.7.42: Severely damaged by near misses during air attack off Novaya Zemlya. Abandoned. Later sunk by submarine (U.88) torpedo 75.08N 45.06E (voyage Reykjavik/N.Russia – tanks, ammunition, food and steel).

6 FRANCIS MARION 4.42 ASB 12.67: Scrapped Oakland, Cal.

7 CHARLES C. PINCKNEY 5.42 GMC 27.1.43: Sunk by submarine (U.514) torpedo off Azores, 36.37N 30.55 W (voyage USA/Casablanca).

8 JOHN CROPPER 6.42 GMC 11.65: Scrapped Portland, Ore.

9 WILLIAM MOULTRIE 6.42 GMC Reserve Fleet, site 4.

10 THOMAS SUMTER 6.42 GMC Reserve Fleet, site 4.

11 JEREMIAH VAN RENSSELAER 6.42 GMC 2.2.43: Sunk by submarine (U.456) torpedo off Cape Farewell, Greenland, 55.13N 28.52W (voyage Halifax/UK).

12 ARTEMAS WARD 6.42 GMC 24.3.44: Severely damaged in collision with t.e. tanker MANASSAS (43/10,195 grt) in position 51.52N 05.31W. Beached Angle Bay, Milford Haven. 8.6.44: Sunk as 'Gooseberry 2' breakwater blockship at Mulberry Harbour A beach-head, St. Laurent, Normandy. 16.7.44: Officially abandoned (foundered and destroyed) after harbour was destroyed by the storms of 19–22.6.44.

13 HUGH WILLIAMSON 7.42 GMC 18.6.46: Ashore on reef at entrance to Pernambuco harbour, Brazil. (Voyage Mobile/Buenos Aires). 27.6.46: Refloated and proceeded Rio de Janeiro, thence Santos. Later laid up, damaged. 6.48: Scrapped Baltimore.

14 WILLIAM R. DAVIE 7.42 GMC Reserve Fleet, site 4.

15 WILLIAM GASTON 7.42 GMC 26.7.44: Sunk by submarine (U.861) torpedo in S.Atlantic 26.42S 46.12W (voyage Rosario/Rio de Janeiro).
Note: This vessel was shown in early official US reports as a blockship at Normandy in June 1944. This report was erroneous and should have referred to the Liberty ship JAMES W.MARSHALL (qv), the name of which was omitted from the early blockship list.

16 WILLIAM A. GRAHAM 7.42 GMC Reserve Fleet, site 4.

17 JAMES K. POLK 8.42 TS 9.3.43: Damaged by submarine (U.510) torpedo off Dutch Guiana, towed to Trinidad (voyage Suez/Paramaribo). 12.45: Towed Mobile and laid up. CTL. 46: Scrapped USA.

18 ALEXANDER MARTIN 8.42 GMC 9.63: Scrapped Terminal Island.

19 RICHARD D. SPAIGHT 8.42 GMC 10.3.43: Sunk by submarine (U.182) torpedo off South Africa, 28.00S 37.00E. (Voyage Suez/Durban – steel).

20 SAMUEL ASHE 9.42 GMC 8.69: Sold to Philadelphia shipbreakers.

21 BENJAMIN WILLIAMS 10.42 TS 12.66: Scrapped Philadelphia.

22 JAMES TURNER 10.42 GMC 3.70: Sold to New York shipbreakers.

23 NATHANIEL ALEXANDER 10.42 GMC 47: SOLFA. 50: NORSE LADY. 53: DANIO. 62: TROYAN. 1.8.67: Arrived Colombo leaking and flooded after plating fractures (voyage Kosseir/ Whampoa – phosphate rock). Later proceeded and 29.10.67: Arrived Singapore for scrap, and 3.68: scrapped Singapore.

24 DAVID STONE 10.42 GMC 8.66: Scrapped Portland, Ore.

25 BENJAMIN SMITH 11.42 GMC 23.1.43: Sunk by submarine (U.175) torpedo off Sassandra, Africa, 04.05N 07.50W. (Voyage Charleston/Accra – general).

26 JOSEPH HEWES 5.42 TS 9.68: Scrapped New Orleans.

27 JOHN PENN 6.42 GMC 13.9.42: Sunk by aircraft torpedo in Greenland Sea, 76.00N 10.00E. (Voyage Lock Ewe/Archangel – military stores).

28 JOHN C. CALHOUN 6.42 GMC 7.9.44: Explosions in holds whilst berthed at Finschaven; beached Madan Island. 2.45: Refloated, towed from Langemak Bay to Mobile, thence Norfolk, Va. CTL. Partially stripped and laid up. 47: Reported scrapped USA.

29 EDWARD RUTLEDGE 7.42 GMC 9.61: Scrapped Mobile.

30 ABEL PARKER UPSHUR 7.42 GMC 6.66: Scrapped Wilmington.

31 WILLIAM HAWKINS 7.42 GMC .58: Scrapped Baltimore.

32 THOMAS PINCKNEY 9.42 GMC 6.60: Scrapped Baltimore.

33 ROGER WILLIAMS 9.42 GMC 47: SONATA. 51: AVRA. 61: THRASYVOULOS. 29.6.65: Last reported in position 09.03N 56.25E on voyage Madras/Constantza with iron ore. Untraced, presumed sunk.

34 JOHN DRAYTON 9.42 GMC 21.4.43: Sunk by Italian submarine DA VINCI south of Durban, 32.10S 34.50E.

35 JAMES B. RICHARDSON 10.42 GMC 16.12.51: Stranded in fog off Urville, west of Cherbourg. 17.12.51: Back broken. 23.12.51: Refloated, towed Cherbourg, (voyage Philadelphia/Cherbourg – coal).

Temporarily repaired, towed USA and laid up, damaged, in Reserve Fleet, site 1. 1.7.68: Scuttled with cargo of obsolete ammunition off New Jersey, approx 39.30N 71.00W.

36 PAUL HAMILTON 10.42 GMC 20.4.44: Sunk by aircraft torpedoes north of Algiers, 37.00N 03.20E (voyage USA/Bizerta – ammunition).

37 HENRY MIDDLETON 11.42 GMC Reserve Fleet, site 1.

38 COLLIS P. HUNTINGTON 11.42 F & S 3.68: Scrapped New Orleans.

39 CORNELIUS HARNETT 11.42 GMC 3.68: Scrapped Portland, Ore.

40 HENRY BACON 11.42 GMC 23.2.45: Sunk by aircraft torpedo in Barents Sea, 67.38N 05.00W (voyage Kola Inlet/Loch Ewe).

41 ABNER NASH 11.42 WPM .64: Scrapped Philadelphia.

42 JOSEPH ALSTON 11.42 WPM 7.67: Scrapped Richmond, Cal.

43 PAUL HAMILTON HAYNE 12.42 TS 47: GOVERNOR SPARKS. 49: DENISE. 58: CHIR-JUCA. 61: ISAAC MANN. 65: U.S. MERRIMAC. 66: ARLENE. 4.67: Scrapped Kaohsiung.

44 MARSHALL ELLIOTT 12.42 WPM 4.68: Scrapped Panama City.

45 JAMES IREDELL 12.42 WPM 14.7.43: Seriously damaged by submarine torpedo and aircraft bombs off Gela, Sicily. Later towed to UK. 8.6.44: Sunk as 'Gooseberry 2' breakwater blockship at Mulberry Harbour A beach-head, St Laurent, Normandy. 16.7.44: Officially abandoned (foundered) after harbour was destroyed by the storms of 19–22.6.44.

46 PENELOPE BARKER 12.42 GMC 25.1.44: Sunk by submarine (U.271) torpedo in Barents Sea, 73.20N 23.20W (voyage Loch Ewe/Kola Inlet – war supplies).

47 ALEXANDER LILLINGTON 12.42 GMC 1.61: Scrapped Hamburg.

48 RICHARD CASWELL 12.42 GMC 16.7.43: Sunk by submarine (U.513) torpedo off Paranagua, Brazil, 28.10S 46.30W.

49 POCAHONTAS 12.42 GMC 9.60: Scrapped Troon.

50 CHRISTOPHER GADSDEN 12.42 GMC 12.69: Sold for scrapping at New Orleans.

51 BETTY ZANE 1.43 GMC 47: ANASTASSIOS PATERAS. 63: ANASTASSIS. 2.68: Scrapped Moji.

52 JAMES J. PETTIGREW 1.43 GMC 5.60: Scrapped Baltimore.

53 DANIEL H. HILL 1.43 GMC 64: Scrapped Richmond, Cal.

54 GEORGE DAVIS 1.43 WPM 6.60: Scrapped Baltimore.

55 WALTER RALEIGH 1.43 F & S 12.67: Scrapped Kearny, NJ.

56 JOHN HARVEY 1.43 F & S 2.12.43: Sunk during German air attack on Bari Harbour, Italy, 41.06N 16.52E. 48: Wreck sold to Genoa shipbreakers.

57 ROBERT HOWE 1.43 WPM Reserve Fleet, site 1.
Note: This was the second Liberty ship to arrive in the Port of London — arriving from New York on 30.3.43.

58 NATHANIEL MACON 1.43 GMC 47: EVGENIA CHANDRIS. 17.8.52: Aground in fog off Aleutian Islands, 51.15N 179.07W, (voyage Moji/Victoria). Refloated and 27.8.52: Arrived Victoria, BC. CTL. Sold and repaired. 53: WILLIAM V.S.TUBMAN. 54: Lengthened at Kure to 511½ ft (8,582 grt). 59: PENN VANGUARD.
11.69: Scrapped Kaohsiung.

59 JOHN WRIGHT STANLY 1.43 F & S 43: LEIV ERIKSSON. 47: VINNI. 54: PROBITAS. 4.69: Scrapped Vado.

60 FRANCIS NASH 1.43 VIW 43: FRIDTJOF NANSEN. 60: OLGA.

61 EPHRAIM BREVARD 2.43 F & S Reserve Fleet, site 4.

62 GEORGE E. BADGER 2.43 GMC Reserve Fleet, site 2.

63 FLORA MACDONALD 2.43 GMC 30.5.43: Damaged by submarine (U.126) torpedo off Sierra Leone, 07.15N 13.20W. 1.6.43: Arrived Freetown; afire and beached. Fire later extinguished but vessel completely gutted and reported as a 'distorted mass of scrap'. Total loss. (Voyage Takoradi/Freetown, — general).

64 JAMES SPRUNT 2.43 GMC 10.3.43: Sunk by submarine (U.185) torpedo south of Cuba, 19.49N 74.38W (voyage Key West/Guantanamo).

65 MATT W. RANSOM 2.43 VIW 15.4.43: Damaged by submarine (U.117) torpedo off Casablanca, proceeded to Gibraltar, thence to UK. 8.6.44: Sunk as 'Gooseberry 1' breakwater blockship at Mulberry Harbour A beach-head, Verreville, Normandy. 16.7.44: Officially abandoned (foundered) after harbour was destroyed by the storms of 19—22.6.44.

66 FURNIFOLD M. SIMMONS 2.43 GMC 47: ELLEN MAERSK. 48: HADA COUNTY. 52: COMET. 12.68: Scrapped Sakaide.

67 EDWARD B. DUDLEY 2.43 GMC 11.4.43: Sunk by submarine (U.615) torpedo in Atlantic, approx 53.00N 38.00W (voyage Halifax/Liverpool).

68 WILLIE JONES 2.43 GMC 68: Reported in USN service. No further details.

69 JAMES MOORE 2.43 GMC 47: SEIN. 61: VELOS. 62: Re-engined at Nantes with oil engine by At. & Ch. de Bretagne. 64: FEDE.

70 ALFRED MOORE 3.43 GMC 2.61: Scrapped Bremerhaven.

71 WOODROW WILSON 3.43 GMC 2.60: Scrapped Philadelphia.

72 WILLIAM D. PENDER 3.43 GMC 2.60: Scrapped Baltimore.

73 WILLIAM D. MOSELEY 3.43 GMC 5.62: Scrapped Panama City.

74 DAVID L. SWAIN 3.43 GMC 47: SIBILLA. 63: SYBIL. 12.68: Scrapped Tsuneishi.

75 JONATHAN WORTH 3.43 GMC 10.69: Scrapped Panama City.

76 MATTHEW T. GOLDSBORO 3.43 GMC 12.69: Scrapped Kearny, NJ.

77 ELISHA MITCHELL 3.43 GMC 4.61: Scrapped Baltimore.

78 CHRISTOPHER GALE 3.43 GMC 62: Scrapped New Orleans.

79 WILLIAM L. DAVIDSON 3.43 GMC 9.3.46: Ashore on rocks 5 miles east of Okso Light, Norway (voyage Copenhagen/New York). Refloated, damaged.

Towed to Stavanger, Copenhagen and thence proceeded USA. 47: Sold to USN and used as hulk. No further trace, presume later scrapped.

80 WALKER TAYLOR 4.43 GMC 12.59: Scrapped Portland, Maine.

81 ROGER MOORE 4.43 GMC Reserve Fleet, site 1.

82 ROBERT ROWAN 4.43 GMC 11.7.43: Damaged by aircraft bombs and artillery fire off Gela, Sicily, 36.47N 14.30E. Caught fire and abandoned, (cargo ammunition). Blew up and sank. 2.48: Wreck sold Italy and scrapped.

83 THOMAS W. BICKETT 4.43 GMC 66: Scrapped Kearny, NJ.

84 HORACE WILLIAMS 4.43 GMC 47: ERASMUS. 47: LEMSTERKERK. 62: KYPROS. 65: STALO.

85 JOSE BONIFACIO 4.43 GMC Reserve Fleet, site 8.

86 THOMAS L. CLINGMAN 4.43 GMC 6.60: Scrapped Baltimore.

87 DAVID CALDWELL 4.43 GMC 4.9.46: Aground in storm 5 miles off La Coubre, near Bordeaux. Broke in three. Total loss. (Voyage Hampton Roads/Pauillac — coal).

88 WAIGSTILL AVERY 4.43 GMC 12.60: Scrapped Troon.

89 CORNELIA P. SPENCER 4.43 GMC 21.9.43: Sunk by submarine (U.188) torpedo in Indian Ocean, 02.08N-50.10E (voyage Aden/Durban).

90 WALTER HINES PAGE 5.43 GMC 45: OPOLE. 47: WALTER HINES PAGE. Reserve Fleet, site 2.

151 JOSEPH A. BROWN 5.43 GMC Reserve Fleet, site 2.

152 ROBERT F. HOKE 5.43 GMC 28.12.43: Damaged by Japanese submarine (I.26) torpedo in Arabian Sea (voyage Abadan/Mombasa). 1.44: Towed Oman; beached. Refloated. 14.1.44: Towed Aden. 28.1.44: Towed Massawa for discharge, but 6.44: Broke back; temporarily repaired. 27.7.44: Left in tow for Suez. 2.8.44: Arrived Port Sudan in distress due to previous damages. 30.9.44: Left in tow for Suez. Encountered heavy weather and cast adrift. 16.10.44: Sighted by RAF 550 miles north of

Massawa in 21.40N 37.16E. Salved and returned to Port Sudan. 20.11.44: Left in tow for Suez. 25.11.44: Arrived; drydocked, but CTL. Hull partially stripped and propeller and tailshaft removed. 25.12.44: Left in tow for Bombay. 45: Taken over by RN at Bombay for use as training ship. 5.47: Discarded by RN, beached Dharamtar Creek, Bombay — still with torpedo damage of a 40 ft hole in her side. Offered for sale. 6.49: Sold to local buyers and scrapped.

153 SALLIE S. COTTEN 5.43 GMC 43: OLE BULL. 59: SOUTH RIVER. 65: KRONOS. 3.67: Scrapped Tsuneishi, Japan.

154 JOHN OWEN 5.43 GMC 8.64: Scrapped Portland Ore.

155 PHILIP DODDRIDGE 5.43 GMC 47: FEGGEN. 61: THEODORA. 3.69: Scrapped Whampoa.

156 JOHN GRIER HIBBEN 5.43 GMC 46: BELFORT 66: KETTARA IX. 6.67: Scrapped Yokosuka.

157 KEMP P. BATTLE 5.43 GMC 47: GOVERNOR GRAVES. 52: SEAHERALD. 54: HERALD. 61: KORTHI. 65: EASTBOUND. 9.68: Scrapped Kaohsiung.

158 ROBERT DALE OWEN 5.43 GMC 47: KALLIOPI. 20.12.47: Struck mines off Rijeka; broke in three and sank, 45.08N 14.16E (Voyage Charleston /Rijeka — ballast).

159 JOHN P. MITCHELL 5.43 GMC Reserve Fleet, site 1.

160 CHARLES D. McIVER 6.43 GMC 23.3.45: Sunk by mine or submarine torpedo off Ostend, Belgium, 51.23N 03.05E.

161 JOHN M. MOREHEAD 6.43 GMC 47: GOVERNOR COMER. 49: POLARUS SAILOR. 51: ALBION. 56: JOSEPH FEUER. 58: ANNE QUINN. 65: BRAZOS TRADER. 6.66: Scrapped Bilbao.

162 HANNIS TAYLOR 6.43 GMC Reserve Fleet, site 2.

163 EDWARD RICHARDSON 6.43 GMC 55: Converted to YAG (same name, USN). (Conversion type EC2-S-22a). USN Reserve Fleet, site 2.

164 WILLIAM T. BARRY 6.43 GMC Reserve Fleet, site 4.

165 LEE S. OVERMAN 6.43 GMC 12.11.44: Sunk by mine off Le Havre, France.

166 THOMAS J. JARVIS 6.43 GMC 8.61: Scrapped Wilmington, NC.

167 JOSEPH LE CONTE 6.43 GMC 46: PANAMANTE. 65: TONY.

168 ARTHUR DOBBS 6.43 GMC 46: HAI LIEH. 56: CHI LUNG. 5.68: Scrapped Kaohsiung.

169 JOHN LAWSON 6.43 GMC 47: BEAUVAIS. 62: Converted at St. Nazaire to liquified gas carrier by the fitting of two methane gas cargo tanks. Used for experiments of 'free-standing' tanks of the type subsequently installed in the French gas tanker JULES VERNE (65/22,292 grt). 5.67: Scrapped Castellon.

170 HILARY A. HERBERT 7.43 GMC 6.4.47: Aground near Philippe Light, River Schelde. 13.4.47: Refloated, towed Antwerp, (voyage Hampton Roads/ Antwerp – coal). CTL. Sold and repaired. 48: PARITA III. 49: KATIE. 60: DOXA. 10.67: Scrapped Hamburg.

171 HUTCHINSON I. CONE 7.43 GMC 5.62: Scrapped Mobile.

172 LAWRENCE D. TYSON 7.43 GMC Reserve Fleet, site 2.

173 DAVID F. HOUSTON 7.43 GMC 7.69: Scrapped Mobile.

174 JOHN MERRICK 7.43 GMC 67: Scrapped Terminal Island.

175 CHARLES A. DANA 7.43 GMC Reserve Fleet, site 5.

176 CLEMENT CLAY 7.43 GMC 2.62: Scrapped Hirao.

177 THOMAS W. OWEN 8.43 GMC 64: Scrapped Kearny, NJ.

178 RICHMOND P. HOBSON 7.43 GMC 47: NUEVA ESPERANZA. 61: TREBISNJICA. 17.7.63: Aground on Hogsty Reef, north of Cabo Maysi, 21.36N 73.50W. Abandoned. Total loss. (Voyage Naples/Cuba – ballast).

179 CHATHAM C. LYON 8.43 GMC 5.67: Scrapped Kearny, NJ.

180 JAMES I. McKAY 8.43 GMC 46: HAI TIEN. 51: MARIA THERESA. 65: INGRID ANNE. 12.67: Scrapped Mukaishima.

181 JOHN N. MAFFITT 8.43 GMC 66: Scrapped Philadelphia.

182 GEORGE DURANT 8.43 GMC 7.61: Scrapped Philadelphia.

183 AUGUSTUS S. MERRIMON 8.43 GMC 10.57: Scrapped Baltimore.

184 MONTFORT STOKES 8.43 VIW Completed as SAMPHIRE. 47: MONTFORT STOKES. 4.62: Scrapped Chickasaw, Ala.

185 THOMAS POLLOCK 8.43 VIW 47: ELSA MAERSK. 49: GIERULV. 54: SUNLONG. 26.12.56: Abandoned, sinking, in North Sea 57.55N 04.40E (voyage Narvik/Rotterdam – iron ore). Presumed sunk.

186 JOHN BRANCH 8.43 VIW Completed as SAMBRIAN. 47: CLAN MACFARLANE. 61: NICHOLAS. 10.10.61: Aground and abandoned in typhoon at Hachinoe, Honshu, Japan, (voyage Kamaishi/Vancouver – ballast). 27.10.61: Refloated, towed Hachinoe harbour. CTL. Sold. 62: Scrapped Yokosuka.

BUILT BY OREGON SHIP BUILDING CORPORATION

Another of the shipyards established by the Kaiser organisation was the eight-way yard of the Oregon Ship Building Corporation at Portland. It was another of the nine yards approved in 1941 and from which 260 ships were expected to be delivered from their total of sixty-five slipways within a two-year period.

One of the first two West Coast yards in operation, it was entirely new and was designed specifically to mass-produce just one type of ship rapidly. Laid out to spacious plans, it included plate shops, assembly bays and extensive storage space. Rapid expansion soon increased the number of slips to eleven, and then to thirteen; but still further space was required and early in 1942 part of the storage area was used for another assembly bay. Small assemblies were made in this building, were then conveyed to the platens at the slipways and there joined into larger units. The increased layout presented many difficulties however, for material first passed to the fabricating shops, moved back to the assembly plant and then forward in sub-assemblies — round the shops — and to the ways. But this essential movement of material caused many transit problems and they were only resolved by use of a strictly regulated traffic control system. Nevertheless, although the yard layout violated the 'straight flow' of an ideal production line it still led many others with its speed records. Later it was further expanded and remodelled and only then did the yard achieve its own particular sensational and spectacular high-speed shipbuilding record. However, all this progress was only achieved at greatly increased cost, for whereas in June 1941 the anticipated cost of its eleven ways was 7¼ million dollars, the actual cost had, by December 1944, escalated to more than 25 million.

As with all shipbuilding contracts, those with this Oregon yard set time schedules for ship production. These the yard attained by about mid-1942 with their quota of ten ships per month. By mid-1943 they produced ships at the steady pace of one every seventeen days (their contracts still allowed twenty-three days) and during the whole of this same year the yard's output averaged sixteen ships per month.

Previously however, in 1942 (September 13–23) the yard had launched one ship (Yard No 581) only ten days after keel-laying. The Richmond No 2 shipyard responded to this with their world-record ship built in even faster time, but these extra-high-speed products were only 'show-piece' stunts and the pace was not maintained or even again contemplated.

The fees paid to shipbuilders were set by statute at a maximum of seven per cent of the ship-cost plus bonuses for speed/performance — but no greater than ten per cent in all.

In March 1941 the average cost of a Liberty ship was estimated at 1¾ million dollars, but as productivity from all the yards increased so the overall costs were reduced. Nevertheless some fifteen months later the contracts of the Oregon Ship Building Corpn. were still fixed at the high maximum fee of 140,000 dollars per ship. In December 1942 this fee was finally halved and four months later was still further reduced, to 60,000 dollars.

After June 1944 the nation's shipbuilding programme was at last given an 'urgency' rating for its manpower requirements and shipyards were more easily able to acquire their necessary quotas of workers. Within five months of this date this Oregon shipyard had increased its manpower from 27,800 to nearly 35,000 and only a few months later more than 31 per cent of its total labour force were women workers.

Overall, the yard had the highest rating for speed (number of ships delivered per slipway) and it led in the lowest number of manhours per ship.

In 1944 this yard turned from Liberty ship construction to the production of Victory type ships.

Liberty ship output : 322 vessels at an average cost of 1,643,000 dollars each

USMC hull numbers : MCE 170– 200 (Yard Nos 170–200) (varied order)
229– 240 (,,   ,, 229–240) (,,   ,,)
543– 630 (,,   ,, 543–630)
1590–1631 (,,   ,, 631–672)
1747–1754 (,,   ,, 673–680) Cancelled.
2003–2098 (,,   ,, 681–776)
2245–2261 (,,   ,, 777–793)
2519–2537 (,,   ,, 794–812)
2568–2584 (,,   ,, 813–829)

170 MERIWETHER LEWIS 1.42 WISC 2.3.43: Sunk by submarine (U.634) torpedo in N.Atlantic, 61.10N 28.25W (voyage New York/UK).

171 STAR OF OREGON 12.41 GMC 30.8.42: Sunk by submarine (U.162) torpedo off Trinidad, 11.48N 59.45W. (Voyage Durban/Trinidad – general).

172 WILLIAM CLARK 2.42 WISC 4.11.42: Damaged during enemy attack, later sunk by submarine (U.354) torpedo in Greenland Sea, approx 71.05N 13.10E.

173 ROBERT GRAY 2.42 GMC 22.4.43: Sunk by submarine (U.306) torpedo in N.Atlantic, approx

The Liberian-flag *Cape Palmas* laid up in the
Zeebrugge Canal in 1958. (Oregon, Yard no 569)

The Greek-flag *Ioannis P. Goulandris* traded under
this name for some 22 years. (Oregon, Yard no 824)

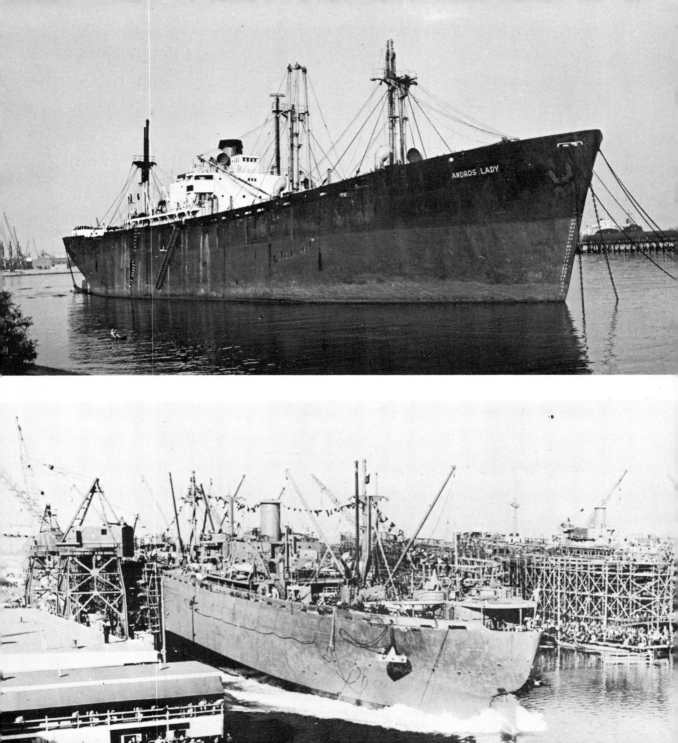

The *Andros Lady* (ex *Henry Adams*) laid up at Rotterdam in June 1958. (Permanente No 1, Yard no 2268)

The *Robert E. Peary,* which established a world ship-building record, being launched on November 12, 1942, only 4 days 15½ hours after her keel was laid. (Permanente No 2, Yard no 440)

57.30N 43.00W (voyage Halifax NS/Loch Ewe).

174 JOHN BARRY 2.42 WISC 28.8.44: Sunk by submarine (U.859) torpedo in Indian Ocean, 15.10N 55.18E.

175 THOMAS JEFFERSON 2.42 GMC 4.61: Scrapped Terminal Island.

176 JOHN HANCOCK 2.42 WISC 18.8.42: Sunk by submarine (U.553) torpedo in Caribbean, 19.41N 76.50W (voyage Trinidad/Key West).

177 PHILIP LIVINGSTON 3.42 WISC 47: NIDAR-DAHL. 50: TINDRA. 53: DONGHAE HO. 57: DONG HAE. 1.69: Scrapped Pusan.

178 STEPHEN A. DOUGLAS 3.42 WISC 66: Scrapped Beaumont, Texas.

179 ROBERT FULTON 3.42 WISC 12.69: Scrapped Mobile.

180 ALEXANDER HAMILTON 3.42 WISC 5.62: Scrapped Seattle.

181 JOHN JAY 3.42 WISC 5.60: Scrapped Troon.

182 THOMAS MACDONOUGH 3.42 F & S 4.67: Scrapped New Orleans.

183 WILLIAM DAWES 4.42 WISC 21.7.42: Sunk by Japanese submarine (I.11) torpedo south of Sydney, NSW, 36.47S 150.16E.

184 PHILIP SCHUYLER 4.42 WISC 6.67: Scrapped New Orleans.

185 GEORGE CLYMER 4.42 WISC 30.5.42: Disabled with machinery trouble 600 miles south west of Ascension Island, (cargo — aircraft and timber). 6.6.42: Damaged by MTB from German raider MICHEL. Abandoned and capsized. 7.6.42: Shelled by HMS ALCANTARA in position 14.32S 20.31W, but remained afloat. Wreck later sank.

186 JAMES WILSON 4.42 GMC 1943: STEROPE AK 96 (USN). 46: Returned to US Govt. 11.64: Scrapped Oakland, Cal., as JAMES WILSON.

187 JOHN HART 4.42 WISC 66: Scrapped Tacoma.

188 HENRY W. LONGFELLOW 4.42 WISC 5.62: Scrapped Chickasaw, Ala.

189 JOHN DICKINSON 4.42 WISC Reserve Fleet, site 2.

190 FISHER AMES 4.42 WISC Reserve Fleet, site 1.

191 ROBERT G. HARPER 4.42 GMC 47: ST. CROIX. 51: MARNA. 54: ASTRON. 62: URANOS. 67: GREAT PEACE.

192 EDGAR ALLEN POE 4.42 WISC 9.11.42: Wrecked at New Caledonia, 22.14S 166.30E. CTL. 11.42: Transferred to USN, renamed E.A.POE, IX 103. 46: EDGAR ALLEN POE. Laid up in Subic Bay. 49: Sold to China for scrap, but 7.9.49: Grounded at Hong Kong in typhoon. 10.50: Reported still aground, but 12.50: Scrapped Hong Kong.

193 NATHANIEL HAWTHORNE 5.42 GMC 7.11.42: Sunk by submarine (U.508) torpedo off Trinidad, 11.34N 63.26W (voyage Paramaribo/New York — bauxite).

194 JOHN G. WHITTIER 5.42 WISC 62: Scrapped Philadelphia.

195 WILLIAM CULLEN BRYANT 5.42 WISC 3.63: Scrapped Philadelphia.

196 JAMES RUSSELL LOWELL 5.42 F & S 15.10.43: Damaged by submarine (U.371) torpedo off Algeria, beached near Philippeville. CTL. Forepart later salved and 4.1.53: Taken in tow for Anzio. 6.1.53: Cast adrift in heavy weather. 12.1.53: Located and sunk by RN as danger to navigation south of Pantellaria, 36.17N 12.23E. 29.3.53: Stern part salved, towed to Italy and scrapped.

197 HENRY D. THOREAU 5.42 WISC Reserve Fleet, site 5.

198 RALPH WALDO EMMERSON 5.42 WISC 8.60: Scrapped Philadelphia.

199 JAMES WHITCOMB RILEY 5.42 F & S Reserve Fleet, site 1.

200 SAMUEL MOODY 5.42 WISC 5.64: Scrapped Richmond, Cal.

229 JOHN SEVIER 5.42 WISC 6.4.43: Sunk by submarine (U.185) torpedo north of Cuba, 20.17N 73.52W. (Voyage Demerara/Mobile — bauxite).

230 JONATHAN EDWARDS 5.42 GMC 1.61: Scrapped Baltimore.

231 OLIVER WENDELL HOLMES 5.42 GMC 3.69: At New Orleans for scrapping.

232 WALT WHITMAN 5.42 F & S Reserve Fleet, site 5.

233 MARK TWAIN 5.42 WISC 9.59: Scrapped Portland, Ore.

234 WASHINGTON IRVING 6.42 WISC Reserve Fleet, site 2.

235 JAMES FENIMORE COOPER 6.42 F & S 51: MOHAWK. 55: ALGONKIN. 56: WORLD LOYALTY. 62: FARO. 4.1.66: Aground in heavy weather 2 miles off Nojima, 34.53N 139.55E (voyage Muroran/Keelung – ballast). CTL. 67: Sold to Japanese shipbreakers 'as lies'. Scrapped.

236 THOMAS BAILEY ALDRICH 6.42 WISC Reserve Fleet, site 4.

237 BRET HARTE 6.42 GMC 12.63: Scrapped Panama City.

238 ANNE HUTCHINSON 6.42 F & S 26.10.42: Sunk by submarine (U.504) torpedo in Indian Ocean, 34.10S 28.30E.

239 JOHN HARVARD 6.42 WISC 47: BERNIERES. 21.4.63: Grounded alongside jetty of Vridi Canal when entering Abidjan (voyage Sassandra/La Pallice – timber). Refloated, severely damaged. CTL. Sold. 63: Scrapped Hendrik-Ido-Ambacht.

240 ELIHU YALE 6.42 WISC 15.2.44: Struck by aerial glider bomb, set on fire, blew up and sank off Anzio, Italy, 41.27N 12.38E, whilst discharging munitions. 47: Wreckage reported raised and scrapped in Italy.

543 CORNELIUS GILLIAM 6.42 F & S 3.70: Sold to New York shipbreakers.

544 GEORGE H. WILLIAMS 6.42 GMC 8.60: Scrapped Philadelphia.

545 MATTHEW P. DEADY 7.42 GMC 6.61: Scrapped Panama City.

546 JASON LEE 7.42 WISC 3.67: Scrapped Oakland, Cal.

547 MARCUS WHITMAN 7.42 F & S 10.11.42: Sunk by Italian submarine DA VINCI torpedo and gunfire off Natal, Brazil, 05.40S 32.11W.

548 JOHN McLOUGHLIN 7.42 WISC Reserve Fleet, site 4.

549 JESSE APPLEGATE 7.42 OWI Reserve Fleet, site 1.

550 GEORGE ABERNETHY 7.42 WISC 10.60: Scrapped Baltimore.

551 JOSEPH LANE 7.42 GMC 2.66: Scrapped Tacoma.

552 HARVEY W. SCOTT 7.42 WISC 3.3.43: Sunk by submarine (U.160) torpedo in Indian Ocean, 31.54S 30.37E (voyage Durban/Bandar Shapur).

553 JAMES W. NESMITH 7.42 F & S 7.4.45: Damaged by submarine (U.1024) torpedo in Irish Sea. Beached at Holyhead. Refloated, towed Liverpool. CTL. 29.8.45: Towed to River Blackwater, laid up. 3.6.46: Transferred to War Department, and towed to Bremerhaven. Loaded with obsolete ammunition, towed to sea and scuttled. Note: This vessel and the WILL ROGERS (qv) were the last vessels to be torpedoed by enemy submarines in the Irish Sea area.

554 JOHN C. AINSWORTH 8.42 GMC 2.61: Scrapped Seattle.

555 WILLIAM P. McARTHUR 8.42 OWI 66: Converted to a crane barge at New Orleans.

556 EUGENE SKINNER 8.42 WISC Reserve Fleet, site 8.

557 DANIEL H. LOWNSDALE 8.42 WISC 3.70: Sold to New York shipbreakers.

558 ELIJAH WHITE 8.42 OWI 7.61: Scrapped, Wilmington, NC.

559 HARRY LANE 8.42 WISC 3.62: Scrapped Baltimore.

560 GEORGE CHAMBERLAIN 8.42 F & S 12.55: Converted to YAG (same name, USN). (Conversion type EC2-S-22a). USN Reserve Fleet, site 1.

561 JONATHAN HARRINGTON 8.42 OWI 8.69: Scrapped Oakland, Cal.

562 WILLIAM H. SEWARD 8.42 WISC 8.60: Scrapped Hirao.

563 GIDEON WELLES 9.42 OWI 47: PIONEER. 49: PUNTA PLAIA. 50: ISA PARODI. 60: KOPALNIA MYSLOWICE.

564 EDWIN M. STANTON 9.42 OWI Reserve Fleet, site 1.

565 CLEVELAND ABBE 9.42 WISC Reserve Fleet, site 2.

566 ANDREW CARNEGIE 9.42 WISC 47: BASTIA. 10.63: Scrapped La Seyne.

567 PIERRE S. DUPONT 9.42 OWI Reserve Fleet, site 5.

568 JAMES DUNCAN 9.42 F & S 11.62: Scrapped Panama City.

569 GEORGE H. THOMAS 9.42 WISC 47: ARISTARCHOS. 48: RESOLUTE. 55: CAPE PALMAS. 63: MARCAR. 15.7.67: Beached at Tarrafal, Cape Verde Islands, after developing leaks (voyage Tampa/Bombay – phosphates). 25.8.67: Refloated, towed St Vincent. 9.67: Arrested for debts to salvors. 3.68: Removed from roadstead to another part of harbour. 4.68: Reported slowly sinking. 17.5.68: Reported submerged forward of bridge and settling by stern. Bridge structure later set afire by vandals, and gutted.

570 WILLIAM S. ROSECRANS 9.42 WISC 6.1.44: Damaged by mines in Gulf of Salerno, 40.10N 14.15E. Wreck sunk by torpedo and gunfire of HM ship. (Voyage Naples/USA, ballast).

571 HENRY VILLARD 9.42 OWI 51: AMPAC OREGON. 55: ARAPAHOE. 57: KETTY D. 61: ATHENOULA T. 24.12.64: Aground in fog at Hook of Holland, (voyage New Orleans/Antwerp – scrap iron). 30.12.64: Refloated, severely damaged. CTL. Sold. 4.65: Scrapped Hamburg.

572 SAMUEL SEABURY 9.42 OWI 61: Scrapped Portland, Ore.

573 MARK HANNA 10.42 WISC 6.61: Scrapped Mobile.

574 HENRY GEORGE 9.42 OWI 47: GRENOBLE. 61: ST JAMES. 66: ESPERANCE. 68: Scrapped Kaohsiung.

575 EDWARD EVERETT 10.42 OWI 2.69: Scrapped Portland, Ore.

576 JAMES McNEILL WHISTLER 10.42 WISC 19.6.46: Ashore at Meshima, 90 miles south west of Nagasaki. Total loss. Stripped of all salvable parts. (Voyage Shanghai/Japan – 3,400 Japanese repatriates).

577 SALMON P. CHASE 10.42 WISC 8.60: Scrapped Beaumont, Texas.

578 STEPHEN GIRARD 10.42 WISC 47: SAINTE MERE L'EGLISE. 62: VIMY. 64: MARGRETHE PAULIN. 3.68: Scrapped Kaohsiung.

579 HENRY DEARBORN 10.42 OWI 12.59: Scrapped Portland, Maine.

580 JAMES B. STEPHENS 10.42 OWI 8.3.43: Sunk by submarine (U.160) torpedo off Durban, 28.53S 33.18E. (Voyage Port Said/Durban – general).

581 JOSEPH N. TEAL 9.42 OWI 63: Scrapped Panama City.

582 TABITHA BROWN 10.42 WISC Reserve Fleet, site 6.

583 ALEXANDER GRAHAM BELL 10.42 WISC 8.62: Scrapped Philadelphia.

584 THOMAS A. EDISON 10.42 OWI 4.12.42: Ashore and wrecked on Vuata Vatoe Island, Pacific. Total loss. (Voyage San Francisco/Suva).

585 SAMUEL COLT 11.42 WISC 7.69: Scrapped New Orleans.

586 JOHN DEERE 10.42 OWI 3.61:Scrapped Hirao.

587 CHARLES GOODYEAR 11.42 WISC 68: Scrapped Kearny, NJ.

588 ELMER A. SPERRY 11.42 OWI 6.63: Scrapped Portland, Ore.

589 JOHN P. HOLLAND 11.42 WISC 11.64: Scrapped Panama City.

590 S.M. BABCOCK 11.42 OWI 8.67: Scrapped Portland, Ore.

591 CHARLES GORDON CURTIS 11.42 OWI 44: SERGEI KIROV. 47: S.KIROV.

592 JAMES B. EADS 11.42 OWI Reserve Fleet, site 1.

593 SAMUEL PARKER 11.42 WISC 68: Scrapped Green Cove Springs, Fla.

This vessel was named after a nineteenth century Congregationalist missionary and explorer of the Oregon territory.

The ship was the first to be awarded a 'Gallant Ship' plaque, and earned this honour for her heroic performances in the Mediterranean theatre of war. She shuttled between various ports for six months during 1943 with troops and every type of military stores and equipment. Frequently she landed her cargoes in the front line of battle; was constantly under heavy air attack; was harassed by exploding mines, torpedo attacks and even by burning petrol from exploding ships.

She finally steamed for home with her hull and superstructure holed in hundreds of places and with many other scars and signs of battle damage.

Her 'Gallant Ship' plaque is now on display in the Merchant Marine Exhibit at the Maritime Administration, whilst the ship's name plate has been presented to the Oregon Historical Society.

594 JOSEPH GALE 11.42 WISC 3.62: Scrapped Bordentown, NJ.

595 PETER SKENE OGDEN 11.42 IFM 22.2.44: Damaged by submarine (U.969) torpedo north east of Algiers, 37.22N 07.17E. Taken in tow and 26.2.44: beached near Bona. CTL. Stripped and later scrapped.

596 JOSEPH L. MEEK 11.42 OWI Reserve Fleet, site 4.

597 SAMUEL J. TILDEN 11.42 WISC 2.12.43: Struck by aircraft bombs, exploded burnt and sunk during German air attack on Bari Harbour, Italy. 48: Wreck sold Genoa shipbreakers and scrapped.

598 ABNER DOUBLEDAY 11.42 OWI 1.68: Scrapped New Orleans.

599 G.W. GOETHALS 12.42 WISC Reserve Fleet, site 2.

600 WILLIAM T. SHERMAN 12.42 OWI 47: COLMAR.

601 FRANK B. KELLOGG 12.42 WISC 62: Scrapped Oakland, Cal.

602 CARL SCHURZ 12.42 OWI 10.61: Scrapped Tacoma.

603 HENRY BARNARD 12.42 WISC 12.61: Scrapped Mobile.

604 JOHN S. COPLEY 12.42 OWI 10.59: Scrapped Portland, Ore.

605 CHARLES WILLSON PEALE 12.42 OWI 27.6.43: Successfully fought off an attack by U-boat U.199 50 miles south of Rio de Janeiro. 6.60: Scrapped Baltimore.

606 EDWIN BOOTH 12.42 WISC 8.69: Scrapped Portland, Ore.

607 JOSEPH JEFFERSON 12.42 OWI 2.61: Scrapped Yokosuka.

608 RICHARD MANSFIELD 12.42 WISC 2.59: Scrapped Seattle.

609 JOHN BURKE 12.42 OWI 28.12.44: Struck by Japanese Kamikaze plane off Mindoro, Philippines. Exploded and sank. (Voyage USA/Mindoro — general). Note: Some early (erroneous) reports show the vessel to have been lost on the same date off Perth, Australia.

610 JIM BRIDGER 12.42 WISC Reserve Fleet, site 5.

611 EZRA MEEKER 12.42 OWI Reserve Fleet, site 4.

612 SACAJAWEA 12.42 OWI 5.61: Scrapped Seattle.

613 CHIEF WASHAKIE 12.42 WISC 50: CHENA.

614 WILLIAM E. BORAH 1.43 OWI 7.61: Scrapped Hirao.

615 M.M. GUHIN 1.43 WISC Reserve Fleet, site 2.

616 LINDLEY M. GARRISON 1.43 OWI 8.61: Scrapped Everett, Wash.

617 JOHN W. WEEKS 1.43 OWI 51: DUPAGE APB 51 (USN). 59: Stricken from USN. No further trace.

618 STEPHEN B. ELKINS 1.43 WISC 1.61: Scrapped Oakland, Cal.

619 DANIEL S. LAMONT 1.43 OWI 10.66: Scrapped Mobile.

620 ALEXANDER J. DALLAS 1.43 OWI 66: Scrapped Tacoma.

621 RICHARD RUSH 1.43 WISC 61: Scrapped Philadelphia.

622 SAMUEL D. INGHAM 1.43 OWI 62: Scrapped Philadelphia.

623 GEORGE W. CAMPBELL 1.43 OWI 47: ST VALERY EN CAUX. 49: SAINT VALERY. 56: SAINT VALERY EN CAUX. 62: HENRIETTE. 8.67: Scrapped Hong Kong.

624 WILLIAM J. DUANE 1.43 OWI 4.61: Scrapped Sakai.

625 THOMAS EWING 1.43 OWI 43: GIANSAR AK 111 (USN). 46: THOMAS EWING. 4.63: Scrapped Baltimore.

626 WALTER FORWARD 2.43 IFM 8.61: Scrapped Beaumont, Texas.

627 FRANKLIN MACVEAGH 2.43 IFM 47: HUGO DE VRIES. 47: LEUVEKERK. 61: MITSA. 63: ATHANASSIOS K. 8.67: Scrapped Shanghai.

628 GEORGE M. BIBB 2.43 IFM 11.62: Scrapped Panama City.

629 ROBERT J. WALKER 2.43 WISC 25.12.44: Sunk by submarine (U.862) torpedo off Sydney, NSW, 36.32S 150.45E.

630 WILLIAM M. MEREDITH 2.43 IFM 9.60: Scrapped Barrow.

631 JOHN WHITEAKER 2.43 IFM 43: SITULA AK 140 (USN). 46: Returned to US Govt. 8.61: Scrapped West coast of USA.

632 SAM JACKSON 2.43 WISC 5.68: Scrapped Mobile.

633 OWEN SUMMERS 2.43 IFM 8.61: Scrapped Baltimore.

634 ARTHUR RIGGS 2.43 IFM 6.62: Scrapped Panama City.

635 LOT WHITCOMB 2.43 IFM 47: FLIGHT LIEUTENANT VASSILIADES R.A.F. 63: MITRO-POLIS. 28.10.66: Put into Manzanillo, Mexico, leaking and with fractured plates (voyage Houston/Korea — scrap). 21.11.66: Proceeded Portland, Ore for repairs. 8.67: Detained at Portland for debt. 1.68: Sold to Portland shipbreakers. Later resold. 24.8.68: Towed to Kaohsiung and 10.68: scrapped.

636 MORTON M. McCARVER 2.43 IFM 8.67: Scrapped Portland, Ore.

637 HALL J. KELLEY 3.43 IFM 47: GOVERNOR HOUSTON. 49: DIDDO. 58: JANET QUINN. 64: U.S. PECOS. 67: GITTEL. 67: Sold and renamed CAPTAIN PARKER, but sale formalities not completed and name reverted. 7.68: Scrapped Kaohsiung.

638 JOHN W. CULLEN 3.43 IFM 23.1.63: Broke adrift from tug whilst being towed from Beaumont to New Orleans for scrapping. Taken in tow again but 27.1.63: again broke adrift. 6.2.63: Located aground in position 29.11N 94.55W. 14.3.63: Refloated, anchored Bolivar Roads. Later proceeded in tow. 6.63: Scrapped New Orleans.

639 NATHANIEL J. WYETH 3.43 IFM 43: DE GRASSE AP 164 (USN). 1945: DE GRASSE AK 223 (USN). 46: NATHANIEL J.WYETH. 2.70: Sold to New York shipbreakers.

640 HENDERSON LUELLING 3.43 IFM 8.59: Scrapped Hirao.

641 E.H. HARRIMAN 3.43 IFM 43: DEKABRIST.

642 CUSHING EELLS 3.43 IFM 47: AGHIOS NICOLAOS. 60: PRAOTIS. 61: JABLANICA.

643 JAMES HARROD 3.43 IFM 16.1.45: Caught fire after collision with anchored Liberty ship RAYMOND B.STEVENS in The Downs, off Deal, Kent. Beached Pegwell Bay. 22.1.45: Fire extinguished. Broke in two, forepart still beached, afterpart submerged. CTL. (Voyage New York/Antwerp — cased petrol and lorries). 30.4.45: Forepart salved, towed to Deal, Sheerness, Holehaven and then beached on Blyth Sands. Later refloated, towed to London, thence to River Blackwater and laid up. 17.5.46: Towed to Bremerhaven. Loaded with obsolete chemical ammunition, towed to sea and scuttled. Afterpart reported later salved and scrapped Antwerp.

644 CHRISTOPHER GREENUP 3.43 IFM 6.62: Scrapped Tacoma.

645 AMOS KENDALL 3.43 IFM 5.61: Scrapped Baltimore.

646 BELVA LOCKWOOD 3.43 IFM 2.62: Scrapped Baltimore.

647 KENNETH A.J. MACKENZIE 3.43 IFM 3.70: Sold to New York shipbreakers.

648 LUCRETIA MOTT 3.43 IFM 10.68: Scrapped Kearny, NJ.

649 PIERRE GIBAULT 3.43 IFM 22.6.45: Damaged by mine off Rhodes, Eastern Mediterranean, 36.08N 29.30E. Beached with bow missing. 11.7.45: Refloated, towed Piraeus. CTL. 8.9.45: Towed Palermo. 7.48: Towed Savona. 1.49: Scrapped Savona.

650 BENJAMIN H. GRIERSON 3.43 IFM Reserve Fleet, site 4.

651 ELIJAH P. LOVEJOY 3.43 IFM 43: ALEXANDR SUVOROV.

652 GRAHAM TAYLOR 3.43 IFM 43: MIKHAIL KUTUSOV.

653 ALBERT B. CUMMINS 3.43 IFM 61: Scrapped Seattle.

654 JAMES W. GRIMES 3.43 IFM Reserve Fleet, site 2.

655 GEORGE L. BAKER 4.43 IFM 47: KAMERLINGH OUNES. 50: TOMINI. 57: TEXEL. 62: SOUTHERN CROSS. 63: MINDANAO MERCHANT. 65: BROTHERS S. 7.69: Scrapped Pusan.

656 CHIEF JOSEPH 4.43 IFM 46: HAI CHANG. 14.10.62: Left Kaohsiung for Keelung and Tacoma with cargo of copper, silver and gold concentrates but disappeared off Pescadores Islands. Presumed seized by crew and taken to Communist Chinese port, but later searches discovered oil and debris — suggesting the vessel foundered east of Tsamou, Penghu Island, approx 23.38N 119.50E.

657 HENRY W. CORBETT 4.43 IFM 43: ALEXANDR NEVSKY.

658 GEORGE FLAVEL 4.43 IFM 8.68: Scrapped Oakland, Cal.

659 JOHN H. COUCH 4.43 IFM 11.10.43: Sunk by air attack off Kola Point, Guadalcanal, 09.38S 160.00E. (Voyage USA/Guadalcanal — war stores).

660 GEORGE H. FLANDERS 4.43 IFM 47: BOERHAAVE. 47: ALAMAK. 58: GEROLAMO CAMPANELLO. 61: HUTA FERRUM.

661 FRANCIS W. PETTYGROVE 4.43 IFM 13.8.43: Damaged by aircraft torpedo in Mediterranean, 36.08N 02.14W (voyage Port Said/Gibraltar — ballast). 15.8.43: Towed Gibraltar. Beached. CTL. Later sold. 21.6.49: Refloated, towed to Algeciras and scrapped.

662 HENRY FAILING 4.43 IFM 7.61: Scrapped Everett, Wash.

663 B.F. SHAW 4.43 IFM Reserve Fleet, site 5.

664 SIMON BOLIVAR 4.43 IFM Reserve Fleet, site 2.

665 LOUIS AGASSIZ 4.43 IFM Completed as EMILIAN PUGACHEV.

666 EDWARD BELLAMY 4.43 IFM Reserve Fleet, site 8.

667 CASS GILBERT 4.43 IFM Completed as STEPAN RAZIN.

668 GOUVERNEUR MORRIS 4.43 IFM 43: LENINGRAD. 62: IVAN KULIBIN.

669 GILBERT STUART 4.43 IFM 47: HELLENIC SKY.

670 DE WITT CLINTON 4.43 IFM Completed as SEVASTOPOL.

671 RICHARD HARDING DAVIS 4.43 IFM 7.67: Scrapped Oakland, Cal.

672 WILLIAM H. McGUFFEY 5.43 IFM 4.67: Towed to Alaska for use as a breakwater to protect a new installation at Nikishka, 65 miles south west of Anchorage.

681 CUSHMAN K. DAVIS 5.43 IFM 6.66: Scrapped Portland, Ore.

682 GEORGE L. SHOUP 5.43 IFM Completed as PSKOV.

683 IGNATIUS DONNELLY 5.43 IFM 4.62: Scrapped Vancouver, Wash.

684 ROBERT NEWELL 5.43 IFM 61: Scrapped Seattle.

685 STANFORD NEWEL 5.43 IFM 1.70: Scrapped Oakland, Cal.

686 WILLIAM G. T'VAULT 5.43 IFM Completed as KUBAN.

687 WILLIAM H. GRAY 5.43 IFM 3.61: Scrapped Everett, Wash.

688 EDWARD EGGLESTON 5.43 IFM Completed as NOVOROSSISK.

689 THOMAS A. HENDRICKS 5.43 IFM 47: ROBERT FRUIN. 47: AMSTELDIEP. 61: EFDEMON. 9.68: Scrapped Kaohsiung.

690 JONATHAN JENNINGS 5.43 IFM 43: TALITA AKS 8 (USN). 1947: Returned to US Govt. 64: Scrapped Oakland, Cal.

691 GEORGE W. JULIAN 5.43 IFM 61: Scrapped Tacoma.

692 HENRY S. LANE 5.43 IFM 6.64: Scrapped New Orleans.

693 JAMES OLIVER 5.43 IFM 10.67: Scrapped Panama City.

694 ERIC V. HAUSER 5.43 IFM 47: IVY G. 48: LIBERTAD. 63: FAIRWINDS. 2.67: Scrapped Split.

695 R.C. BRENNAN 5.43 IFM 4.60: Scrapped Portland, Ore.

696 FRANCIS E. WARREN 5.43 IFM Reserve Fleet, site 4.

697 GEORGE DAVIDSON 6.43 IFM 3.62: Scrapped Baltimore.

698 JOSEPH C. AVERY 6.43 IFM 43: KHERSON. 3.7.43: Wrecked between Cape Povorothi and Akhomten Bay on east coast of Kamchatka, on delivery trip to USSR (voyage Portland, Ore/ Vladivostock). Broke in two; both sections re-floated and towed to Petropavlovsk 'for scrapping'. No further official trace.
Note: See also HARVEY CUSHING and JAY COOKE.

699 JOHN MINTO 6.43 IFM Completed as VITEBSK.

700 PLEASANT ARMSTRONG 6.43 IFM Completed as VLADIVOSTOCK. 62: UELEN.

701 WILSON P. HUNT 6.43 IFM 10.64: Scrapped Oakland, Cal.

702 BEN HOLLADAY 6.43 IFM 10.58: Scrapped Oakland, Cal.

703 JOEL PALMER 6.43 IFM 9.64: Scrapped Philadelphia.

704 THOMAS NUTTALL 6.43 IFM Reserve Fleet, site 2.

705 JOHN A. JOHNSON 6.43 IFM 29.10.44: Sunk by Japanese submarine (I.12) torpedo in Pacific, 29.55N 141.25W (voyage San Francisco/Pearl Harbour).

706 EPHRAIM W. BAUGHMAN 6.43 IFM 5.60: Scrapped Philadelphia.

707 EDWARD CANBY 6.43 IFM 61: Scrapped Hirao.

708 SAMUEL A. WORCESTER 6.43 IFM Completed as SOVETSKAYA GAVAN.

709 JOHN F. STEFFEN 6.43 IFM 11.59: Scrapped Wilmington, NC.

710 THOMAS CONDON 6.43 IFM 47: LEONTIOS. 10.67: Scrapped Hirao.

711 SIMON BENSON 6.43 IFM 48: Sold commercial (same name). 53: SEAMERIT. 54: AGIA TRIADA. 56: ANDROS TRIDENT. 63: SAN BENITO. 1.69: Scrapped Hirao.

712 IRVING W. PRATT 6.43 IFM Completed as NAKHODKA.

713 NICHOLAS J. SINNOTT 6.43 IFM 47: HAI CHIAO. 8.66: Scrapped Kaohsiung.

714 HENRY L. PITTOCK 7.43 IFM Completed as ASKOLD.

715 FELIX HATHAWAY 7.43 IFM 59: Scrapped Oakland, Cal.

716 JAMES WITHYCOMBE 7.43 IFM 19.12.43: Aground off Margarita Point, outside Cristobal, Panama Canal Zone, 08.58N 79.32W (voyage Galveston/Melbourne — general). Broke in two. Stripped and abandoned. Total loss.

717 BINGER HERMANN 7.43 IFM Reserve Fleet, site 1.

718 DONALD MACLEAY 7.43 IFM 12.67: Scrapped Portland, Ore.

719 HENRY L. HOYT 7.43 IFM 10.67: Scrapped Panama City.

720 JOSEPH WATT 7.43 IFM Completed as EREVAN.

721 DELAZON SMITH 7.43 IFM 12.67: Scrapped Mobile.

722 SAMUEL K. BARLOW 7.43 IFM 4.61: Scrapped Everett, Wash.

723 JOHN P. GAINES 7.43 IFM 24.11.43: Broke in two off Shumagin Island, Aleutians, 55.15N 159.00W. Forepart presumed sunk, afterpart later drifted ashore at Koniuji Island, Alaska. Total loss. (Voyage Adak/Pleasant Island).

724 WILLIAM C. LANE 7.43 IFM Completed as SAMPLER. 47: PORT ALBANY. 51: TENI. 53: GLORIANNA. 9.68: Scrapped Shanghai.

725 DAVID DOUGLAS 7.43 IFM Completed as BAKU.

726 GEORGE H. HIMES 7.43 IFM 47: GEORGIOS PANORAS. 56: NICOLAOS EPIPHANIADES. 15.3.61: Exploded and caught fire whilst loading at Odessa; aground and abandoned (voyage Odessa/Djakarta – anthracite). 10.61: Refloated but detained at Ilichevsk by Soviet Authorities due to damage caused to Odessa port installation. 9.64: Reported scrapped by USSR.

727 J.D. ROSS 7.43 IFM 47: GOVERNOR MILLER. 49: IRENESTAR. 60: LAMPSIS. 11.1.66: Sprung leak in heavy weather in N.Atlantic. 12.1.66: Sank 600 miles east north east of Bermuda, 34.18N 51.22W (Voyage Casablanca/Philadelphia – ore).

728 JAMES K. KELLY 7.43 IFM 6.63: Scrapped Panama City.

729 THOMAS W. SYMONS 7.43 IFM 10.61: Scrapped Tacoma.

730 WILLIS C. HAWLEY 7.43 IFM Completed as STALINABAD. 62: DUSHAMBE.

731 GEORGE L. CURRY 8.43 IFM 47: RUNA. 53: PEGASUS. 64: EASTWARD. 66: UNITED FORWARD. 5.68: Scrapped Kaohsiung.

732 WILLIAM HUME 8.43 IFM 12.11.45: Damaged by mine off Salvore Point, Istria. Taken in tow but sank in Adriatic 45.36N 14.41E (voyage Baltimore/Trieste – wheat).

733 ANTON M. HOLTER 8.43 IFM Completed as SAMBAY. 47: SENATOR. 64: AJAX. 5.68: Scrapped Kaohsiung.

734 CLINTON KELLY 8.43 IFM 3.62: Scrapped Seattle.

735 EDWARD D. BAKER 8.43 IFM 59: Scrapped Beaumont, Texas.

736 SAMUEL LANCASTER 8.43 IFM 11.64: Scrapped Oakland, Cal.

737 JOHN JACOB ASTOR 8.43 IFM 47: JALA-KANYA. 1.63: Scrapped Bombay.

738 CHARLES M. RUSSELL 8.43 IFM 47: JALA-KENDRA. 61: HERACLES. 4.68: Scrapped Onomichi.

739 JOSEPH SIMON 8.43 IFM 6.60: Scrapped Baltimore.

740 R.P. WARNER 8.43 IFM 47: SYROS. 20.1.55: Dragged anchor and grounded in gale at Cherrystone Hill, Bermuda. 1.2.55: Refloated, towed Hamilton. CTL. (Voyage Amsterdam/Hampton Roads – ballast). Sold and repaired; renamed ALBA. 62: ZAFIRO. 67: TILLIE. 68: Scrapped Kaohsiung.

741 HENRY L. ABBOTT 8.43 IFM 7.9.49: Grounded in typhoon at Hong Kong. Later refloated, damaged. CTL. 50: Sold to Shanghai shipbreakers, but 26.9.50: Intercepted by Chinese Nationalist warships in international waters 180 miles off Keelung when in tow of tug CHRISTINE MOLLER (voyage Hong Kong/Shanghai). Tug ordered to cut loose tow; vessel cast adrift in position 28.05N 123.00E. 4.10.50: Salved by Chinese Nationalist tug, towed Keelung. 24.8.51: Released, towed Hong Kong. 9.51: Scrapped Hong Kong.

742 C.J. JONES 8.43 IFM Completed as SAMBUT. 6.6.44: Sunk by gunfire from enemy shore battery in Straits of Dover, 51.08N 01.33E (voyage River Thames/Normandy beaches – troops and vehicles).

743 DAVID THOMPSON 8.43 IFM 4.61: Scrapped Everett, Wash.

744 DUNHAM WRIGHT 8.43 IFM 4.61: Scrapped Tacoma.

745 B.F. IRVINE 8.43 IFM 65: Converted at Portland, Ore. into a crane barge.

746 DAVID F. BARRY 8.43 IFM 47: OAKLAND. 56: ARTA. 59: KOPALNIA BOBREK.

747 THOMAS J. WALSH 8.43 IFM 47: ATALANTI. 62: TRAMPROVER. 66: BOREAL. 4.69: Scrapped Kaohsiung.

748 PETER DE SMET 8.43 IFM 9.68: Scrapped Philadelphia.

749 JAMES M. CLEMENTS 9.43 IFM 1.60: Scrapped Terminal Island.

750 EDWARD N. WESTCOTT 9.43 IFM 2.60: Scrapped Mobile.

751 CHARLES A. BROADWATER 9.43 IFM
Completed as SAMTHAR. 47: BARRANCA. 57:
CESCO CORRADO. 7.67: Scrapped Spezia.

752 JOSEPH W. FOLK 9.43 IFM Reserve Fleet, site
1.

753 JAMES L. BRECK 9.43 IFM 7.60: Scrapped
Hirao.

754 SIDNEY EDGERTON 9.43 IFM 47: ATLANTIC
CAPTAIN. 62: WHITE CLOUD. 14.10.62: Ashore
at entrance to Humboldt Bay, Calif. 22.10.62:
Refloated, damaged, and towed Eureka. (Voyage
Coos Bay/Eureka). CTL. Sold. 63: Scrapped Seattle.

755 ROBERT S. BEAN 9.43 IFM 47: CLEO. 51:
ARSENA. 25.7.58: Aground on Maio Island, C.V.,
15.18N 23.60W (voyage Takoradi/USA). 5.8.58: Refloated, damaged, towed Dakar. 18.9.58: Towed
Rotterdam. CTL. Sold. 7.59: Scrapped Rotterdam.

756 NATHANIEL CROSBY 9.43 IFM
1.70: Sold for scrapping at Portland, Ore.

757 JOHN I. NOLAN 9.43 IFM 1947: Reported
severely damaged by striking reef in Pacific, (no
further details). Proceeded USA and laid up at Suisun
Bay, Calif. CTL. 4.49: Scrapped Oakland, Cal.

758 BEN T. OSBORNE 9.43 IFM 6.66: Scrapped
Portland, Ore.

759 JAMES S. LAWSON 9.43 IFM
4.69: Scrapped Kearny, NJ.

760 MIDWEST FARMER 9.43 IFM 5.61: Scrapped
Baltimore.

761 VICTOR C. VAUGHAN 9.43 IFM Completed
as SAMZONA. 61: Reported scrapped in USA.

762 WILLIAM S. LADD 9.43 IFM 10.12.44: Sunk
by Japanese Kamikaze aircraft attack in Leyte
Harbour, Philippines (voyage Oro Bay/Hollandia).

763 FREDERICK BILLINGS 9.43 IFM 5.61:
Scrapped Oakland, Cal.

764 ANTHONY RAVALLI 9.43 IFM 61: Scrapped
Philadelphia.

765 EDMUND F. DICKINS 9.43 IFM 5.45:
Damaged by mine 'in Pacific'. Towed USA and laid
up in James River. CTL. 9.47: Scrapped Baltimore.

766 JOHN F. MYERS 9.43 IFM 47: SANTORINI.
65: CAPTAMIHALIS. 8.69: Scrapped Bilbao.

767 DAVID B. HENDERSON 9.43 IFM 62:
Scrapped Oakland, Cal.

768 JOHN M. BOZEMAN 9.43 IFM Reserve Fleet,
site 2.

769 THOMAS HOWELL 9.43 IFM 5.64: Scrapped
Oakland, Cal.

770 JAMES D. DOTY 9.43 IFM 8.61: Scrapped
Yokosuka.

771 PRINCE L. CAMPBELL 9.43 IFM Reserve
Fleet, site 1.

772 MANASSEH CUTLER 9.43 IFM Completed
as SAMOURI. 26.1.44: Sunk by submarine (U.188)
torpedo in Gulf of Aden, 13.04N 55.45E.

773 JOHN G. BRADY 10.43 IFM 11.60: Scrapped
Baltimore.

774 JEAN NICOLET 10.43 IFM 2.7.44: Sunk by
Japanese submarine (I.8) torpedo and gunfire south
of Maldive Islands, 03.28S 74.16E (voyage Los
Angeles/Calcutta — army stores).

775 W.B. AYER 10.43 IFM 47: MARIT. 55: ANDROS.
62: MARIA. 67: PANAGIOTIS K.

776 CHARLES NORDHOFF 10.43 IFM
4.70: Sold to Spanish shipbreakers.

777 WILLIAM L. SUBLETTE 10.43 IFM 47:
TOULON. 12.66: Scrapped Bilbao.

778 WILLIAM H. ASHLEY 10.43 IFM 56:
Converted to YAG (same name, USN). (Conversion
type EC2-S-22a). USN Reserve Fleet, site 2.

779 W.W. McCRACKIN 10.43 IFM 47: MARIA
G. CULUCUNDIS. 61: CAPTAIN GEORGE.
14.11.62: Abandoned in heavy weather after fire
and explosion 300 miles north east of Bermuda.
18.11.62: Sank in position 36.49N 61.24W (voyage
New Orleans/Umm Said — sulphur, carbon nitrate,
dynamite and general).

780 FRANCIS N. BLANCHET 10.43 IFM 11.61:
Scrapped Portland, Ore.

781 CHARLES F. AMIDON 10.43 IFM 3.61:
Scrapped Tacoma.

782 JOSEPH M. CAREY 10.43 IFM Reserve Fleet, site 5.

783 WATSON C. SQUIRE 10.43 IFM 4.61: Scrapped Oakland, Cal.

784 STEPHEN G. PORTER 10.43 IFM 12.61: Scrapped Oakland, Cal.

785 ABBOT L. MILLS 10.43 IFM 10.11.45: Damaged by mine off Dubrovnik; towed into port. CTL. Sold. 7.48: Towed Venice; repaired. 49: CORALLO. 50: Converted to oil engine at Trieste by Fiat. 64: MARI-NUCCI. 65: AQUILA.

786 ALBERT A. MICHELSON 10.43 IFM 47: PANAGHIA KATHARIOTIS. 49: PANAGHIA K. 9.12.66: In distress due to leaking holds in Pacific, 27.51N 126.41E; escorted to Okinawa, damaged. 2.67: Scrapped Kaohsiung.

787 EDMUND G. ROSS 10.43 IFM 5.61: Scrapped Oakland, Cal.

788 PETER WHITE 10.43 IFM 8.45: Damaged by mine off Leyte, 14.25N 123.45E. Temporarily repaired, towed to Portland and laid up. CTL. 6.49: Scrapped Portland, Ore.

789 J. WARREN KEIFER 11.43 IFM 61: Scrapped Philadelphia.

790 WILLIAM H. DALL 11.43 IFM 47: CANNA-REGGIO. 64: AMILLA. 65: TRADEWAYS II. 21.10.65: Sprung leak in heavy weather 200 miles north of Azores. 22.10.65: Broke in two; forepart sank. 23.10.65: Afterpart sank. (Voyage Antwerp/Montreal — steel products).

791 JAMES H. LANE 11.43 IFM 49: OCEAN NAVIGATOR. 55: PLEIADES. 56: CAPTAIN GEORGE. 16.10.57: Aground off Ilha de Maio, Cape Verde Islands, 15.21N 23.10W (voyage Kassa Island/Port Alfred — bauxite). CTL. 58: Wreck reported sold for scrap.

792 WILLIAM D. HOARD 11.43 IFM 47: EURYME-DON. 56: PANAGIOTIS D. 63: KATINA T.H. 3.68: Scrapped Kaohsiung.

793 FRANCIS W. PARKER 11.43 IFM 65: Scrapped Philadelphia.

794 HORACE V. WHITE 11.43 IFM 3.61: Scrapped Oakland, Cal.

795 ELISHA P. FERRY 11.43 IFM 6.69: Scrapped Tacoma.

796 LUCIUS FAIRCHILD 11.43 IFM 47: BERLAGE 50: AMSTELVAART. 60: COSMOPOLITAN. 63: VIGILANT. 68: Scrapped Kaohsiung.

797 JANE G. SWISSHELM 11.43 IFM 10.67: Scrapped Mobile.

798 HENRY T. RAINEY 11.43 IFM Reserve Fleet, site 2.

799 THOMAS CRAWFORD 11.43 IFM 9.59: Scrapped Seattle.

800 GEORGE P. McKAY 11.43 IFM 47: HEMONY. 47: LEOPOLDSKERK. 62: ATTICOS. 5.69: Scrapped Shanghai.

801 RICHARD J. OGLESBY 11.43 IFM 58: Scrapped Alameda, Cal.

802 JOHN BALL 11.43 IFM 6.65: Scrapped Portland, Ore.

803 SEGUNDO RUIZ-BELVIS 12.43 IFM 47: PRESIDENT REITZ. 27.11.47: Ashore on South African coast, 5 miles east of Zitzihamma River, (voyage Table Bay/Durban — ballast). CTL. Wreck sold locally and stripped of all removable parts.

804 FRANK B. LINDERMAN 12.43 IFM 2.62: Scrapped Bellingham, Wash.

805 JOHN B. KENDRICK 12.43 IFM 47: PIETRO B. 48: PIETRO BIBOLINI. 63: EVER PROTECTOR. 5.67: Scrapped Kaohsiung.

806 SIMEON G. REED 12.43 IFM 3.68: Converted at Jersey City into a crane barge.

807 LEWIS L. DYCHE 12.43 IFM 4.1.45: Sunk by Japanese Kamikaze aircraft attack at Mindoro, Philippines. (Voyage USA/Mindoro — war supplies).

808 JOHN STRAUB 12.43 IFM 19.4.44: Broke in two and sank 20 miles off Sannak Island, south of Alaska peninsular, 54.22N 163.24W (voyage Port Townshend/Dutch Harbour — oil & petrol).

809 WILBUR O. ATWATER 12.43 IFM 48: OYONNAX. 59: LEONIDAS VOYAZIDES. 65: TRIADA. 6.68: Scrapped Shanghai.

810 ISAAC McCOY 12.43 IFM 5.61: Scrapped Tampa, Fla.

811 JOHN W. DAVIS 12.43 IFM 8.61: Scrapped Mobile.

812 ENOS A. MILLS 12.43 IFM 7.61: Scrapped Tampa, Fla.

813 GRACE R. HEBARD 12.43 IFM 5.66: Scrapped Philadelphia.

814 JAMES B. MILLER 12.43 IFM 61: Scrapped Philadelphia.

815 RALPH BARNES 12.43 IFM 47: ST JAN. 51: ARTEMIDI. 52: PANTOKRATOR. 55: Lengthened at Kobe to 511½ ft (8,520 grt). 61: PANAGATHOS. 27.10.65: Aground off Ameland Island, Holland, (voyage Rotterdam & Hamburg/USA — steel products). Abandoned. CTL. 1970: Wreck remains 'in situ'.

816 GABRIEL FRANCHERE 12.43 IFM 47: ARGENTAN.

817 WILLIAM A. HENRY 12.43 IFM 60: Scrapped Mobile.

818 GRANT P. MARSH 12.43 IFM Completed as VALERY CHKALOV.

819 NARCISSA WHITMAN 1.44 IFM 61: Scrapped Portland, Ore.

820 ISAAC I. STEVENS 1.44 IFM 47: SAINT DIE. 65: VARA. 67: Scrapped Yokosuka.

821 WILLIAM I. CHAMBERLAIN 1.44 IFM 47: MARIA PARODI. 61: GENERAL TSAKALOTOS. 18.8.66: Sailed from Bombay after repairing cracks in hull. 22.8.66: Further cracks developed, requested assistance in Arabian Sea, 18.52N 63.40E (voyage Bombay/Aden). Leaks later controlled, vessel proceeded. 7.11.66: Grounded in Plencia River, north east of Bilbao (voyage Emden/Bilbao — ballast). 8.11.66: Refloated, towed Bilbao and laid up, damaged. 68: Scrapped Bilbao.

822 MARY E. KINNEY 1.44 IFM 63: Dismantled at Philadelphia for use as a storage tank.

823 HARRINGTON EMERSON 1.44 IFM 9.10.45: Aground and wrecked in typhoon at Okinawa (voyage Port Hueneme/Okinawa). 48: Reported sold and scrapped.

824 ELWOOD MEAD 1.44 IFM 47: IOANNIS P. GOULANDRIS. 11.68: Scrapped Itozaki, Japan.

825 SAMUEL V. STEWART 1.44 IFM 47: SWEELINCK. 47: ALUDRA. 60: MARIA. 61: Lengthened at Maizuru to 511½ ft (8,685 grt). 25.12.61: Aground outside Maizuru whilst on trials after lengthening. Abandoned. CTL. Sold. 5.62: Refloated and scrapped in Japan.

826 JOHN W. TROY 1.44 IFM 47: ELENI D. 61: OCEAN MARINER. 3.67: Scrapped Sakai.

827 ABIGAIL S. DUNIWAY 1.44 IFM 47: VIRAGO. 49: ANGELO PARODI. 62: ARMOSY. 10.63: Scrapped Osaka.

828 EDWARD LANDER 2.44 IFM 58: Scrapped Oakland, Cal.

829 PETER MORAN 2.44 IFM 6.61: Scrapped Osaka.

BUILT BY PERMANENTE METALS CORPORATION, YARD NO 1

In December 1940 the syndicate known as the Todd-California Shipbuilding Corporation — a division of the Permanente Metals Corporation and the very first Kaiser-managed shipyard — contracted to build thirty British 'Ocean' type vessels in a new yard to be specially built for the purpose. This yard was located on a swamp on the north-east shore of San Francisco Bay near Richmond, California, and the dredging, filling and construction work on the site began in January 1941. It was laid out with ample spacing between its seven slipways (each with a large assembly platform at its head) and the assembly shops, and this pattern was soon adopted as one of the basic principles of all the mass-production yards. But nevertheless, even here, more space was soon needed for expansion.

Early in 1941 the managements of both the firms building for the British (the other yard was at Portland, Maine) were given contracts to construct new yards adjacent to those already being built. At Richmond the new yard, known as Richmond No 2 (see Permanente No 2) was managed by the Richmond Shipbuilding Corporation — also a subsidiary of Kaiser's Permanente Metals Corporation, in which all of Kaiser's 'Six Services' group owned shares.

During November 1941 the Maritime Commission approved the leasing of the Todd-California yard by the Richmond Shipbuilding Corporation, with the intention of developing the facilities when all the 'Oceans' were launched. Soon afterward, when Kaiser organised his own shipyards in which Todd had no interest, he acquired full ownership of the yards he was managing and sold to Todd his interests in Todd-managed yards situated elsewhere. Thus the yard came under direct Permanente Metals control and became known as Richmond No 1.

Along with the Oregon shipyard at Portland, Richmond No 1 was one of the first two new shipyards to be in operation on the West Coast, and it was subsequently to achieve outstanding records in Liberty construction.

One of the early expansion schemes saw a huge fabricating shop set up halfway between No 1 and No 2 yards in which whole upper structures of ships were built in only three units. This shop served both the yards and the fabricated sections were transported to the slipways for installation.

By June 1942 vessels were being delivered in an average time of 69 days, against a contract maximum of 76 days. Six months later, contract time was down to 30 days and the deliveries to only 23 days. At the same time, anticipated labour per ship was 622,300 man-hours but actual output was achieved in only 406,400 hours. In the commission's scheme for suggested improvements to the efficiency of all yards, Permanente Metals ranked first in total saving. During 1944 the yard turned to the production of 'Victory' type ships.

Liberty ship output: 138 vessels at an average of 1,875,300 dollars each.

USMC hull numbers: MCE: For the constructions at this yard the MCE numbers were used as the yard numbers.

483 EDWARD ROWLAND SILL 8.42 GMC 11.67: Scrapped Oakland, Cal.

484 JOAQUIN MILLER 8.42 GMC Reserve Fleet, site 4.
Note: The first Liberty ship to arrive in the Port of London — on 21.3.43 from Jacksonville.

485 LEW WALLACE 9.42 GMC
4.70: Sold to New York shipbreakers.

486 O. HENRY 9.42 JHIW 1.62: Scrapped Mobile.

487 F. MARION CRAWFORD 9.42 JHIW
10.69: Sold for scrapping at New Orleans.

488 JOSEPH RODMAN DRAKE 9.42 GMC Reserve Fleet, site 2.

489 WILLIAM DEAN HOWELLS 9.42 GMC 5.60: Scrapped Baltimore.

490 JOHN HOWARD PAYNE 9.42 GMC 6.63: Scrapped Baltimore.

491 ANDREW FURUSETH 10.42 JHIW 47: ESSI. 59: NIOBE. 6.67: Scrapped Hirao.

492 MOSES ROGERS 10.42 JHIW
9.69: Sold to New York shipbreakers.

493 WILLIAM K. VANDERBILT 10.42 GMC
16.5.43: Sunk by Japanese submarine (I.19) torpedo

west of Suva, Pacific, 18.41S 175.07E.

494 JAMES J. HILL 10.42 JHIW Reserve Fleet, site 2.

495 JOHN RUTLEDGE 10.42 JHIW 6.66: Scrapped Portland, Ore.

496 WILLIAM CUSHING 10.42 JHIW 8.69: Scrapped Philadelphia.

497 JOHN BLAIR 10.42 JHIW 4.66: Scrapped Oakland, Cal.

498 ROBERT H. HARRISON 11.42 JHIW 1966: Scrapped Bordentown, NJ.

499 JOHN McLEAN 11.42 JHIW 47: BREST. 60: GALAXY. 69: ELIOS.

500 NOAH H. SWAYNE 11.42 JHIW 43: ARIDED AK73 (USN). 46: Returned US Govt (same name). 8.62: Scrapped Terminal Island.

501 SAMUEL F. MILLER 11.42 GMC 11.66: Scrapped Portland, Ore.

502 DAVID DAVIS 11.42 GMC 42: CARINA AK74 (USN). 3.5.45: Damaged by Japanese PT boats at Okinawa. Later returned to USA. Laid up. 12.52: Scrapped Terminal Island.

503 MORRISON R. WAITE 11.42 JHIW 7.63: Scrapped Kearny, NJ.

504 MELVILLE W. FULLER 11.42 OWI 42:
CASSIOPEIA AK75 (USN). 46: MELVILLE W.
FULLER. 6.61: Withdrawn from James River Reserve
Fleet and 28.6.61: Torpedoed and sunk by US
submarine CUTLASS (SS 478) 100 miles east of
Norfolk, Va, during tests of new torpedoes.

505 STANLEY MATTHEWS 11.42 JHIW 12.63:
Scrapped Philadelphia.

506 DAVID J. BREWER 12.42 JHIW 8.62: Scrapped
Oakland, Cal.

507 PIERRE LA CLEDE 12.42 JHIW
3.70: Sold to New York shipbreakers.

508 FREDERIC REMINGTON 12.42 GMC Reserve
Fleet, site 4.

509 WALTER COLTON 12.42 GMC 3.68: Scrapped
Portland, Ore.

510 J. STERLING MORTON 12.42 JHIW Reserve
Fleet, site 1.

511 GEORGE H. DERN 12.42 GMC 47: CALAIS.
60: ALMAVITA. 5.69: Scrapped Kaohsiung.

512 KEY PITTMAN 12.42 JHIW 43: LEONIS AK
128 (USN). 46: KEY PITTMAN.
6.69: Scrapped Wilmington, Del.

513 CHIEF OURAY 1.43 JHIW 43: DEIMOS AK
78 (USN). 22.6.43: Sunk by Japanese submarine
(RO-103) torpedo near Guadalcanal, 11.35S 162.08E.

514 GEORGE S. BOUTWELL 1.43 JHIW 49: Sold
commercial (same name). 53: SEAGLIDER. 55:
RAYVAH. 61: CARA SEA. 1962: DIANA B. 4.64:
Scrapped Portland, Ore.

515 BENJAMIN H. BRISTOW 1.43 JHIW
9.69: Scrapped Mobile.

516 WILLIAM WINDOM 1.43 JHIW 8.64: Scrapped
New Orleans.

517 CHARLES J. FOLGER 1.43 JHIW 4.60:
Scrapped Baltimore.

518 CHARLES S. FAIRCHILD 1.43 JHIW 43:
KRASNOGVARDEETS.

519 JOHN G. CARLISLE 1.43 WISC 65: Scrapped
USA.

520 LYMAN J. GAGE 2.43 JHIW 43: CHELEB AK

138 (USN). 46: Returned to US Govt (same name).
Reserve Fleet, site 6.

521 WILLIAM H. ASPINWALL 2.43 JHIW Reserve
Fleet, site 5.

522 GRENVILLE M. DODGE 2.43 WISC Reserve
Fleet, site 2.

523 JULIEN DUBUQUE 2.43 WISC Reserve Fleet,
site 4.

524 ADONIRAM JUDSON 3.43 JHIW Reserve
Fleet, site 5.

525 JOHN G. NICOLAY 3.43 JHIW 43: ALBIREO
AK 90 (USN). 46: JOHN G. NICOLAY. 47:
PRESIDENT STEYN. 51: HIDALGO. 54: OCEAN
SAILOR. 4.67: Scrapped Etajima, Japan.

526 EDWARD BATES 3.43 JHIW 1.2.44: Damaged
by aircraft torpedo off Tenes, 36.38N 00.50E.
Abandoned, taken in tow but sank. (Voyage Hampton
Roads/Palermo — flour).

527 JOSIAH B. GRINNELL 3.43 WISC 8.66:
Scrapped Terminal Island.

528 HENRY H. RICHARDSON 3.43 JHIW 4.60:
Scrapped Philadelphia.

529 NATHANIEL CURRIER 3.43 WISC Reserve
Fleet, site 4.

530 JAMES IVES 3.43 JHIW 46: AXIOS. 2.67:
Scrapped Kaohsiung.

531 THOMAS CORWIN 4.43 WISC 11.64:
Scrapped Portland, Ore.

532 JAMES GUTHRIE 4.43 JHIW 17.4.44:
Damaged by mine off Salerno. Towed in and
beached Naples, broke in two. CTL. 47: Scrapped
Naples.

533 HOWELL COBB 4.43 JHIW 66: Sunk (with
EDWARD A.FILENE, qv) and used as a combination
breakwater and dock at Cook Inlet, Alaska.

534 HUGH McCULLOCH 4.43 JHIW 3.62:
Scrapped Baltimore.

535 MATTHEW LYON 4.43 WISC 11.8.43:
Damaged by Japanese submarine (I.11) torpedo in
Pacific, 22.30S 166.30E on voyage to Espiritu Santo.
12.8.43: Arrived in tow. 1944: Transferred to USN,
renamed ZEBRA, IX 107 (engines removed, used as

hulk). 1945: Repaired and re-engined (WISC), renamed ZEBRA, AKN 5 (USN). 1946: MATTHEW LYON. Reserve Fleet, site 2.

536 GEORGE D. PRENTICE 4.43 JHIW
11.69: Scrapped Portland, Ore.

537 WILLIAM A. JONES 5.43 JHIW Reserve Fleet, site 2.

538 HOMER LEA 4.43 JHIW 12.58: Scrapped Seattle.

539 ANSON BURLINGAME 5.43 JHIW 47: KOSTIS LEMOS. 31.12.50: Ashore 1 mile south of Lagayan Point, Camiguin Island. Broke in two. (Voyage Vancouver/Bombay – grain). Total loss.

540 LOUIS HENNEPIN 5.43 WISC 4.61: Scrapped Tampa, Fla.

541 JOSIAH SNELLING 5.43 JHIW 7.61: Scrapped Tampa, Fla.

542 GEORGE WASHINGTON CARVER 5.43 JHIW 11.43: Converted at New York and renamed DOG-WOOD (US Army hospital ship, 7,933 grt). 1.46: Converted at San Francisco to transport for troops and military dependants (see Part Six) with capacity for 948 persons. Reverted to name GEORGE WASHINGTON CARVER. 1946: Returned to US Govt. 1.64: Scrapped Oakland, Cal.

1552 JAMES A. BAYARD 5.43 JHIW 4.63: Scrapped Philadelphia.

1553 MARY CASSATT 5.43 JHIW 43: ODESSA.

1554 MICHAEL PUPIN 6.43 JHIW 3.62: Scrapped Philadelphia.

1555 CYRUS HAMLIN 6.43 JHIW 43: LYRA AK 101 (USN). 46: CYRUS HAMLIN. 47: VIRGINIA. 64: AMEDEO. 4.67: Scrapped Kaohsiung.

1556 HENRY BERGH 6.43 JHIW 31.5.44: Ashore in fog on Farallon Island, 30 miles west of San Francisco. Broke in two, abandoned. Total loss. (Voyage Pacific/San Francisco – 1000 naval personnel).

1557 JOHN CARROLL 6.43 WISC 47: KRONVIKEN. 60: SOLMAR. 63: POMONA. 65: UNION PROSPER. 6.67: Scrapped Kaohsiung.

1558 JONATHAN P. DOLLIVER 6.43 JHIW Reserve Fleet, site 2.

1559 JAMES HARLAN 6.43 JHIW 46: NUEVA FORTUNA. 56: THEOFOROS. 9.9.62: Aground on Kuradimuna Rocks, off Tallinn, Gulf of Bothnia. (Voyage Leningrad/Cuba – trucks). 10.9.62: Refloated, towed in. CTL. 11.62: Scrapped Helsinki.

1560 ROBERT LUCAS 6.43 JHIW Reserve Fleet, site 2.

1561 EDWIN T. MEREDITH 6.43 JHIW Reserve Fleet, site 2.

1562 MARIA SANFORD 7.43 WISC 2.60: Scrapped Terminal Island.

1563 CHRISTOPHER C. ANDREWS 7.43 JHIW 43: HYPERION AK 107 (USN). 46: CHRISTOPHER C.ANDREWS. 8.61: Scrapped Baltimore.

1564 LEONIDAS MERRITT 7.43 JHIW
9.69: Sold to New York shipbreakers.

1565 FLOYD B. OLSON 7.43 JHIW 12.61: Scrapped Hirao.

1692 FRANCIS G. NEWLANDS 7.43 WISC 8.65: Scrapped New Orleans.

1693 AMBROSE BIERCE 7.43 JHIW 10.58: Scrapped Oakland, Cal.

1694 JAMES FERGUS 7.43 JHIW
2.70: Sold to Spanish shipbreakers.

1695 WILLIAM N. BYERS 7.43 WISC 47: NICOLAS. 4.64: Scrapped Vado.

1696 JOSHUA HENDY 7.43 JHIW 11.64: Scrapped Kearny, NJ.

1697 MARCUS DALY 8.43 JHIW 8.68: Scrapped National City, Cal.

1698 JOHN CONSTANTINE 8.43 JHIW 47: ANTONIS. 62: DELIS. 63: BUDHA JAYANTI. 5.66: Scrapped Bombay.

1699 WILLIAM F. VILAS 8.43 JHIW Completed as SAMANA. 47: WILLIAM F.VILAS. 10.59: Scrapped Philadelphia as SAMANA.

1700 MYRON T. HERRICK 8.43 IFM 3.61: Scrapped Everett, Wash.

1701 RING LARDNER 8.43 JHIW 59: Scrapped Oakland, Cal.

1702 HORACE WELLS 8.43 JHIW 47: JANNA. 59: CHORZOW.

1703 WINFIELD S. STRATTON 8.43 IFM Reserve Fleet, site 2.

1704 JAMES LICK 8.43 JHIW 50: Sold commercial (same name). 57: WANG TRADER. 60:ROCKLAND. 60: GIANNIS. 62: AGIOS IOANNIS. 13.6.63: Aground, 3 miles off Ohara, 35.10N 140.23E (Voyage San Francisco/Japan). 9.7.63: Broke in two. Total loss. 13.7.63: Stern part refloated and towed to Tateyama. 19.7.63: Towed Yokosuka and later scrapped there.

1705 FLOYD BENNETT 8.43 IFM Reserve Fleet, site 1.

1706 DAVID BELASCO 9.43 WISC 4.66: Scrapped Portland, Ore.

1707 JOHN S. BASSETT 9.43 WISC 47:CAVAL-AIRE. 1964: Renamed AKRI for delivery to ship-breakers. 5.64: Scrapped Etajima, Japan.

2099 JOHN REED 9.43 JHIW Completed as SAMPFORD. 47: ROWANBANK. 59: TAIWIND. 25.7.66: In collision in fog with tanker ST MATHEW (50/14,376 grt) 8 miles east of Irosaki 34.33N 139.01E (Voyage Chiba/Wakamatsu). Holed and flooded, towed Uraga. CTL. 1.67: Sold and scrapped Yokosuka.

2100 VACHEL LINDSAY 9.43 JHIW Reserve Fleet, site 5.

2101 MICHAEL CASEY 9.43 JHIW 47: GEORGIOS F.ANDREADIS.

2102 MURAT HALSTEAD 9.43 IFM Completed as CHUNG CHENG. 5.2.44: Sunk by submarine (U.188) torpedo 13.26N 54.30E (Voyage Cochin/USA – ore).

2103 HENRY WELLS 9.43 WISC 47: BRITTA. 51: CHALLENGER. 56: PLANET. 10.66: Scrapped Onomichi.

2104 JAMES J. O'KELLY 9.43 IFM 47: COSTIS LOS. 55: AFRICAN KING. 5.63: Scrapped Onahama.

2105 REINHOLD RICHTER 9.43 JHIW 47: SIMON STEVIN. 47: LISSEKERK. 61: MARIA DE LOURDES.

2106 WILLIAM SHARON 10.43 WISC 47: ARIS.

48: CNOSA. 65: AETHALIA. 5.69: Scrapped Todotsu, Japan.

2107 JOHN G. NORTH 10.43 JHIW Completed as SAMARK. 47: JOHN G.NORTH. 60: Scrapped Philadelphia.

2108 SIMON BAMBERGER 10.43 JHIW 47: ONDA. 63: ANTOJO. 2.70: At Split for scrapping.

2109 CYRUS T. BRADY 10.43 WISC Reserve Fleet, site 2.

2110 SAMUEL BRANNON 10.43 WISC 59: Scrapped Oakland, Cal.

2111 CHIEF CHARLOT 10.43 IFM 12.58: Scrapped Seattle.

2112 CASPER S. YOST 10.43 JHIW 48: SULPHUR MINES. 55: WESTPORT. 61: FERORE. 63: SORABOL.

2113 WILLIAM J. PALMER 10.43 JHIW 4.8.45: Struck mine and sank when entering Trieste harbour. (Voyage New York/Trieste – general). 1.49: Reported refloated, towed S.Bartolomeo and scrapped.

2114 PETER COOPER HEWITT 10.43 JHIW 47: CITTA DI VIAREGGIO. 62: SEA SPRAY. 2.67: Scrapped Spezia.

2115 ETHAN A. HITCHCOCK 10.43 WISC Reserve Fleet, site 4.

2116 MARY BICKERDYKE 11.43 JHIW 46: ATLANTIC OCEAN. 28.3.48: Aground near Outer Beacon, Great Pass, Alexandria Harbour. (Voyage Iquique/Alexandria – nitrate). 1.4.48: Refloated. CTL. Repurchased by owner, repaired (same name). 61: WHITE MOUNTAIN. 16.2.66: In collision with mv FUNABASHI (45/7,325 grt) 9 miles from Singapore, 01.19N 104.18E. Capsized and sank. (Voyage Bangkok/Colombo – rice).

2117 WILLIAM W. CAMPBELL 11.43 JHIW 47: NEDON. 63: NEW KAILUNG. 3.67: Scrapped Kaohsiung.

2118 MICHAEL C. KERR 11.43 WISC 6.69: Scrapped New Orleans.

2119 HARRY LEON WILSON 11.43 WISC 47: COSTANTIS. 67: ARAGON.

2120 JOHN W. MELDRUM 11.43 WISC Reserve Fleet, site 5.

2121 CLYDE L. SEAVEY 11.43 JHIW 1.66:
Scrapped Richmond, Cal.

2122 WILLIAM A. COULTER 11.43 JHIW 3.65:
Scrapped Oakland, Cal.

2123 LOUIS PASTEUR 12.43 WISC 48: Sold
commercial (same name). 63: STELLA AZZURRA.
3.67: Scrapped Venice.

2124 WILLIAM C. RALSTON 12.43 WISC
10.12.45: Aground off Okinawa in typhoon. CTL.
Later returned to USA. Laid up. 15.4.58: Loaded
with chemical munitions and scuttled off California.

2125 LAWRENCE GIANELLA 12.43 WISC 47:
MARY G. 48: JALAKALA. 60: CHIPBEE. 64:
STANWOOD. 3.65: Scrapped Osaka.

2126 GEORGE H. POWELL 12.43 WISC 47:
GRONLAND. 51: BARKA. 58: SIRACUSANO.
9.62: Scrapped Vado.

2127 JOSE J. ACOSTA 12.43 JHIW 46: DELFIN.
63: KHIBINY.

2128 HEBER M. CREEL 12.43 JHIW 2.61: Scrapped
Seattle.

2129 MILLEN GRIFFITH 12.43 WISC 58:
Scrapped Oakland, Cal.

2130 OTIS SKINNER 1.44 WISC 47: VALHALL.
65: SIMONE. 4.67: Scrapped Castellon.

2131 JOHN SHERMAN 1.44 WISC 47: ATLANTIC
COAST. 61: DEMOS. 9.67: Scrapped Osaka.

2132 HENRY R. SCHOOLCRAFT 2.44 JHIW 47:
SAN MARCO QUARTO. 56: SETTEMARI. 61:
CHRISTITSA. 18.4.67: In collision with mv CITTA
DI BEIRUT (40/1,535 grt) off Zourva Point, Hydra
Island, Greece. Beached at Kynosoura, severely
damaged. Refloated, towed Eleusis Bay. (Voyage
Algeirs/Eleusis — ore). 9.67: Sold. 68: Scrapped
Castellon.

2133 JOSEPH E. WING 2.44 JHIW 47: EMANUELE
V. PARODI. 62: ROBY. 9.63: Scrapped Yokosuka.

2134 HARRIET MONROE 2.44 WISC 47:
MONTELLO. 59: MIDDLE RIVER. 61: LOUSSIOS.
68: Sold for scrapping at Whampoa, but 1.69: Boiler,
machinery and steering gear trouble on delivery
voyage; resold Hong Kong shipbreakers.

2135 FRANK J. CUHEL 3.44 JHIW 47: FORTINI.
55: AVRA. 18.7.65: Developed leaks in two holds,
140 miles north of Cochin (voyage Mormugao/Japan
— iron ore). Abandoned. 19.7.65: Sank in position
11.57N 75.13E.

2136 DAULTON MANN 3.44 WISC 47: JALAKETU.
8.64: Scrapped Bombay.

2262 ALEXANDER MAJORS 3.44 JHIW 47:
TRITONE.

2263 JAN PIETERSZOON COEN 3.44 IFM 47:
SALLY STOVE. 53: Converted to oil engines at
Spezia by Fiat. 60: SUSQUEHANNA. 63: NEPTUNE.
3.68: Scrapped Kaohsiung.

2264 AUGUSTIN DALY 4.44 IFM 4.67: Scrapped
Portland, Ore.

2265 JAMES H. BREASTED 4.44 WISC 26.12.44:
Sunk by aircraft bombs at Mindoro, Philippine
Islands. (Voyage Hollandia/Mindoro).

2266 WALTER WYMAN 4.44 JHIW 47: ITALCIELO.
50: Converted to oil engines at Genoa by Fiat. 65:
GREENPORT.

2267 JOHN ROACH 3.44 IFM 46: SAPHO. 11.67:
Scrapped Kaohsiung.

2268 HENRY ADAMS 4.44 WISC 47: WASHINGTON
49: CATHERINE M. GOULANDRIS. 57: ANDROS
LADY. 4.63: Scrapped Inverkeithing.

2269 GEORGE COGGESHALL 4.44 JHIW
Completed as SUKHONA.

2270 JOHN ISAACSON 4.44 JHIW Reserve Fleet,
site 4.

2271 SILVESTRE ESCALANTE 4.44 JHIW 9.61:
Scrapped Terminal Island.

BUILT BY PERMANENTE METALS CORPORATION, YARD NO 2

In 1941 the management of Todd-California (later Richmond No 1), already building a yard to construct 'Ocean'
type ships, was given a contract by the Maritime Commission to construct an adjacent six-way yard to be known

The *John L. Sullivan* as *YAG 37*, shown using her deck-mounted aircraft engines for propulsion. (Permanente No 2, Yard no 1121)

The lengthened Liberty ship *Capetan Costis I* (ex *Henry M. Stephens)* in the Manchester Ship Canal before towage to Spanish shipbreakers. Her deplor- able condition was accentuated by having her ventilators removed and her masts and funnel chopped down to mere stumps. Topmasts, cross-trees and ventilators were lashed to her deck and steel fore- and-aft girders were fitted to strengthen her for the trip to Spain. The vessel had been previously damaged by grounding in August 1966. (Permanente No 2, Yard no 2762)

The US Navy's repair and supply ship *Baham* (ex *Elizabeth C. Bellamy*) in August 1944. (St Johns, Yard no 25)

as Richmond No 2 under the Richmond Shipbuilding Corporation, a subsidiary of Kaiser's Permanente Metals Corporation. This new yard, under the same management, was therefore in line with the Commission's plans which, at that time, were not to commence new yards but to expand existing facilities. Shortly afterward, the slips were extended to nine in number and in February 1942 increased, yet again, to twelve. So, at the spacious deep-water location of Richmond (not far from Oakland, the Kaiser headquarters), four Kaiser yards totalling twenty-seven ways very quickly replaced the one original seven-way yard. By 1943 the population of Richmond had increased to over 100,000 from its 1940 figure of 23,000 and additional facilities in the town included roads and transport and a ferry service to carry workers to the yards.

The shortest time of the many different but steadily-maintained averages of Liberty deliveries from all yards was about 17 days, but some previous special efforts had sometimes cut this time to much less. At the Oregon Shipyard one vessel was launched only ten days after keel laying, and Richmond No 2 responded with an effort which established a Liberty building record, assembling a ship in just over four days and outfitting her in another three. This was yard No 440, the *Robert E.Peary,* on slip between 8 and 12 November, 1942. This pace was not, of course, maintained and no effort was made so to do, but the speed of this construction did focus attention on shipyard achievements and methods and gave quite a boost to morale.

Here, a brief study of overall building times will, perhaps, put the building of these record vessels and all the other emergency shipbuilding into perspective. A vast amount of prefabrication work was carried out before the construction of any ship actually commenced on the slipway. For example, when a contract stipulated a building limit of, say, fifty days per ship, the materials involved had been undergoing prefabrication for an average of some thirty-five days prior to keel-laying, thus giving a total of some eighty-five days for complete construction. Undoubtedly the material for the record ships underwent an even greater amount of preparatory work, whilst all the subsequent reductions in contract times were met by greater efficiencies in pre-keel work.

When, later, the military authorities called for LSTs in a hurry, half of the requirements were assigned to Kaiser-controlled yards. But objections to breaking the production flow in these major yards were upheld and a new, smaller yard (originally Richmond No 3A, later No 4) was built so that continuity of Liberty production at both the Richmond and the Oregon shipyards was maintained. However, military types gradually filled more and more slipways and nearly all the West Coast yards were constructing these types by mid-1944. By August of the same year no Liberty ships at all were being built on this coast and of the total production for the year, military types formed 29 per cent and Liberty ships only 32 per cent.

Richmond No 2 turned to the production of 'Victory' ships during 1944, but their previous Liberty output had shown a very great and progressive drop in time and costs per ship. The original contracts estimated 622,300 man-hours per ship, but this figure reduced to as low as 347,500 during production and whereas the December 1942 slipway time was allowed at 30 days per ship, the figure was reduced to some 19 days.

Liberty ship output: 351 vessels at an average cost of 1,667,500 dollars each.

USMC hull numbers:

Built by Richmond Shipbuilding Corporation

MCE 241–264 (Yard Nos 41–64)
321–332 (" " 65–76)

Built by Permanente Metals Corporation

For the constructions at this yard the MCE number was used as the yard number.

41 JAMES OTIS 3.42 JHIW 6.2.45: Aground off coast of Devon. CTL. 5.46: Transferred to US Army on "as is, where is" basis at Falmouth. 7.46: Towed to sea and scuttled.

42 JOHN ADAMS 3.42 F & S 5.5.42: Sunk by Japanese submarine (I.21) torpedo off New Caledonia, 23.30S 164.35E (Voyage Noumea/Brisbane).
Note: This was the first Liberty ship to be sunk by enemy action.

43 KIT CARSON 3.42 GMC 2.66: Scrapped Portland, Ore.

44 ZACHARY TAYLOR 4.42 JHIW 10.61: Scrapped Staten Island, NY.

45 ANTHONY WAYNE 4.42 F & S 3.60: Scrapped Baltimore.

46 TIMOTHY PICKERING 4.42 JHIW 13.7.43: Damaged by aircraft torpedo off Avola, Sicily, 37.00N 15.21E. Caught fire and abandoned. Shelled by Allied warships, sank in shallow water. (Voyage Alexandria/ Avola — army stores). 48: Wreck sold to Genoa shipbreakers.

47 STEPHEN HOPKINS (I) 5.42 JHIW 27.9.42: Sunk in action with German raider STEIR, in position 28.08S 11.59W. (Voyage Cape Town/Bahia).

This ship fought — and won — a very gallant and fierce action with the armed German raider STEIR (36/4,778 grt, ex-Atlas Levante Line's CAIRO). She fought so fiercely that although she herself was overwhelmed and sunk with heavy loss of life, the raider also sank.

On the morning of Sunday, September 27, 1942, the STEIR and her supply ship TANNENFELS were lying together, and stopped, in the S.Atlantic in an area 'through which no ship ever passed' and overside painting was in progress. Visibility was down to only two miles when the STEPHEN HOPKINS was sighted, and the raider opened fire at long range at 0856 hours. Four minutes later the freighter replied with, states the German War Diary, "six 4.7 inch guns and lighter weapons". In fact the Liberty ship had replied with her only armament — a single 4-inch gun giving a 31 lb. 'broadside' — to an adversary armed with six 5.9 inch guns and six smaller ones, two torpedo tubes and two Arado seaplanes and with a speed of 14 knots.

As the STEPHEN HOPKINS turned so the STEIR followed, only to be hit by two shells. One jammed her rudder to starboard and the other exploded in her engine room, stopping her engines and setting fire to fuel oil. The way on the ship brought her round in a half-turn, her portside guns were brought to bear and these kept up a heavy rate of fire despite a complete absence of power. Her torpedo tubes remained inoperative due to the damaged electrical systems.

The American ship was soon afire and stopped, and by 0918 when firing finally ceased, both vessels lay side by side, silenced and heavily damaged. At 10 a.m. the STEPHEN HOPKINS sank. But the raider had been hit fifteen times in less than ten minutes and her plight increased as burning oil spread rapidly through the ship. Flames shot from among the nineteen torpedoes stored in No 2 hold, decks became red hot, and the vessel was abandoned. Her survivors were picked up by the TANNENFELS and as they reached her deck so the STEIR blew up and sank. Fifteen survivors of the STEPHEN HOPKINS reached the coast of Brazil thirty-one days later;

the remaining forty-two of her crew were lost.

This somewhat embarrassing finalé to the raider's career was preceded by a similar luckless period. She sailed from Rotterdam on May 12, 1942, disguised as SPERRBRECHER 171, was fired on by the long-range guns of the Dover Battery and lost some of her escort in an attack by British MTBs in the Dover Straits. She finally broke out into the Atlantic on May 20 and, later, followed this by a tedious session of refuelling from a supply ship with hoses which failed to fit the couplings — and the discovery that the new 'fuel'contained over 90 per cent water. In over four months of operations, however, the STEIR sank only four Allied ships totalling 29,406 grt, this figure including the STEPHEN HOPKINS.

48 SAMUEL HUNTINGTON 5.42 JHIW 29.1.44: Damaged by bombs whilst anchored off Anzio, Italy. Caught fire, blew up and sank. (Voyage Naples/ Anzio — ammunition). 48: Sold Genoa shipbreakers.

49 WILLIAM ELLERY 5.42 GMC 9.68: Scrapped New Orleans.

50 LEWIS MORRIS 6.42 JHIW 1.61: Scrapped Oakland, Cal.

51 JOHN WISE 6.42 JHIW Reserve Fleet, site 4.

52 GEORGE ROSS 7.42 JHIW 11.66: Scrapped Portland, Ore.

53 JAMES SMITH 7.42 JHIW 9.3.43: Damaged by submarine (U.510) torpedo in Atlantic (voyage Bahia/Trinidad — ballast). Abandoned. Reboarded, towed Trinidad thence New Orleans. Repaired. 23.9.43: Sank submarine U.260 by shell fire in Atlantic. 2.63: Scrapped Panama City.

54 GEORGE TAYLOR 7.42 JHIW 8.61: Scrapped Alameda, Cal.

55 WILLIAM WHIPPLE 8.42 JHIW 10.58: Scrapped Baltimore.

56 OLIVER WOLCOTT 8.42 JHIW 7.61: Scrapped Oakland, Cal.

57 FRANCIS LEWIS 8.42 JHIW 7.69: Sold to New York shipbreakers.

58 JOHN MORTON 8.42 JHIW Reserve Fleet, site 2.

59 GEORGE READ 8.42 JHIW Reserve Fleet, site 2.

60 ROGER SHERMAN 8.42 JHIW 9.61: Scrapped Baltimore.

61 RICHARD STOCKTON 8.42 JHIW 45: BELGIAN

LOYALTY. 47: RICHARD STOCKTON. Reserve Fleet, site 2.

62 MATTHEW THORNTON 8.42 JHIW Reserve Fleet, site 5.

63 WILLIAM WILLIAMS 9.42 JHIW 5.5.43: Damaged by Japanese submarine (I.19) torpedo in Pacific, 20.09S 178.04W. Abandoned. Reboarded, towed Fiji thence to Auckland. (Voyage Espiritu Santo/Auckland). Repaired, then 43: VENUS AK 135 (USN). 46: VENUS. 8.61: Scrapped Oakland, Cal.

64 ELI WHITNEY 9.42 JHIW 1956: Converted to YAG (same name) (USN) (conversion type EC2-S-22a). Reserve Fleet, site 5.

65 IRVIN MACDOWELL 6.42 JHIW 2.70: Sold to Spanish shipbreakers.

66 GEORGE B. McCLELLAN 6.42 JHIW Reserve Fleet, site 5.

67 JOSEPH HOOKER 7.42 JHIW 10.67: Scrapped Portland, Ore.

68 AMBROSE E. BURNSIDE 9.42 JHIW 12.65: Scrapped Wilmington, NC.

69 PETER J. McGUIRE 9.42 JHIW 3.68: Scrapped Terminal Island.

70 PHILIP H. SHERIDAN 9.42 JHIW 7.69: Scrapped Portland, Ore.

71 DAVID BUSHNELL 9.42 JHIW 51: MOJAVE. 56: ULYSSES II. 57: Lengthened at Kobe to 511½ ft (8,608 grt). 62: ULYSSES. 65: NARCEA.

72 JOHN FITCH 9.42 JHIW 4.67: Scrapped Portland, Ore.

73 JAMES RUMSEY 9.42 JHIW 14.5.46: Stranded at San Salvador 27.00N 77.30W. Later refloated, towed Mayport, Fla. in leaking condition. (Voyage Savannah/Santos). CTL. 12.47: Scrapped Baltimore.

74 JOHN STEVENS 10.42 JHIW 2.62: Scrapped Baltimore.

75 SAMUEL F.B. MORSE (I) 10.42 JHIW 1943: YUCCA (assigned name of hospital ship – not used). 11.43: Converted at New York and renamed JARRETT M. HUDDLESTON (US Army hospital ship). 12.45: Converted at New York to transport

for military dependants (see Part Six) with capacity for 326 women and 150 children. (Same name, as former name allocated to another construction). 6.46: Returned to US Govt. Reserve Fleet, site 2.

76 CYRUS H. McCORMICK 10.42 JHIW 18.4.45: Sunk by submarine (U.1107) torpedo in English Channel 48.05N 06.28W (Voyage New York/Antwerp).

418 JAMES B. FRANCIS 10.42 JHIW 3.66: Scrapped Kearny, NJ.

419 RICHARD JORDAN GATLING 10.42 JHIW 4.69: Scrapped Oakland, Cal.

420 JOHN JAMES AUDUBON 10.42 JHIW 42: CRATER AK 70 (USN). 45: JOHN JAMES AUDUBON. Reserve Fleet, site 6.

421 JOHN F. APPLEBY 10.42 JHIW Reserve Fleet, site 1.

422 CHARLES M. HALL 10.42 JHIW 6.10.45: Damaged by striking submerged object in river Seine. Returned to USA, laid up (damaged) in James River. CTL. 58: Scrapped Baltimore.

423 GEORGE WESTINGHOUSE 10.42 JHIW 9.61: Scrapped Panama City.

424 JOHN BARTRAM 10.42 JHIW Reserve Fleet, site 5.

425 G.H. CORLISS 11.42 WISC 42: ADHARA AK 71 (USN). 45: G.H. CORLISS. Reserve Fleet, site 2.

426 RICHARD MARCH HOE 11.42 GMC 42: PRINCE GEORGES AP 165 (USN). 45: PRINCE GEORGES AK 224 (USN). 46: RICHARD MARCH HOE. 11.69: Scrapped Oakland, Cal.

427 ELIHU THOMSON 11.42 GMC 11.69: Scrapped Kearny, NJ.

428 GEORGE B. SELDEN 11.42 GMC 12.60: Scrapped Tsuneishi.

429 NATHANIEL BOWDITCH 11.42 JHIW 1.60: Scrapped Oakland, Cal.

430 CHARLES M. CONRAD 11.42 GMC 8.63: Scrapped Tacoma.

431 JOHN B. FLOYD 11.42 JHIW 1.65: Scrapped Terminal Island.

432 JOSEPH HOLT 11.42 GMC 4.61: Scrapped Yokosuka.

433 JOHN M. SCHOFIELD 11.42 JHIW 8.62: Scrapped Portland, Ore.

434 JOHN A. RAWLINS 12.42 GMC 17.9.45: Ashore in typhoon at Okinawa. Total loss. Stripped and abandoned. Later reported scrapped by China Merchants & Engineers Inc, China.

435 GEORGE W. McCRARY 12.42 GMC 12.67: Scrapped Kearny, NJ.

436 ALEXANDER RAMSEY 12.42 GMC Reserve Fleet, site 2.

437 ROBERT T. LINCOLN 12.42 JHIW 42: ALUDRA AK72 (USN). 23.6.43: Sunk by Japanese submarine (RO-103) torpedo off San Cristobal Island 11.35S 162.08E.

438 WILLIAM C. ENDICOTT 12.42 GMC 1.65: Scrapped Portland, Ore.

439 REDFIELD PROCTOR 12.42 JHIW 42: CELENO AK76 (USN). 19 : Severely damaged by enemy action in Pacific, returned to USA and laid-up Suisun Bay. CTL. 46: REDFIELD PROCTOR. 3.61: Reported scrapped Panama City.

440 ROBERT E. PEARY 11.42 JHIW 6.63: Scrapped Baltimore.

441 DAVID GAILLARD 12.42: JHIW Reserve Fleet, Site 5.

442 HENRY J. RAYMOND 12.42 GMC Reserve Fleet, site 5.

443 WILLIAM G. McADOO 12.42 GMC 43: GRUMIUM AK112 (USN). GRUMIUM IX174 (USN). 44: Adapted for carrying aviation stores GRUMIUM AVS3 (USN). 46: Returned US Govt (same name). Reserve Fleet, site 2.

444 LESLIE M. SHAW 12.42 JHIW 10.61: Scrapped Baltimore.

445 GEORGE B. CORTELYOU 1.43 JHIW 43: CETUS AK77 (USN). 46: GEORGE B. CORTELYOU. Reserve Fleet, site 2.

446 FREDERICK JACKSON TURNER 1.43 WPMC 3.62: Scrapped Baltimore.

447 JOSEPH G. CANNON 1.43 JHIW Reserve Fleet, site 2.

448 GEORGE ROGERS CLARK 1.43 JHIW 47: ORLEANS. 9.63: Scrapped Hamburg.

449 LOUIS JOLIET 1.43 JHIW 47: ALIKI. 60: RIO. 10.68: Scrapped Whampoa.

450 SAMUEL DE CHAMPLAIN 1.43 JHIW 47: LA ROCHELLE. 9.67: Renamed JUPITER for voyage to Taiwan breakers. 3.68: Arrived Kaohsiung and scrapped.

451 JOHN A. LOGAN 1.43 GMC 43: ALNITAH AK127 (USN). 46: JOHN A.LOGAN. 5.61: Scrapped Portland, Ore.

452 PERE MARQUETTE 1.43 GMC Reserve Fleet, site 4.

453 JOHN M. PALMER 1.43 JHIW 43: DRACO AK79 (USN). 46: JOHN M.PALMER. 47: PRESIDENT KRUGER. 51: RIVIERA. 53: EFFIE. 58: PRESIDENT PRETORIUS. 4.68: Scrapped Kaohsiung.

454 RICHARD YATES 1.43 JHIW Reserve Fleet, site 1.

455 NANCY HANKS 2.43 JHIW 58: Scrapped Baltimore.

456 EDWARD P. COSTIGAN 2.43 WISC 8.59: Scrapped Portland, Ore.

457 SIEUR DULUTH 2.43 WISC 43: TUNGUS.

458 RICHARD HENDERSON 2.43 WISC 26.8.43: Sunk by submarine (U.410) torpedo off Sardinia, approx 37.15N 08.24E.

459 BENJAMIN BONNEVILLE 2.43 JHIW 47: NICOLAOS PATERAS. 53: EVANGELISMOS. 66: MANNA DESPOINA. 68: Reported scrapped Shanghai.

460 CHARLES WILKES 2.43 JHIW 43: KOLKHOSNIK.

461 JUSTIN S. MORRILL 2.43 JHIW 2.62: Scrapped Baltimore.

462 THOMAS KEARNS 2.43 WISC 12.61: Scrapped Jacksonville, Fla.

463 VITUS BERING 2.43 JHIW 10.61: Scrapped Baltimore.

464 DAN BEARD 2.43 JHIW 10.12.44: Damaged by submarine (U.1202) torpedo off Strumble Head, N. Wales. Broke in two. Afterpart sank, forepart drifted ashore and wrecked.

465 JANE A. DELANO 3.43 JHIW 12.69: Sold New York shipbreakers.

466 JOHN R. PARK 3.43 JHIW 21.3.45: Sunk by submarine (U.399) torpedo off Brest, 49.58N 05.45W (voyage Southampton/USA).

467 JAMES B. HICKOK 3.43 WISC 48: PRESIDENT PRETORIUS. 52: CENTURION. 54: PRODROMOS. 3.12.58: In collision in fog with mv KING MINOS (58/11,156 grt) 12 miles off Dungeness. Broke in two, forepart taken in tow and beached 2½ miles south of Rye Harbour, 50.46N 00.55E (voyage Montreal/Helsinki – grain). Afterpart presumed sunk. 10.12.58: Forepart refloated, towed Boulogne. CTL. 1.59: Scrapped Antwerp.

468 HIRAM S. MAXIM 3.43 WISC 8.65: Scrapped Portland, Ore.

469 WILLIAM B. OGDEN 3.43 JHIW 1.7.43: Ashore Sacremento Shoal, near Vizagapatam. 6.7.44: Refloated, towed Calcutta. Repaired. 8.64: Scrapped New Orleans.

470 DAVID DUDLEY FIELD 4.43 JHIW 2.70: Sold for scrapping at Portland, Ore.

471 CHARLES P. STEINMETZ 3.43 JHIW 5.62: Scrapped Panama City.

472 DAVID STARR JORDAN 4.43 JHIW Reserve Fleet, site 4.

473 JACQUES LARAMIE 3.43 JHIW Reserve Fleet, site 5.

474 LUCY STONE 3.43 WISC Reserve Fleet, site 4.

475 FRANCES E. WILLARD 3.43 WISC 9.61: Scrapped Hirao.

476 BETSY ROSS 3.43 JHIW 43: COR CAROLI AK91 (USN). 46: BETSY ROSS. Reserve Fleet, site 2.

477 ABIGAIL ADAMS 4.43 JHIW Reserve Fleet, site 5.

478 ELIZABETH BLACKWELL 4.43 JHIW 47: ATLANTIC AIR. 62: MATIJA IVANIC. 66: MAR. 7.67: Scrapped Hualien, Formosa.

479 S. HALL YOUNG 4.43 JHIW 47: BREDERO. 48: LEKKERKERK. 61: MARIA SANTA. 6.67: Scrapped Kaohsiung.

480 J.H. KINCAID 4.43 JHIW 66 (circa): Scrapped USA.

481 ALEXANDER BARANOF 4.43 JHIW 43: VALERY CHKALOV. 12.12.43: Broke in two in heavy weather in N.Pacific, 54.22N 164.49E (voyage Port Sovetskaya/Portland, Ore). Both parts salved, towed Adak, Alaska. 4.44: Towed Kodiak, thence Vancouver and both parts rejoined and renamed ALEXANDER BARANOF (US flag). 46: Placed in Wilmington Reserve Fleet. 65: Scrapped Philadelphia.

482 SHELDON JACKSON 4.43 JHIW 66: Scrapped Richmond, Cal.

1099 LUTHER BURBANK 4.43 JHIW 43: ERID-ANUS AK92 (USN). 46: LUTHER BURBANK. 47: PANAGIOTIS. 15.11.55: Grounded Kunsan, Korea. (Voyage Baltimore/Inchon – coal). 21.11.55: Broke in two. CTL. Sold. 56: Both parts refloated, towed Pusan, thence Shimonoseki, Japan. 57: Rejoined at Tokio, lengthened to 448½ ft (7,321 grt) and renamed SILLA.

1100 GEORGE M. PULLMAN 4.43 JHIW 47: SILVANA. 54: ZEPHYR. 60: SEIRIOS. 12.63: Scrapped Chiba, Japan.

1101 WILBUR WRIGHT 4.43 JHIW 10.66: Reported scrapped Oakland, Cal.

1102 WILLIAM THORNTON 4.43 JHIW 51: WESTERN TRADER. 57: WESTERN RANGER. 57: WANG RANGER. 58: PACIFIC NAVIGATOR. 60: EQUITABLE SAILOR. 60: BACKUS. 61: AVRA. 65: DELFINI. 16.2.68: Broke adrift in gales from anchorage at Kaizuka and grounded. Later arrested and 8.68: refloated on orders of Japanese Govt, anchored off Kure. Sold. 69: Scrapped Aioi.

1103 GLENN CURTISS 5.43 JHIW 46: ABSIRTO. 59: ALBINO. 61: MALOU.

1104 GEORGE EASTMAN 5.43 JHIW 52: Converted to experimental minefield sweeper YAG 39 (same name) (USN).

This vessel served as an atomic fall-out sampling ship during Pacific tests, being fitted with 'bird-bath' collecting tubs on masts. Engines and steering were remote-controlled from shielded interior compartment to permit entry into dangerous radiation zones. Later used as a storeship. 62: Replaced into service as research ship. Now reported laid up.

1105 CYRUS W. FIELD 5.43 JHIW 11.61: Scrapped Wilmington, NC.

1106 ISAAC BABBITT 5.43 JHIW 43: ETAMIN AK 93 (USN). 27.4.44: Damaged by Japanese aircraft torpedo in Aitape Roads, New Guinea. Towed Finschafen for temporary repairs. Became storage hulk IX 173 (USN). 49: Scrapped by Asia Development Co of Shanghai.

1107 CHARLES E. DURYEA 5.43 JHIW 43: OREL. 49: IVAN POLZUNOV.

1108 BENJAMIN HOLT 5.43 JHIW 58: Scrapped Oakland, Cal.

1109 OLIVER EVANS 5.43 JHIW 12.59: Scrapped Portland, Maine.

1110 ELISHA GRAVES OTIS 5.43 JHIW 9.64: Scrapped Panama City.

1111 KNUTE ROCKNE 5.43 JHIW Reserve Fleet, site 4.

1112 JAMES J. CORBETT 5.43 JHIW 7.64: Scrapped Panama City.

1113 WALTER CAMP 5.43 WISC 25.1.44: Sunk by submarine (U.532) torpedo in Indian Ocean, 10.00N 71.49E (voyage New York/Calcutta).

1114 HOBART BAKER 5.43 JHIW 28.12.44: Sunk by Japanese air attack near Mindoro, Philippines.

1115 CHRISTY MATHEWSON 5.43 F & S 9.60: Scrapped Tsuneishi.

1116 GEORGE GIPP 5.43 JHIW Reserve Fleet, site 4.

1117 MATTHEW B. BRADY 5.43 WISC 9.60: Scrapped Port Glasgow.

1118 EDWARD A. MACDOWELL 6.43 WISC 47: KENT COUNTY. 58: GIBSON. 59: TWINFOX. 4.67: Scrapped Kaohsiung.

1119 JOSEPH SMITH 6.43 JHIW 11.1.44: Abandoned sinking after developing cracks in hull, 44.30N 43.10W (voyage Liverpool/New York). Sunk by gunfire from HM ship.

1120 TECUMSEH 6.43 JHIW 47: AVRANCHES. 66: AVRANCHOISE. 4.70: At Split for scrapping.

1121 JOHN L. SULLIVAN 6.43 WISC 57: Converted to experimental minesweeper YAG 37 (no name, USN).

Used in Chesapeake Bay for tests carried out by the Underwater Explosion Research Division of the Norfolk Naval Shipyard to determine the degree of resistance of the hull to underwater explosions. Four T34 turbo-prop aircraft engines were fitted on gunmounts on deck – two forward and two aft – and were solely to provide for minor movements of the ship. All other propelling machinery was removed; it was claimed that the air engines with their 24,000 hp gave the vessel a speed of 8 knots. After the tests these engines were removed and holes in the hull repaired at Newport News to enable the ship to be towed to Wilmington, where, in 1958 she was scrapped.

1122 GERONIMO 6.43 JHIW 60: Scrapped Tacoma, Wash.

1566 IRVING M. SCOTT 6.43 JHIW 1.60: Scrapped Portland, Ore.

1567 JOSEPH S. EMERY 6.43 F & S 6.60: Scrapped Jersey City.

1568 GEORGE BERKELEY 6.43 JHIW 12.60: Scrapped Kobe.

1569 ADOLPH SUTRO 6.43 JHIW 5.61: Scrapped Tacoma.

1570 JOHN W. MACKAY 6.43 JHIW 5.69: Scrapped Oakland, Cal.

1571 JAMES W. NYE 6.43 JHIW 43: GANYMEDE AK 104 (USN). 47: GANYMEDE. Reserve Fleet, site 6.

1572 WILLIAM W. MAYO 6.43 JHIW 1.60: Scrapped Baltimore.

1573 JOHN LIND 6.43 IFM Reserve Fleet, site 2.

1574 OLE E. ROLVAAG 6.43 JHIW Reserve Fleet, site 2.

1575 JOHN T. McMILLAN 6.43 JHIW 3.70: Sold for scrapping at Portland, Ore.

1576 FREMONT OLDER 6.43 IFM 47: ASTRO. 47: ZENEIZE. 60: CINAN. 64: ARTEMIDA. 5.10.67: Developed severe leaks in holds, beached off Sungei Muar, Malacca Strait, 02.30N 102.29E. (Voyage Safaga/China – phosphate rock). 18.10.67: Refloated, towed Singapore. Later towed Shanghai. 30.11.67: Broke adrift from anchorage in heavy weather, grounded Woosung Quarantine Anchorage. Broke in two, sank. Total loss.

1577 CONRAD KOHRS 6.43 JHIW 46: AEQUITAS
II. 9.63: Scrapped Hirao.

1578 STEPHEN CRANE 7.43 JHIW 5.44: Bombed
by Japanese in salved US plane in Pacific. Severely
damaged but proceeded. Later reported grounded
and again damaged. Refloated, but CTL. Later towed
James River and laid up. 58: Scrapped Baltimore.

1579 WILLIAM BEAUMONT 7.43 JHIW Reserve
Fleet, site 5.

1580 JOHN H. ROSSETER 7.43 JHIW 10.66:
Scrapped Tacoma, Wash.

1581 HENRY DODGE 7.43 JHIW 46: GIOVANNI
AMENDOLA. 61: ALHELI. 22.4.68: Abandoned
sinking 900 miles east of Bermuda after leaks in holds.
24.4.68: Sank 33.15N 45.50W. (Voyage Almeria/
Wilmington, Del).

1582 JOHN S. SARGENT 7.43 JHIW
10.69: Sold to New York shipbreakers.

1583 CHARLES ROBINSON 7.43 JHIW 47:
SARONNO. 9.63: Scrapped Spezia.

1584 INCREASE A. LAPHAM 7.43 JHIW 43: ALKES
AK110 (USN). 46: INCREASE A. LAPHAM. Reserve
Fleet, site 2.

1585 CLARENCE KING 7.43 JHIW 47: ATLANTIC
PILOT. 53: PILOT. 59: ANASTASIA IV. 64:
AMAZON RIVER. 17.5.64: Aground Serranilla Bank,
200 miles south west of Jamaica. (Voyage Cuba/Japan
– sugar). 27.5.64: Refloated. Towed Kingston. 10.64:
Towed Curacao, CTL. Sold. 65: RIVER. 25.12.66:
Arrived Genoa, in tow, for scrap. 18.2.67: Moved to
Vado where she sank in shallow water after ranging
alongside the quay in heavy weather and developing
leaks. Presumably later scrapped.

1586 WILLIAM PROUSE 7.43 IFM 11.60: Scrapped
Baltimore.

1587 M.H. DE YOUNG 7.43 JHIW 14.8.43: Damaged
by Japanese submarine (I.19) torpedo in Pacific,
21.50S 175.10E (voyage Port Hueneme/Espiritu Santo).
4.9.43: Towed into Tongatubu Island. 5.44:
Transferred to USN, renamed ANTELOPE IX 109
(engines removed, used as a hulk). 46: M.H. DE
YOUNG. 48: Sold to China for scrap. 23.8.50:
Towed from Hong Kong to Shanghai. Later scrapped.

1588 JOHN E. WILKIE 7.43 JHIW Completed as
SAMBRIDGE. 18.11.43: Sunk by Japanese submarine
(I.27) torpedo in Arabian Sea 11.25N 47.25E (voyage
Madras/USA).

1589 JOHN ROSS 7.43 IFM 47: HELLENIC WAVE.

1708 JOSEPH A. HOLMES 7.43 JHIW 9.65:
Scrapped Portland, Ore.

1709 LUTHER S. KELLY 7.43 WISC 47: GIOA-
CCHINO LAURO. 12.68: Scrapped Spezia.

1710 CHARLES N. McGROARTY 7.43 IFM
12.59: Scrapped Oakland, Cal.

1711 THOMAS M. COOLEY 7.43 IFM 51: SEA
LEGEND. 53: OCEAN BETTY. 55: OCEAN ROSE.
59: PACIFIC RANGER. 60: DOMINGA. 62: SANTA
MARIA I. 65: IONIC CREST. 4.2.67: Reported
leaking and flooded due to heavy weather damage and
fractured plates on voyage Mormugao/Japan — iron
ore. Sold. 28.2.67: Arrived Nagoya for scrap but resold and renamed JULIE II for voyage to breakers.
12.67: Scrapped Hirao.

1712 JOHN EVANS 7.43 JHIW 3.61: Scrapped
Philadelphia.

1713 FRANK D. PHINNEY 7.43 WISC Completed
as SAMOVAR. 47: KANSI. 49: COLONIAL. 61:
PLANTER. 63: GARGI JAYANTI. 67: SAM-
UDRA JYOTI.

1714 WILLIAM H. ALLEN 8.43 JHIW Reserve
Fleet, site 5.

1715 MELVILLE E. STONE 8.43 JHIW 24.11.43:
Sunk by submarine (U.516) torpedo south of Panama,
10.36N 80.19W (voyage Antofagasta/New York).

1716 HENRY V. ALVARADO 8.43 JHIW
47: ITALMARE. 50: Converted at Genoa to 6 cyl
oil engine by Fiat. 66: EASTPORT.

1717 GEORGE INNESS 8.43 WISC Completed as
SAMBRE. 48: GEORGE INNESS. 4.61: Scrapped
Baltimore.

1718 H.G. BLASDEL 8.43 JHIW 29.6.44: One of
four Liberty ships (see JAMES A. FARRELL, etc)
torpedoed by U.984 in English Channel whilst in
convoy with troops to Normandy. USS LST.326
(already carrying 900 German POWs) detached from
her UK-bound convoy to rescue survivors, amounting

to nearly 300 troops. Towed in and beached near Southampton. Broke in two. Subsequently refloated and 13.11.44: arrived in tow at Briton Ferry for scrapping. 47: Scrapped.

1719 THOMAS C. POWER 8.43 WISC 12.65: Scrapped Wilmington, NC.

1720 WILLIAM MATSON 8.43 JHIW 2.62: Scrapped Everett, Wash.

1721 BRANDER MATTHEWS 8.43 JHIW 47: VALERIUS. 50: ARUNDO. 55: KHIOS BREEZE. 59: NYMFEA. 5.67: Scrapped Ikeda.

1722 WILLIAM KEITH 8.43 WISC 10.66: Scrapped Tacoma, Wash.

1723 JOSEPH K. TOOLE 8.43 WISC 47: TRANVIK. 54: MARINA GABRIELLA PARODI. 55: MARINA G. PARODI. 9.65: Scrapped Spezia.

1724 JEREMIAH M. DAILY 8.43 JHIW 47: GOVERNOR KILBY. 48: ATLANTICUS. 56: SAG HARBOR. 4.62: Scrapped Jersey City.

1725 MARY PATTEN 8.43 JHIW 43: AZIMECH AK124 (USN). 45: MARY PATTEN. Reserve Fleet, site 2.

1726 HIRAM BINGHAM 8.43 JHIW 47: VULCANO. 65: AGIOGALUSENA. 4.69: Scrapped Split.

1727 WILLIAM D. BURNHAM 8.43 WISC 23.11.44: Damaged by mine or submarine torpedo in English Channel, 49.46N 01.15W. (Voyage St Helens Roads/ Cherbourg — vehicles & army stores). Towed to Cherbourg and beached. 5.1.45: Refloated, towed Falmouth. CTL. Sold. 17.7.48: Towed Antwerp and scrapped.

1728 ANTOINE SAUGRAIN 8.43 WISC 5.12.44: Damaged by Japanese aircraft torpedoes in Leyte Gulf, (voyage New Guinea/Leyte). Taken in tow but 6.12.44: Again torpedoed and sank near Surigas Strait.

1729 STEPHEN W. KEARNY 8.43 JHIW Reserve Fleet, site 4.

1730 JAMES ROWAN 8.43 JHIW 43: ALLIOTH AK 109 (USN). 44: ALLIOTH IX 204 (USN) 44: Converted to Aviation Store ship ALLIOTH AVS 4 (USN). 47: JAMES ROWAN. 5.65: Scrapped Kearny, NJ.

1731 RICHARD MOCZKOWSKI 8.43 WISC 66: Scrapped Kearny, NJ.

2137 JOHN COLTER 9.43 IFM 46: BRIANCON. 60: ZEPHYROS. 66: SAILOR STAR. 6.67: Scrapped Shanghai.

2138 MARY M. DODGE 9.43 JHIW 9.43: MOLEN-GRAAF. 47: PRINS WILLEM II. 53: DAYROSE. 56: ARETI S. 63: DIMOS. 12.69: Scrapped Whampoa.

2139 EMILE BERLINER 9.43 WISC 47: FROSTVIK. 50: ARNETA. 63: SUSAN PAULIN. 65: KYRA. 5.69: Scrapped Bilbao.

2140 CHARLES G. COUTANT 9.43 JHIW 46: ATLANTIC SEA. 62: SPLENDID SEA.

2141 JOHN W. HOYT 9.43 JHIW 9.61: Scrapped Oakland, Cal.

2142 WAYNE MACVEAGH 9.43 IFM Reserve Fleet, site 4.

2143 HARMON JUDSON 9.43 JHIW Completed as SAMWASH. 47: MAPLEBANK. 57: AFRICAN LORD. 4.69: Scrapped Kaohsiung.

2144 HENRY M. TELLER 9.43 WISC Completed as CHUNG SHAN. 47: HENRY M. TELLER. Reserve Fleet, site 2.

2145 JEREMIAH M. RUSK 9.43 JHIW 2.70: Sold to Spanish shipbreakers.

2146 BENJAMIN H. BREWSTER 9.43 JHIW 46: ANGELINA LAURO. 64: LILY LAURO. 5.69: Scrapped Spezia.

2147 CHARLES E. SMITH 9.43 JHIW 47: ALGA. 4.69: Scrapped Spezia.

2148 CHARLES DEVENS 9.43 JHIW Completed as SAMORE. 43: SAMDEL. 47: Returned US Govt. 2.59: Scrapped Baltimore.

2149 LOUIS A. SENGTELLER 9.43 JHIW 46: CORACERO. 48: ARRIERO. 63: AKTI.

2150 DONALD M. DICKINSON 9.43 WISC 8.65: Scrapped Philadelphia.

2151 AUGUSTUS THOMAS 9.43 JHIW 24.10.44: Severely damaged when USN tug SONOMA (alongside) was struck by crashing Japanese bomber in San Pedro Bay, Leyte. Beached. 17.11.44: Further damaged in air attack. Refloated, towed Hollandia. CTL. Towed Newcastle (NSW), thence Suisun Bay, Calif, (laid up). 1.47: Offered for sale for scrap. 57: Reported scrapped Oakland, Cal.

2152 GEORGE STERLING 9.43 JHIW 6.58: Scrapped Portland, Ore.

2153 WILLIAM H. MOODY 9.43 WISC 47: MARIA B. 48: MARIA BIBOLINI. 63: BOOTES. 3.67: Scrapped Hong Kong.

2154 HENRY C. PAYNE 9.43 JHIW 47: RIALTO. 2.67: Scrapped Trieste.

2155 GEORGE VON L. MEYER 10.43 WISC 12.59: Scrapped Portland, Ore.

2156 JAMES D. PHELAN 10.43 JHIW 47: JALAK-ANTA. 9.63: Scrapped Bombay.

2157 OTTO MEARS 10.43 WISC 47: NAPOLI. 48: POSILLIPO. 54: FEDERICO COSTA. 56: BIANCA C. 57: BICE COSTA. 60: ENOSIS. 22.11.67: Afire in after holds, put aground in Krabi River, Thailand, 07.52N 98.56E (Voyage Chingwangtao/India — coal). Fire spread throughout ship, vessel abandoned. 4.12.67: Refloated unaided, drifted, still afire. 11.12.67: Taken in tow, beached off Penang, fire extinguished. Refloated. 26.1.68: Arrived Singapore in tow, completely gutted. CTL. Sold for scrapping at Jurong, Singapore.

2158 FRANK NORRIS 10.43 JHIW Reserve Fleet, site 4.

2159 FRANCIS M. SMITH 10.43 JHIW 2.62: Scrapped Baltimore.

2160 FRANK A. MUNSEY 10.43 JHIW Reserve Fleet, site 5.

2161 FREDERIC A. EILERS 10.43 IFM 47: Sold commercial (same name). 55: PORTORIA. 61: ELENI SECONDA. 3.65: Scrapped Spezia.

2162 WILLIAM S. CLARK 10.43 JHIW 47: PUNTA MESCO. 7.65: Scrapped Spezia.

2163 SAMUEL W. WILLISTON 10.43 JHIW 47: ATLANTIC SEAMAN. 60: WHITE CLIFFS. 3.67: Scrapped Kaohsiung.

2164 EDGAR W. NYE 10.43 JHIW 3.62: Scrapped Terminal Island.

2165 FRANK C. EMERSON 10.43 WISC Reserve Fleet, site 8.

2166 JOHN W. FOSTER 10.43 JHIW Reserve Fleet, site 2.

2167 NORMAN HAPGOOD 10.43 WISC 47: NEREIDE.

2168 BERNARDO O'HIGGINS 10.43 JHIW 12.59: Scrapped Oakland, Cal.

2169 NORMAN E. MACK 10.43 JHIW Reserve Fleet, site 4.

2170 HENRY H. BLOOD 10.43 JHIW 8.61: Scrapped Baltimore.

2171 JOHN SWETT 10.43 WISC 2.65: Scrapped Philadelphia.

2172 VERNON L. PARRINGTON 10.43 JHIW 47: PHILIPS VAN MARNIX. 47: LOOSDRECHT. 61: CRESCENT. 1.9.62: Aground during typhoon Tolo Harbour, Hong Kong. Total loss. Scrapped 'in situ'.

2173 GEORGE K. FITCH 10.43 WISC 47: GOVERNOR BIBB. 48: NORTH SKY. 54: AGIA THALASSINI. 20.9.65: Arrived Montevideo after severe grounding damage on voyage Necochea/ Civitavecchia. Cargo discharged, vessel laid-up unrepaired. 66: MARIA TERESA (still laid-up). 9.68: Towed Santander for scrap.

2174 FRANCIS A. WARDWELL 10.43 WISC Reserve Fleet, site 1.

2175 KATE DOUGLAS WIGGIN 10.43 JHIW 1.61: Scrapped Oakland, Cal.

2176 DAVID HEWES 11.43 JHIW 47: PUNTA ALICE. 64: ISPAHAN. 12.69: Scrapped Gandia.

2177 FERDINAND A. SILCOX 11.43 JHIW 9.69: Sold for scrapping at Mobile.

2178 SARA TEASDALE 11.43 JHIW 47: ORA-DOUR. 59: LEOTRIC. 60: HERA. 63: CALIFORNIA SUN. 64: ZANETA. 19.6.66: Foundered in Arabian Sea after springing leaks, 17.56N 58.20E (voyage Mormugao/Trieste — ore).

2179 JAMES KING 11.43 JHIW 11.61: Scrapped Portland, Ore.

2180 R.F. PECKHAM 11.43 WISC 31.12.45: In collision with Liberty ship JESSE COTTRELL, 10 miles east of Gibraltar, 36.03N 04.55W. Towed into Gibraltar, severely damaged. CTL. (Voyage Palermo/Hampton Roads). Sold. 27.9.48: Arrived Cadiz in tow for scrapping. Resold and repaired and 1950: RIO TAJO (7,696 grt).

2181 PETER TRIMBLE ROWE 11.43 JHIW 2.62: Scrapped Baltimore.

2182 KEITH VAWTER 11.43 WISC 47: HELLENIC STAR.

2183 JAMES G. MAGUIRE 11.43 JHIW 47: NINETTO GAVARONE. 60: CADORE SECONDO. 62: HUTA LABEDY.

2184 ROBERT LOUIS STEVENSON 11.43 WISC 8.67: Sank off Alaska.

In July 1967 the US Defence Department announced a series of some forty underwater detonations to be conducted during a three-month period in an area extending from 1100 miles south west to 500 miles north east of Amchitka, Aleutian Islands. In the following month the ROBERT LOUIS STEVENSON was laden with 5,000 tons of old military cargo (including 2,000 tons of mines and torpedoes) at the Naval Air Depot, Bangor Bremerton, Washington and was towed to a point 34 miles off Amchitka to be scuttled in 4,000 feet and with a pressure detonator to set off an explosion at this depth.

This controlled sinking was to be the largest planned underwater non-nuclear explosion in history and was to help improve nuclear detection techniques and to enable the study of seismic wave action.

On 10th August however, the vessel was declared a hazard to navigation when she failed to sink after her sea-valves were opened, for she rolled over on her side and drifted off into a fog bank. Later, she sank during heavy weather and was finally located in 'shallow' water 20 miles south of Rat Island. The depth of 2,800 feet was not sufficient to detonate the charge and in an attempt to create enough pressure to set off her detonator, the US Navy sent out attack bombers in its frustrating campaign to blow up the old ship. The first bombs dropped proved to be duds — the ship defied further action and remains intact in the Pacific waters off Alaska.

2185 FRANCISCO M. QUINONES 11.43 JHIW 9.68: Scrapped Green Cove Springs, Fla.

2186 FERDINAND WESTDAHL 11.43 JHIW 6.67: Scrapped Portland, Ore.

2187 WILLIAM F. EMPEY 11.43 JHIW 47: PORTOROSE. 7.68: Scrapped Trieste.

2272 GEORGE CLEMENT PERKINS 4.44 WISC 51: SEAMONITOR. 57: GRAIN TRADER. 58: MARIA H. 59: MOUNT RAINIER. 62: Lengthened at Tokio to 511½ ft (8,584 grt), renamed DUVAL. 8.69: Scrapped Kaohsiung.

2273 GILBERT M. HITCHCOCK 4.44 JHIW 2.67: Scrapped Portland, Ore.

2274 HENRY WHITE 4.44 JHIW 47: DESPINA. 53: ELGA. 8.67: Scrapped Kaohsiung.

2275 EMMET D. BOYLE 5.44 JHIW 44: INGUL. 50: INGUL II.

2276 ALEXANDER WOOLCOTT 5.44 JHIW 8.63: Scrapped Tacoma, Wash.

2277 E.A. CHRISTENSEN 5.44 JHIW 51: SEAFORT. 57: ANDROS FORT. 61: SAMOTHRAKI. 63: THRACE. 8.68: Scrapped Hirao.

2278 HENRY J. WATERS 5.44 JHIW Intended to be completed as JAN TROMP but completed as RODINA.

2279 WILLIAM E. RITTER 5.44 JHIW 44: BRIANSK. 44: BRIANSK II. 67: BRIANSK.

2280 JOE HARRIS 5.44 JHIW 57: Scrapped Baltimore.

2281 MELLO FRANCO 5.44 JHIW 46: BAYEAUX. 65: SINOE. 4.69: Scrapped Castellon.

2282 WILLIAM ALLEN WHITE 5.44 JHIW 51: TRANSPACIFIC. 59: TALKEETNA. 12.67: AMICUS. 2.69: Scrapped Kaohsiung.

2283 STEPHEN HOPKINS (II) 5.44 JHIW 6.67: Scrapped New Orleans.

2284 CECIL G. SELLERS 5.44 JHIW 29.2.48: On fire, abandoned, 200 miles south west of Cocos Island. (Voyage Fremantle/Cobh — wheat). Fire extinguished. 19.3.48: Towed Fremantle. CTL. 2.49: Towed Hong Kong. 11.50: Scrapped Shanghai.

2285 NORMAN J. COLMAN 5.44 JHIW Reserve Fleet, site 2.

2286 WILLIAM SPROULE 5.44 JHIW 51: CHRISTINE. 54: FELICIA. 55: ALEXANDRA. 56: MADISON BELLE. 6.63: Scrapped Hirao.

2287 JOHN L. STODDARD 11.43 JHIW 47: SAMOS. 6.67: Scrapped Hsinkang.

2288 FRANK H. DODD 11.43 JHIW 47: VALEN-
TINA B. 48: VALENTINA BIBOLINI. 62:
KATERINA SAMONA. 66: PALOMA. 66: AGIOS
GIORGIS. 9.67: Scrapped Kaohsiung.

Toward the end of 1964 the KATERINA SAMONA
commenced a voyage which was to be a curtain-raiser to a
new timber trade between Canada and Plymouth but delivered
her 10,000 ton cargo in 120 days instead of the estimated 44.
On voyage from Port Alberni she first broke down and was
repaired at Panama. Then, in early December she suffered
boiler and machinery damage, her cargo shifted and she
almost foundered in a storm in the Atlantic. The tug MAAS
took her in tow in 37.13N 30.17W for the Azores. Repairers
there thought the ship should never sail again, but she was
repaired and sailed. On 28.12.64 she was again in distress,
leaking, listing and sinking from fractured plates and
damaged by shifting cargo in high seas off Spain in 44.30N
12.40W. The tug ATLANTIC met her and she was towed to
Ferrol. Attempts to get her engine going were abandoned and
on 4.2.65 she arrived at Plymouth in tow of the tug SERVICE-
MAN. Again repaired, she changed her name twice during
1966. On 25.7.67 she was yet again in distress and sinking in
a gale after cracks in her hull in position 08.50N 83.42E on a
voyage from Calcutta to Japan with iron ore. Later she
arrived at Colombo. Many cracks were reported in her hull
and her plates were stated to be 'knife-edge' thin. Further
repairs were commenced but on 2.8.67 she sailed without
them being completed on her final voyage to the shipbreakers
yard.

2289 MARY WALKER 11.43 WISC 47: LOULA
NOMIKOS. 59: PRESIDENT HOFFMAN. 10.63:
Scrapped Osaka.

2290 J. MAURICE THOMPSON 11.43 IFM
47: MOUNT ATHOS. 62: EUXEINOS. 27.2.66:
Abandoned after developing leaks about 360 miles
south west of the Azores, 33.05N 31.10W (voyage
Evi Gocek/Baltimore). Presumed sunk.

2291 WALTER WILLIAMS 11.43 JHIW 7.60:
Scrapped Portland, Ore.

2292 MARY A. LIVERMORE 11.43 IFM 47:
MYRTO. 5.48: Converted to tanker by Bethlehem
Steel Co, Baltimore. 54: Converted to dry cargo by
Howaldtswerke, Hamburg. 60: WORLD LEADER.
63: CONCORD. 64: OCEANIC EXPLORER. 67:
Renamed PACMOON for delivery trip from Saigon
for scrapping. 3.68: Scrapped Kaohsiung.

2684 GEORGE CRILE 5.44 JHIW Reserve Fleet,
site 2.

2685 RALPH T. O'NEIL 5.44 JHIW 2.66: Scrapped
Oakland, Cal.

2686 GEORGE B. McFARLAND 5.44 JHIW 3.64:
Scrapped New Orleans.

2687 WILLIAM H. CLAGETT 5.44: JHIW 68:
Converted at Portland, Ore, into a crane barge.

2688 JOSE PEDRO VARELA 5.44 JHIW 49: ELLY.
52: MARVEN. 55: ARION. 12.68: Scrapped
Etayima.

2689 SAMUEL L. COBB 6.44 JHIW 46: VOLUN-
TEER STATE. 55: FORTUNA.

2690 EDWARD P. RIPLEY 6.44 JHIW 49: FLORA
C. 57: ARTHUR FRIBOURG. 58: DOROTHY
BOYLAN. 66: DOROTHY. 10.68: Scrapped
Santander.

2691 CHARLES J. COLDEN 6.44 JHIW Reserve
Fleet, site 1.

2692 HENRY T. SCOTT 6.44 JHIW 11.65: Scrapped
Panama City.

2693 OVID BUTLER 6.44 JHIW 8.65: Scrapped
New Orleans.

2694 JAY COOKE 6.44 JHIW 44: GENERAL
VATUTIN. 66: MIKLUKHO-MAKLAI.
(See HARVEY CUSHING and JOSEPH C. AVERY).

2695 TERRY E. STEPHENSON 6.44 JHIW Reserve
Fleet, site 1.

2696 THOMAS F. HUNT 6.44 JHIW 5.64:
Converted at Portland, Ore, to a barge.

2697 GEORGE E. GOODFELLOW 6.44 JHIW
44: GENERAL PANFILOV.

2698 JUSTO AROSEMENA 7.44 JHIW
4.70: Sold to Seattle shipbreakers.

2699 SAMUEL GOMPERS (II) 7.44 JHIW 6.60:
Scrapped Baltimore.

2700 BENJAMIN WARNER 7.44 JHIW Reserve
Fleet, site 1.

2701 SEAMAN A. KNAPP 11.43 IFM Reserve Fleet,
site 2.

2702 JAMES ROLPH 12.43 WISC 47: SPIGA. 63:
ALA-TAU. 67: Deleted from USSR Register.

2703 ANTONIN DVORAK 12.43 JHIW 3.59: Sold
for scrap but 28.3.59: Broke adrift from tug

OILTRANSCO whilst in tow from Wilmington NC to Baltimore for scrapping. Aground near Cape Hatteras. Salved. 24.4.59: Arrived Baltimore and scrapped there the same year.

2704 ALBERT A. ROBINSON 12.43 JHIW 58: Scrapped Oakland, Cal.

2705 RICHARD B. MOORE 12.43 WISC 47: SAN GIUSTO. 63: MASHUK.

2706 ALEXANDER WILSON 12.43 IFM 47: ALFIOS. 5.4.52: Struck wreck outside Saigon, 10.20N 107.03E. Aground, broke in two, submerged. Total loss. (Voyage Dunkirk/Saigon — general). 3.54: Stern part refloated, towed Hong Kong and scrapped.

2707 JOSE C. BARBOSA 12.43 JHIW 3.60: Scrapped Tacoma.

2708 ALEXANDER MITCHELL 12.43 JHIW 47: SIRENA. 4.67: Scrapped Trieste.

2709 J.C. OSGOOD 12.43 IFM 47: BIANCA CORRADO. 63: BESHTAU.

2710 FRANK H. EVERS 12.43 JHIW 46: ENRICO C. 63: NICOLAS A. 4.67: Scrapped Kaohsiung.

2711 JAMES OLIVER CURWOOD 12.43 JHIW 47: NAZARIO SAURO. 63: HUTA ZYGMUNT. 1.9.67: Used as grain store at Szczecin.

2712 EDWARD G. ACHESON 12.43 WISC 47: VERSILIA. 62: SEA URCHIN. 5.67: Scrapped Osaka.

2713 FRANCIS WILSON 12.43 WISC 3.62: Scrapped Baltimore.

2714 CLAUS SPRECKELS 12.43 JHIW 46: HUMANITAS. 62: ALBADA. 64: RENEKA. 4.66: Renamed SAN CARLOS for delivery to breakers. 5.66: Scrapped Spezia.

2715 DAVID LUBIN 12.43 JHIW 46: FLORESTA. 49: LUIGI. 2.63: Scrapped Vado.

2716 FRANK J. SPRAGUE 12.43 WISC 2.68: Scrapped Portland, Ore.

2717 JEAN P. CHOUTEAU 12.43 JHIW 47: DUINO. 8.68: At Trieste for scrapping.

2718 JULIA L. DUMONT 12.43 JHIW 4.66: Scrapped Portland, Ore.

2719 ROBERT G. COUSINS 12.43 WISC 47: MONGINEVRO. 63: AVACHA.

2720 GEORGE B. PORTER 12.43 JHIW 47: ASPROMONTE. 10.66: Scrapped Spezia.

2721 WILLIAM FORD NICHOLS 1.44 WISC Reserve Fleet, site 2.

2722 LILLIAN WALD 1.44 IFM 47: GIORGIO. 60: DORCOL. 2.70: At Split for scrapping.

2723 GEORGE LUKS 1.44 WISC 5.61: Scrapped Kobe.

2724 WILLIAM VAUGHN MOODY 1.44 WISC 7.69: Scrapped New Orleans.

2725 OLIVER KELLEY 1.44 JHIW 8.59: Scrapped Seattle.

2726 ABRAM S. HEWITT 1.44 WISC 47: QUEMAR. 47: ITALO MARSANO. 57: GOLFO DI TRIESTE. 14.12.64: Sank after developing leaks, 11.10N 112.31E off South Vietnam. (Voyage Gijon/Japan — pig iron).

2727 WILLIAM PEFFER 1.44 JHIW 47: LISIEUX. 52: BAR DE LUC. 54: ANDREA PARODI. 60: ALBUR. 1.69: Scrapped Shanghai.

2728 ADA REHAN 1.44 JHIW 47: MONVISO. 67: Scrapped Spezia.

2729 URIAH M. ROSE 1.44 JHIW 47: AURAY. 61: Converted to oil engine at Nantes by At. & Ch. Bretagne. Renamed PAN. 64: ORCHIDEA.

2730 JOHN W. BURGESS 1.44 IFM 11.64: Scrapped Tacoma.

2731 MOSES G. FARMER 1.44 JHIW 3.62: Scrapped Tacoma.

2732 ALFRED C. TRUE 1.44 WISC 47: FRANCESCO BARBARO. 49: LUISIANA. 60: SERENITAS. 61: ARKAS. 9.69: At Trieste for scrapping.

2733 WILLIAM B. LEEDS 1.44 JHIW 54: Scrapped Baltimore.

2734 FRANCISCO MORAZAN 1.44 JHIW 47: CHRYSSI. 52: HARALAMPOS HADJIPATERAS. 63: AEGAION. 4.67: Scrapped Shanghai.

2735 WILLIAM D. BOYCE 1.44 IFM 47: MONROSA. 63: MALAKHOV KURGAN.

2736 W.B. RODGERS 1.44 JHIW 47: AKTI. 60: JENNY III. 6.8.62: Aground in River Guayas.

15.8.62: Refloated. 28.8.62: Aground again on Serrana Bank, (Voyage Guayaquil/New Orleans — sugar). 8.9.62: Refloated, towed New Orleans. CTL. 6.63: Scrapped New Orleans.

2737 CARL B. EIELSON 1.44 WISC 3.62: Scrapped Portland, Ore.

2738 ALICE H. RICE 2.44 WISC 23.8.45: Ashore Kinabatangan Reef, nr Subic Bay. (Voyage Los Angeles/Lingayen and Manila). 16.9.45: Refloated, temporary repairs at Lingayen, thence to USA and laid-up Suisun Bay. CTL. 10.47: Scrapped Terminal Island.

2739 ELWOOD HAYNES 1.44 JHIW 47: LAURA LAURO. 1.69: Scrapped Spezia.

2740 NATHAN S. DAVIS 2.44 IFM 46: GIACOMO FASSIO. 62: Scrapped Spezia.

2741 MORGAN ROBERTSON 2.44 JHIW 47: STROMBOLI.

2742 JOHN HOPE 2.44 WISC 47: TERGESTE. 59: RAVNI KOTARI. 7.67: Scrapped Hirao.

2743 DANIEL G. REID 2.44 JHIW Reserve Fleet, site 4.

2744 CORNELIUS VANDERBILT 2.44 IFM 47: STELLA. 47: SPUMA. 11.67: Scrapped Trieste.

2745 JAMES DEVEREUX 2.44 JHIW 47: MONT-BELLIARD. 66: GEOWILKA. 12.12.67: Aground off Gedser, Denmark, 54.29N 12.06E. (Voyage India/Poland — general). 16.12.67: Refloated, severely damaged, proceeded Szczecin. CTL, sold. 1.3.68: Arrived Hamburg in tow for scrap.

2746 JOHN H. THOMAS 2.44 WISC 47: SANTA RITA. 62: ALBORADA.

2747 PERCY E. FOXWORTH 2.44 JHIW 10.69: Scrapped Panama City.

2748 CARL G. BARTH 2.44 JHIW 47: FALAISE. 1.64: Scrapped Ferrol.

2749 EDWIN C. MUSICK 2.44 JHIW 12.58: Scrapped Portland, Ore.

2750 SARA BACHE 2.44 JHIW 4.61: Scrapped Portland, Ore.

2751 HANS HEG 2.44 WISC 3.61: Scrapped Seattle.

2752 FRANZ SIGEL 2.44 JHIW 47: GOVERNOR O'NEAL. 48: SEAFAIR. 62: SMITH CRUSADER. 9.64: Scrapped Ferrol.

2753 ARTHUR A. PENN 2.44 JHIW 1.59: Scrapped Portland, Ore.

2754 ALLEN JOHNSON 2.44 JHIW 11.58: Scrapped Seattle.

2755 GEORGE A. POPE 2.44: WISC 46: PACIFIC OCEAN. 52: ALIKI P. 55: PANAGIOTIS XILAS. 63: RAZANI. 8.63: Scrapped Onomichi.

2756 JOSEPH J. KINYOUN 2.44 JHIW 46: GRAN-VILLE. 61: GRANIKOS. 19.9.66: Grounded, Buffalo Rock, Pulo Sambu, Indonesia. (Voyage China/Chittagong — rice). 21.9.66: Refloated, towed Singapore, laid up in damaged condition. 3.68: Scrapped Hong Kong.

2757 JUAN PABLO DUARTE 2.44 JHIW 46: ETNA. 6.63: Scrapped Palermo.

2758 JOHN F. SHAFROTH 3.44 WISC 64: Scuttled by US Navy.

This vessel was taken from Suisun Bay Reserve Fleet and towed to the Naval Weapons Station, Concord, Cal, for stripping and loading. Her cargo included bombs, torpedo warheads, mines, cartridges, projectiles, fuses, detonators, boosters and over-age Polaris missile motors and contaminated 'cake-mix' for deep sea disposal. She departed in tow on 22.7.64 and reached the deep-water dumping site, 47 miles west of Golden Gate next morning. Seacocks were opened at 11.35 am and at 14.03 she slid beneath the surface carrying her 9,800 tons of cargo safely to an 8,000 feet depth.

2759 CLEVELAND FORBES 3.44 JHIW 46: LANCERO. 48: RESERO. 64: FRANCISCO-HACHE. 64: MARNIC. 15.11.64: Aground at San Salvador, Bahamas. (Voyage Maracaibo/New York — ballast). 17.11.64: Refloated. CTL. Sold. 3.65: Scrapped Aviles.

2760 SIDNEY H. SHORT 3.44 JHIW 2.70: Sold for scrapping at New Orleans.

2761 E.A. BRYAN 3.44 JHIW 17.7.44: Exploded whilst loading munitions at Port Chicago harbour, 35 miles north of San Francisco.

The terrific explosion of this vessel's 5,000 tons of cargo also detonated the munitions being loaded into the Victory-type ship QUINALT VICTORY (44/7,608 grt). Both vessels completely disintegrated, only a small section of one and a few twisted remains of the other remaining visible at the site. Later, other pieces were discovered many miles away.

The piers and buildings of Port Chicago were almost completely destroyed. Other damage was widespread and reached a distance of 50 miles, whilst the blast from the explosion was felt more than 200 miles away. The devastation and loss was estimated at many millions of dollars, and in addition the two shattered ships were together valued at nearly 4½ million dollars.

Other vessels involved were Coast Guard vessels, fire and patrol boats and a tanker, which were either sunk or damaged. Many hundreds of lives were lost in the catastrophe and thousands of naval and military personnel were injured.

2762 HENRY M. STEPHENS 3.44 JHIW 51: SEA-FAITH. 56: Lengthened at Sasebo to 511½ ft, (8,453 grt). 57: ANDROS FAIRPLAY. 60: MESSINIAKOS. 62: POLYKTOR. 63: CAPETAN COSTIS I. 4.67: Scrapped Gandia.

2763 WILLET M. HAYS 3.44 WISC 47: COURS-ELLES. 4.64: Scrapped Hamburg.

2764 EDWARD E. HALE 3.44 JHIW 47: DOM-FRONT. 65: SAINT LYS. 3.67: Scrapped Hiroshima.

2765 CHARLES JOHN SEGHERS 3.44 JHIW 46: CAPRERA. 12.68: Scrapped Vado.

2766 WILLIAM J. GRAY 3.44 JHIW 3.69: Scrapped Portland, Ore.

2767 AMERIGO VESPUCCI 3.44 JHIW 1.62: Scrapped Portland, Ore.

2768 GEORGE MIDDLEMAS 3.44 JHIW 60: Scrapped Philadelphia.

2769 ROBERT D. CAREY 3.44 JHIW 47: PERLA. 1.69: Scrapped Spezia.

2770 H. WEIR COOK 3.44 WISC 3.68: Scrapped Portland, Ore.

2771 LOUIS WEULE 3.44 JHIW 7.67: Scrapped Portland, Ore.

2772 JOSE M. MORELOS 3.44 JHIW Reserve Fleet, site 5.

2773 BENJAMIN WATERHOUSE 3.44 JHIW Reserve Fleet, site 4.

2774 WILLIAM SCHIRMER 3.44 JHIW 10.69: Scrapped Kearny, NJ.

2775 J.S. HUTCHINSON 3.44 WISC 11.64: Scrapped Mobile.

2776 EDWARD S. HOUGH 4.44 JHIW 8.69: Sold to Philadelphia shipbreakers.

2777 E.A. BURNETT 4.44 JHIW 3.67: Scrapped Panama City.

2778 WALLACE R. FARRINGTON 4.44 JHIW 4.69: Scrapped Mobile.

2779 LOUIS SLOSS 4.44 JHIW Reserve Fleet, site 5.

2780 TOUSSAINT LOUVERTURE 4.44 JHIW 5.59: Scrapped Baltimore.

2781 LOUIS SULLIVAN 4.44 JHIW 1.70: At Mobile for scrapping.

2782 LUCIEN LABAUDT 4.44 WISC 47: CALI-FORNIA. 49: PACIFICUS. 62: SMITH CONQUEROR. 65: U.S. CONQUEROR. 67: MARIETTA. 9.69: Scrapped Kaohsiung.

2783 JAMES A. DRAIN 4.44 JHIW 47: OLYMPIC PIONEER. 62: WILDCAT. 63: Returned to US Govt. Reserve Fleet, site 2.

2784 THOMAS F. FLAHERTY 4.44 JHIW Completed as STALINGRAD. 62: VOLGOGRAD.

2785 ROBERT S. ABBOTT 4.44 JHIW Completed as KAMENETS-PODOLSK.

2786 BENJAMIN CARPENTER 4.44 WISC 11.60: Scrapped Barrow.

2787 CHARLOTTE CUSHMAN 4.44 JHIW 3.61: Scrapped Tacoma.

2788 HENRY MEIGGS 4.44 WISC Reserve Fleet, site 4.

2789 MARISCAL SUCRE 4.44 JHIW 3.68: Scrapped Portland, Ore.

BUILT BY ST JOHNS RIVER SHIPBUILDING COMPANY

The St Johns River shipyard at Jacksonville, in Florida, was established in 1942, being constructed by a local ship repair firm which combined with a New York firm of contractors to build this southernmost East Coast yard.

The plans for construction here closely followed those adopted by the Marinship yard, this being a lay-out known as a 'horizontal yard with a turning flow'. Its basis was that the transit of steel and components was parallel to the shoreline until it reached the head of the ways. Then it turned and flowed across the assembly platens down to the shipways. There was, in fact, no duplicated transit of materials — it was a straight flow, although not in a straight line.

This form of yard lay-out was generally used when inland expansion was not practicable and growth had to be spread along the shoreline.

In August 1942 the Maritime Commission offered rewards for suggested improvements to efficiency. All suitable suggestions were shared between the yards and by the end of 1944 the overall savings to the Commission amounted to some forty-five million dollars and thirty-one million man-hours. In this drive for reductions in cost, the St Johns River yard ranked second in total savings.

As with most types of war material, the profits from wartime shipbuilding, taking into account the fact that many contracts were not re-negotiable, were always the subject of criticism and shipbuilders were frequently singled out for attack because many of them operated plant owned by the government.

At a Congress hearing of 'Investigations in Shipyard Profits' in 1946 it was reported that from a total investment of only twenty-three million dollars by shipyard operators, profits had totalled 356 million dollars. Also in these hearings one of the Kaiser companies was alleged to have made a profit of 11,600 per cent; Bethlehem Fairfield was charged with a profit of a mere 1,200 per cent and in the extreme case, the private interests in the St Johns River company supposedly made 50,000 per cent on an investment of only 400 dollars. However, all these figures were strongly contested by the builders, whose sound basis of argument was that they had backed their efforts with all their resources and that the putting of their specialised 'know-how' into the new companies was sufficient justification for profits.

Liberty ship output: 82 vessels, at an average cost of 2,100,000 dollars each.

USMC hull numbers: MCE 1193–1222 (Yard Nos 1–30)
                           2467–2518 ("   "   31–82)

1 PONCE DE LEON 4.43 GMC 10.62: Scrapped Mobile, Ala.

2 JOHN GORRIE 5.43 GMC 9.67: Scrapped Portland, Ore.

3 FRANCIS ASBURY 5.43 GMC 3.12.44: Mined in North Sea, 51.21N 03.00E. Beached off Blankenberg, Belgium. Broke in two. Total loss. 10.53: Reported scrapped 'in situ'.

4 JOHN J. CRITTENDEN 6.43 GMC 3.68: Sold for scrapping at Mobile.

5 SIDNEY LANIER 7.43 GMC 8.61: Scrapped Bellingham, Seattle.

6 ROBERT Y. HAYNE 7.43 GMC 47: CITTA DI SAVONA. 58: CENTERPORT.

7 RICHARD MONTGOMERY 7.43 SMF 8.44: Damaged by enemy aircraft in Thames Estuary approaches. Towed in, but 20.8.44: Aground Nore Sands, Medway Channel. Broke in two, abandoned.

CTL. (Voyage New York/Sheerness — ammunition).

8 JOHN PHILIP SOUSA 8.43 F & S 46: ERATO. 54: TAXIARCHIS. 60: PROTOSTATIS. 30.9.65: Aground 2 miles from Point Traverse, Lake Ontario (voyage Detroit/Genoa — scrap). 12.10.65: Refloated, towed Kingston, Ont. 16.11.65: Aground Wolfe Island, St Lawrence, 44.14N 76.11W whilst in tow to Genoa for repairs. Abandoned. CTL. 31.1.66: Refloated, sold. 7.66: Scrapped Valencia.

9 HENRY WATTERSON 8.43 F & S 47: SPURT. 61: SPARTAN. 13.12.61: Aground in fog, Pasa Buenavista, Cuba. 29.5.62: Refloated, towed Havana. CTL. (Voyage Gdansk/Cienfuegos — cement). Taken over by salvors. Reported scrapped.

10 GEORGE DEWEY 8.43 GMC Reserve Fleet, site 5.

11 WILLIAM BYRD 9.43 F & S Reserve Fleet, site 2.

12 RUFUS C. DAWES 9.43 GMC 3.68: Scrapped Tacoma, Wash.

13 THOMAS SULLY 9.43 GMC 47: ACTOR. 49: CITTA DI PALERMO. 4.63: Scrapped Vado.

14 DWIGHT W. MORROW 10.43 GMC 12.69: Scrapped Mobile.

15 JOHN S. MOSBY 10.43 GMC Reserve Fleet, site 1.

16 GRANT WOOD 10.43 GMC 47: ORSOLINA.

17 EDWARD M. HOUSE 11.43 GMC 29.6.44: One of four Liberty ships torpedoed by U-boat U.984 in English Channel (see JAMES A. FARRELL, etc). Towed in, thence towed to Tyne and repaired. 47: BLUE MASTER. 54: DICORONIA.

18 HARVEY CUSHING 11.43 GMC 47: ERETTEO. 20.9.65: Aground on rocks near Uglegorsk, Sakhalin Island (voyage Tanoura/Vancouver). Abandoned. 2.10.65: Further damaged in typhoon, broke in two. CTL. 10.65: Refloated by USSR, towed Gavan. No further official trace.

At one time official shipping records did not confirm the accuracy of Soviet ship names and it was thought that this vessel had been repaired and renamed MIKLUKHO MAKLAI. However, the recent availability of the Russian Ship Register shows that this name is carried by the ex JAY COOKE (qv), and presumably therefore the remaining two vessels from this group have now been scrapped. (See also JOSEPH C. AVERY).

19 WILLIAM G. SUMNER 11.43 GMC 44: ALKAID AK 114 (USN). 46: WILLIAM G. SUMNER. 4.64: Scrapped Terminal Island.

20 PETER STUYVESANT 11.43 GMC 44: CRUX AK 115 (USN). 46: PETER STUYVESANT. 3.62: Scrapped Oakland, Cal.

21 JAMES SCREVEN 12.43 GMC 44: SHAULA AK 118 (USN). 46: JAMES SCREVEN. 47: OLIMPIA. 1.69: Scrapped Spezia.

22 NAPOLEON B. BROWARD 12.43 GMC 44: MATAR AK 119 (USN). 46: Returned to US Govt (same name). Reserve Fleet, site 6.

23 ARTHUR M. HUDDELL 12.43 F & S Reserve Fleet, site 6.

24 OWEN WISTER 12.43 GMC 12.64: Scrapped Portland, Ore.

25 ELIZABETH C. BELLAMY 12.43 GMC 43: BAHAM AK 122 (USN). 44: BAHAM AG 71 (USN). 47: ELIZABETH C.BELLAMY. Reserve Fleet, site 6.

26 JOHN WHITE 1.44 GMC 44: MENKAR AK 123 (USN). 46: JOHN WHITE. 5.64: Scrapped Oakland, Cal.

27 ROYAL S. COPELAND 1.44 GMC 47: LES GLIERES. 59: NICTRIC. 14.6.67: Afire in holds at Chittagong (voyage Chinwangtao/Chittagong — coal). Repairs uneconomic. Sold. 9.68: Scrapped Kaohsiung.

28 JOHN EINIG 1.44 GMC 47: AIDA LAURO. 3.69: Scrapped Spezia.

29 EDWIN G. WEED 2.44 F & S 46: EUGENIO C. 63: ARIS. 5.67: Scrapped Kobe.

30 ANDREW TURNBULL 2.44 F & S 6.68: Scrapped Portland, Ore.

31 HENRY S. SANFORD 3.44 GMC Reserve Fleet, site 8.

32 JAMES L. ACKERSON 3.44 GMC 47: CAPTAIN J. MATARANGAS. 52: ARTEMIS. 3.67: Scrapped Ikeda, Japan.

33 EDWARD W. BOK 3.44 GMC 47: PAOLINA. 59: NANDO. 59: Re-engined at Genoa with oil engines by Fiat. 60: KIM. 65: SUN.

34 THOMAS A. McGINLEY 3.44 F & S Completed as MELUCTA AK 131 (USN). 46: THOMAS A. McGINLEY. 4.70: Sold to Spanish shipbreakers.

35 FREDERICK TRESCA 4.44 GMC Completed as PROPUS AK 132 (USN). 46: FREDERICK TRESCA. 47: NICOLAOU GEORGIOS. 22.5.51: On fire and abandoned in Red Sea, 21.01N 38.19E (voyage Dairen/Trieste — maize). Fire extinguished, towed to Suez. CTL. Sold and repaired and 1952: Re-engined at Trieste with oil engines by Harland & Wolff; renamed GABBIANO. 1.70: Scrapped Spezia.

36 EDWARD A. FILENE 4.44 F & S 66: Sunk (along with HOWELL COBB, qv) and used as a combination breakwater and dock at Cook Inlet, Alaska.

37 RICHARD K. CALL 4.44 GMC 1.70: Sold to New York shipbreakers.

The *John White* as the US Navy's cargo ship *Menkar* in July 1944. (St Johns, Yard no 26)

The Israel-flag *Fenice,* a re-engined Liberty ship. Note the enlarged funnel — a feature common to such motorised vessels. (Southeastern, Yard no 17)

The Norwegian *Belfri,* owned by Belships A/S, (Christian Smith & Co) in the Bristol Channel at the time of her sale in August 1960. (Todd Houston, Yard no 89)

38 AUGUST BELMONT 4.44 F & S Reserve Fleet, site 2.

39 ARTHUR R. LEWIS 5.44 JHIW 1.65: Scrapped Philadelphia.

40 GEORGE E. MERRICK 5.44 F & S 51: SAXON. 61: PANAGIA KOUNISTRA.

41 JAMES K. PAULDING 5.44 GMC 11.64: Scrapped New Orleans.

42 THOMAS J. LYONS 6.44 GMC 11.63: Scrapped Portland, Ore.

43 RAYMOND CLAPPER 6.44 F & S 47: T.J. STEVENSON. 54: SHAMROCK. 54: MASTER NICKY. 60: THRYLOS. 65: ELIAS DAYFAS II. 5.7.66: Abandoned sinking after developing leaks off Yucatan Peninsula, Mexico (voyage Galveston/Saigon – flour). Taken in tow by tanker SEA PIONEER (49/17,943 grt) but broke adrift and presumed sunk 21.11N 86.26W.

44 HUGH J. KILPATRICK 6.44 JHIW 46: HOOSIER STATE. 55: TRANSAMERICAN. 63: A & J MID-AMERICA. 65: GRAND HOPE. 67: UNION TIGER.

45 NOAH BROWN 6.44 JHIW 49: HENRY STEVEN-SON. 55: ALDERSHOT. 60: KAROLINA. 63: VRONTADOS PIONEER. 1.69: Scrapped Gandia.

46 HENDRIK WILLEM VAN LOON 6.44 JHIW 5.65: Scrapped Portland, Ore.

47 STEPHEN BEASLEY 7.44 JHIW 3.61: Scrapped Beaumont, Texas.

48 JASPER F. CROPSEY 7.44 JHIW 49: OCEANIC. 61: Lengthened at Tokio to 511½ ft (8,312 grt). 67: Traded in under Ship Exchange Act for T2 tanker COHOCTON. 11.67: Scrapped Spezia.

49 WILLIAM CRANE GRAY 7.44 GMC Reserve Fleet, site 5.

50 ETHELBERT NEVIN 7.44 GMC 3.60: Scrapped Baltimore.

51 W.S. JENNINGS 8.44 GMC Reserve Fleet, site 2.

52 FILIPP MAZZEI 8.44 F & S 3.60: Scrapped Baltimore.

53 HENRY HADLEY 8.44 GMC Reserve Fleet, site 4.

54 ALFRED I. DU PONT 8.44 F & S Reserve Fleet, site 4.

55 IRVIN S. COBB 8.44 GMC 67: Scrapped Panama City.

56 NEGLEY D. COCHRAN 9.44 GMC 47: SURNA. 59: MARINGA. 16.6.69: Sank off Brazil, 11.30S 37.15W (voyage   /   – salt).

57 ANNA DICKINSON 9.44 GMC 6.62: Scrapped Panama City.

58 JOHN RINGLING 9.44 GMC Reserve Fleet, site 5.

59 MICHAEL DE KOVATS 9.44 GMC Reserve Fleet, site 4.

60 JOHN H. McINTOSH 9.44 GMC Reserve Fleet, site 1.

61 JERRY S. FOLEY 10.44 GMC Reserve Fleet, site 5.

62 ROBERT MILLS 10.44 GMC Reserve Fleet, site 4.

63 MORRIS C. FEINSTONE 10.44 GMC Reserve Fleet, site 2.

64 DAVID L. YULEE 10.44 GMC Reserve Fleet, site 1.

65 GEORGE E. WALDO 10.44 GMC 47: HAWAII-AN FORESTER. 55: C.R. MUSSER. 69: RELIANCE SERENITY.

66 HENRY B. PLANT (I) 11.44 GMC Completed as HARALD TORSVIK. 47: GREY COUNTY. 51: AEGEAN SAILOR. 59: Re-engined at Newport (Mon) with two oil engines by Mirrlees, Bickerton. 60: KYRAMAROUKO. 64: SPALMATORI. 66: ANASTASSIOS. 67: STYMFALOS. 4.68: Scrapped Kaohsiung.

67 FREDERIC W. GALBRAITH 11.44 GMC Reserve Fleet, site 4.

68 C.W. POST 11.44 GMC Reserve Fleet, site 2.

69 JUNIUS SMITH 11.44 GMC 11.65: Scrapped New Orleans.

70 ISAAC M. SINGER 11.44 GMC Reserve Fleet, site 4.

71 TELFAIR STOCKTON 11.44 GMC 49:

EUGENIE. 56: TRANSPORTER. 61: Lengthened at Tokio to 511½ ft (8,636 grt). 66: ZANETA II. 69: SFAKIA.

72 LOUIS BAMBERGER 12.44 GMC 47: HORACE IRVINE. 68: RELIANCE AMITY.

73 ISAAC MAYER WISE 12.44 GMC Reserve Fleet, site 4.

74 HENRY B. PLANT (II) 12.44 GMC 6.2.45: Sunk by submarine (U.245) torpedo 17 miles east of Ramsgate, Straits of Dover, (voyage New York/Antwerp).

75 WALTER M. CHRISTIANSEN 12.44 GMC 51: SEA COMET. 52: OCEAN ULLA. 58: VALIANT HOPE. 60: OCEAN ROVER. 60: PACIFIC VENTURE. 5.67: Scrapped Kaohsiung.

76 GROVER C. HUTCHERSON 12.44 GMC Reserve Fleet, site 2.

77 FRED C. STEBBINS 1.45 GMC 61: Reported transferred USN and disposed of.

78 HAROLD A. JORDAN 1.45 GMC 66: Scrapped Kearny, NJ.

79 JOHN MILLER 1.45 GMC Reserve Fleet, site 5.

80 JAMES H. COURTS 1.45 GMC Completed as NIKI. 47: HADIOTIS. 65: ACHILLES. 21.11.65: Aground at Muroran after anchor chain broke in heavy weather. 2.12.65: Refloated, damaged. CTL. 1.66: Scrapped Osaka.

81 FRED HERRLING 2.45 GMC 5.69: Scrapped Mobile.

82 THOMAS L. HALEY 2.45 GMC Completed as SPETSAE. 47: CAPTAIN K. PAPAZOGLOU. 54: PANTANASSA. 61: GIORGOS TSAKIROGLOU. 5.69: Scrapped Whampoa.

BUILT BY SOUTHEASTERN SHIPBUILDING CORPORATION

Just prior to the United State's entry into the war the Maritime Commission awarded shipbuilding contracts to Savannah Shipyards Inc, this company having made good progress in building its own three-slipway yard without commission aid. But these contracts carried many special provisions, for both the management and the capital structure of the company had not given the commission much confidence. The firm was required to recruit a full staff, show full capital and to complete their facilities within thirty to sixty days. In normal times failure to comply would have meant cancelled contracts and nothing more. In fact, these builders did fail to meet these conditions and the 'intervention' of Pearl Harbour enabled the commission, as per the contract, to take possession of the yard, complete the site to a six-way yard and award management of it to a new company.

In January 1942 a leading construction company was given the task of completing the yard and in the same month management was vested in a team of experienced ship equipment manufacturers, who organised the yard, now renamed Southeastern Shipbuilding Corporation.

As a boost to the shipbuilding programme, the yard was considered on the same basis as all the other, new, six-way yards. The half-built facilities acted as a spur and the yard finally delivered more ships during 1943 than any of these rivals, but fewer vessels in 1944 due to a rather poor use of man-hours. The 1943 contracts for the future delivery of ships allowed 573,700 man-hours per ship, but in fact the actual delivery time of these vessels averaged 706,600 man-hours each — one of the highest figures of all the yards.

In April 1943, contracts were awarded to the yard for the construction of C.1 type vessels and AP type transports.

The commission's seizure of the yard raised many legal complications; the case subsequently went to trial and Savannah Shipyards Inc were awarded a very substantial compensation.

Liberty ship output: 88 vessels at an average cost of just over 2 million dollars each

USMC hull numbers: MCE 341– 352   (Yard Nos 1–12)
                    1051–1074   (”   ” 13–36)

2432–2447 (Yard Nos 37–52)
2863–2898 (” ” 53–88)
2899–2907 (” ” 89–97) (Cancelled)

1 JAMES OGLETHORPE 2.43 CB 17.3.43: Sunk by submarine (U.91) torpedo in NW Atlantic, 50.38N 34.46W (voyage New York/UK).

2 GEORGE HANDLEY 3.43 CB 12.64: Scrapped Kearny, NJ.

3 JAMES JACKSON 3.43 GMC Reserve Fleet, site 4.

4 GEORGE WALTON 3.43 GMC 6.11.51: On fire, abandoned, about 350 miles west of Cape Flattery. (Voyage Portland, Ore/Bombay — wheat). Taken in tow. 18.11.51: Tow broke, sank 40 miles north west of Cape Flattery.

5 LYMAN HALL 4.43 GMC 10.63: Scrapped Philadelphia.

6 JOHN MILLEDGE 4.43 GMC 65: Scrapped USA.

7 ROBERT TOOMBS 4.43 F & S 59: Scrapped Baltimore.

8 ROBERT M.T. HUNTER 5.43 F & S Reserve Fleet, site 1.

9 CRAWFORD W. LONG 5.43 VIW 7.69: Scrapped Kearny, NJ.

10 JOHN C. BRECKENRIDGE 5.43 GMC 1.60: Scrapped Baltimore.

11 BUTTON GWINNETT 5.43 VIW 12.68: Scrapped Panama City.

12 FELIX GRUNDY 6.43 GMC 5.65: Scrapped New Orleans.

13 LANGDON CHEVES 6.43 GMC 1.61: Scrapped Baltimore.

14 NICHOLAS HERKIMER 7.43 VIW 9.67: Scrapped Green Cove Springs, Fla.

15 CASIMIR PULASKI 7.43 GMC Reserve Fleet, site 2.

16 HAMLIN GARLAND 7.43 VIW Reserve Fleet, site 2.

17 ANDREW PICKENS 8.43 VIW 47: CAEN. 61: Re-engined at Nantes with oil engine by At. & Ch. de Bretagne; renamed FENICE. 70: ARENDAL.

18 WILLIAM L. YANCEY 8.43 F & S 47: ELENI STATHATOS. 64: CEBOLATTI. 69: Renamed CEBOLLA for voyage to Shanghai shipbreakers.

19 GEORGE WHITEFIELD 8.43 VIW 47: WILFORD. 57: ORATA. 63: DARYAL.

20 JOSEPH E. BROWN 8.43 F & S Reserve Fleet, site 4.

21 DUDLEY M. HUGHES 9.43 F & S 47: ALIAK-MON. 62: CAVTAT. 65: SHEIK BOUTROS. 5.69: Scrapped Whampoa.

22 JEROME K. JONES 9.43 F & S 47: VINDAF-JORD. 51: GLADIATOR. 60: SOLTA. 68: PANAGHIA KYKKOU.

23 HOKE SMITH 9.43 GMC 47: THORA DAN. 48: SPALMATORI. 60: MASTRO STELIOS II. 65: WENDY H. 11.67: Scrapped Valencia.

24 WILLIAM BLACK YATES 10.43 GMC 1.70: Sold to New York shipbreakers.

25 JAMES H. COUPER 10.43 VIW 8.65: Scrapped Portland, Ore.

26 JOSEPH HABERSHAM 10.43 VIW 5.61: Scrapped Tsuneishi, Japan.

27 JOSEPH H. MARTIN 10.43 GMC Reserve Fleet, site 2.

28 ROBERT FECHNER 11.43 GMC 47: VAN DER WAALS. 50: ENGGANO. 57: AMSTELLAAN. 61: SILVER STATE. 11.66: Scrapped Kaohsiung.

29 CHARLES C. JONES 11.43 VIW 10.60: Scrapped Rosyth.

30 FLORENCE MARTUS 11.43 VIW 5.60: Scrapped Baltimore.

31 CHARLES H. HERTY 12.43 VIW 67: Scrapped Panama City.

32 JOHN E. WARD 12.43 VIW Reserve Fleet, site 1.

33 EDWIN L. GODKIN 12.43 GMC 47: KONISTRA. 61: ERETRIA. 68: ERATO.

34 A. FRANK LEVER 12.43 VIW 47: BROTT. 51:

FINNBORG. 54: ARCHANAX. 67: MISTRAL. 5.68: Scrapped Kaohsiung.

35 THOMAS WOLFE 12.43 VIW 6.65: Scrapped New Orleans.

36 LOUIS A. GODEY 12.43 GMC Completed as SAMVANNAH. 48: Returned to US Govt. 61: Scrapped Orange, Texas.

37 BEN ROBERTSON 1.44 VIW 47: KASTOR. 12.68: Scrapped Hirao.

38 SAMUEL T. DARLING 1.44 GMC 2.61: Scrapped Seattle.

39 ISAAC S. HOPKINS 2.44 VIW 5.61: Scrapped Baltimore.

40 SAMHORN 2.44 VIW 48: Returned US Govt. 60: Scrapped Orange, Texas.

41 A. MITCHELL PALMER 2.44 VIW 48: Sold commercial (same name). 51: WAIMEA. 54: ANNITSA A. 64: JUSTICE. 5.68: Scrapped Kaohsiung.

42 SAMDART 3.44 GMC 47: SEDGEPOOL. 54: BOBARA. 56: FLEVARIOTISSA. 58: KAPETAN ANDREAS. 65: KITSA. 2.67: Scrapped Kaohsiung.

43 JOHN E. SWEET 3.44 VIW 6.65: Scrapped Philadelphia.

44 CLARK HOWELL 3.44 VIW 47: EPTANISSOS. 5.67: Scrapped Shanghai.

45 EARL LAYMAN 4.44 GMC 46: IONIAN TRADER. 5.67: Scrapped Kure.

46 JOHN A. TREUTLEN 4.44 VIW 29.6.44: One of four Liberty ships (see JAMES A. FARRELL, etc) torpedoed by U.984 in English Channel. Beached near Southampton. CTL. Refloated, and 9.44: Scrapped Briton Ferry.

47 BEN A. RUFFIN 4.44 VIW 46: HAI HSUAN. 58: JULIA. 60: BRUCE THOMAS. 63: CAICARA.

48 WILLIAM D. HOXIE 5.44 VIW Reserve Fleet, site 8.

49 SAMCEBU 5.44 GMC 47: REYNOLDS. 51: ST NICOLAS. 56: PANAGOS. 60: AMAZON. 24.12.63: Aground near Cape Bon, 36.43N 10.58E. 8.1.64: Refloated, severely damaged. CTL. (Voyage Venice/Buenos Aires). 3.64: Scrapped Spezia.

50 HARRY L. GLUCKSMAN 5.44 VIW 22.9.66: Arrived at Erie, Penn. Stripped to bare hull. Later towed to Lorain, Ohio for conversion to minesweeper FY 66 (USN) for use in Saigon harbour and other river areas of Vietnam. In conversion was filled with plastic foam and fitted with eight special outboard motors mounted on her hull. This enables her to manoeuvre sideways up and down rivers and clear mines to a width of water equal to her own length. A bridge mounted on shock-absorbers was constructed on her bow. Reclassified MSS–1. 8.69: Conversion reported completed.

51 JULIETTE LOW 5.44 VIW Reserve Fleet, site 5.

52 FRANCIS S. BARTOW 6.44 GMC Completed as THEMISTOCLES.

53 JACOB SLOAT FASSETT 6.44 GMC 3.65: Scrapped Portland, Ore.

54 RICHARD UPJOHN 6.44 GMC Reserve Fleet, site 4.

55 WILLIAM G. LEE 7.44 GMC 49: DORIAN PRINCE. 49: NADINA. 64: Converted into container ship (175 24-ft containers).

56 RUBEN DARIO 7.44 JHIW 3.63: Scrapped Philadelphia.

57 BENJAMIN BROWN FRENCH 7.44 JHIW 4.67: Scrapped Philadelphia.

58 STEPHEN LEACOCK 7.44 JHIW 9.69: Sold for scrapping at New Orleans.

59 CHARLES A. KEFFER 8.44 GMC Reserve Fleet, site 2.

60 RISDEN TYLER BENNETT 8.44 JHIW 4.63: Scrapped Philadelphia.

61 ALEXANDER R. SHEPERD 8.44 JHIW 6.65: Scrapped Philadelphia.

62 JAMES SWAN 8.44 JHIW 51: QUARTETTE. 21.12.52: Aground on Pearl and Hermes Reef, 90 miles east of Midway Island (voyage Baltimore/ Pusan – grain). Broke in two. Total loss.

63 MARTHA BERRY 8.44 JHIW Reserve Fleet, site 2.

64 FRANK P. WALSH 9.44 JHIW 51: BLUESTAR. 54: MELODY. 60: IKAROS. 10.66: Scrapped Hirao.

65 FLOYD GIBBONS 9.44 GMC 4.66: Scrapped Kearny, NJ.

66 JONAS LIE 9.44   9.1.45: Damaged by submarine (U.1055) torpedo in Bristol Channel approaches 51.45N 05.26W (voyage Swansea/New York). Abandoned. Taken in tow. Tow rope later broke. Ship not located, presumed sunk.

67 JOHN P. HARRIS 10.44 JHIW 51: GEORGE M. CULUCUNDIS. 52: SEAVICTOR. 54: EVIBELLE. 65: GRETHE. 4.67: Scrapped Tsuneishi, Japan.

68 RICHARD COULTER 10.44 GMC 7.60: Scrapped Baltimore.

69 ADDIE BAGLEY DANIELS 10.44 GMC Reserve Fleet, site 2.

70 WILLIAM H. EDWARDS 10.44 GMC 5.67: Scrapped Portland, Ore.

71 JOSEPH MURGAS 10.44 GMC Reserve Fleet, site 2.

72 MILTON J. FOREMAN 11.44 GMC 51: SHINNE-COCK BAY. 60: MOUNT SHASTA. 63: SHANKARA JAYANTI. 7.65: Scrapped Bombay.

73 JOSEPH S. McDONAGH 11.44 GMC 31.3.46: Ashore, mouth of River Canete, south of Cerro Azul. (Voyage Talcahuano and Callao/Havre — flax, etc). Total loss.

74 JOSIAH TATTNALL 11.44 GMC 4.70: Sold to Spanish shipbreakers.

75 MOINA MICHAEL 11.44 GMC Reserve Fleet, site 4.

76 ROBERT PARROT 11.44 GMC 4.68: Scrapped Portland, Ore.

77 JOSIAH COHEN 12.44 GMC 47: THEMONI. 61: NICOLAOS FRANGISTAS. 64: NICOLAOS F.

69: KOUNISTRA.

78 RUDOLPH KAUFFMANN 12.44 GMC Reserve Fleet, site 5.

79 JAMES H. PRICE 12.44 GMC 11.64: Scrapped Portland, Ore.

80 WILLIAM L. McLEAN 12.44 GMC 4.64: Scrapped Portland, Ore.

81 EDWARD J. BERWIND 1.45 GMC 9.61: Scrapped Jacksonville, Fla.

82 WILLIAM W. SEATON 1.45 GMC 51: SEA-MERCHANT. 53: MENITES. 63: TEMPO. 30.5.66: Driven aground off Kaohsiung in typhoon. Abandoned, severely damaged. CTL. Scrapped 'in situ'.

83 MACK BRUTON BRYAN 1.45 GMC 51: TRANS-UNION. 63: JIAN. 64: ENTELLA. 1.67: Scrapped Aioi.

84 WILLIAM TERRY HOWELL 1.45 GMC 11.60: Scrapped Faslane.

85 WILLIAM LEROY GABLE 1.45 GMC 47: CIMON. 55: ARCHIGETIS. 60: WESTERN VENTURE. 5.69: At Kaohsiung for scrapping.

86 HARRY KIRBY 2.45 GMC 49: CHRISTINE. 50: SEAVETERAN. 53: KAPARIA. 54: PORT-ARIA. 62: COSMOS ALTAIR.

87 ARLIE CLARK 2.45 GMC 46: PALMETTO STATE. 55: FLOMAR. 64: Returned to US Govt under Ship Exchange Act (with five other Liberty ships) in exchange for six C4 type vessels. Reserve Fleet, site 2.

88 THOMAS W. MURRAY 2.45 GMC 51: SEA-GLAMOR. 54: BARBARA MICHEL. 54: OCEAN ALICE. 59: BARBARA MICHEL. 59: PACIFIC ISLE. 59: OCEAN ALICE. 61: LISA B. 64: GRAND GRACE. 12.68: Scrapped Kaohsiung.

BUILT BY TODD HOUSTON SHIPBUILDING CORPORATION

This yard commenced in 1941 as the Houston Shipbuilding Corporation. It was a six-way yard situated at Irish Bend Island, Houston, Texas, and it was one of the commission's initial contracts for nine yards in different parts of the country. These yards, which had a total of sixty-five ways, were expected to build some 260 ships in the first phase of production.

The yard was among the first five approved (the others were the emergency yards at Portland, Ore, and South Portland, Maine; the California Shipbuilding and Todd California yards) and management of them was divided between the Kaiser group and Todd Shipyards Corporation. The latter concern, subsequently to figure prominently in emergency construction, were already shipbuilders and they were also one of the largest ship repair groups, having yards on all coasts.

For its lay-out the yard adapted plans generally used for a 'vertical' yard (i.e. a small frontage launching many ships, much work being carried out away from the waterfront) to one incorporating an extra, small, launching basin. Renamed Todd Houston Shipbuilding Corporation, the slips were soon increased to nine in number, but whereas the anticipated cost of these was some 7½ million dollars, the final cost was twice this figure.

When the first Liberty contracts were awarded, they anticipated ships to be built in 210 days and the next 'round' of deliveries in 150 days. Generally however, first deliveries took around 250 days and although following contracts reduced the limit still further to 105 days, a slower schedule of 132 days still applied to Houston, whose yard was still very far from complete when their first keel was laid. With these time limits, each day ahead of schedule earned the yard a bonus — each day beyond, a penalty. Seven of the initial nine yards earned maximum fees but the Houston yard, for the reasons stated, was one of the slowest, their first vessel delivered in May 1942 taking some 300 days. Even by the latter part of 1943, when the nation's overall Liberty production had about reached its zenith, the Houston contracts still allowed 45 days-per-ship construction schedules.

Liberty ship output: 208 vessels at an average cost of 1,833,400 dollars each

USMC hull numbers:

Built by Houston Shipbuilding Corporation: MCE 95–119 (Yard Nos 1–25)
            265–276 (” ” 26–37)

Built by Todd Houston Shipbuilding
 Corporation: MCE 828– 859 (” ” 38– 69)
           1936–1966 (” ” 70–100)
           2420–2431 (” ” 101–112)
           2908–3003 (” ” 113–208)(varied order)

1 SAM HOUSTON 5.42 CB 28.6.42: Sunk by submarine (U.203) torpedo and gunfire in West Indies, approx 19.21N 62.22W (voyage Houston/Bombay).

2 DAVY CROCKETT 6.42 NT 3.69: Sold for scrapping at Portland, Ore.

3 MATTHEW MAURY 6.42 NT 3.61: Scrapped Terminal Island.

4 WINFIELD SCOTT 6.42 GMC 7.66: Scrapped New Orleans.

5 MICHAEL J. STONE 6.42 GMC 3.60: Scrapped Baltimore.

6 DAVID S. TERRY 7.42 NT Reserve Fleet, site 1.

7 BENJAMIN BOURN 8.42 GMC 11.69: Sold for scrapping at New Orleans.

8 DANIEL CARROLL 8.42 NT 3.60: Scrapped Philadelphia.

9 NICHOLAS GILMAN 8.42 GMC 63: Scrapped Philadelphia.

10 SAMUEL GRIFFIN 8.42 NT 11.61: Scrapped Baltimore.

11 THOMAS HARTLEY 8.42 GMC 66: Converted to a floating platform by Railwater Terminal Co, Seattle for use at Seattle. Bow and stern sections removed to give a hull section 173 feet long. Equipped with a 200 ton sheerleg derrick.

12 DANIEL HIESTER 9.42 GMC Reserve Fleet, site 2.

13 BENJAMIN HUNTINGTON 9.42 GMC Reserve Fleet, site 1.

14 JOHN LAURANCE 10.42 NT 7.63: Scrapped Panama City.

15 SAMUEL LIVERMORE 10.42 GMC 12.59: Scrapped Jersey City.

16 HOUSTON VOLUNTEERS 10.42 NT 66: Scrapped Oakland, Cal.

17 A.P. HILL 10.42 GMC 10.65: Scrapped Panama City.

18 JAMES LONGSTREET 10.42 F & S 27.10.43: Ashore on New Jersey coast 40.27N 74W (Voyage Southampton/New York). 23.11.43: Refloated. Towed to New York. Dismantled. Hulk towed to

Cape Cod Bay and sunk as gunnery target.

19 JOSEPH E. JOHNSTON 11.42 GMC
5.69: Scrapped Kearny, NJ.

20 J.E.B. STUART 12.42 GMC
7.69: Scrapped Portland, Ore.

21 JOHN B. HOOD 12.42 GMC 3.65: Scrapped
Wilmington, NC.

22 FITZHUGH LEE (I) 12.42 GMC Completed as
BIG FOOT WALLACE. 8.65: Scrapped Panama City.

Big Foot Wallace, a hero of both Texas history and Texas
legend was recalled in January 1966 at Galveston when the
Texas Maritime Academy received the builders nameplate
from the ship which bore his name. The brass plate was
donated under the Liberty Ship Memorial Programme.

The ship entered service at the peak of the German
U-boat campaign, but her career, like those of many
Liberty ships, was unspectacular but nevertheless essential.
Until 'VJ' day she delivered supplies, fuel, munitions and
troops and thereafter carried urgent relief cargoes to war-
torn countries and brought troops home.

Having survived three years of gunfire, bombs and
torpedoes, BIG FOOT WALLACE was retired into lay-up
in 1945, but was recalled for service in 1946 and again
during the Korean war. In 1952 she received her third and
last discharge and thereafter lay at Mobile until her sale
for scrap.

The ship was named after William Alexander Anderson
Wallace, born in Virginia in 1817. He went to Texas at the
time of her struggle for independence from Mexico and won
fame as a patriot, scout and Indian fighter. Reportedly his
nickname was gained during imprisonment in Mexico when
his shoes wore out and his small-footed jailers were
astounded at the heroic proportions of the replacements.

23 AMELIA EARHART   12.42 GMC 10.11.48:
Ashore off Borneo, 02.47N 108.36E 20.11.48:
Refloated, towed Singapore. CTL. (Voyage Nagoya/
Mobile — bauxite and plywood). Sold and repaired.
51: MODENA. 51: PRZYSZLOSC. 65: JIADING.

Under the name of JIADING she is owned by the People's
Republic of China and was one of the first vessels to display
the "Thoughts of Mao" emblazoned in brilliant colours across
her bridge when in Britain in 1967. This was at the time this
cult was suddenly becoming popular among the Chinese
officials in the Western Hemisphere.

24 CHAMP CLARK 1.43 NT 58: Scrapped Terminal
Island.

25 JOSEPH T. ROBINSON 1.43 GMC 4.67: Scrapped
Panama City.

26 STEPHEN F. AUSTIN 7.42 GMC 9.67: Scrapped
New Orleans.

27 WILLIAM B. TRAVIS 7.42 NT 12.64: Scrapped
Panama City.

28 MIRABEAU B. LAMAR 7.42 ASB 1.63:
Scrapped Mobile.

29 THEODORE SEDGWICK 9.42 NT 3.61: Scrapped
Hirao.

30 THOMAS T. TUCKER 10.42 GMC 28.11.42:
Ashore at Olifants Bosch Point between Slangkop and
Cape Point, 34.16S 18.23E. (Voyage New Orleans/
Table Bay and Suez). Broke in three, total loss.

31 JEREMIAH WADSWORTH 10.42 NT 27.11.42:
Sunk by submarine (U.178) torpedo off South
Africa 39.22S 22.23E. (Voyage New Orleans/Bombay).

32 JAMES BOWIE 11.42 GMC Reserve Fleet, site 5.

33 THOMAS J. RUSK 11.42 NT Reserve Fleet, site
4.

34 LAMBERT CADWALADER 11.42 GMC 1.60:
Scrapped Baltimore.

35 JAMES MADISON 1.43 NT 5.66: Scrapped
Oakland, Cal.

36 WILLIAM L. SMITH 1.43 GMC 8.64: Scrapped
Panama City.

37 STEPHEN C. FOSTER 1.43 NT 6.61: Scrapped
Oakland, Cal.

38 WILLIAM EUSTIS 1.43 GMC 17.3.43: Sunk by
submarine (U.91) torpedo in N.Atlantic, 50.38N
34.46W (Voyage New York/UK).

39 JOHN ARMSTRONG 2.43 GMC 7.64: Scrapped
Mobile.

40 WILLIAM H. CRAWFORD 2.43 GMC
12.69: Scrapped Terminal Island.

41 JAMES BARBOUR 2.43 NT Reserve Fleet,
site 8.

42 JOHN H. EATON 2.43 GMC 46: MYRIAM.
57: NEW KAOHSIUNG. 3.68: Scrapped Kaohsiung.

43 JOEL R. POINSETT 2.43 GMC 4.3.44: Broke in
two, abandoned 43.30N 56.30W. (Voyage Southampton and Liverpool/New York). 21.3.44: Afterpart
towed to Halifax, NS. Later shaft and propeller
removed. Became a depot ship.

44 JOHN BELL 3.43 GMC 27.8.43: Sunk by submarine (U.410) torpedo off Sardinia, 37.15N 08.24E.

45 JOHN C. SPENCER 3.43 JHIW 62: Scrapped Baltimore.

46 JAMES M. PORTER 3.43 GMC 10.61: Scrapped Bellingham, Seattle.

47 WILLIAM WILKINS 3.43 GMC 6.63: Scrapped Panama City.

48 FITZHUGH LEE (II) 3.43 JHIW 9.59: Scrapped Baltimore.

49 JUBAL A. EARLY 4.43 NT 47: NICOLAOS G. KULUKUNDIS. 64: CAPTAIN NICOLAS. 6.68: Scrapped Shodoshima.

50 RICHARD S. EWELL 4.43 WISC 65: Scrapped Camden, NJ.

51 GEORGE E. PICKETT 4.43 JHIW 3.69: Scrapped Kearny, NJ.

52 WILLIAM N. PENDLETON 4.43 WISC Reserve Fleet, site 1.

53 MOSES AUSTIN 4.43 JHIW 47: CHERBOURG. 54: ANTONIOS. 66: DIMOS. 7.69: Scrapped Whampoa.

54 BENITO JUAREZ 4.43 WISC 47: JALAKIRTI. 56: CHRYSANTHI. 17.8.66: Grounded Loculan Shoals, near Misamis (voyage Philippines/Europe — copra). Refloated, damaged; later proceeded. 11.9.66: Grounded when departing Singapore. 21.10.66: Refloated, damaged; returned Singapore and laid up. Later sold. 8.68: Scrapped Hong Kong.

55 DAVID G. BURNET 5.43 WISC 6.64: Scrapped New Orleans.

56 JAMES S. HOGG 5.43 WISC Completed as PAVO AK 139 (USN). 46: JAMES S. HOGG. Reserve Fleet, site 2.

57 JANE LONG 5.43 WISC Reserve Fleet, site 2.

58 JAMES B. BONHAM 5.43 WISC 11.66: Scrapped Portland, Ore.

59 JAMES W. FANNIN 5.43 NT 47: SAINT MALO. 63: TEGEAN. 28.11.66: Aground on Sister Rocks, about 16 miles south of Halifax, NS 42.47N 63.32W (Voyage Glasgow/USA). Abandoned. 20.12.66: Broke in tow. Total loss.

60 ANSON JONES 5.43 WISC 46: LAPPLAND. 50: CASPIANA. 69: Scrapped Shanghai.

61 FREDERICK L. DAU 5.43 WISC 47: STYLI-ANOS N. VLASOPULOS. 64: PLATE TRADER. 65: ANTONIA II. 4.69: Scrapped Kaohsiung.

62 JAMES E. HAVILAND 6.43 WISC Reserve Fleet, site 2.

63 EDWARD BURLESON 6.43 WISC 4.63: Scrapped Oakland, Cal.

64 LORENZO DE ZAVALA 6.43 GMC 10.64: Scrapped Philadelphia.

65 BENJAMIN R. MILAM 6.43 NT 8.3.45: Explosion in boiler room and sank at Locust Point, Baltimore. Raised and repaired. 47: HYERES. 61: DUERO. 64: FANOR. 10.68: Scrapped Santander.

66 SIDNEY SHERMAN 6.43 ASB 8.59: Scrapped Baltimore.

67 JOHN MARY ODIN 6.43 NT 5.61: Scrapped Panama City.

68 MARY AUSTIN 6.43 IFM Reserve Fleet, site 2.

69 E.A. PEDEN 7.43 WISC 47: SOUNION. 49: MARIA LOS. 55: MARIEL. 58: NORTHPORT. 66: SAGITTARIUS.

70 SAM HOUSTON II 7.43 IFM 12.59: Scrapped Portland, Maine.

71 GEORGE C. CHILDRESS 7.43 WISC 47: K. HADJIPATERAS. 27.7.67: Aground on reef near Koronje Island, 35 miles north of Pagoda Point off Bassein, Burma 16.32N 94.14E. Sank. (Voyage Calcutta/Rangoon — coal).

72 J. PINCKNEY HENDERSON 7.43 IFM 18.8.43: In collision (on maiden voyage Gulf/Mersey — combustible war cargo) off Newfoundland, 44.12N 53.58W with tanker J.H. SENIOR (31/11,065 grt) which was laden with high octane aviation spirit. Both vessels drenched in petrol and raging fires started, the flames spreading so quickly that only nine persons from both crews survived. 31.8.43: Arrived Sydney, NS, in tow. Beached. For three weeks flames and explosions racked the ship and when finally extinguished the vessel was completely gutted. Later refloated, towed Halifax. 14.1.44: Towed to New York. CTL. 7.44: Scrapped Philadelphia.

73 GEORGE P. GARRISON 7.43 IFM 45: BELGIAN LIBERTY. 47: GEORGE P. GARRISON. Reserve Fleet, site 2.

74 ORAN M. ROBERTS 8.43 WISC Reserve Fleet, site 4.

75 ROBERT T. HILL 8.43 IFM 5.63: Scrapped Wilmington, NC.

76 FREDERICK H. NEWELL 8.43 WISC 3.68: Scrapped Portland, Ore.

77 JOHN H. REAGAN 8.43 IFM 4.67: Scrapped Kearny, NJ.

78 R.M. WILLIAMSON 8.43 NT 47: NICOLAS KAIRIS. 5.5.59: Aground near Kuchino Shima. 30.4N 129.52E. (Voyage Haifa/Tokio — scrap). Broke in two. Sank.

79 JESSE BILLINGSLEY 8.43 WISC 49: LAGUNA. 50: Re-engined at Trieste to 6 cyl oil engine by Fiat. 64: MARILU. 65: ORIONE. 3.2.69: Engine breakdown and holds flooded in storm near Azores (voyage Bourgas/Galveston — ore). Abandoned. Towed Fayal thence Vigo to discharge cargo. Sold and scrapped Bilbao.

80 EDWIN W. MOORE 8.43 WISC 3.60: Scrapped Baltimore.

81 GEORGE BELLOWS 9.43 GMC 47: EVANTHIA. 60: EVIE. 65: ALBINO. 12.69: Scrapped Bilbao.

82 DAVID WILMOT 9.43 IFM 47: ANTHONY LEEWENHOEK. 47: LAURENSKERK. 60: GROSVENOR TRADER. 67: GLORIA. 12.68: Scrapped Shanghai.

83 SAMUEL H. WALKER 9.43 NT 10.64: Scrapped Kearny, NJ.

84 ERASTUS SMITH 9.43 GMC 47: KYMA. 60: RODOS. 9.67: Scrapped Shanghai.

85 JOSE NAVARRO 10.43 IFM 26.12.43: Sunk by submarine (U.178) torpedo in Indian Ocean, 08.20N 70.35E (voyage Houston/Calcutta).

86 JOSHUA A. LEACH 10.43 GMC 47: EVROS. 61: BAR. 17.2.67: Aground off Split in heavy weather (voyage Split/Augusta). Salvage uneconomical. CTL. 27.2.67: Sold 'as lies' and scrapped.

87 HARVEY C. MILLER 10.43 IFM 2.60: Scrapped Hirao.

88 GEORGE W. LIVELY 10.43 F & S 6.66: Scrapped Philadelphia.

89 THOMAS W. GREGORY 10.43 WISC 49: BELFRI. 54: Converted to oil engines at Spezia by Ansaldo, Genoa. 60: ROMANCE.

90 WILL R. WOOD 10.43 NT 6.61: Scrapped Yokosuka.

91 WILLIAM M. RAYBURN 10.43 F & S 10.66: Scrapped Philadelphia.

92 L.H. McNELLY 10.43 F & S 47: ZEEMAN. 50: TROMPENBURG. 59: SANTA FE. 59: Lengthened at Yokosuka to 511½ ft (8,327 grt). 13.8.67: Lost radio contact in storm 30 miles north of Isla Huamblin 44.40S 75.00W; missing in Straits of Magellan. (Voyage Coquimbo/San Nicolas — iron ore). Untraced, but 17.11.67: Wreckage sighted off Rowlett Island presumed to be from this ship.

93 LUCIEN B. MAXWELL 10.43 F & S 6.8.45: Aground in Seine Estuary (voyage New Orleans/Havre and Rouen — cotton). Broke in two, sank into quicksands, salvage abandoned. Total loss.

94 ALBERT S. BURLESON 11.43 F & S Reserve Fleet, site 2.

95 JOSEPH H. KIBBEY 11.43 JHIW Completed as PHOBOS AK 129 (USN). 46: JOSEPH H. KIBBEY. 2.70: Sold to New York shipbreakers.

96 OSCAR CHAPPELL 11.43 F & S 3.58: Scrapped Baltimore.

97 J.S. CULLINAN 11.43 NT Completed as ALDERAMIN AK 116 (USN). 46: J.S. CULLINAN. 65: (circa) scrapped USA.

98 HUGH YOUNG 11.43 NT Completed as ZAURAK AK 117 (USN). 46: HUGH YOUNG. 6.63: Scrapped Oakland, Cal.

99 MATTHEW J. O'BRIEN 11.43 F & S 7.66: Scrapped Panama City.

100 HENRY AUSTIN 12.43 F & S 10.64: Scrapped Tacoma.

101 CHARLES MORGAN 12.43 IFM 10.6.44: Sunk by aircraft bombs off 'Utah' beach-head, Normandy, France.

102 JOHN W. GATES 12.43 F & S 47:

ARISTOTELIS. 10.68: Scrapped Onomichi.

103 ANTHONY F. LUCAS 11.43 IFM Completed as ZANIAH AK 120 (USN). Later ZANIAH AG 70 (USN). 47: Returned to US Govt (same name). Reserve Fleet, site 6.

104 WILLIAM BECKNELL 12.43 IFM Completed as SABIK AK 121 (USN). 46: WILLIAM BECKNELL. 11.61: Scrapped Oakland, Cal.

105 HARRY PERCY 12.43 GMC 47: IRA. 7.3.47: Aground on Goodwin Sands, broke in two. Total loss. (Voyage Hampton Roads/Antwerp — coal).

106 REBECCA BOONE 12.43 NT 48: Sold commercial (same name). 50: VENERATOR. 58: GIGA. 60: CUYANO. 60: Lengthened at Trieste to 511½ ft (8,184 grt) and converted to bulk carrier. 61: PALOS. 63: EVMAR.

107 CHARLES GOODNIGHT 1.44 IFM 47: BACCARAT. 54: MARGALITIS. 64: WINONA. 12.68: Scrapped Aioi.

108 ANDREW BRISCOE 1.44 IFM 47: CRETE. 2.69: Scrapped Sakaide.

109 WILLIAM M. EASTLAND 1.44 IFM 47: LE HAVRE. 48: VILLE DU HAVRE. 60: LE HAVRE. 64: ALMAR. 67: TEGEAN.69: Scrapped Shanghai.

110 JOHN G. TOD 1.44 IFM 47: DORADO. 60: GLYFADA. 69: PLATRES.

111 CHARLES J. FINGER 1.44 F & S 47: ST THOMAS. 51: CAVOSTARAS. 53: DESPINA. 59: AMFITHEA. 64: MARATHA EXPLORER. 66: SAMUDRA VIJAY.

112 MORRIS SHEPPARD 2.44 NT 47: GIULIANO. 62: KOPALNIA SIEMIANOWICE. 66: Converted in Poland into a floating warehouse.

113 KATHERINE L. BATES 2.44 IFM 47: COUTANCES. 54: MARIBLANCA. 4.69: Scrapped Kaohsiung.

114 JACOB PERKINS 2.44 IFM 46: HAI TEE. 63: SINCERE CARRIER. 64: KONDOR. 17.7.66: Grounded outside Onahama. Refloated, severely damaged; towed to Hakodate. (Voyage Kaohsiung/ Onahama — salt). 9.66:Scrapped Hirao.

115 JOSE G. BENITEZ 2.44 F & S 47: PANAGIO-

TIS COUMANTAROS. 65: FILIA. 2.1.67: Collision with mv TAYGA (61/7,311 grt) in mouth of Red Sea, 13.15N 43.12E (voyage Tegal/Rotterdam — tapioca). Beached 2 miles west of Mokha. Abandoned. CTL. No salvage due to inaccessible position.

116 ROBERT HENRI 3.44 IFM 58: Scrapped Baltimore.

117 KEITH PALMER 3.44 IFM 8.68: Scrapped Kearny, NJ.

118 ANNA H. BRANCH 3.44 IFM 47: ARTHUR STOVE. 55: KOSTIS. 3.6.68: Stranded on Bissagos Island, 230 miles south of Dakar, 11.18N 16.48W. Afire and gutted; flooded and partially submerged. Abandoned. Later reported to have broken up. (Voyage Sfax/China — phosphates).

119 GEORGE STEERS 3.44 IFM 61 (circa) scrapped Baltimore.

120 JOHN GIBBON 3.44 IFM 7.68: Scrapped Kearny, NJ.

121 THOMAS SAY 3.44 IFM 46: ATLANTIC TRADER. 62: SPLIT. 7.67: Scrapped Split.

122 ISAAC VAN ZANDT 3.44 NT 66: Transferred from Reserve Fleet to US Navy and loaded at the Naval Ammunition Depot, Bangor, Bremerton, Washington, with obsolete cargo and explosives. 23.5.66: Towed to sea for scuttling. Towrope parted and the vessel became a hazard to shipping as she drifted off with some 400 tons of high explosives in her cargo. The USN tugs TATNUCK and KOKA spent several anxious hours searching for the ship, which was finally located, recovered and towed to the dumping site. Four and a half hours after the seacocks were opened she sank, and shortly afterwards her cargo detonated at the 4,000 feet level as planned. Although she did not sink in the precise location required, the scientific operation was nevertheless declared a success.

123 DANIEL E. GARRETT 4.44 IFM 1944: MAJOR GENERAL ROBERT OLDS (US Army aircraft repair ship). 1946: DANIEL E. GARRETT. 4.60: Scrapped Baltimore.

124 CHRISTOPHER S. FLANAGAN 4.44 IFM 11.63: Scrapped Portland, Ore.

125 JOHN IRELAND 4.44 IFM 3.67: Scrapped New Orleans.

126 HENRY M. ROBERT 4.44 IFM 46: ATLANTIC WIND. 53: WIND. 60: GALINI. 3.68: Scrapped Kaohsiung.

127 SUL ROSS 4.44 IFM 47: ASTRA. 63: SIL. .2.68:Scrapped Kaohsiung.

128 JULIUS OLSEN 4.44 IFM 47: BLUE GRASS STATE. 55: AUBURN. 57: MARSHALL. 61: MAREILEEN. 1.67: Deck and hull plating cracked during heavy weather whilst on voyage Vancouver/ Ceylon. Put into Osaka for temporary repairs; later proceeded. 3.67: Sold to Japanese shipbreakers. Re-sold. 12.68: Scrapped Kaohsiung.

129 FELIPI DE BASTROP 4.44 IFM 2.61: Scrapped Tampa, Fla.

130 RICHARD O'BRIEN 5.44 IFM 1944: BRIGADIER GENERAL ASA N. DUNCAN (US Army aircraft repair ship). Reserve Fleet, site 2.

131 O.B. MARTIN 5.44 IFM Reserve Fleet, site 6.

132 HENRY D. LINDSLEY 5.44 IFM Reserve Fleet, site 2.

133 MINOR C. KEITH 5.44 IFM 47: GOVERNOR BRANDON. 49: AKTION. 51: OMEGA. 54: OMNIUM FREIGHTER. 57: Lengthened at Yoko-hama to 511½ ft (8,596 grt). 65: OMNIUM TRADER. 68: THOR. 7.69: At Yawata for scrapping.

134 NICHOLAS D. LABADIE 5.44 IFM 5.62: Scrapped Mobile.

135 ARTHUR ST. CLAIR 5.44 IFM 5.63: Scrapped Wilmington, NC.

136 RUFUS CHOATE 5.44 IFM Reserve Fleet, site 2.

137 GUS W. DARNELL 5.44 IFM 23.11.44: Damaged by aircraft torpedo off Samar Island, Pacific. (Voyage USA/Leyte — troops and stores). Beached. Later refloated. CTL. 12.45: Towed San Francisco, acquired by USN, renamed JUSTIN IX 228. 46: GUS W. DARNELL. 6.54: Scrapped Terminal Island.

138 ELEAZAR LORD 6.44 WISC 67: Scrapped Richmond, Cal.

139 JUAN N. SEGUIN 6.44 WISC 9.66: Scrapped New Orleans.

140 BERTRAM G. GOODHUE 6.44 WISC 67: Scrapped Richmond, Cal.

141 OLIVER LOVING 6.44 WISC 1.70: Sold for scrapping at New Orleans.

142 ANDREW W. PRESTON 6.44 WISC 51: NORTH-PORT. 57: ABALONE. 61: Lengthened at Tokio to 511½ ft (8,565 grt). 62: NORWALK. 9.69: Scrapped Kaohsiung.

143 NATHANIEL SCUDDER 6.44 WISC 44: ALFRED J. LYON. 44: BRIGADIER GENERAL ALFRED J. LYON (US Army aircraft repair ship). 64: Converted to depot ship at Portland, Ore.

144 JOHN B. HAMILTON 6.44 WISC Reserve Fleet, site 4.

145 NATHANIEL SILSBEE 6.44 JHIW Reserve Fleet, site 5.

146 ROBERT WATCHORN 7.44 JHIW 47: AMERICAN ROBIN. 57: PACIFIC STAR. 60: ROVER. 60: HWA AN. 3.68: Scrapped Kaohsiung.

147 TOMAS GUARDIA 7.44 JHIW 64: Scrapped New Orleans.

148 LAURA DRAKE GILL 7.44 JHIW 47: HAWAIIAN LUMBERMAN. 60: CAPE HENRY. 62: TRIKERI. 65: DAHLIA. 2.67: Scrapped Kaohsiung.

149 ANGUS McDONALD 7.44 JHIW 10.69: Scrapped Seattle.

150 WYNN SEALE 7.44 JHIW 5.64: Sold, vessel stripped, hull converted into floating crane barge with 125 ton crane on deck; renamed ZIDELL'S DELIGHT.

151 T.E. MITCHELL 7.44 JHIW 1.70: Sold for scrapping at Portland, Ore.

152 CARLOS J. FINLAY 8.44 JHIW Reserve Fleet, site 5.

153 KYLE V. JOHNSON 8.44 JHIW Reserve Fleet, site 4.

154 JACOB A. WESTERVELT 8.44 GMC Reserve Fleet, site 4.

155 ROBERT S. LOVETT 8.44 GMC 51: WESTERN RANCHER. 54: CHRYSSI S.M. 9.65: Scrapped Hamburg.

156 IDA STRAUSS 8.44 JHIW 3.60: Scrapped Baltimore.

157 THOMAS BULFINCH 8.44 JHIW Reserve Fleet, site 8.

158 LORADO TAFT 8.44 JHIW 9.66: Scrapped Philadelphia.

159 HOWARD L. GIBSON 9.44 JHIW 14.10.44: Afire after collision with tanker GEO. W. McKNIGHT (33/12,502 grt), 250 miles north west of Madeira 34.07N 21.24W. (Voyage Galveston/Karachi). Abandoned. Reboarded and 15.10.44: Fire extinguished. Towed Casablanca, thence New York. CTL. 10.45: Scrapped Philadelphia.

160 THOMAS EAKINS 9.44 WISC 8.60: Scrapped Baltimore.

161 ROBERT E. CLARKSON 9.44 JHIW 1.65: Scrapped Portland, Ore.

162 IRVING BABBITT 9.44 WISC 9.61: Scrapped Philadelphia.

163 MICHAEL J. OWENS 9.44 WISC 49: POLARUS TRADER. 50: BURCO TRADER. 60: MONTEGO SUN. 61: DISKOS. 2.11.61: Grounded, Panama City, Fla. Refloated with bottom damage but proceeded. 1.62: Suffered heavy weather damage on voyage USA/Kobe. 5.62: Scrapped Hirao.

164 EDWARD G. JANEWAY 9.44 GMC 51: SANTA VENETIA. 30.12.63: Main deck fractured and machinery trouble in heavy weather near Midway Island. Temporarily repaired, proceeded Yokohama. Sold. 9.64: Scrapped Oppama, Yokosuka.

165 HERBERT D. CROLY 9.44 WISC Reserve Fleet, site 8.

166 FREDERIC E. IVES 10.44 GMC 47: RANA. 52: TURMOIL. 59: VALIANT POWER. 60: PANTAZIS L. 8.68: Scrapped Hirao.

167 WALTER WELLMAN 10.44 WISC Reserve Fleet, site 2.

168 RICHARD J. HOPKINS 10.44 JHIW 51: ATLANTIC WATER. 62: KOUMIOTISSA. 63: AGIA ERINI L. 3.2.64: Foundered 30.22N 153E, 600 miles south east of Yokohama after developing hull leaks and fractures in heavy weather. (Voyage Portland/Kawasaki -- scrap iron).

169 J.D. YEAGER 10.44 JHIW 4.67: Scrapped Kearny, NJ.

170 JOHNNY APPLESEED 10.44 WISC 3.64: Scrapped Philadelphia.

171 PAUL BUNYAN 10.44 GMC 23.1.64: Sold for scrap. 12.69: At Philadelphia still awaiting scrapping due to Vietnam situation.

172 ANSON MILLS 10.44 JHIW Reserve Fleet, site 1.

173 ROBERT NEIGHBORS 10.44 GMC 2.70: Sold to Spanish shipbreakers.

174 FRANCIS B. OGDEN 11.44 JHIW 8.65: Scrapped Kearny, NJ.

175 EDWIN S. NETTLETON 11.44 GMC Reserve Fleet, site 2.

176 PONTUS H. ROSS 11.44 JHIW 5.69: Scrapped Portland, Ore.

177 CLARENCE ROBERTS 11.44 JHIW 23.1.64: Sold for scrap. 12.69: At Philadelphia still awaiting scrapping due to Vietnam situation.

178 OTIS E. HALL 11.44 GMC 1.68: Scrapped Oakland, Cal.

179 CHARLES L. McNARY 11.44 GMC 4.66: Scrapped Terminal Island.

180 CYRIL G. HOPKINS 11.44 WISC Completed as NAVARCHOS KOUNDOURIOTIS. 20.10.64: Aground when leaving Mar del Plata for Marseilles (wheat). Broke in two. CTL. Both parts later re-floated and sold locally for scrapping.

181 I.B. PERRINE 11.44 JHIW Completed as ELEFTHERIA. 23.3.45: Mined in North Sea after leaving River Schelde (voyage Ghent/Thames). Aground, north of Ostend. Broke in two. Total loss.

182 PAUL DAVID JONES 12.44 WISC 67: Scrapped Panama City.

183 WILL B. OTWELL 12.44 JHIW 12.64: Scrapped Panama City.

184 JACOB CHANDLER HARPER 12.44 JHIW 3.70: Towed to Santander for scrapping.

185 HAROLD D. WHITEHEAD 12.44 JHIW 51: Sold commercial (same name). 59: JACKIE HAUSE.

60: GLORIA DUNAIF. 60: RAINBOW. 61: Lengthened at Tokio to 511½ ft (8,549 grt). 68: ASIDOS.

186 CLYDE AUSTIN DUNNING 12.44 JHIW 51: BOY. 58: JOAN O'BERG. 61: ELDERMERE. 61: OCEAN MERCHANT. 63: UNION SKIPPER.

187 JAMES KYRON WALKER 12.44 WISC Reserve Fleet, site 2.

188 WALTER FREDERICK KRAFT 12.44 JHIW 47: GLOBAL FARMER. 47: EVERGREEN STATE. 55: MARCELL M.H. 6.67: Scrapped Aioi.

189 WILLIAM R. LEWIS 12.44 JHIW 50: POLARUS CARRIER. 50: NORCUBA. 54: EVICYNTHIA. 56: Lengthened at Innoshima to 511½ ft (8,342 grt). 61: SPARTAN. 62: ELAINE. 1.68: Scrapped Onomichi.

190 WILLIAM ASA CARTER 1.45 JHIW 12.61: Scrapped Panama City.

191 JAMES ROY WELLS 1.45 JHIW 51: SEA-PIONEER. 52: LAMYRA. 63: COSMOS BETEL-GEUSE. 2.68: Scrapped Kaohsiung.

192 WILLIAM K. KAMAKA 1.45 WISC 12.67: Scrapped Kearny, NJ.

193 DANIEL L. JOHNSTON 1.45 WISC 2.63: Scrapped Panama City.

194 LLOYD S. CARLSON 1.45 JHIW 51: MARY ADAMS. 55: WIND RUSH. 59: DEBARDELEBEN MARINE I. 60: Converted at Baltimore to bulk chemical carrier. 62: TEXAS GULF SULPHUR I. 68: Returned to US Govt under Ship Exchange Act in exchange for C4-type troopship GENERAL W.C. LANGFITT. 3.69: Sold for scrapping at New Orleans.

195 RUSSELL R. JONES 1.45 JHIW 51: PEGOR. 58: PACIFIC WAVE. 60: CHING YUNG. 2.67: Scrapped Kaohsiung.

196 JOHN MARTIN MILLER 1.45 JHIW Reserve Fleet, site 5.

197 WALLACE M. TYLER 2.45 JHIW 51: SEA-STAR. 60: ARCHON. 11.66: Scrapped Edajima, Japan.

198 WILLIAM W. JOHNSON 2.45 JHIW 51: SEA-

Todd Houston Shipbuilding Corporation

GARDEN. 17.4.61: Grounded off Tobago. 19.4.61: Re-floated, severely damaged. Sold. 9.61: Scrapped Bilbao.

199 BERNARD L. RODMAN 2.45 JHIW 51: SEA-FIGHTER. 53: MELIDA. 67: JUPITER. 29.3.68: Grounded at Cabo San Lazaro, Mexico, 24.48N 112.19W (voyage Osaka/Mazatlan — ballast). Abandoned.

200 LEONARDO L. ROMERO 2.45 JHIW 51: CHIAN TRADER. 57: COAL MINER. 60: PETER BLIX. 61: Lengthened at Tokio to 511½ ft (8,539 grt), renamed METEOR. 68: ASITRES.

201 WILLARD R. JOHNSON 2.45 JHIW 51: NEPTUNUS. 52: APOLLO. 54: EVIMAR. 58: THEOKEETOR. 64: RIVERHEAD. 65: MARU. 4.67: Scrapped Hong Kong.

202 SAMUEL L. JEFFERY 2.45 — 45: Damaged on war service (no further details); towed in and laid-up at Mobile. CTL. 47: Scrapped Port Arthur, Texas.

203 CLIFFORD E. ASHBY 2.45 JHIW 51: PECONIC BAY. 52: TROJAN TRADER. 57: ARMONK. 60: MARINE RICE QUEEN, (converted to self-unloader specially fitted to carry rice). (7,365 grt). 63: SEJ.LO ROJO. 64: ALNFIELD. 67: Reported to be renamed CERES.

204 ALFRED L. BAXLAY 2.45 JHIW Completed as LEKTOR GARBO. 47: N.O. ROGENAES. 60: KALU.

205 FRANCIS E. SILTZ 3.45 JHIW 47: PORTLAND TRADER. 5.1.61: Aground on Tubbataha Reef, 400 miles south of Manila. (Voyage Vancouver, Wash/Calcutta — wheat). Re-floated. CTL. Sold. 4.61: Scrapped Hong Kong.

206 CHARLES H. LANHAM 3.45 JHIW 51: THUNDERBIRD. 61: WATLING. 63: NEW KAILING. 12.67: Scrapped Kaohsiung.

207 MARK A. DAVIS 3.45 JHIW Completed as PSARA. 5.67: Scrapped Osaka.

208 EDWARD N. HINTON 3.45 JHIW 47: LES ANDELYS. 54: CORMORANT. 6.69: Scrapped Onomichi.

BUILT BY WALSH-KAISER COMPANY

At a time when the New England area had been selected as the location of new shipyards, (these being dependent upon the availability of labour and good sites) the management of one yard was vested in the Rheem Manufacturing Company. This company was experienced in the manufacture of water heaters and, later, in the production of ammunition, but had no shipbuilding knowledge.

Its own preference for a site was at Stockton in California, but this was overruled due to 'overcrowding' in that State and the company was forced to take a site at Providence, Rhode Island. It proved, however to be a most difficult one and Rheem were unable to complete the facilities, even with the very high costs allowed. Instead of the original estimate of six million dollars, the company spent eighteen million and yet the six-slipway yard was still far from complete in February 1943. The Maritime Commission then installed new management, this being formed by the Kaiser group and the Walsh Construction Company. The Rheem contract was cancelled and only the first six vessels from the thirty-two ship order were subsequently completed, the first by Rheem themselves and the remainder under the auspices of the new management.

Later the construction of frigates commenced and in mid-1944 the yard further contracted with the USN for thirty-two Attack Cargo ships (AKA's). But the designs of these vessels were delayed and Providence was awarded a 'fill-in' contract for six Liberties. Late deliveries of material, trouble with the frigates and the consequent delays in outfitting so retarded deliveries, however, that by the spring of 1944 the yard was working on frigates, AKA's and Liberties at the same time.

Ultimately the Liberty contract was reduced to the five vessels which had found their way onto the stocks during the period of congestion.

Liberty ship output: 11 vessels

USMC hull numbers:

Built by Rheem Manufacturing Company:	MCE 1457	(Yard No 1)
	1463—1488	(cancelled)
Built by Walsh-Kaiser Company:	MCE 1458—1462	(Yard Nos 2—6)

For the remaining constructions at this yard the MCE number was used as the yard number. (No 3124 was cancelled).

1 WILLIAM CODDINGTON 2.43 GMC 3.67: Scrapped Portland, Ore.

2 JOHN CLARKE 4.43 GMC 5.68: Scrapped Panama City.

3 SAMUEL GORTON 5.43 HMC 3.68: Scrapped Kearny, NJ.

4 JAMES DE WOLF 6.43 VIW 6.61: Scrapped Seattle.

5 LYMAN ABBOTT 5.43 HMC Reserve Fleet, site 4.

6 MOSES BROWN 6.43 WPM 9.61: Scrapped Panama City.

3119 MELVILLE JACOBY 3.44 GMC 47: VICTORIA. 50: NORTH QUEEN. 53: DOMINATOR.

13.3.61: Aground in fog near Palos Verdes Point, 12 miles north of Los Angeles, 33.46N 118.26W. (Voyage Vancouver, Wash/Algiers — wheat). CTL. Wreck later sold for scrapping.

3120 FRANK GILBRETH 4.44 GMC 47: NICOLAAS WITSEN. 47: AMSTELLAND. 61: ERNA STATHATOS. 65: ALBADORO.

3121 CORNELIUS FORD 5.44 GMC Reserve Fleet, site 1.

3122 JESSE H. METCALF 5.44 GMC Reserve Fleet, site 1.

3123 NELSON W. ALDRICH 4.44 GMC 11.68: Scrapped Kearny, NJ.

PART TWO

Liberty Ships, Tankers, Z—ET1—S—C3 Type

Towards the end of 1942, when the need to transport more oil, and to replace the many tankers sunk by the enemy became an urgent problem, the Maritime Commission explored the possibility of converting some Liberty type dry cargo ships to carry oil in bulk. The original intention was to convert existing vessels and to redesign some of the new hulls then under construction, but it was found that the requirements could be satisfied by confining the conversions to new, forthcoming, ships.

The Delta Shipbuilding Company of New Orleans was allotted the task of designing the tankers and preparing the specifications, and this Company was then awarded contracts for fifty-two vessels of the type. At the same time the California Shipbuilding Corporation received a contract for fifty such vessels. Within a few months conditions and requirements had changed and these figures were reduced to thirty-two and to thirty, respectively.

As material became available construction commenced and after the usual initial production problems their building times were only slightly more than the times for the standard ships. Nearly all were built during 1943, only the final few being delivered early in the following year.

In outward appearance these tankers were very similar to the basic Liberty type and the two were not easily distinguishable from either the sea or the air. To aid the deception the deck piping was concealed and dummy cargo gear — booms and winches — were installed. The oil hatches were small and low and could easily be covered and hidden.

No major change was made in the machinery installation, and most fuel and ballast tanks were also unaltered. But the forward deep tanks were eliminated and part of the midship deep tank became a pump room. The main transverse bulkheads were redesigned into oiltight ones and additional ones were added midway in hold Nos 1, 2, 4 and 5 and at the after end of No 3. These extended up to the second deck only, except in the way of the trunks — which were so formed when the original hatchways were trunked-in between the second and upper decks. A longitudinal centre-line bulkhead was fitted in the cargo spaces, this extending from the inner bottom to the second deck and to the upper deck at the trunks. This arrangement gave nine cargo tanks, port and starboard, and two main fuel tanks.

Into the latter were recessed the two pump rooms, one forward and one aft and both adjacent to the engine room. The second deck space around the trunks remained 'void' although situated in it were manifolds, control valves and piping, thus avoiding exposure of these on the upper deck.

Additional structural strength was gained by the fitting of a stringer at the sides and in way of the bulkheads and web frames at each cargo tank. Reinforcement of the second deck — which now formed the cargo tank tops — was by means of a longitudinal girder on the upper side. Such strengthening thus allowed the use of second deck plating and beams which were already in hand as part of the standard Liberty construction programme.

The original hatches were plated over, so forming the tops of the cargo tank expansion trunks, and each compartment was fitted with a 4 ft diameter oiltight hatch. The forward cargo tanks were arranged for the carriage of either petrol or heavier oils, whilst the after ones handled heavy oils only. The cargo-handling system was cross-connected but so arranged that the three forward tanks, both port and starboard, could carry one grade of oil and the remaining forward tanks a different grade.

Each pump room was equipped with two 14 x 14 x 12 in vertical duplex piston pumps, and the steam supply and cargo handling valves were operated from within upper deck enclosures. Exhaust ventilators and blowers assured the pump rooms a constant supply of fresh air, this equipment automatically closing when the carbon dioxide fire-extinguishing system was operated.

Cargo oil tanks were fitted with vent lines which converged to single vents and were then taken up the masts to a height of 25 ft above the upper deck. Petroleum tank vents were also fitted with pressure relief valves and flame arresters. Each cargo tank was provided with some 8,000 ft of 1½ in diameter heating coils and a tank cleaning system, and to assist the latter the normal Liberty ship ballast pump was replaced by another of the duplex type. The cargo tanks themselves were safeguarded by a steam smothering system and fire-main hose connections at each expansion trunk.

Liberty tankers proved extremely efficient in operation and whilst not quite so convenient as the machinery-aft bulk-oil tanker built specially for the job, they served their arduous wartime duties well. In addition to their normal oil cargoes they frequently carried heavy deck loads and aircraft to the various theatres of war. Subsequently, some of these vessels then being operated by the USN were converted into distilling ships and were able to store large quantities of drinking water.

Post-war analysis of earlier wartime situations often raised the question of why, when Liberty ships underwent extensive redesign into tankers, the one further step of locating the machinery aft was not taken. But these tankers were emergency ships for an emergency situation and there was simply no more time for further change. Of course, later in the war the Liberty collier design did have such a re-arrangement of machinery, and had the lessons learned from this been available in earlier times, more consideration might have been given to relocating the tanker machinery.

It will be noted that the Liberty tanker design was prefixed 'ET–1'. In this instance the letters 'ET' indicated 'Emergency Tanker', whilst the figure 1 represented a length of under 450 ft and not under 400 ft as with the dry cargo vessels.

It is thought that the designation Z–EC2–S–C3 may have been the provisional one allocated to the (then) already-completed dry cargo Liberties which were intended to be converted into tankers, although in the event such conversions were not undertaken. This design number does not, however, figure in the official Maritime Commission/Administration records.

Details

Tonnages:	Registered	7,219 gross (approx), 4,409 nett
	Deadweight	10,674
	Lightweight	3,571
	Defence equipment	138
Capacities:	Oil cargo, gallons	2,722,692
	" " barrels	64,826
	Fixed ballast tons	nil
	Fuel oil, tons	2,087 (approx)

Remaining details as EC2–S–C1 type, as applicable.

The *Brigadier General Alfred J. Lyon,* an ex-US Army aircraft repair ship, tied up at dolphins in Portland, Oregon, harbour awaiting a decision regarding her (then) future use. Note that a helicopter platform has replaced the foremast, the superstructure lengthened to give more accommodation and that the numerous gun-tubs are devoid of armament. (Todd Houston, Yard no 143)

The converted tanker *Alan Seeger* as the *Sealady.* Note addition of a third mast on the lengthened foredeck. (California, Tankers, Yard no T10)

The *Andrew Marschalk* off the East Coast of the USA in March 1944. Note the small circular oil-tank hatches grouped in pairs on top of the original cargo hatches. Each oil-tank hatch served a different cargo tank within the hull. (Delta, Tankers, Yard no 66)

The *Leif Ericson* as the US Navy's station tanker *Porcupine* in October 1944. (Delta, Tankers, Yard no 91)

BUILT BY CALIFORNIA SHIPBUILDING CORPORATION
USMC hull numbers: MCE 1880-1909 (Yard Nos T1 —T30)
                    ?   ? ("   " T31—T50) cancelled.

T1 JOHN GOODE 9.43 JHIW 48: Sold commercial (same name). 54: ANDRIOTIS. 55: Converted to dry cargo at Schiedam. 55: Lengthened at Kure to 511½ ft (8,395 grt). 57: ANDROS PATRIOT. 60: LOUDIAS. 6.67: Scrapped Kaohsiung.

T2 HENRY C. WALLACE 9.43 JHIW 51: Sold commercial (same name). 54: TROCADERO. 55: PERCY JORDAN. 56: Converted to dry cargo at Kure and lengthened to 511½ ft (8,494 grt). 65: CALIFORNIA SUN. 16.11.67: Afire after engine room explosion off Nicobar Islands; abandoned 01.38N 59.39E (voyage Belekeri/Germany). 28.11.67: Salved and towed to Seychelles by mv JALARAJAN (66/11,323 grt). CTL.

T3 ALBERT J. BERRES 9.43 JHIW 48: STRATH-MORE. 50: Converted to dry cargo at Savannah, re-named NIKOKLIS. 53: CAPTAIN N.B. PALMER. 54: NATIONAL UNITY. 55: Lengthened at Kobe to 511½ ft (8,562 grt). 61: SERRE. 63: UNITY. 65: EVIE W. 68: EASTERN VENTURE. 12.68: Scrapped Canton.

T4 RICHARD J. CLEVELAND 10.43 JHIW 50: MATA REDONDA. 68: Scrapped at Tampico, Mexico.

T5 JOSIAH G. HOLLAND 10.43 JHIW 48: CYGNET III. 49: Converted to dry cargo at Baltimore. 52: BATSI. 54: EKATERINI G. 17.10.65: Lost propeller in heavy weather 700 miles north of Midway Island. Taken in tow but broke adrift and grounded on Great Sitkin Island, 20 miles from Adak. CTL. (Voyage Niigata/W.coast N.America).

T6 OSCAR F. BARRETT 10.43 JHIW 48: PACO. 54: GAYETY. 55: Converted to dry cargo at Greenock. 56: Lengthened at Sasebo to 511½ ft (8,394 grt) and renamed APOLLONIUS. 57: ANDROS CHAMPION. 60: PAGASTIKOS. 62: PORTORAFTI. 64: NAVIA.

T7 JAMES COOK 10.43 IFM 47: Sold commercial (same name). 55: Converted to dry cargo at Greenock, renamed ANTIPOLIS. 56: Lengthened at Kure to 511½ ft (8,540 grt). 57: ANDROS CITY.

60: THERMAIKOS. 63: CALLIOPE. 65: VANCALT. 66: MICHIKO. 16.6.67: Aground 4 miles south of Algeciras. 26.6.67: Refloated, severely damaged, towed Algeciras, Carthagena thence Genoa. CTL. (Voyage Gela/P.Cabello, sulphate). Sold. 8.67: Scrapped Vado.

T8 CHRISTOPHER L. SHOLES 10.43 IFM 50: ESCOLIN. 50: CIUDAD MADERO. 66: Scrapped Tampico, Mexico.

T9 ORSON D. MUNN 10.43 JHIW 48: HALCYON III. 49: Converted to dry cargo at Baltimore. 52: GAVRION. 57: LILLA. 60: SYRA. 62: Lengthened at Maizuru to 511½ ft (8,364 grt). 17.7.64: Aground north of Callao, 06.07S 81.06W (voyage Chimbote/Rotterdam — fish meal). 23.8.64: Refloated, towed Callao. 8.10.64: Towed Rotterdam. CTL, sold. 65: Scrapped Bilbao.

T10 ALAN SEEGER 10.43 JHIW 52: Sold commercial (same name). 54: BENGT H. LARSON. 55: Converted to dry cargo at Kure and lengthened to 511½ ft (8,471 grt). 59: SEALADY. 68: Sold, towed from Panama City for scrapping at Rijeka (cargo — scrap iron) but, 9.8.68: damaged by surfacing US ballistic missile submarine VON STEUBEN in 36.34N 06.16W. Holed and flooded, grounded in Cadiz Bay, Spain. Awash and abandoned. 4.69: Submerged and reported settling deeper into the sand.

T11 HORACE SEE 10.43 JHIW 50: SEATHRILL. 52: STENIES. 54: Converted to dry cargo at Greenock. 56: Lengthened at Maizuru to 511½ ft (8,518 grt). 57: ANDROS SEAMAN. 60: KIFISSOS. 62: NIRITOS. 62: CAVOURI. 64: MARIA T.

T12 CARLETON ELLIS 10.43 JHIW 47: CATA-HOULA. 54: Converted to dry cargo at Schiedam, renamed MESSARIA. 55: Lengthened at Kure to 511½ ft (8,466 grt). 57: ANDROS MERCHANT. 60: LAKONIKOS. 4.67: Scrapped Sakaide, Japan.

T13 CHARLOTTE P. GILMAN 10.43 JHIW 44: APSHERSON. 48: CHARLOTTE P. GILMAN. 51: HESS BUNKER. 54: AEGEUS. 55: Converted to dry cargo at Schiedam. 55: Lengthened at Maizuru to 511½ ft (8,394 grt). 57: ANDROS EAGLE. 60:

Key to Elevation

1 Stores
2 Fore peak
3 Oil tank No 1 (P & S)
4 Oil tank No 2 (P & S)
5 Oil tank No 3 (P & S)
6 Oil tank No 4 (P & S)
7 Oil tank No 5 (P & S)
8 Fuel oil tank No 1 (P & S)
9 Forward pump room
10 Fuel oil settling tank (P & S)
11 Machinery space
12 Fresh water tank (P & S)
13 Fuel oil tank No 2 (P & S)
14 After pump room (P & S)
15 Oil tank No 6 (P & S)
16 Oil tank No 7 (P & S)
17 Oil tank No 8 (P & S)
18 Oil tank No 9 (P & S)
19 Shaft tunnel

20 Tunnel recess
21 Shaft tunnel escape trunk
22 After peak
23 Steering gear compartment
24 5-ton boom (P & S)

Double-bottom tanks:

25 Fuel oil or ballast tank No 1 (P & S)
26 Fuel oil or ballast tank No 2 (P & S)
27 Fuel oil or ballast tank No 3 (P & S)
28 Ballast tank
29 Reserve fresh water tank No 4 (P & S)
30 Fuel oil or ballast tank No 5 (P & S)
31 Fuel oil or ballast tank No 6 (P & S)

P & S = Port & Starboard

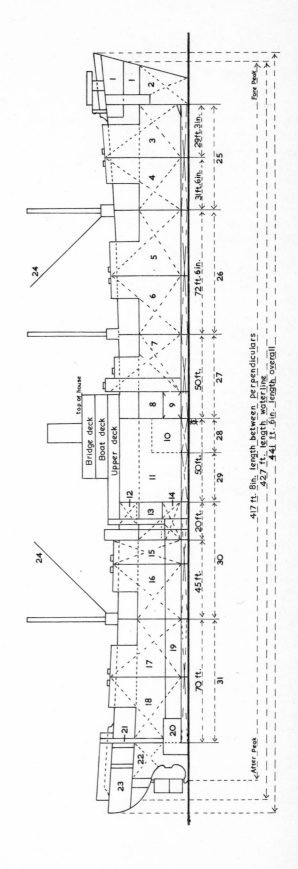

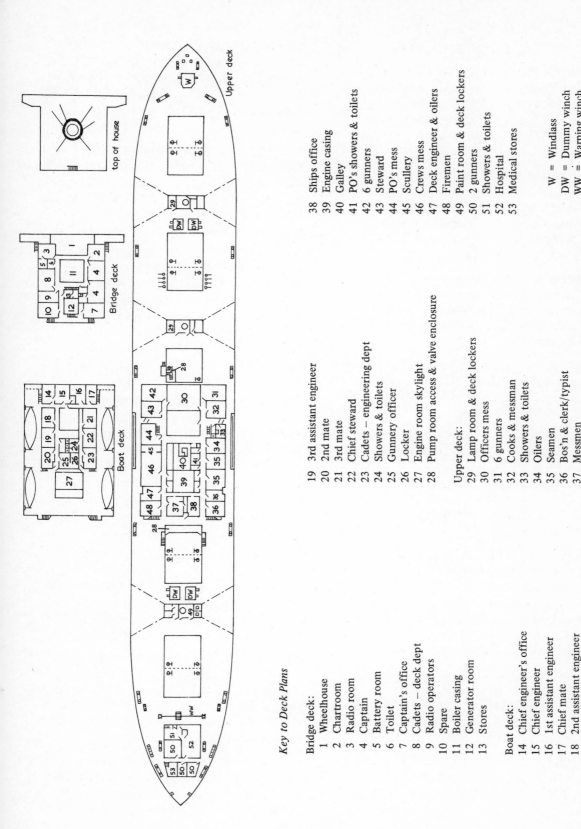

top of house

Upper deck

Bridge deck

Boat deck

Key to Deck Plans

Bridge deck:
1 Wheelhouse
2 Chartroom
3 Radio room
4 Captain
5 Battery room
6 Toilet
7 Captain's office
8 Cadets – deck dept
9 Radio operators
10 Spare
11 Boiler casing
12 Generator room
13 Stores

Boat deck:
14 Chief engineer's office
15 Chief engineer
16 1st assistant engineer
17 Chief mate
18 2nd assistant engineer

19 3rd assistant engineer
20 2nd mate
21 3rd mate
22 Chief steward
23 Cadets – engineering dept
24 Showers & toilets
25 Gunnery officer
26 Locker
27 Engine room skylight
28 Pump room access & valve enclosure

Upper deck:
29 Lamp room & deck lockers
30 Officers mess
31 6 gunners
32 Cooks & messman
33 Showers & toilets
34 Oilers
35 Seamen
36 Bos'n & clerk/typist
37 Messmen

38 Ships office
39 Engine casing
40 Galley
41 PO's showers & toilets
42 6 gunners
43 Steward
44 PO's mess
45 Scullery
46 Crews mess
47 Deck engineer & oilers
48 Firemen
49 Paint room & deck lockers
50 2 gunners
51 Showers & toilets
52 Hospital
53 Medical stores

W = Windlass
DW = Dummy winch
WW = Warping winch

LIBERTY TANKER, Z – ET1 – S – C3 TYPE

EVINOS. 62: VARI. 65: SYRA. 67: HALLA.

T14 MORTON PRINCE 10.43 JHIW 47: CARRA-
BULLE. 54: Converted to dry cargo at Amsterdam,
renamed MESSATHOURI. 56: Lengthened at Kure
to 511½ ft (8,435 grt). 57: ANDROS MENTOR.
60: LOUROS. 62: AGIOS NIKOLAOS II. 66:
AKIKO.

T15 HARVEY W. WILEY 10.43 JHIW 48: Sold
commercial (same name). 50: MANDOIL. 54:
NATIONAL FORTUNE. 55: Converted to dry
cargo at Amsterdam. 55: Lengthened at Nagasaki
to 511½ ft (8,393 grt). 61: EVVIA. 68: BLUE
SURF. 10.69: Scrapped Sakaide.

T16 JOHN H. MARION 11.43 JHIW 49: Sold
commercial (same name); converted to dry cargo
at Newport News. 52: COMPASS. 55: MARY P.
57: P.PREKLA. 63: PERDIKA. 66: NEBRASKAN.
12.67: Scrapped Hirao.

T17 JOHN P. ALTGELD 11.43 JHIW 51: ANDROIL.
55: Converted to dry cargo at Nagasaki and lengthened
to 511½ ft (8,428 grt), renamed NATIONAL HOPE.
63: KAVALA. 67: PACIFICA.

T18 PAUL DUNBAR 11.43 JHIW 44: BYEL-
GOROD. 48: PAUL DUNBAR. 51: MORRIS HESS.
54: Converted to dry cargo at Greenock, renamed
PALATIANI. 56: Lengthened at Sasebo to 511½
ft (8,371 grt). 57: ANDROS PEARL. 60: ILISSOS.
62: ELENA. 66: ORIENT IMPORTER. 1.69:
Scrapped Hirao.

T19 THOMAS H. GALLAUDET 11.43 JHIW
44: MAIKOP. 48: THOMAS H.GALLAUDET.
51: AMBERSTAR. 54: ELMIRA. 55: Converted to
dry cargo at Greenock. 60: PONTOS. 65: SAMUEL
S. 25.3.69: Aground on Kuchinoerabu Island, Japan,
30.25N 130.14E (voyage Guam/Pusan — scrap iron).
Later broke in two; sank. Total loss.

T20 SCHUYLER COLFAX 11.43 JHIW 16.8.46:
Grounded whilst proceeding between Hawaiian
ports, damaged and laid up at Hawaii. 8.47:
Transferred to USN and sunk as target ship by aircraft bombs and submarine torpedoes in Pacific.

T21 SIDNEY HOWARD 11.43 JHIW 43: ARMA-
DILLO IX III (USN). 46: SIDNEY HOWARD. 48:
DEAN H. 54: CHRIS H. 55: Converted to dry cargo
at Jacksonville. 63: Returned to US Govt. Reserve
Fleet, site 2.

T22 DAVID RITTENHOUSE 11.43 JHIW
43: BEAGLE IX 112 (USN). 46: DAVID RITTEN-
HOUSE. 48: EDISON SKIPPER. 55: Converted to
dry cargo at Baltimore, renamed GEORGE S. 60:
GEORGIOS SIDERATOS. 64: MARIA G.L. 3.69:
Scrapped Hirao.

T23 WILLIAM H. CARRUTH 11.43 JHIW 43:
CAMEL IX 113 (USN). 46: WILLIAM H. CARRUTH.
48: Sold commercial (same name). 49: Converted to
dry cargo at Savannah. 59: PENN SHIPPER. 62:
HALCYON PIONEER. 63: Returned to US Govt.
63: Scrapped Tacoma.

T24 NATHANIEL B. PALMER 11.43 JHIW
43: CARIBOU IX 114 (USN). 46: NATHANIEL
B.PALMER. 49: Converted to dry cargo at Newport
News. 51: Sold commercial (same name). 31.5.52:
Aground in Martin Garcia Channel, Buenos Aires.
(Voyage Constitucion/Montevideo — ballast).
2.11.52: Refloated.CTL, sold. Repaired. 53:
MANOLITO. 61: MANEGINA. 11.62: Scrapped
Savona.

T25 WILLIAM WINTER 11.43 JHIW 43: ELK IX
115 (USN). 46: WILLIAM WINTER. 51: SEA-
PEARL. 53: KORTHI. 54: Converted to dry cargo
at Greenock. 56: Lengthened at Sasebo to 511½ ft
(8,390 grt). 57: ANDROS COUNTY. 60:
KALAMAS. 3.9.60: Ashore on Oregon coast.
12.10.60: Refloated, towed Coos Bay thence San
Francisco, (voyage Chemainus/Australia — lumber).
Sold. 62: Scrapped Oakland, Cal.

T26 CYRUS K. HOLLIDAY 11.43 JHIW
43: GAZELLE IX 116 (USN). 46: CYRUS K.
HOLLIDAY. 48: EVISTAR. 49: CHRYSSTAR.
50: CHRYSANTHY. 55: Converted to dry cargo
at Antwerp, renamed RHAPSODY. 60: FOS. 66:
PACIFIC LOGGER. 9.68: Scrapped Kaohsiung.

T27 CARL R. GRAY 12.43 JHIW 43: GEMS-
BOK IX 117 (USN). 46: CARL R.GRAY. 48:
ALPHA. 51: STRATH BAY. 53: Converted to dry
cargo at Savannah. 55: COLUMBIA TRADER. 63:
PILOT ROCK. 65: Returned to US Govt. 3.66:
Scrapped Portland, Ore.

T28 SANFORD B. DOLE 12.43 JHIW
43: GIRAFFE IX 118 (USN). 46: SANFORD B.
DOLE. 48: Sold commercial (same name). 49:
Converted to dry cargo at Newport News. 50:

EILEEN. 51: SEAPENDOR. 53: RAGNAR NAESS. 55: OCEAN DAPHNE. 61: ORIENT LAKES. 11.67: Scrapped Hirao.

T29 NICHOLAS LONGWORTH 12.43 JHIW 43: IBEX IX 119 (USN). 46: NICHOLAS LONG-WORTH. 48: HELEN STEVENSON. 49: Converted to dry cargo at Norfolk, Va. 57: ELDERFIELDS. 61: WINNER. 10.9.65: Aground in typhoon at Wakanoura, Japan. 25.9.65: Refloated, repairs

uneconomic; sold. 2.66: Scrapped Hirao.

T30 CHARLES T. YERKES 12.43 JHIW 43: JAGUAR IX 120 (USN). 46: CHARLES T. YERKES. 48: HARRY PEER. 49: Converted to dry cargo at Mobile, renamed TINI. 51: ILLENAO. 4.6.54: Aground near Prongs Lighthouse, Bombay (voyage Fremantle/Bombay — wheat). Refloated. CTL. Sold to Indian shipbreakers and scrapped.

BUILT BY DELTA SHIPBUILDING COMPANY
USMC hull numbers: MCE 1734–1746 (Yard Nos 64–76)
1916–1934 (” ” 77–95)

64 GEORGE W. KENDALL 9.43 GMC 49: Converted to dry cargo at Mobile, renamed DOROTHY STEVENSON. 54: CAMBRIDGE. 56: WOLNA POLSKA. 57: CAMBRIDGE. 61: YI MING. 3.68: Scrapped Kaohsiung.

65 MARY ASHLEY TOWNSEND 9.43 IFM 48: DAVID T.WILENTZ. 55: SWEETVILLE. 56: Converted to dry cargo at Kure and lengthened to 511½ ft (8,602 grt). 57: BERKSHIRE. 64: DELOS GLORY. 68: Scrapped Kaohsiung.

66 ANDREW MARSCHALK 10.43 ASB 50: SEA-GLORIOUS. 55: Converted to dry cargo at Schiedam. 56: Lengthened at Kure to 511½ ft (8,433 grt). 57: ANDROS GLIDER. 60: EVROTAS. 62: KINI. 65: THREE SISTERS. 68: KRITI.

67 JOHN STAGG 9.43 ASB 47: Sold commercial (same name). 50: TAKOIL. 54: NATIONAL SERVANT. 55: Converted to dry cargo at Schiedam. 56: Lengthened at Maizuru to 511½ ft (8,544 grt). 61: YIANNINA. 10.68: Scrapped Hirao.

68 JACOB THOMPSON 10.43 WISC 50: ATZCA-POTZALCO. 68: Scrapped Minatitlan, Mexico.

69 TOBIAS E. STANSBURY 9.43 ASB 48: WANDA. 54: KYRA. 57: Converted to dry cargo at Baltimore, re-named TAXIARCH. 58: PANDORA. 63: PONDEROSA. 17.2.67: Aground at Topar Island, Concepcion Channel, Chile. (Voyage Necochea/Callao — grain). Refloated and grounded several times. 7.3.67: Beached Molyneux Bay, abandoned. CTL. 16.5.67: Refloated and later sold for service as fish factory ship.

70 LAFCADIO HEARN 9.43 GMC 48: POLARU-SOIL. 55: Converted to dry cargo at Jacksonville, renamed MYCENAE. 59: Lengthened at Kobe to 511½ ft (8,588 grt). 60: HYDROUSSA. 64: DROMON. 66: MYCENAE. 69: Scrapped Kaohsiung.

71 DAVID HOLMES 10.43 GMC 49: Sold commercial (same name). 55: Converted to dry cargo at Amsterdam, renamed ALPHEUS. 56: Lengthened at Kure to 511½ ft (8,479 grt), renamed ANDROS STREAM. 60: PATRAIKOS. 62: TILEMACHOS. 63: ARGOLIKOS. 63: TILEMACHOS. 64: ARGOLIKOS. 8.67: Scrapped Mukaijima, Japan.

72 WILLIAM E. PENDLETON 10.43 GMC 48: NATICO. 54: CASINO. 55: Converted to dry cargo at Amsterdam, renamed AMALIAS. 56: Lengthened at Maizuru to 511½ ft (8,531 grt). 57: ANDROS VALLEY. 60: CORINTHIAKOS. 64: GEORGIOS P. 68: PACSTAR. 4.4.69: Aground in storm on north shore of Toshima, Japan (voyage Kure/Portland, Ore — ballast). Abandoned. Total loss. To be sold 'as lies'.

73 IRWIN RUSSELL 10.43 ASB 47: ELIZABETH H. 2.62: Scrapped Hirao.

74 HENRY L. ELLSWORTH 11.43 GMC 50: REYNOSA. 68: Scrapped Minatitlan, Mexico.

75 REGINALD A. FESSENDEN 10.43 GMC 48: KINGSTON. 50: SEAMAGIC. 53: STRAPOU-RIES. 54: Converted to dry cargo at Schiedam. 55: THEOTOKOS. 24.10.63: Severely damaged in collision with BRITISH STATESMAN (59/27,896 grt) 30 miles north west of Lisbon, 39.20N 09.40W

(voyage Ymuiden/Genoa). Sold. 3.64: Scrapped Vado.

76 WILLIAM CROMPTON 11.43 GMC 48: CARIB-STAR. 50: SEADREAM. 52: LIVADIA. 54: Converted to dry cargo at Schiedam. 55: THEON-YMPHOS. 4.69: Scrapped Spezia.

77 ANDREW A. HUMPHREYS 11.43 ASB 48: Sold commercial (same name). 54: Converted to dry cargo at Kure and lengthened to 511½ ft (8,615 grt), renamed WILLIAM R.TOLBERT. 61: OCEAN LEADER. 11.69: Scrapped Onomichi.

78 JOSEPH GOLDBERGER 10.43 GMC 48: GEORGE OGDEN. 49: TALON. 50: SEACOMET. 54: Converted to dry cargo at Amsterdam. 55: Lengthened at Kure to 511½ ft (8,426 grt). 57: ANDROS COMET. 60: ALPHEIOS. 64: ANNIE. 3.69: Scrapped Kaohsiung.

79 OSCAR S. STRAUS 11.43 F & S 47: Sold commercial (same name). 55: Converted to dry cargo at Rotterdam, renamed AMERICUS. 55: Lengthened at Kure to 511½ ft (8,509 grt). 57: ANDROS NAVIGATOR. 60: LADON. 62: ARIETTA. 67: POPEYE.

80 THOMAS F. CUNNINGHAM 12.43 GMC 49: Converted to dry cargo at Hoboken, renamed PAUL REVERE. 54: CHRIS. 11.65: Scrapped Hirao.

81 JEAN BAPISTE LE MOYNE 12.43 GMC 48: WALTER DU MONT. 54: Converted to dry cargo at Schiedam, renamed PANACHRANDOS. 55: Lengthened at Maizuru to 511½ ft (8,444 grt). 57: ANDROS PILGRIM. 60: AMVRAKIKOS. 23.11.61: Aground during fog at Pancake Shoal, Lake Superior. 26.11.61: Refloated, damaged. Temporary repairs made, proceeded on voyage (Toledo/Japan — scrap iron). Sold, and 6.62: Scrapped Sakai.

82 ALBERT G. BROWN 11.43 ASB 47: Sold commercial (same name). 6.60: Scrapped Hirao.

83 ELIZA JANE NICHOLSON 11.43 ASB 51: Sold commercial (same name). 54: AETNA. 55: Converted to dry cargo at Amsterdam. 56: DRURY L.S. 58: IRINI STEFANOU. 4.2.65: Aground off San Benito Islands, Baja California 28.20N 115.32W (voyage Vancouver/London — timber). 25.2.65: Refloated, towed Los Angeles. CTL. 2.67: Sold for scrapping at Terminal Island.

84 PAUL TULANE 12.43 GMC 43: KANGAROO IX 121 (USN). 46: PAUL TULANE. 48: MOSTANK. 50: SEABRAVE. 54: Converted to dry cargo at Schiedam, renamed NIBORIO. 57: ANDROS SEA-FARER. 63: SAN PABLO. 3.69: Scrapped Kaohsiung.

85 HORACE H. HARVEY 12.43 GMC 48: GROTON TRAILS. 49: Converted to dry cargo at Baltimore. 57: VALLEY FORGE. 31.12.59: Aground near Berlangkap, 65 miles south east of Singapore, 01.00N 104.50E (voyage Portland, Ore/Madras — wheat). 1.1.60: Abandoned, total loss.

86 CHARLES A. WICKLIFFE 12.43 ASB 51: Sold commercial (same name). 55: OMNIUM CARRIER. 57: Converted to dry cargo at Yokohama and lengthened to 511½ ft (8,196 grt). 68: LAVENHAM.

87 WILLIAM B. BANKHEAD 12.43 ASB 43: LEOPARD IX 122 (USN). 46: WILLIAM B. BANKHEAD. 48: YANKEE FIGHTER. 49: Converted to dry cargo at Staten Island. 51: FIGHTER. 55: CARRETO. 60: ZOE. 14.7.65: Struck submerged object, sprank leak 33.30S 52.27W (voyage Chimbote/Rio Grande — salt). 17.7.65: Arrived at Rio Grande, but CTL. Sold to Porto Alegre shipbreakers.

88 JUDAH TOURO 12.43 IFM 43: MINK IX 123 (USN). 46: JUDAH TOURO. 51: SEAVALOR. 52: APIKIA. 54: Converted to dry cargo at Greenock, renamed ELENI V. 9.67: Scrapped Sakaide, Japan.

89 MASON L. WEEMS 1.44 ASB 44: MOOSE IX 124 (USN). 46: MASON L.WEEMS. 48: YANKEE PIONEER. 49: Converted to dry cargo at Brooklyn. 51: W.L. McCORMICK. 61: ANJI. 5.9.64: Grounded and damaged in typhoon at Hong Kong. 24.11.64: Refloated. 3.65: Scrapped Hong Kong.

90 OPIE READ 12.43 IFM 43: PANDA IX 125 (USN). 46: OPIE READ. 48: WESTPORT. 49: Converted to dry cargo at Hoboken. 54: PARDA-LINA. 63: SAN ANTONIO. 2.68: Scrapped Hirao.

91 LEIF ERICSON 12.43 IFM 43: PORCUPINE IX 126 (USN). 30.12.44: Sunk by Japanese Kamikaze suicide aircraft attack off Mindoro, Philippine Islands.

92 J.C.W. BECKHAM 1.44 ASB 44: RACCOON IX 127 (USN). 46: J.C.W. BECKHAM. 48: CHRYSAN-THYSTAR. 49: Converted to dry cargo at Brooklyn, renamed JUPITER. 51: SEARANGER. 53: SARIZA.

63: SARA. 65: ASIA MARINER. 11.68: Scrapped Kaohsiung.

93 NORMAN O. PEDRICK 2.44 IFM 44: STAG IX 128 (USN). 44: STAG AW1 (USN). 46: Returned US Govt. USN Reserve Fleet, site 2.

94 EUGENE W. HILGARD 1.44 ASB 44: WHIPPET IX 129 (USN). 46: EUGENE W. HILGARD. 51: Sold commercial (same name). 55: Converted to dry cargo at Savannah, renamed LOIDA. 56: Lengthened at Kobe to 511½ ft (8,536 grt). 65: NERVION.

95 LEON GODCHAUX 2.44 IFM 44: WILDCAT IX 130 (USN). 44: WILDCAT AW2 (USN). 46: Returned US Govt. 3.68: Scrapped Portland, Ore.

PART THREE

Liberty Ships, Colliers, EC2–S–AW1 Type

Early in 1944 the Delta Shipbuilding Company was requested by the Maritime Commission to design and build a group of Liberty colliers from plans and specifications which had been previously prepared in Washington.

Although ultimately forming a part of the tail-end of the Liberty ship programme, these ships were really planned with a very definite future and were not intended merely for wartime emergency use.

They were designed specifically to operate on America's East Coast domestic coal trade between Hampton Roads and New England, the need being both to replace vessels lost by enemy action and to replace a fleet which was already obsolete and expensive to operate. The urgency of the latter need was made apparent by the fact that of the survivors of the forty colliers serving the Eastern seaboard at the outbreak of the war, only two were less than twenty years old and eleven were more than thirty years old.

In the preliminary stages of design both the commission and the builders carefully considered the views and requirements of experienced collier operators and every effort was made to construct vessels which would stand up to the severe rigors of the trade. One view was that these colliers should be coal-burners — this being the operating companies own product — but of course such divergence could not be tolerated with the Liberty hull, nor could the necessary sacrifice of cubic and deadweight capacity.

At one time during construction, the procurement of certain materials gave cause for considerable concern. For although it was important to use as much standard Liberty equipment as possible, most of this was already under manufacture for the basic type of ship — or even lying surplus in other yards. But some new and different sections still had to be manufactured within a tight time schedule, and this presented some complications.

Generally the dimensions of the collier were the same as those of the basic Liberty ship type, but the overall length was slightly increased due to the addition of a poop deck 95 ft 10½ in long and a resultant slight overhang at the stern.

Two main differences between the two types were that the collier had its machinery located aft instead of in the customary midship position, and that it was designed as a long-range ship. The latter point enforced compliance with certain rules and regulations in that all bulkheads, doors and furniture were of steel or steel and asbestos instead of the wood used for much similar outfitting in the basic dry cargo type of ship.

For two main reasons it became essential, when using the Liberty hull for this type of ship, to locate the propelling machinery aft. The first was that the fine lines of the type and the confined space aft, if used for cargo, would create a serious hindrance to economic discharge. The second was the knowledge that colliers with machinery amidships usually required extensive manual trimming in the final stages of discharge and were also very prone to damage — especially in the area of the shaft tunnel — from discharging grabs.

Therefore, the machinery space, fitted with the normal Liberty ship triple expansion engine, occupied the same space and position as No 5 hold of the standard type.

The arrangement in the limited space of the Liberty collier's engine room was that the main engine, condensers and large pumps were situated at the customary 'low level' whilst the boilers, evaporators, generators, compressors and all other auxiliaries were located on a raised platform 21 ft above. The boilers, aft of the main engine, faced inboard, and although of standard Liberty design the backs of the fireboxes had to be cut off at an angle of 60 degrees due to space restriction. Nevertheless, considering the fineness of the ships at the stern, this arrangement of machinery gave a surprising amount of space.

The ships had five main cargo holds, each with two 30 ft by 20 ft hatches and to each of these was fitted a steel one-piece hatch cover hinged at the transverse coaming. On deck the steel hatch coamings were 3 ft high and continuous, thus giving a trunk deck between the hatches. The longitudinal hatch coaming angle bar and the gunwale bar were the only parts which were rivetted — the ships otherwise being of all-welded construction.

A new design of steel king posts, these being an improvement over the previously-used tubular or box type which gave no access for maintenance, assisted the operating of the hatch covers, which were controlled by sets of sheaves and steel cables leading to winches at the foot of the bridge structure. The location of these winches under cover, rather than in the customary position of adjacent to the hatches, considerably reduced the maintenance problem and gave safer working conditions. Four winches were fitted to each ship and were of the same type as those of the Liberty cargo ship.

In addition to the main holds there were also three deep tanks. Two were situated under No 1 hold and the third, being the full depth of the vessel and 15 ft long, was located between Nos 2 and 3 holds and immediately beneath the midships four-deck-high bridge superstructure. Fuel oil was carried in tanks in the double bottom under Nos 3, 4 and 5 holds, whilst No 2 double bottom and No 3 deep tank were for emergency fuel or ballast.

At the after part of the ships the two-deck poop reached from No 5 hold to the stern.

With the interior construction the bottom shell in way of the ballast tanks was covered in a layer of concrete and an extra side stringer, fitted at the normal second deck level, permitted the use of standard side frames.

From the after end of No 1 hold to the engine room bulkhead longitudinal sloping bulkheads formed topside wing ballast tanks, these being situated between the main deck and the side stringer of the original 'tween deck. They fitted into this otherwise wasted, 'triangular' space formed in the upper holds by the ship's side, the deck and the normal angle of repose of the cargo, and as well as providing for the essential ballast necessary when 50 per cent of their seatime was without cargo they also added great strength to these ships serving a trade which subjected them to alternate sagging and hogging strains.

Midway in each hold heavy web frames arched across the deck and eliminated hatch-end pillars. The brackets of these frames were angled, and these features, combined with the angled side ceilings and a complete absence of any horizontal surfaces in the holds helped to produce a collier of the self-trimming type.

Also in the holds the heavy transverse bulkheads were fitted with continuous vertical stiffeners and these, plus the extra heavy protection on other structures, was expected to not only well-withstand the onslaught of the heavy discharging machinery but to create a respect for the structure by the unloading personnel — and perhaps even stir the thought that extra care would also safeguard their own equipment.

Experience with colliers showed the need for heavier ground tackle than that provided for the basic Liberty, for when in ballast their great freeboard created the serious problem of holding them safely at anchor in a heavy blow. So the Liberty collier anchors were increased in size, to 11,410 lb each, with $2\frac{5}{16}$ in chain. Mooring and windlass fittings were correspondingly heavier and included a steam capstan capable of a 20,000 lb pull at 30 ft per minute.

Accommodation was provided for a crew of forty-six, with additional space for any necessary gun crews. Classed as a long range vessel, the quarters, galleys and messrooms and other interior arrangements were very much larger than in the basic ship.

The central bridge structure included accommodation for the captain and deck officers, owners stateroom, radio room, lounge, ships office and quarters for cadets, clerk and radio operator. Engineer officers were accommodated on the boat deck aft; steward, cooks, boatswain and hospital on the poop deck, and seamen, messmen and engine room crew on the upper deck aft.

Key to Elevation

1 Stores
2 Fore peak
3 Deep tank No 1 (P & S)
4 Deep tank No 2 (P & S)
5 Deep tank No 3
6 Wing ballast tank No 1 (P & S)
7 Wing ballast tank No 2 (P & S)
8 Wing ballast tank No 3 (P & S)
9 Wing ballast tank No 4 (P & S)
10 Machinery space
11 Machinery flat
12 Fresh water tank
13 Fuel oil settling tank

14 After peak
15 Steering gear compartment
16 1-ton boom (P & S)

Double-bottom tanks:

17 Emergency fuel oil or ballast tank No 1 (P & S)
18 Fuel oil or ballast tank No 2 (P & S)
19 Fuel oil or ballast tank No 3 (P & S)
20 Fuel oil or ballast tank No 4 (P & S)
21 Boiler feed water tank No 5 (P & S)

P & S = Port & Starboard

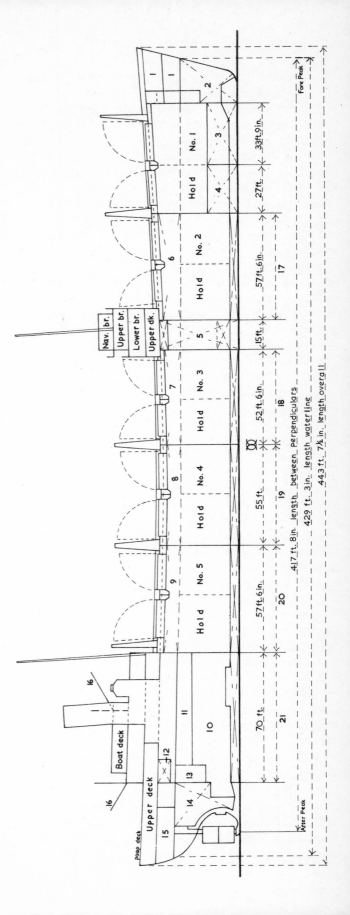

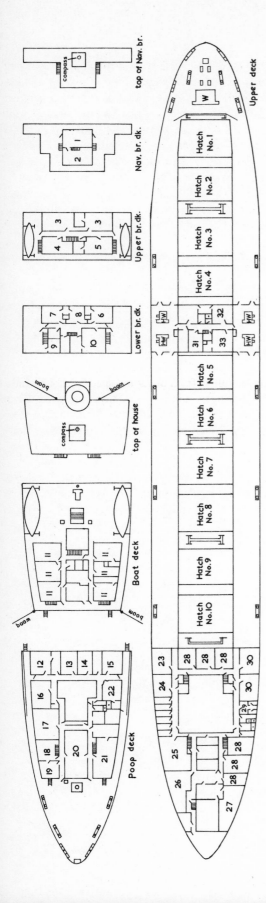

top of Nav. br.

Nav. br. dk.

Upper br. dk.

Lower br. dk.

top of house

Boat deck

Poop deck

Upper deck

Hatch No.1

Hatch No.2

Hatch No.3

Hatch No.4

Hatch No.5

Hatch No.6

Hatch No.7

Hatch No.8

Hatch No.9

Hatch No.10

Key to Deck Plans

Navigating bridge deck:
1 Wheelhouse
2 Chartroom

Upper bridge deck:
3 Captain
4 Radio room
5 Office

Lower bridge deck:
6 Chief mate
7 2nd mate
8 3rd mate
9 Radio operators
10 Officers lounge

Boat deck:
11 Engineers

Poop deck:
12 Steward
13 Cooks
14 Spare
15 Bos'n
16 Store room
17 Crews mess
18 Crews pantry
19 PO's mess
20 Galley
21 Officers mess
22 Hospital

Upper deck:
23 Oilers
24 Spare
25 Machine shop
26 Stores
27 Messmen
28 Engine room crew
29 Showers & toilets
30 Seamen
31 Clerk
32 Owner's staterooms
33 Cadets

W = Windlass
HW = Hatch-cover winch

LIBERTY COLLIER, EC2 – S – AW1 TYPE

All outside surfaces of the accommodation were ceiled and insulated. Also fitted was a diesel-driven interior ventilating and heating system, this being essential for comfort in a coastal trade, where, both at loading and discharge ports, the accommodation had to be tightly closed-up due to the heavy dust from coal and other cargoes.

The large size of ballast pumps was regulated by the large amount of water necessary on this type of vessel, and also by the limited time in which the ballast had to be discharged, for in heavy weather the ships had to retain their ballast until arriving inside the capes of the prime loading port — Hampton Roads — and then to complete discharge before reaching the coal piers. The topside ballast tanks were also fitted with sluicing valves, so permitting direct overboard discharge.

Lifesaving equipment included two thirteen-person, 18-ft lifeboats with crescent-type davits on the upper bridge deck and two fifty-two person, 28-ft motor lifeboats with gravity davits on the boat deck aft. All the lifeboats were constructed of aluminium alloy — the first time such material had been used for American standard-ship boats.

The draft of the Liberty-type collier was 10¼ in greater than the basic type, and this gave a corresponding increase in deadweight tonnage, although on a reduced gross tonnage.

Within the first few months of operation these colliers proved to be extremely efficient. They were loading more coal in less time per ton; they averaged 12 knots, or two knots faster than pre-war colliers and on a reduced fuel consumption; they employed a smaller crew than many of the small coal-fired colliers, and they had a rapid discharge rate coupled with complete elimination of stevedoring or trimming labour. Also, although having the same hull lines as the standard Liberty, they proved to be more seaworthy both under full load and extreme ballast conditions.

The placing into service of twenty-four new colliers within a period of a few months made a big impact in the trade, but nevertheless there still remained the need for smaller vessels. The one feature that restricted the use of the Liberty as a collier was its size, for many of the discharging berths then in use could not accommodate ships of this length or draft. It was this fact which had previously kept the average collier down to a maximum deadweight of some 8,000 tons.

These colliers were named after well-known American coal seams.

In the early stages of collier design Delta yard numbers 97—115 (nineteen vessels) were re-allocated to Liberty colliers. But later this design change was cancelled and the numbers were again used for basic-type vessels. Subsequently, when collier production was about to commence, a later series of numbers were substituted for those previously allocated.

Details

Measurements:			
	Length overall	443 ft	$7\frac{1}{2}$ in
	” waterline	429 ”	3 ”
	Draft, international	28 ”	$7\frac{1}{8}$ ”
	” coastwise, emergency	29 ”	$3\frac{5}{8}$ ”
	Freeboard	8 ”	$10\frac{1}{2}$ ”

Tonnages:		
	Registered	6,643 gross, 3,740 nett
	Deadweight	11,047
	Displacement	14,730
	” light ship	3,600 (at 8 ft 5 in draft)
	Lightweight	3,683
	Defence equipment	20

Capacities: Coal, cu ft:
(measured at 45 cu ft per ton)

No 1 hold	84,611	=	1,880 tons
” 2 ”	103,133	=	2,292 ”
” 3 ”	91,300	=	2,029 ”
” 4 ”	95,491	=	2,122 ”
” 5 ”	98,264	=	2,184 ”

Totals   472,799 =   10,507 ”

General stores, cu ft	14,594
Refrigerated stores, cu ft	2,983

Water ballast, tons	4,200 (approx)
Fixed ” ”	nil
Fuel oil, ”	2,000 (approx)
Freshwater, ”	466

Masts:

Mainmast, height above poop deck	65 ft
Foremast, ” ” bridge ”	49 ft 11 in

Remaining details as EC2–S–C1 type, as applicable.

BUILT BY DELTA SHIPBUILDING COMPANY

USMC hull numbers:

MCE 2816	(Yard No 142)
2824	(”	150)
2832	(”	158)
2836	(”	162)
2840	(”	166)
2842	(”	168)
2844	(”	170)
2846–2862	(”	172–188)

142 JAGGER SEAM 3.45 JHIW 47: BOSTON. 8.68: Scrapped Kaohsiung.

150 SEWANEE SEAM 4.45 JHIW 47: NEWTON. 63: Converted at Baltimore to barge (boilers and machinery removed); renamed EASTERN 2. 25.12.69: Broke adrift from tug and later grounded near Shark river, 12 miles from Sandy Hook, NJ (voyage Hampton Roads/   , coal). Broke in two.

158 HERRIN SEAM 6.45 JHIW 46: THOMAS TRACY. 60: MARINE LEADER. 62: CANTERBURY LEADER. 4.67: Scrapped Kaohsiung.

162 LA SALLE SEAM 3.45 JHIW 47: MARINE TRADER. 4.67: Returned to US Govt. Sold to ship-breakers under Ship Sale Act. 3.68: Scrapped Santander.

166 STREATOR SEAM 8.45 JHIW 47: LEXING-TON. 63: Converted at Baltimore to barge (boilers and machinery removed); renamed EASTERN 1. 22.1.69: Broke adrift from tug and stranded Kitty Hawk beach, NC (voyage New York/Norfolk). Re-floated, sold unrepaired. 7.69: At Bilbao for scrapping.

168 LINTON SEAM 4.45 JHIW 48: SEACONNET. 63: SEACOMET. 7.64: Scrapped Bilbao.

170 REDSTONE SEAM 5.45 JHIW 46: BERWIND-VALE. 63: POINT VINCENTE. 4.65: Scrapped Castellon, Spain.

172 JEWELL SEAM 5.45 JHIW 48: WINCHESTER. 67: Returned to US Govt under Ship Exchange Act in exchange for C4 troopship MARINE PHOENIX. 12.67: Scrapped Sakaide.

173 MERRIMAC SEAM 5.45 JHIW 49: MARINE SHIPPER. 66: Returned to US Govt. Reserve Fleet, site 4.

174 JELLICOE SEAM 10.45 F & S 48: CHARLES-TOWN. 54: BRANT. 61: HAJDUK. 4.67: Scrapped Hamburg.

175 BON AIR SEAM 5.45 GMC 48: PENOBSCOT. 62: MARINE COASTER. 10.65: Scrapped Hirao.

176 GLAMORGAN SEAM 6.45 JHIW 48: PLYMOUTH. 63: MARINE MERCHANT. 7.68: Scrapped Kaohsiung.

177 SEWELL SEAM 6.45 GMC 47: CONCORD. 64: Converted at New Orleans to barge (boilers and machinery removed); renamed EASTERN 4.

178 BECKLEY SEAM 7.45 GMC 47: MALDEN. 63: Converted at New Orleans to barge, (boilers and machinery removed); renamed EASTERN 3.

179 POCAHONTAS SEAM 6.45 GMC 48: MED-FORD. 54: OSPREY. 64: ANDROMEDA.

180 EAGLE SEAM 7.45 JHIW 47: MARINE TRANSPORT.

181 POWELLTON SEAM 7.45 GMC 46: EVELYN. 3.63: Scrapped Hirao.

182 CHILTON SEAM 8.45 JHIW 46: MAE. 5.63: Scrapped Hirao.

183 BANNER SEAM 7.45 JHIW 46: MICHAEL TRACY. 7.62: Scrapped Kearny, NJ.

184 RODA SEAM 10.45 F & S 47: MOUNT TAMALPAIS. 47: EVERETT. 54: GULL. 64: ALGOL.

185 IMBODEN SEAM 8.45 JHIW 47: READING.

186 FREEPORT SEAM 9.45 F & S 46: EDITH. 1.63: Scrapped Hirao.

187 MINGO SEAM 9.45 F & S 46: MOUNT SUNAPEE. 47: MELROSE. 54: TERN. 61: USKOK. 6.67: Scrapped Split.

188 PITTSBURG SEAM 9.45 JHIW 47: ARLING-TON. 62: Converted at Houston to barge, (propeller removed); (same name).

PART FOUR

Section A

Liberty Ships, Boxed Aircraft Transports, Z–EC2–S–C5 Type

During the war a large number of Liberty ships were turned over to the US army and navy for special services and a number were extensively converted.

In most cases the ships were converted after their delivery from the builder's yard to the Maritime Commission, but with these vessels already earmarked for forward delivery to the armed forces, certain 'deletion' instructions were given to the builders, this preventing the installation of unnecessary outfit and an undue amount of tear-out work at the conversion yard.

The boxed aircraft transport was a re-design of the basic type of Liberty ship, and it was also very similar to those re-designed as tank carriers (see Part Four, Section B). But with the aircraft transports four hatches (two forward and two aft) replaced the customary five of the standard ship and they were also increased in size over those of their counterpart. Three hatches had dimensions of 23 ft by 42½ ft and the fourth was 20 ft by 20 ft.

Instead of the customary three steel masts, the masting was arranged to handle loads of up to 30 tons, and this involved the fitting of four sets of goal-post type masts – one set forward of each hatch – and a pair of king posts fitted at the bridgefront. Two 30 ton and two 15 ton cargo booms were located at each large hatch, whilst No 4 hatch was equipped with two 5 ton derricks.

Forty vessels of this type were ordered and the first one was delivered in January 1945. Others followed during the following ten months, but by the latter part of this period the need for the vessels had faded. Only thirty-six were actually delivered and the remaining four contracts were cancelled. After the war the majority of these ships remained under military jurisdiction, and later many were further converted for varying purposes.

The modification of a group to naval auxiliaries commenced in the mid-1950's, when they became Ocean Radar Station Ships (YAGR). Prior to this the first four vessels of the programme had been designated YAG (miscellaneous).

These radar vessels were a new conception in the USN and were employed primarily to provide the United States seaward approaches with radar coverage as part of the air defence system of the American continent. They were, in fact, the first vessels to carry equipment specifically designed for this purpose.

The conversion of each ship included the installation of additional communication equipment, air and surface search radar, a combat information centre and much improvement in the accommodation, both to the berthing and in the recreational areas.

In this new guise the complement of each vessel totalled 151, made up of thirteen officers and 138 ratings.

Conversion of the first eight vessels began in 1955-56, and the four vessels YAGR 9-12 were dealt with under the 1957 naval appropriations programme. The final four came under the following year's programme.

In September 1958 all the YAGR vessels were reclassed AGR (Radar Picket ships) but retained their names and numbers.

During 1965 the vessels were stricken from active fleet status and placed in USN Reserve.

Other interesting conversions by the USN concerned three vessels of the New England shipyard's output of eight of this type. At New York in September 1960, conversion began of Yard No 3127 into a Hydrographic and Research vessel, and the ship commissioned in July of the following year.

Later, similar conversions of the remaining two (Nos 3125 and 3126) were carried out at Newport News and both entered service late in 1963.

All three ships were used for various experiments as well as for research; the latter work undertaken particularly involving radio communications and electro-magnetic radiation.

In April 1964 these three vessels were reclassed as Technical Research ships.

BUILT BY J.A. JONES CONSTRUCTION CO, PANAMA CITY

USMC hull numbers: MCE 2334—2349 (Yard Nos 75— 90)
                    3137—3148 (”   ” 97—108)

75 FREDERICK E. WILLIAMSON 1.45 F & S Reserve Fleet, site 8.

76 MICHAEL JAMES MONAHAN 1.45 F & S 67: Transferred to USN, loaded at Naval Ammunition depot, Charleston, W.Virginia, with over-age Polaris missile motors and 30.4.67: Scuttled in Atlantic.

77 CHARLES A. DRAPER 1.45 JHIW 56: INVESTIGATOR YAGR 9 (USN). 9.58: INVESTIGATOR AGR 9 (USN). USN Reserve Fleet, site 1.

78 RAFAEL R. RIVERA 1.45 JHIW 55: SKYWATCHER YAG 43 (USN). 57: SKYWATCHER YAGR 3 (USN). 9.58: SKYWATCHER AGR 3 (USN). USN Reserve Fleet, site 1.

79 JAMES W. WHEELER 2.45 JHIW 55: SEARCHER YAG 44 (USN). 57: SEARCHER YAGR 4 (USN). 9.58: SEARCHER AGR 4 (USN). USN Reserve Fleet, site 1.

80 RAYMOND VAN BROGAN 2.45 F & S 56: VIGIL YAGR 12 (USN). 9.58: VIGIL AGR 12 (USN). USN Reserve Fleet, site 1.

81 WILLIAM J. RIDDLE 2.45 JHIW 9.57: INTERRUPTER YAGR 15 (USN). 9.58: INTERRUPTER AGR 15 (USN). 9.59: TRACER AGR 15 (USN). USN Reserve Fleet, site 6.

82 DUDLEY H. THOMAS 2.45 F & S 9.57: INTERPRETER YAGR 14 (USN). 9.58: INTERPRETER AGR 14 (USN). USN Reserve Fleet, site 6.

83 JOHN L. McCARLEY 2.45 JHIW Reserve Fleet, site 4.

84 VERNON S. HOOD 3.45 JHIW 9.57: WATCHMAN YAGR 16 (USN). 9.58: WATCHMAN AGR 16 (USN). USN Reserve Fleet, site 6.

85 EDWIN D. HOWARD 3.45 GMC 55: SCANNER YAGR 5 (USN). 9.58: SCANNER AGR 5 (USN). USN Reserve Fleet, site 6.

86 WESLEY W. BARRETT 3.45 JHIW 4.65: Scrapped New Orleans.

87 WARREN P. MARKS 3.45 GMC 56: PROTECTOR YAGR 11 (USN). 9.58: PROTECTOR AGR 11 (USN). USN Reserve Fleet, site 1.

88 FRANK O. PETERSON 4.45 GMC 55: LOCATER YAGR 6 (USN). 9.58: LOCATER AGR 6 (USN). USN Reserve Fleet, site 6.

89 BARNEY KIRSCHBAUM 4.45 JHIW Reserve Fleet, site 4.

90 MARY CULLOM KIMBRO 4.45 JHIW 19 : CORPORAL ERIC G.GIBSON (US Army repair ship). 67: Loaded with miscellaneous cargo of obsolete military equipment and 15.6.67: Scuttled in Atlantic, 39.37N 70.57W.

97 JAMES G. SQUIRES 5.45 JHIW 55: GUARDIAN YAG 41 (USN). 57: GUARDIAN YAGR 1 (USN). 9.58: GUARDIAN AGR 1 (USN). USN Reserve Fleet, site 1.

The *Jagger Seam* off the US East Coast in April 1945. (Delta, Colliers, Yard no 142)

James G. Squires as the *USS Guardian* arriving at Boston, Mass., in August 1960. (Jones, Panama City, Yard no 97)

The *Sturgis* (ex *Charles H. Cugle*), the US Army's floating nuclear power plant. Note the power lines leading ashore from the foredeck gantry. (Jones, Panama City, Yard no 105)

The *Sarah J. Hale,* a conversion for the transport of Army tanks. Note the four sets of goal-post masts and four long hatches instead of the basic-types' three 'pole' masts and five hatches. (Jones, Panama City, Yard no 20)

98 JAMES F. HARRELL 6.45 JHIW 55: PICKET YAGR 7 (USN). 9.58: PICKET AGR 7 (USN). USN Reserve Fleet, site 6.

99 CLAUDE KITCHIN 6.45 F & S 55: LOOKOUT YAG 42 (USN). 57: LOOKOUT YAGR 2 (USN). 9.58: LOOKOUT AGR 2 (USN). USN Reserve Fleet, site 1.

100 FRANCIS J. O'GARA 6.45 F & S 56: OUTPOST YAGR 10 (USN). 9.58: OUTPOST AGR 10 (USN). USN Reserve Fleet, site 1.

101 FRANK FLOWERS 7.45 F & S Reserve Fleet, site 5.

102 EDWIN H. DUFF 7.45 F & S 8.57: INTERDICTOR YAGR 13 (USN). 9.58: INTERDICTOR AGR 13 (USN). USN Reserve Fleet, site 6.

103 JOSEPH V. CONNOLLY 8.45 F & S 1946: (Same name, US Army transport). 12.1.48: On fire and abandoned in Atlantic 900 miles east of New York. 24.1.48: Taken in tow but broke adrift and 29.1.48: Sank in position 40.47N 52.48W (voyage New York/Antwerp – 4,500 coffins).

104 WALTER W. SCHWENK 8.45 F & S Reserve Fleet, site 4.

105 CHARLES H. CUGLE 8.45 F & S 64: Converted into a floating nuclear power plant; renamed STURGIS.

The conversion of this vessel, a surplus one withdrawn from the Reserve Fleet, into a seagoing atomic power station at a cost of some 18 million dollars, was commenced at Mobile in 1964 by the Alabama S.B. & D.D. Co. The ship was jumbo-ised by the insertion of a new 212 ft long mid-section, and was also widened to 65 ft – this affording some measure of protection to the reactor in the event of collision.

The superstructure was replaced with one containing a nuclear ventilation funnel, a refuelling room, navigation bridge and offices and accommodation both for the 15-man towage crew and for the ship's operating crew of 44 technicians.

Located beneath this superstructure is the control room, operating both the ship and the power plant. The nuclear power plant is situated in the new mid-body. The reactor's core and heat exchanger are located within a container and this, 44 ft long and 31 ft in diameter, is designed to afford utmost protection in the event of accident. Another barrier – of concrete, lead and plastic – reduces radiation to normal occupational level. This power plant, in which reactor heat converts either sea or fresh water into steam and thence, via turbines, generates electricity, develops 10,000 kilowatts and power is sent ashore by overhead lines or underwater cable.

The plant is able to operate for one year without refuelling, and new fuel – in the form of a core of 32 elements of enriched uranium dioxide – is kept aboard in a storage vault.

The vessel now has a draught of 18 feet, a displacement of 9,400 tons and a speed of nine knots when in tow of her customary 1,800 hp tug, her original propelling machinery having been removed.

Now owned and operated by the United States Army Corps of Engineers and renamed STURGIS, the ship is designated MH–1A (mobile high-powered operational plant number one) and provides bulk power to military complexes. As originally proposed the vessel was to be deployed in the Vietnam area, but subsequent strategy and the risk of 'an incident' deemed this move imprudent.

Seagoing power stations are not a new concept. The first, JACONA, entered service back in 1929. Four were used by the US Army during the Second World War and, post-war, the US Navy built a 35,000 kw generator ship – which now operates near the Thule Air Force base in Greenland. However, all these latter ships required normal periodic refuelling.

106 ROBERT F. BURNS 9.45 F & S 12.68: Scrapped New Orleans.

107 EDWARD W. BURTON 9.45 F & S 55: INTERCEPTER YAGR 8 (USN). 9.58: INTERCEPTER AGR 8 (USN). USN Reserve Fleet, site 6.

108 ORA ELLIS 9.45 F & S 47: CORAL SEA. 51: SEACORAL. 55: Lengthened at Kure to 511½ ft (8,577 grt). 57: ANDROS CORAL. 18.5.60: Aground south east of Dona Sebastiana Isle, entrance to Chacao Channel, Chile. 20.5.60: Sank in shallow water. Abandoned. CTL. (Voyage San Juan/Buenos Aires – ore).

BUILT BY NEW ENGLAND SHIPBUILDING CORPORATION

Vessels built at the East Yard:

USMC hull numbers: For the following constructions at this yard the MCE number was used as the yard number.

Note: MCE 3133–3136 were cancelled contracts.

3125 ROBERT W. HART 8.45 GMC 63: Converted at Newport News, renamed GEORGETOWN AG 165 (USN). 4.64: Reclassed (same name) AGTR 2.

3126 J. HOWLAND GARDNER 8.45 GMC 63: Converted at Newport News, renamed JAMESTOWN AG 166 (USN). 4.64: Reclassed (same name) AGTR 3. 12.69: Stricken from USN.

3127 SAMUEL R. AITKEN 8.45 F & S 60: Converted at New York, renamed OXFORD AG 159 (USN). 4.64: Reclassed (same name) AGTR 1.

3128 LORENZO C. McCARTHY 9.45 F & S Reserve Fleet, site 4.

3129 CARDINAL O'CONNELL 9.45 F & S 19 : (same name) T–AKV 7 (USN). 19 : Returned to US Govt. Reserve Fleet, site 8.

3130 TOM TREANOR 10.45 F & S 4.68: Scrapped Terminal Island.

3131 WALTER F. PERRY 10.45 F & S Reserve Fleet, site 2.

3132 ALBERT M. BOE 10.45 F & S 64: Sold for scrapping at Portland, Ore, but converted to floating fish cannery for non-transportation use. Renamed STAR OF KODIAK and stationed at Kodiak, Alaska. Note: This was the last Liberty ship to be built.

PART FOUR

Section B

Liberty Ships, Army Tank Transports, Z–EC2–S–C2 Type

The Liberty ships adapted for use as transports for army tanks were also a re-design of the basic type of ship, and these — the so-called 'zipper ships' — were then designated as the Z–EC2–S–C2 type.

The addition of the letter 'Z' and its use as a prefix to a design type was intended to indicate modifications to the standard ships, so making them special purpose ships. Nevertheless, the records of the Maritime Commission show that the Z prefix/designation was not consistently used for this purpose, although it was applied both to these ships and to those which were re-designed as aircraft transports.

Military requirements and anticipated future operations included plans for the use of a small number of army tank transport vessels in certain theatres of war, and so only eight of this type were actually built. Even so, it was necessary for the Maritime Commission to re-arrange their shipbuilding schedules and to allow a break in the production flow of the basic type of ship at the particular shipyard, for the construction and outfitting of these special vessels.

In emergency or as occasion demanded orthodox cargo ships — perhaps with more difficulty — were able to supplement them, as had already been proven in earlier times. Subsequently vessels of the boxed aircraft transport type (Z–EC2–S–C5), (see Part Four, Section A) also became available as supplementary ships, although their completion during the first ten months of 1945 proved too late for very much serious wartime activity.

In point of fact, these tank carriers were so similar to the aircraft transports that each type could readily substitute for the other, and, generally, they were regarded as one type for operational planning.

The prime intention of the tank carrier design was to ensure speedy, easy handling and transportation of vehicles with a maximum weight of 30 tons each. Therefore the masting arrangement was similar to that of the aircraft transports, being a set of goal-post (or bridge type) masts situated at the forward end of each hatch and a pair of bridge-front king posts — these latter being cross-connected only by wire stays — instead of the three single centreline masts of the normal Liberty ships. The tops of the goal-posts at No 3 hatch were fitted with cowl ventilators but the tops of the remaining posts were sealed with flush plating. Matching the normal Liberty type ships, two top masts (generally) were carried, although on both the tank-carrying and aircraft-carrying vessels they were fitted on the centreline but above the cross beam of the masts serving Nos 2 and 3 hatches. Again, the customary foremast crows nest was still fitted to these special vessels, but it was resited to a central position on the cross beam of the foremast.

The cargo handling gear also generally conformed to that of the boxed aircraft transports, this consisting of extra-length booms necessary for the working of heavy loads at long hatches, plus the usual 30 and 15-ton derricks. Additional gear fitted to some of the ships consisted of the British-style 'Admiralty Net Device', this being long booms hinged to both port and starboard of the forward and after masts. These booms, lowered when attack was threatened, had a steel net hung between them parallel to the sides of the ship — so placing an underwater 'screen' between the vessel and its opponent's torpedoes. However, this equipment was not a great success, for it reduced a ship's speed and spoilt its steering qualities at a time when, perhaps, these two qualities were most needed.

A main difference in the deck arrangement concerned the hatches, for although these numbered four — as with the aircraft transports — three were of slightly smaller dimensions. Hatches Nos 1, 2 and 3 measured 40 ft by 20 ft, this being a reduction in length of some 2½ ft and in breadth of some 3 ft over their counterparts. The dimensions of No 4 hatch remained unaltered at 20 ft square.

Internally the only difference was the installation of a platform deck beneath the second deck.

Other modifications jointly concerning these two types of special purpose ships involved the superstructure, for here the main deckhouse was slightly lengthened and two 36 ft lifeboats on gravity davits replaced the after pair of standard boats and their screw davits.

These eight vessels were built by only one shipyard and were delivered within the four month period commencing in November 1943. After the war they came under the control of the Department of Commerce and are currently laid up in the Reserve Fleet.

BUILT BY J.A. JONES CONSTRUCTION CO, WAINWRIGHT YARD, PANAMA CITY

USMC hull numbers: MCE 1534–1541   (Yard Nos 16–23)

16 MARY BALL 11.43 F & S Reserve Fleet, site 4.

17 JOHN BARTON PAYNE 11.43 F & S Reserve Fleet, site 4.

18 FREDERIC C. HOWE 12.43 GMC Reserve Fleet, site 2.

19 WILLIAM B. WILSON 12.43 GMC Reserve Fleet, site 2.

20 SARAH J. HALE 12.43 GMC Reserve Fleet, site 2.

21 NATHAN B. FORREST 12.43 GMC Reserve Fleet, site 2.

22 STEPHEN R. MALLORY 1.44 F & S Reserve Fleet, site 1.

23 EDGAR E. CLARK 2.44 GMC Reserve Fleet, site 2.

PART FIVE

The 'Sam' Ships

'Sam' ships were a group of Liberty ships loaned to Britain during the war on lease lend terms, and consisted entirely of vessels of the EC2-S-C1 type. The terms were those of the Defense Aid Supplemental Appropriation Act, approved by Congress on 27 March, 1941, which provided for the transfer of merchant ships and other forms of aid to Britain under a lease lend formula.

In all, these loaned Liberties totalled some 200 vessels, this figure representing nearly 7½ per cent of the entire Liberty programme.

They were given a British form of nomenclature, this being the prefix 'Sam' to each name. It is generally believed that they derived this prefix from the fact that the ships came under the 'red duster' by the courtesy of 'Uncle Sam'. This no doubt lent a great deal of weight to the decision to use names with a prefix which acknowledged Britain's gratitude to the United States, but the basis of such naming was in reality a much more mundane and realistic one to the officialdom of the British Ministry of War Transport. Here, the vessels were given the type description of 'Superstructure Aft of Midships' and the initials of this description were applied to form the prefix to the class name.

However, this is not an absolutely accurate description if an exact half-length is taken into account, for the bridge-fronts of the ships occupy a position just forward of a precise mid-length line. But nevertheless, with midships being regarded merely as the waist of the ships, there is certainly no superstructure forward of this position.

For a time after the war the surviving lease lend vessels continued to trade under the British flag, thus playing an important role in the economy of the country at a time when the merchant fleet still had insufficient tonnage to meet all its requirements. Then, early in 1947, and in a sudden burst of nationalism partially prompted by the knowledge that Britain was able to operate these ships to and fro' across the Atlantic (and elsewhere) at a considerably lower cost ratio than that enjoyed by the USA for their own similar ships, America presented an ultimatum ...... Britain must return all the ships to United States ownership, but might be permitted to buy some of them outright.

Following lengthy discussions, the British Government finally allowed British owners to bid for one hundred of the ships, at £135,000 for each one.

Some British experts claimed that this was too high a price to pay for mass-produced wartime tonnage, but in the light of the situation and the urgent need to acquire tonnage, some of the finer points of 'sale and purchase' had to be overlooked.

In fact, the sale price of each ship was finally agreed at some £2,000 more than the 'permitted' figure.

All the British-flag Liberties were then 'technically' returned to America, although in practice many were still retained by their operators whilst the legalities of outright purchase were performed. The others were returned to America and many of these were placed into the reserve fleet. Some of them, with no previous name, retained their 'Sam' title whilst others reverted to their former names. A third group, intended to revert, did not in fact do so, and in course of time met their fate whilst still carrying British-style nomenclature.

Liberties were constructed as 'stiff' ships. To counteract this feature in the 'Sams' — and in particular those which sailed from certain British ports — there grew the wartime (and subsequent) practice of using solid ballast in the 'tween decks, sometimes even at the expense of stability, and certainly leading to a series of mishaps.

After a number of dangerous experiences with unsecured ballast had occurred, the British Ministry of War Transport issued a notice regarding the dangers of using stone, shale, slag and sand, and inferring that other ballasts were at least more stable. The notice recommended that ballast be kept well-trimmed and spread almost flat, but it gave no mention of the necessity of using shifting boards to control its movement, or of the fact that all solid ballasts might move if not controlled.

The question of stability arose again in 1944 when the *Sameveron* — in ballast and in convoy — nearly capsized off Newfoundland. She had previously loaded 2,000 tons of Thames ballast — not among the proscribed types — and this was divided between her lower holds and her 'tween decks. (Thames ballast was a mixture of small-sized stones and wet sand. Its known 'angle of repose' of some 40 degrees generally suggested that it might solidify and might even require to be broken up with pickaxes prior to removal.) With no shifting boards fitted, the ship sailed on a North Atlantic voyage and during a storm and in a beam sea her 'tween deck ballast suddenly shifted, rolling the ship on to her beam ends and to an angle of 55 degrees. Fortunately she rolled no further and when the gale abated her crew were able to venture below and shift the ballast back 'up-hill', after placing her shifting boards firmly, but belatedly, in position.

On another wartime occasion, and not for the first time in her life, the *Samsoaring* developed a severe list, this time when outward bound for Philadelphia. Her ballast, too, had shifted, but the ship luckily survived the ordeal.

Tragedy struck in post-war years with the loss of the *Samkey*. This Liberty ship loaded 1,500 tons of Thames ballast and stowed it all in the 'tween decks. She sailed from London for Panama in January 1948; was sighted in good order on the 29th and reported by radio two days later. Then she disappeared without trace. The vessel had passed through severe storms, and, later, a Court of Enquiry presumed that her uncontrolled ballast had suddenly shifted, high seas had overwhelmed her and the ship had gone straight down.

Notwithstanding, another near-disaster occurred only a few months later, when the shifting boards of the British-flag Liberty ship *Leicester* (ex *Samesk*, qv) actually carried away during an Atlantic hurricane and the vessel listed to 70 degrees. Luckily she survived the ordeal, and was towed in to the safety of Bermuda seventeen days later.

One exception to the ships which sailed with 'Sam' names under the British flag was the Liberty laid down as the *Adolph S. Ochs*. Completed as a 'Sam', she reverted to her original name within a very short time. Adolph S. Ochs was a famous editor of the New York Times, and a plea from influential Americans that the name be retained in his honour was accepted.

Later, on the occasions when the ship visited New York the newspaper concerned feted the crew at banquets, theatres and on tours — although in the interim periods the ship gave normal wartime service to various theatres of war.

After the war the ship reverted to American jurisdiction and was laid up in the Wilmington reserve fleet. Assigned to the shipbreakers in 1968, the vessel was one of the batch of twenty-two sold in a block sale involving all the remaining Liberties at this anchorage. The site was closed down after their transfer to the purchasers.

For the benefit of readers a complete list of 'Sam'-named vessels is included in the index.

PART SIX

Section A

Liberty Ships Converted to Hospital Ships

During the war twenty-four hospital ships served with the American army and seventeen with the USN, and all were operated under the provisions of the Hague Convention, Article X, of 1907, and in accordance with international practice.

Later a sub-convention was called by the USA for the purpose of adapting to maritime warfare the principles established at a previous (Geneva) convention for the conduct of Red Cross and other medical personnel during war. Although Article V of the Hague Convention prescribed specific identifying marks for hospital ships, the character of World War II and the progress of aviation made such markings alone inadequate and it was necessary to give supplementary means of identification. The major one was the addition of illuminated Red Cross signs on deck.

The army hospital ships were operated under the jurisdiction of their War Department and of the total of twenty-four vessels six were Liberty type ships which had been in commercial cargo service, and which were selected in November 1943 for conversion into hospital ships. The names allocated to these vessels were in accordance with the then existing policy of the Surgeon General's Office to have hospital ships named after flowers, although in the event all these names were not taken up.

The crews of these six ships were civilian employees of the Transportation Corps; all hospital staffs were assigned from the Medical Department and these complements functioned in the same way as shore-based hospitals. The arrangement of wards, rooms and other detail of hospital design were agreed between the Chief of Transportation and the Surgeon General.

Hospital ships were listed without cargo capacity, although international agreement permitted them to carry medical supplies, even for ultimate use in battle.

Patients on hospital ships were carried not more than two decks below the one on which the lifeboats were situated.

Hospital ship names:

BLANCHE F. SIGMAN (California, Yard No 163) — named in honour of First Lieut Blanche F. Sigman, the first army nurse killed in action at the Anzio beach-head.

JARRETT M. HUDDLESTON (Permanente No 2, Yard No 75) — named in honour of Colonel Jarrett M. Huddleston, Corps Surgeon of the Fifth Army, killed in action in Italy in 1944.

JOHN J. MEANY (North Carolina, Yard No 1) — named in honour of Major John J. Meany, killed in action in N.Africa in 1943.

ST. OLAF (Bethlehem, Yard No 2020).

DOGWOOD (Permanente No 1, Yard No 542).

WISTERIA (Bethlehem, Yard No 2104).

The following details particularly apply to the conversion of the *William Osler* into the army hospital ship *Wisteria,* but they are nevertheless typical of the work involved on other similar conversions from this type of vessel.

The *William Osler* had been in commercial service for some months when taken over by the army. All her cargo-handling gear (derricks, winches etc.) were removed and the vessel ballasted down for the removal of super-structure, bulkheads, piping and insulation, until little but the bare shell remained. Some of the double-bottom fuel tanks were converted to fresh-water tanks and additional ones added to Nos 4 and 5 holds.

Thereafter a 'lower deck' was erected within the hull and the vessel strengthened by the addition of a steel band, 18 in wide and 1 in thick, rivetted around 80 per cent of the hull. Similar plating was rivetted over the upper deck. Steel girders were installed at points of stress and further strength was gained by the erection of steel bulk-heads and partitions: work then commenced on the new decks required for a ship of this type.

Hatch openings on the second and main decks — the only original ones — were closed, and then a third deck, superstructure deck, bridge deck and a special top deck were added.

All this work completely transformed both the internal and external appearance of the ship, for she now had more than three hundred separate areas of rooms, corridors, wards, clinics and laboratories. Five miles of insulation, from both heat and cold, was fitted, as was distilling equipment to supply a daily 160 tons of fresh water. Other equipment included sterilizing units, over 400 radiators, twenty-eight separate ventilating units and eight refrigerated spaces totalling over 15,000 cu ft.

The plans called for the ship to handle nearly 600 patients, and for this a total of forty-four wards were built, these handling from two to 108 beds. Thirty-five rooms were built for the medical staff and forty-one for the crew of the ship. Others were morgue, autopsy, biological and X-ray rooms and operating theatres.

Special attention was given to wards designated for mental patients and cells were provided for violent cases.

After completion of the superstructure the ship was given new 75 ft high masts and a new funnel wide enough to display 12 ft Red Cross symbols was fitted. Similar signs were displayed on the upper deck and on the hull.

The medical staff consisted of seventeen officers, thirty-nine nurses and 159 attendants. In addition the ship carried chaplains, signal corps men and a crew of 123.

PART SIX

Section B

Liberty Ships Converted to Troopships

During the war the USA operated over 300 vessels which, for an appreciable time, transported personnel on military and naval schedules. These vessels, which were intended to be regularly despatched on more than one voyage from embarkation ports in the USA to overseas destinations, were classified (in the true sense of the word) as troopships.

In addition, other miscellaneous vessels, including very many Liberty ships, came under this classification. Some of the latter were fully converted for the purpose; many others of the same type were converted to become troopships of only limited troop capacity.

Omitted from this troopship-group are other types of transport, generally those for Marines, Sea Bee's etc (designated AP's) and Navy Attack Transports (APA's), and the Liberty ships which were rapidly outfitted in the Pacific for bringing troops home quickly. These latter ones remained essentially cargo ships and their troop accommodations were removed upon arrival in the USA and after only the one homeward voyage.

Except for the Liberties which were fully converted to troopers (of which three did in fact serve for a while as AP's), the first use of this type of vessel for passenger-carrying followed Allied successes in North Africa, when it was arranged to convey large numbers of prisoners-of-war to America.

Accordingly many ships were nominated for this service and it was planned to accommodate, with only slight alteration, 308 POWs in each. A later decision increased the capacity to 504, but by this time 113 ships had already been fitted to the original requirements. Of these fifty-seven were left unaltered and the balance of fifty-six adjusted to take the higher figure. The remaining vessels from those selected and which had not commenced alteration, went directly into conversion for 504 persons.

The re-arrangement of cargo ships for troop use involved the installation of berths into selected compartments and the provision of evaporation plant, galleys and quarters for military, medical and signal personnel. Other major requirements were heavy-lift equipment, strong rooms and equipment storage spaces.

Defence features included de-gaussing gear, camouflage painting and an armament with gun crews at first supplied by the army but later manned by navy gunners.

Lifesaving equipment took the form of extra lifeboats, instant-release liferafts and lifefloats and a lifejacket for each person.

All troop accommodation was provided with heating and ventilation and two escape stairways. Generally, troops were not berthed lower than the waterline.

However, even with these ships so altered, they were still regarded essentially as freighters.

In due time it became obvious that once the conveyance of POWs had ceased this large fleet would be available for the transport of American troops. Therefore an improvement in carrying conditions involved more alterations and included reducing the berths from 5 high to 3 high tiers, and this reduced capacity to 350 troops.

Ships with this lower capacity were already in service when victory in Europe was achieved, and it was decided to re-deploy the vessels in the south-west Pacific. For this yet a further adjustment planned an increase in troop capacity to 550, and some 206 vessels from the original list were intended for such conversion. This work was completed on 200 of them; the remaining six were either lost or had not reached an American repair yard by V-J Day.

Despite these official capacity figures however, it may be noted that the *Benjamin Contee,* when damaged by an enemy torpedo in the Mediterranean, was carrying some 1,800 Italian POWs — albeit on only a short voyage, from which 320 were lost.

In the same theatre of war the *Paul Hamilton,* when lost, had 504 American servicemen killed, the majority of these being a special demolition squad on its way to the Anzio beach-head.

After the war many of these troopers were laid up when no longer required, for their troop accommodation made them unsuitable for cargo-carrying purposes.

Liberty ships fully converted to troopships:-

Built by Bethlehem,	Yard No 2019	
” ” California,	Yard Nos 16, 27, 60, 123, 170(a), 182, 197(b)	
” ” Delta,	Yard No 49	
” ” Kaiser,	Yard No 47	
” ” North Carolina,	Yard Nos 10, 26, 157, 163	
” ” Oregon,	Yard Nos 188, 554, 602, 612, 616, 617, 639(c), 644, 658, 662, 681, 691.	
” ” Permanente No 1,	Yard Nos 485, 1556	
” ” Permanente No 2,	Yard Nos 418, 426, 431, 480	
” ” Walsh Kaiser,	Yard No 5	

    (a) later LIVINGSTON AP 163 (USN)
    (b) later KENMORE AP 162 (USN)
    (c) later DE GRASSE AP 164 (USN)

Liberty ships converted to troopships of limited capacity:-

Built by Alabama,	Yard Nos 240, 281, 282, 285*
” ” Bethlehem,	Yard Nos 2013, 2021, 2022, 2025, 2028, 2033, 2036, 2038, 2042, 2044, 2048*, 2049, 2050, 2055, 2057, 2058, 2059, 2062, 2076, 2083, 2089, 2097, 2098, 2105, 2108, 2112*, 2119, 2122, 2126, 2134, 2136*, 2137, 2140, 2142, 2144, 2145, 2146*, 2148, 2151, 2156
” ” California,	Yard Nos 8, 12, 13, 19, 21, 22, 23, 24, 33*, 42, 46, 47, 50, 51, 53, 64, 67, 72, 73, 79,

	Yard Nos 82, 84, 90, 93, 95*, 98, 102, 106, 107, 109, 118, 124, 134, 155
t by Delta,	Yard Nos 3, 5*, 6*, 8, 9, 10, 11, 12, 15*, 18, 23, 26, 27, 30, 31, 33, 37*, 48, 51
" Jones, Panama City,	Yard No 2
" Marinship,	Yard Nos 1, 6
" New England,	Yard Nos 214, 225, 265, 266, 270, 275
" North Carolina,	Yard Nos 6, 8, 16, 20, 22, 29, 35, 36*, 37, 39, 42, 44, 45*, 47, 51, 53, 54, 56*, 69, 70, 72, 73, 75, 83, 158, 159, 161, 162, 164, 169, 170
" Oregon,	Yard Nos 178, 181, 189, 196, 199, 230, 237, 239, 240*, 543, 553*, 557, 563, 569, 570*, 581, 582, 583, 587, 594, 597*, 615, 621, 623, 626, 628, 648
" Permanente No 1,	Yard Nos 484, 487, 491, 494, 496, 497, 498, 511, 522, 526*
" Permanente No 2,	Yard Nos 48*, 65, 66, 67, 68, 69, 74, 419, 435, 461
" St Johns,	Yard No 1
" Southeastern	Yard Nos 2, 3, 6, 8, 10, 11, 12
" South Portland,	Yard Nos 204, 205, 217, 221, 254, 257, 259, 260, 262, 263, 264, 267
" Todd Houston,	Yard Nos 3, 9, 10, 13, 15, 17, 21, 22, 25, 27, 28, 34, 36, 41, 53, 59, 65
" Walsh Kaiser,	Yard No 2

asterisk * marked above, indicates a vessel not increased to a capacity of 550 troops.

te: the design Z—EC2—S—C4 was intended as a troopship designation, but no vessels with this particular classifi-
ion were constructed.

PART SIX

Section C

Liberty Ships further converted to carry War Brides and Military Dependants

Built by Bethlehem,		Yard No 2020
,,	,, North Carolina,	Yard No 1
,,	,, Permanente No 1,	Yard No 542
,,	,, Permanente No 2,	Yard No 75

PART SIX
Section D

Liberty Ships converted to Animal Transports

Built by Bethlehem,		Yard Nos 2106, 2111
”	” California,	Yard Nos 31, 222
”	” Delta,	Yard Nos 110, 123
”	” Oregon,	Yard No 579
”	” Permanente No 1,	Yard Nos 1696, 2113
”	” Permanente No 2,	Yard No 1105
”	” St Johns,	Yard No 4
”	” Todd Houston,	Yard Nos 83, 85

PART SEVEN

'THE MOTHBALL FLEET' – The US Merchant Fleet Reserve

As early as 1943 the Maritime Commission and the War Shipping Administration appointed a Post-War Planning Committee to survey the country's probable post-war shipping requirements and to prepare plans for a merchant marine adequate both for commerce and for defence of the country.

The outcome of this planning, combined with actual post-war requirement, the use of all types of ships and the dispersal of a great many vessels among America's allies still left the United States with a vast shipping surplus.

So the National Defense Reserve Fleet was created by an Act of Congress in 1946, and in the same year the Maritime Commission was granted permission to sell surplus government-owned war-built vessels for commercial operation.

During the war and in the immediate post-war period many vessels were operated on behalf of the American Government as vast tonnages needed conveyance to all parts of the world, but within a year or two of the cessation of hostilities the shipping industry as a whole was beginning to find its way towards a peace-time standard, and government-operated ships were therefore needed less.

Accordingly, more Liberties retired into honourable lay-up and joined the many others which had gone straight into 'mothball' reserve from the holocaust of war. Some however, still under government ownership, did continue to operate at differing times over the forthcoming years as circumstances and occasions demanded.

Generally, during the war, vessels were placed in service under General Agency Agreement. Under this agreement a private shipowner was appointed as a general agent and was responsible for providing crews and stores for the ship, overseeing repairs and carrying out similar services in return for government compensation for expenses, plus a fee for overheads.

In post-war times some agreements were changed to bareboat charter, but usually such charters were only granted in times of severe commercial shipping shortage, and permitted private companies to charter government-owned ships to provide an essential service.

Some Liberty ships, therefore, although generally classified under reserve status, did have spells of active service between times, and one vessel, the *Harry L. Glucksman* serves to illustrate this point.

From her completion in 1944 until November 1946 she was operated under an agency agreement by the Merchants & Miners Transportation Company. From the latter date and until May 1948, when she went into the reserve fleet at Wilmington, she operated under bareboat charter by the Isthmian Steamship Company.

Returning to service from November 1951 until June 1952 she ran for the United States Navigation Company under agency terms. After another stay in the Wilmington fleet she was again withdrawn, in November 1956, and bareboat chartered to the American Coal Shipping Inc. She returned to reserve, this time the James River site, in March 1958.

In fact this vessel, during this same year, was one of the last laid-up Liberties to pass a Special Survey. Subsequently her peak condition over the fast-fading qualities of other vessels made her an obvious choice when she was later transferred to the USN, but even then she was stripped to a bare hull when rebuilt as a special conversion.

The reserve fleet, therefore, was originally formed with surplus war-built vessels and included those vessels which remained unsold when the authority for their sale expired in 1951.

In all, a total of eight separate sites were established to accommodate the ships of this large fleet. These sites were situated at:

(1) Hudson River, near Nyack, New York.
(2) James River, near Newport News, Virginia.
(3) Wilmington, North Carolina.
(4) Mobile, Alabama.
(5) Beaumont, Texas.
(6) Suisun Bay, San Francisco, California.
(7) Columbia River, Astoria, Oregon.
(8) Puget Sound, Olympia, Washington.

Note: The numbers shown against each of these sites have been added by the authors purely for the purpose of reference to this text. Where applicable, vessels still in reserve are shown as such whilst the number used as a suffix indicates the site of lay-up.

From these fleets of maintained vessels of all types were drawn the surplus merchantmen to meet supply needs during emergencies such as the Korean crisis, the first Suez Canal closing — and latterly for use in supplying the armed services in Vietnam.

During 1954 a large number of laid-up Liberty ships were used as grain storage ships during an American grain surplus. Eighty-four vessels of the Astoria fleet were loaded at that port or at Portland; forty-three from Olympia were similarly loaded at Seattle and Tacoma, and other vessels from the Hudson and James River sites were loaded at Baltimore. The first vessel loaded, at Seattle in mid-March of the year, was the *George D. Prentice*.

Many of the first Liberties to go into reserve still carried scars and signs of war damage. Yet others, damaged by marine hazards, had been laid aside as unworthy of even minor repair whilst so many could readily take their place, so it was that the earliest disposals for scrapping were those in a generally poor condition. A random example of such minor damage — readily repairable under normal circumstances, shows that the *R.S. Wilson* (qv) was declared a constructive total loss in 1946 mainly because, with such a surfeit of tonnage, this one particular ship was not really needed and therefore any repairs would have been uneconomic. And yet, although a CTL she remained laid-up for thirteen more years before her final disposal.

As time progressed through the 1950s and 1960s and Liberties became further obsolete due to age and condition, the Maritime Administration continued to eliminate the remaining war-damaged, weakened and unstrengthened ships, and in the period from 1957 to 1966 sold 832 of them for scrap.

Block disposals became the customary replacement of uneconomic single-ship deals, and an interesting block deal involving the purchase, for scrap, of thirty-five Liberties by Bethlehem Steel Co included the famous first-ever Liberty ship, the *Patrick Henry*. And so, after some twelve years of idleness the very first product from the world's greatest production line met the inglorious fate of being scrapped by those who actually built her, for she was towed to Baltimore and demolished by an associated company of her builders.

Another interesting 'potential' deal occurred in 1960 when tenders were invited for the block purchase of 219 laid-up ships — mostly Liberties — intended for scrapping in the USA, as well as for an additional fifty for scrapping abroad. But at expiry time no bids for the ships had been received.

Early in 1968 the Maritime Administration announced the block sale, for 900,000 dollars, of the last remaining twenty-two ships, all Liberties, at the Wilmington site. Among these were vessels with very famous commemorative names, as for instance the *Henry Ward Beecher* (a Brooklyn clergyman), the *Button Gwinnett* (a signatory of the Declaration of Independence), the *Joseph E. Johnston,* the *George E. Pickett* and the *Pierre Soule* (Confederate generals) and the *Dwight W. Morrow* (a diplomat).

The removal of these vessels from the Cape Fear river was to effect the closing-down of this location, for all the other vessels — as many as 427 Liberty ships were once anchored at this site — had previously been sold either for scrap or for non-transportation use. The purchasers of the twenty-two ships, Union Minerals & Alloys Corporation of New York, had just previously bought thirty-four other ships from the US Government and this total of fifty-six vessels formed a total investment of some 2½ million dollars within a twelve-month period. These buyers do not have their own shipbreaking premises but instead use 'outside' breakers on a contract basis. Many of their purchases are demolished at two scrapyards which also figure prominently in the shipbreaking industry, namely those at Kearny and at Panama City. At the time of the Wilmington site closure the Astoria site was undergoing a similar fate, this following the removal, also for scrap, of the last of the laid-up vessels from the location.

At the time of writing therefore, six reserve fleet sites remain, and even these are gradually being depleted with the continuing sale of obsolete vessels.

An earlier form of disposal of Liberty ships from the reserve fleets commenced in 1958 when the US Army, faced with the problem of disposing of many tons of chemical warfare gas, loaded it into the hulk of the *William C. Ralston* (qv) and then scuttled the ship at sea.

Prior to this the two usual methods of disposing of deteriorated explosives and armaments were those of dumping at sea by use of hopper-door barges or the loading of it aboard a ship, which was then towed to sea and the material then man-handled over the side. A third but minor method of disposal was to burn explosives ashore purely for the residual scrap metal value of its containers, but all these methods were costly and extremely dangerous.

In 1963 the authorities enquired into the condition of ammunition stocks — much of which had been in store since the Korean crisis, and some of which dated from the days of World War II. The majority was found in good order but some deteriorated material required immediate and cheap disposal.

And so 'Operation Chase' was conceived, and in this the USN acquired, through the Military Sea Transportation Service, obsolete vessels from the reserve fleet. Stripped of all useful gear, they were loaded with the unwanted material, towed to sea and scuttled in deep water.

The first vessel so used was the *John F. Shafroth* (qv), scuttled west of the Golden Gate. The second 'Chase' ship, the *Village* (ex *Joseph N. Dinand*, qv) exploded shortly after sinking. The detonation registered on seismic equipment throughout the world and it also aroused the interest of the (American) Office of Naval Research. Subsequently sinkings were instrumented and deliberate detonations carefully controlled. From these experiments were monitored distinctions between man-made and natural seismic shocks — invaluable information in the detection of underwater nuclear explosions.

Further Liberty ships scuttled under 'Chase' were the *Santiago Iglesias,* the *Isaac Van Zandt,* the *Horace Greeley,* the *Michael J. Monahan* and the *Corporal Eric G. Gibson.* The *Robert Louis Stevenson,* also destined to be scuttled and detonated, defied the might of the USN and chose her own demise instead of her allotted doom.

So far, more than 50,000 tons of volatile materials have been disposed of, and at time of writing three further 'Chase' sinkings are still scheduled. These will conclude the present series of operations.

Reserve ships (of all types) not destined for the scrapyard or for sale for non-transportation use are in clearly defined categories of 'emergency reserve' or 'priority'. Priority ships have the designation of one to six, in accordance with their age, type and condition. Those in Priority One receive the most intensive maintenance, whilst those at the other end of the scale in Priority Six and in Emergency Reserve receive much less.

At the eight reserve fleet sites crews of skilled technicians were engaged in administering, policing and preserving the ships and carrying out a carefully regulated programme of maintenance, preservation and minor repair. This work served the dual purpose of keeping ships in varying states of readiness and enabled them to be put back into service at a minimal cost.

However, it should be remembered that maintenance work on Liberty ships was generally abandoned many years ago, and most of them now receive no attention at all.

The preservation work was scheduled in four phases. Hulls and decks were painted; boilers, engines and auxiliaries were coated internally with metal-conditioning compound; motors and generators were stripped and cleaned, treated with preservatives and re-assembled, and underwater areas were fitted with anodes to arrest corrosion.

The *Samsoaring* while undergoing outfitting at one of the piers of the Bethlehem-Fairfield yard suffered an internal explosion, cause unknown, resulting in considerable damage to the hull and causing the vessel to list heavily to port. (Bethlehem, Yard no 2361)

The US Army Hospital ship *St Olaf,* built at the Bethlehem-Fairfield shipyard as Yard No 2020. (See Part Six)

The troopship *Henry Failing,* built at the Oregon shipyard as Yard No 662. Note the greatly increased number of liferafts and the many hundreds of service personnel aboard. (See Part Six)

Part of the Mothball Fleet. Ships — mostly Liberties — laid up in the Reserve Fleet at Stony Point, New York

An interesting sidelight on subsequent re-activation was the recent American concern at the cost of bringing ships from reserve for service to Vietnam. The first decision to re-activate vessels – mainly of the fast 'Victory' type but including the odd Liberty – estimated recommissioning costs at 325,000 dollars per ship. But rising costs soon increased the figure to over half a million dollars each, this resulting largely from ship repairers complaints of inadequate funds and which, in turn, resulted in costly breakdowns among the first batch delivered.

By the end of 1966 and whilst still looking for more tonnage, the Pentagon was reluctant to consider bringing forward the remaining ships (of all types) in reasonable condition in the reserve fleets, and in fact preferred to charter ships already in service.

But to return for a moment to the year of 1961: American Public Law 86–575, the Ship Exchange Act, permitted non-subsidised obsolete US-flag tonnage to be traded in, on a price differential basis, for better class war-built ships from the reserve fleets.

By mid-1961 the first three exchanges had been effected and these included the Liberty ship *Albatross* (ex *Stage Door Canteen*).

Usually the returned ships joined the laid-up tonnage and afterwards were generally very soon sold to ship-breakers.

Meantime, sales for scrapping continued unabated, further assisted by the Ship Sale Act which permitted disposal of laid-up tonnage for scrap by foreign nationals. A peak was reached during 1961, when 176 Liberties (including 'active' ones) were disposed of. However, it should be borne in mind that the year of sale does not necessarily indicate the actual date of scrapping, for particularly in the USA, vessels are often not scrapped until several years after their purchase by the shipbreakers. Interesting examples of this are two Liberties built by Todd Houston under yard Nos 171 and 177 and which were sold for scrap early in 1964. And yet during 1969 both vessels were still lying at Philadelphia, their scrapping postponed 'due to the Vietnam situation'.

In January of 1962 the total of 1,872 reserve vessels still included 1,051 Liberties, but the momentum of scrapping them slackened so that three years later this latter figure was only down to 859.

By mid-1965 some 800 Liberties were listed in a laid-up total of 1,579 ships, of which 231 were earmarked for scrap, 388 were in emergency grade and the remaining 960 were priority vessels. Twelve months later the figure for reserve Liberties was 722, although some others still came under the jurisdiction of the US armed forces and many of these were in military reserve.

It is of interest that at the same date nearly 700 Liberties were still flying the flags of many nations throughout the world, representing over 25 per cent of all those built.

Further reductions to the reserve fleet showed that the previous figure of 722 Liberty ships had reduced, at the end of December 1968, to 462 vessels. In addition 83 vessels of the same type still remained in military reserve.

During the same period of time the world-wide commercially-owned Liberty ship fleet had, of course, also been further depleted. Later – in July 1969 – those remaining under this form of ownership numbered some 300 vessels, whilst the 462 reserve ships had reduced to 428. Those in military reserve remained unaltered.

With the ceaseless advance of time the great laid-up fleets began to diminish, first in a trickle, then with greater rapidity until the question was raised – were the surviving ships to be regarded merely as scrap potential or historic fact?

It was then that the Liberty Ship Memorial Programme was formed. Its two sponsors – the American Merchant Marine Institute and the American Institute of Marine Underwriters – are, respectively, the major trade associations in the fields of American-flag ocean shipping and in marine insurance. Their combined efforts to preserve the memory of Liberty ships and to call public attention to the war service of the American Merchant Marine receives the full co-operation of the Maritime Administration.

As part of this programme the builders nameplates from ships destined for scrap are formally presented with proper ceremony and publicity to towns, organisations, communities or areas of the country associated with the famous Americans after whom the ships were named.

A number of such presentations are noted, for interest, within the text.

As will be seen, many vessels have reached the end of their lives and have been detailed as 'scrapped'. However, in some cases this could be more accurately described as 'dismantled' – although it has not proved possible in this text to differentiate between the two descriptions for individual vessels.

At one time reserve fleet ships were sold, except in some special cases, with the proviso that they be scrapped within the USA, but permitting the residual steel plates and structural members to be used in the construction and repair of other vessels – providing that they were reduced to individual pieces when removed from the old hulls.

In 1965 a modification to these conditions allowed a wider use of the materials. The revision permitted re-use of portions of the hulls and hull assemblies in whatever size sections the purchaser wished, providing essential structural parts were demolished and the ships ceased to exist in their usual forms.

And so some Liberties, having been only dismantled, do in fact almost 'sail again', though in a somewhat different form and guise.

Concerned in this new business venture of using materials so salved are a number of firms and localities which figure prominently in the Liberty ship shipbreaking programme.

A new five-acre shipyard with three building ways was recently constructed at Green Cove Springs, Florida, and was (initially) to build fifty cargo barges by using the steel plates obtained from scrapped Liberty ships.

The order for these barges was placed by a group of metal merchants formed by Southeastern Rail & Steel Company of Jacksonville, Zidell Explorations Inc, of Portland, Oregon, and steel merchants Hugo Neu of New York. The president of Southeastern Rail is the owner of the large shipbreaking yard at Panama City, Florida – the site of the J.A. Jones Liberty ship shipyard – whilst Southeastern, Zidell and Neu are themselves sole suppliers of all material used in the new barge construction.

Steel plates taken from the scrapped ships are rolled and shaped at Panama City for welding into prefabricated sections some 60 ft by 20 ft. These sections are then taken by barge to the new shipyard for incorporation in the new barges – which are 150 ft long, have a beam of 40 ft, a depth of 11 ft and a deadweight of some 1,800 tons.

Barges of a different type were due to figure in the builders itinerary after completion of their initial programme.

About the time this new Florida yard commenced operations the shipyard of Zidell Explorations at Portland also started the construction of cargo barges using similar Liberty ship steel plates.

Here the initial order was for eighteen barges, these being vessels 200 ft long by 45 ft beam and with a depth of 15 ft.

At this same location Zidell have operated their large shipbreaking yard for very many years.

Perhaps the most important point of these ventures – at least to historians – is that these barge-building enterprises will yet preserve 'remains' of Liberty ships when even the memories of the ships themselves have all but faded.

According to the present plans of the Maritime Administration, only thirty-seven ships will remain in reserve after 1971. All the Liberty ships still currently laid up will have been disposed of by that time, together with hundreds of other types of ships. The thirty-seven vessels considered useful beyond 1971 – but only until 1975 – will all be 30 years of age by then, and are all 'Victory' type cargo ships.

In the light of the foregoing, a decision reached by the United States Court of Appeals during December 1968 was an interesting one. The result of this decision was that America's 'mothball' fleet of merchant ships had to be considered for use in moving military cargo before foreign-flag vessels.

The Court's ruling came in a case brought by the National Maritime Union, which protested against the use by the Military Sea Transportation Service of foreign ships to transport military cargo to Vietnam, without first considering the use of United States vessels out of commission, but being kept in reserve for future use in emergencies.

However, the judgment left the American Government 'with wide discretion to determine the availability, or otherwise, of mothballed ships for military purposes'.

'They mark our passage as a race of men,
Earth will not see such ships as those again'.
John Masefield

ADDENDUM

Built by Alabama

234 ARTHUR MIDDLETON Voyage: New York/
Oran — munitions.

286 WILLIAM C. GORGAS Voyage: Mobile/
Swansea — general.

Built by Bethlehem

2004 ROGER B. TANEY Sunk by submarine U.160
in position 22.00S 07.45W on voyage Suez/Bahia —
ballast.

2016 GEORGE CALVERT (II) Voyage: Baltimore/
Bandar Shapur — general.

2023 ALEXANDER MACOMB Voyage: New York/
Archangel — military equipment.

2030 THEODORE FOSTER 4.70: sold for scrapping
at Bilbao.

2031 JAMES GUNN 11.69: sold for scrapping at
New Orleans.

2043 JOHN CARTER ROSE Voyage: New York/
Accra — gasoline and general.

2045 BENJAMIN CHEW Now laid up in Reserve
Fleet, site 4.

2051 THOMAS McKEAN Voyage: Philadelphia/
Bandar Shapur — war supplies.

2084 ANDREW G. CURTIN Voyage: Iceland/
Murmansk — military supplies.

2085 MOLLY PITCHER Voyage: Baltimore/
Casablanca — war supplies.

2099 JAMES W. DENVER Voyage: Baltimore/
N.Africa — war supplies.

2114 CHARLES M. SCHWAB 3.70: sold to New
York shipbreakers.

2127 WILLIAM W. GERHARD Vessel was only
damaged by submarine torpedo, then caught fire
and broke in two. Forepart sank, afterpart sunk by
naval gunfire. Voyage: Casablanca/Salerno — petrol
and ammunition.

2137 KARPATY 12.69: Scrapped Split.

2145 SIKHOTE ALIN 3.70: at Split for scrapping.

2149 CHARLES BULFINCH 1.70: sold to Canadian
buyers. 5.70: Resold to Italian shipbreakers.

2151 KOLASIN 21.1.70: Stranded 35 miles south of
Tuapse. Salvage attempts failed; vessel abandoned.

2159 ROBERT ERSKINE Voyage: New York/Naples
— military stores. 1948: wreck sold to Genoa shipbreakers.

2162 BLUE SAND 11.69: Scrapped Sakaide.

2164 GEORGE W. CHILDS 1.2.44: Put into Clyde
due to shifting of cargo, voyage: New York/UK.
15.2.44: Anchored off Loch Sunart, Scotland,
leaking and with machinery damage; requested tug
assistance. Remained in position for twelve days,
and 27.2.44: towed to Greenock.

2220 GALLETTA 10.4.70: Grounded 60 miles off
Chalna, 21.48N 89.29E on voyage Chittagong/Chalna
— rice. By 12.5.70: some cargo discharged, refloating
attempts failed and later abandoned. Salvage again
undertaken and 21.5.70: refloated and towed Chalna.
Later proceeded Singapore.

2227 TUTUILA 1970: Still in USN service.

2240 CONCORD VENTURE 1.70: Scrapped Sakaide.

2243 PAMYATI KIROVA Converted to a fish carrier at Murmansk 1948-1955.

2274 TITANUS 12.69: Scrapped Mihara.

2319 VASSILIKI 31.3.70: Stranded on Mayaguana Island, Bahamas, on voyage Sicily/Havana — fertiliser. Holed, leaking, flooded and abandoned. Offered for sale 'as lies'.

2334 SPLENDID SKY 4.10.69: Grounded off Bats, river Schelde on voyage Antwerp/Spezia — silversand. Refloated, but cracked and buckled amidships and leaking. Towed to Antwerp. Repairs uneconomic. 1.70: Scrapped Antwerp.

2346 VOLUSIA 11.69: Scrapped Hong Kong.

2361 IOANNIS K. Voyage: Saigon/Singapore — ballast.

2377 SAMSYLARNA Voyage: USA/Bombay — war supplies and silver bars.

2380 RELIANCE HARMONY 6.11.69: Sank off Hososhima, 32.18N 131.54E after collision with ss MARITIME EXPRESS (46/8,942 grt) on voyage Ube/West India — fertiliser.

Built by California
9 ALBERT GALLATIN Voyage: New York/ Bandar Shapur — general.

17 HENRY KNOX Voyage: Philadelphia/Bandar Shapur — explosives.

39 GEORGE THACHER Voyage: Charleston/ Mombasa — military stores.

97 FRANK JOSEPH IRWIN 4.70: Sold for scrapping at Bilbao.

119 PHOEBE A. HEARST Voyage: Noumea/Samoa — munitions.

128 JAMES ROBERTSON Voyage: Durban/USA.

142 THEODORE DWIGHT WELD Voyage: Manchester/New York — ballast.

145 LYDIA M. CHILD Voyage: San Francisco/Suez — general.

151 ALICE F. PALMER Voyage: Calcutta/Durban — ballast.

227 INA COOLBRITH 3.70: Sold to Philadelphia shipbreakers.

232 SAMBO Voyage: Iquique via New Zealand/Suez — nitrate.

251 AYIA MARINA 2.69: Arrested for debt at Rio de Janeiro. 12.69: Sold to local shipbreakers.

292 JOHN DOCKWEILER Was sold 1.70 for scrapping at Portland, Ore.

Built by Delta
7 GEORGE GALE 1.70: Sold for scrapping at Portland, Ore.

16 THOMAS SINNICKSON Voyage: Bandar Shapur/USA — ballast.

17 JONATHAN STURGES Voyage: Liverpool/ New York — ballast.

18 JONATHAN TRUMBULL 3.70: Sold to New York shipbreakers.

34 BLACK HAWK 1967: Remains of wreck moved 300 yards along sea bed by explosives to enable a pipeline to be laid across the bay.

36 WALTER Q. GRESHAM Voyage: New York/ Clyde — general.

133 GEORGE POMUTZ 4.70: Sold for scrapping outside USA.

Built by Jones (Brunswick)
139 SAMSELBU Voyage Antwerp/Thames — ballast.

153 EUGENE T. CHAMBERLAIN 1.69: Scrapped Philadelphia.

175 M.E. COMERFORD Was sold 1.70 for scrapping at Portland, Ore.

186 ST DEMETRIUS 9.69: Scrapped Hong Kong.

188 GRAND DOLPHIN 2.70: At Kaohsiung for scrapping.

Built by Jones (Panama City)
6 ELIHU ROOT 10.69: At Kearny, NJ for scrapping.

41 JEAN RIBAUT 3.70: Sold to New York shipbreakers.

71 RANSOM A. MOORE 4.70: Sold to Cleveland, Ohio, shipbreakers.

74 WENDELL L. WILLKIE Was sold 1.70 for scrapping at Mobile.

Built by Kaiser
2 ELIAS HOWE Voyage: Valparaiso/Suez — nitrate.

Built by Marinship
8 FRANCIS PRESTON BLAIR At 2.70: Wreck reported still in good condition, even after long use as a target by Royal Australian Air Force — using dummy bombs.

11 SEBASTIAN CERMENO Voyage: Suez/Bahia — ballast.

Built by New England (East Yard)
266 ALBATROS 10.69: Scrapped Vado.

268 WILLIAM PHIPS 3.70: Sold to New York shipbreakers.

273 CHARLES W. ELIOT Voyage: Normandy beaches/UK — ballast.

282 EZRA WESTON Voyage: Avonmouth/ Normandy beaches — army stores.

3017 SAMWAKE Voyage: Normandy beaches/ Thames — ballast.

3061 JAMES T. FIELDS Was sold 2.70 for scrapping at Portland, Ore.

Built by New England (West Yard)
203 THOMAS HOOKER Voyage: Bona/New York.

206 WILLIAM KING Voyage: Basrah/Cape Town — barrels of oil.

222 RICHARD HOVEY Voyage: Calcutta/USA — jute.

226 GEORGE F. PATTEN Was sold 2.70 to Seoul shipbreakers.

3033 KORTHI 10.69: Scrapped Hirao.

3036 ARAM J. POTHIER 3.70: Sold to Cleveland, Ohio, shipbreakers.

3093 UNION TRANSPORT 1.70: At Kaohsiung for scrapping.

Built by North Carolina
1 ZEBULON B. VANCE 3.70: Sold to Genoa shipbreakers.

2 NATHANAEL GREENE Vessel was only

damaged, not sunk, by submarine torpedo. Vessel was beached but was a total loss; voyage Mostaganem/ Algiers — food.

22 JAMES TURNER Was sold 1.70 to New York shipbreakers.

34 JOHN DRAYTON Voyage: Khorramshahr/Cape Town — barrels of oil.

37 HENRY MIDDLETON 3.70: Sold to New York shipbreakers.

48 RICHARD CASWELL Voyage: Buenos Aires/ New York — ore.

81 ROGER MOORE 1.70: Sold to New York shipbreakers.

160 CHARLES D. McIVER Voyage: Antwerp/New York — ballast.

165 LEE S. OVERMAN Voyage: New York/ Normandy — ammunition.

Built by Oregon
172 WILLIAM CLARK Voyage: Iceland/N.Russia — war supplies.

174 JOHN BARRY Voyage: Philadelphia/Bahrain — mixed 'aid to Russia' cargo, including silver valued at 26 million dollars.

183 WILLIAM DAWES Voyage: San Francisco/ Brisbane — army stores. 1966: Wreck acquired by a finance company and offered for sale for scrapping.

190 FISHER AMES 3.70: Sold to New York shipbreakers.

238 ANNE HUTCHINSON Voyage: Ismailia/New York — barrels of oil.

547 MARCUS WHITMAN Voyage: Port Sudan/ Paramaribo — ballast.

563 KOPALNIA MYSLOWICE Later became a non-propelled storeship, and, 12.69: Scrapped Gdansk.

569 MARCAR 11.69: Vessel sold to Lisbon buyers — who hoped to refloat her; but at 4.70: vessel remained in sunken position with only her superstructure visible above water.

595 PETER SKENE OGDEN Voyage: Naples/Hampton Roads — ballast.

629 ROBERT J. WALKER Voyage: Calcutta/Sydney — ballast.

772 SAMOURI Voyage: Bombay/New York
– ballast.

775 MARIA 1962: Lengthened at Maizuru to 511½
ft (8,426 grt).

818 VALERY CHKALOV Deleted from USSR
Register by 1964.

Built by Permanente No 1
493 WILLIAM K. VANDERBILT Voyage Port
Vila/Suva – ballast.

1702 CHORZOW 1968: Converted to floating
warehouse at Gdansk, renamed MP–PZZ–11.

2105 MARIA DE LOURDES 2.70: Scrapped
Shanghai.

2127 KHIBINY 1967: Deleted from USSR Register.

Built by Permanente No 2
75 JARRETT M. HUDDLESTON 2.70: Sold to
Genoa shipbreakers.

443 GRUMIUM 4.70: Sold as WILLIAM G.
McADOO for scrapping outside USA.

458 RICHARD HENDERSON Voyage: Philadelphia/
Bandar Shapur – war supplies.

1103 MALOU 11.69: Scrapped Shanghai.

1114 HOBART BAKER Sunk by Japanese air attack
whilst discharging cargo off Bug Bug Point, Mindoro.
Voyage: USA/Mindoro – 3,000 tons of steel landing
nets for airstrip runways.

2149 AKTI 10.69: Scrapped Hirao.

2711 HUTA ZYGMUNT 1969: Reported scrapped
Szczecin.

2729 ORCHIDEA 1970: renamed ARDENA.

2746 ALBORADA 8.69: At Savona for scrapping.

Built by St. Johns
3 FRANCIS ASBURY Voyage: New York/Antwerp.

17 DICORONIA 1.70: At Shanghai for scrapping.

33 SUN 4.70: Sold to Japanese shipbreakers.

44 UNION TIGER 4.69: Scrapped Inchon, Korea.

51 W.S. JENNINGS 3.70: Sold to Genoa shipbreakers.

Built by Southeastern
18 CEBOLLA 1969: Scrapped Shanghai.

86 COSMOS ALTAIR 9.69: Scrapped Kaohsiung.

Built by Todd Houston
2 DAVY CROCKETT 1969: Resold and converted
at Richmond, Cal. to a pipelaying vessel.

44 JOHN BELL Voyage: Philadelphia/Bandar Shapur
– war supplies.

69 SAGITTARIUS 25.9.69: Sank in Indio Channel,
Buenos Aires, after collision with mv SCHWARZBURG
(68/8,810 grt) on voyage Rosario/Ravenna – grain.
10.69: Refloated, towed Buenos Aires. 12.69: Sold
for scrapping at Campana.

89 ROMANCE 10.69: Sold to Formosan shipbreakers,
but 31.10.69: Severely damaged by fire in engine room
whilst at Naples. 3.70: Resold, towed to Split and
scrapped.

130 BRIGADIER GENERAL ASA N. DUNCAN
1946: renamed RICHARD O'BRIEN.

185 ASIDOS 12.69: Scrapped Chittagong.

186 UNION SKIPPER 11.69: Scrapped Kaohsiung.

198 SEAGARDEN Voyage: Brazil/Puerto Rico.

200 ASITRES 7.69: At Chittagong for scrapping.

203 ALNFIELD 1967: Reported to be renamed
CERES, but 9.69: At Vado for scrapping, still as
ALNFIELD.

Built by Walsh-Kaiser
5 LYMAN ABBOTT 1.70: Sold for scrapping at
Mobile.

3120 ALBADORO 9.69: At Vado for scrapping.

TANKERS

Built by California
T2 CALIFORNIA SUN At 3.70: vessel remains at
Seychelles.

T17 PACIFICA 10.69: Scrapped Kaohsiung.

COLLIERS

Built by Delta
179 ANDROMEDA 1970: renamed SLAVIANKA.

185 READING 4.70: Sold to Panamanian buyers.
To be renamed ?

BOXED AIRCRAFT TRANSPORTS

Built by New England
3125 GEORGETOWN 12.69: Stricken from USN.

3127 OXFORD 12.69: Stricken from USN. Later towed to Taiwan shipbreakers.

PART SEVEN

'The Mothball Fleet' (Re 'Operation Chase'), Two further scuttlings were carried out towards the end of 1969, these being of the C1 type of ship and bringing the total of disposed material in excess of 60,000 tons. Therefore only one further controlled sinking then remained scheduled, and this was finally carried out at the end of May 1970. The vessel involved was the Liberty ship FREDERICK E. WILLIAMSON (See Part Four, section A) which was towed out of the Olympia Reserve Fleet (site 8) to the Bangor Ammunition Depot at Bangor, Washington. Here she was loaded with obsolete ammunition and then towed to sea and scuttled off the Washington coast.

BIBLIOGRAPHY

Charles, Roland W. *Troopships of World War II* (1947, Washington, D.C.)

Lane, Frederic C. *Ships for Victory* (1951, Baltimore, Md.)

Stanford, Commander Alfred, USNR. *Force Mulberry* (1951, New York.)

Corporation of Lloyd's shipping publications

Lloyd's Registers of Shipping

Marine News

Military Sea Transportation Service publications

Record of American Bureau of Shipping

Sea Breezes

Shipbuilding and Shipping Record

Official lists of shipping losses of various countries

INDEX

Note: Italic numerals indicate an illustration
under an original or subsequent name

DATE DUE

OCT 1 2			
NOV 22 1993			
GAYLORD.			PRINTED IN U.S A